Global Tensions
Challenges and Opportunities in the World Economy

Edited by
Lourdes Benería and Savitri Bisnath

ROUTLEDGE
New York and London

Published in 2004 by
Routledge
29 West 35th Street
New York, NY 10001
www.routledge-ny.com

Published in Great Britain by
Routledge
11 New Fetter Lane
London EC4P 4EE
www.routledge.co.uk

Library of Congress Cataloging-in-Publication Data
Global tensions: challenges and opportunities in the world economy/ edited by Lourdes Benería and Savitri Bisnath
   p. cm.
   Includes bibliographical references and index.
   ISBN 0-415-93440-0 (alk. paper) — ISBN 0-415-93441-9 (pbk.: alk. paper)
     1. Free trade. 2. Foreign trade and employment. 3. Globalization—Economic aspects. 4. Globalization—Social aspects. 5. Anti-globalization movement. 6. International economic relations. I. Benería, Lourdes. II. Bisnath, Savitri, 1965–
HF1713.G5615 2003
337—dc21

                      2003046662

Contents

Acknowledgments

The editors would like to thank Manuel Montes and the Ford Foundation for the generous grant that made it possible to organize the international conference in which the papers in this collection were presented. At Cornell University, many individuals and programs contributed to making the conference a success; many thanks to Ravi Kanbur and the Poverty, Inequality and Development Initiative, Philip McMichael and Rural Sociology, David Lelyveld and Donna Decker of the Mario Einaudi Center for International Studies, Ben Kohl and the International Studies in Planning Program, the Women's Studies Program, Thomas P. Braun, Salah Hassan, and Dean Porus Olpadwala. The conference also could not have taken place without the assistance of many graduate students who contributed their skills and time: Rhodante Ahlers, Joyce Altobelli, Florion O. Arguillas, Jr., Joy Arguillas, Betty Iroku, Razack Karriem, Naoko Mizuno, Michael L. Ristorucci, Susanna Schaller, and Leslie Feazell Schill. The Global Tensions conference was organized through the Gender and Global Change Program.

Introduction

LOURDES BENERÍA AND SAVITRI BISNATH

During the past decade much has been written, from a variety of fields and perspectives, on globalization and its glories and discontents. Rapid changes resulting from the increasingly internationalized areas of production, finance, and trade, coupled with parallel technological, social, political, and cultural shifts, require continuous study and practical understandings. Certainly, the degree of globalization is not homogeneous across these areas or within and between regions and nation-states. For example, financial markets are most globalized and have been leading other sectors in the same direction. Multinational corporations (MNCs) have been instrumental in globalizing production, investments, and trade in goods and services. The G7 countries have played key roles, not only as home to most MNCs, but also in the creation of regional and international institutions and regulatory agreements that foster economic and political integration within and across countries. In particular, the so-called Anglo-Saxon model of neoliberal policies has set the tone for the emphasis on free markets and the promotion of the Washington Consensus in the developing world.

Trade liberalization registered a significant leap forward with the shift from the trade regime that was prevalent under the General Agreement on Tariffs and Trade and the Bretton Woods period to the regime that was institutionalized through the Uruguay Round of trade negotiations, which led to the creation of the World Trade Organization (WTO). As a result, new areas of economic activity, including services and intellectual property rights, are incorporated in the processes of trade liberalization. Further, the WTO's Trade Policy Review Mechanism and its Dispute Settlement

Mechanism make it increasingly difficult for member-states to resist economic liberalization. It is in this sense that the WTO is viewed as the institution that most symbolizes the consolidation of the current globalization process.

Alternatively, labor markets have not been globalized to the degree that they would if the free flow of persons was allowed. On the contrary, and as a result of increasing flows of migrants from low-wage to high-wage countries, including those in the former Soviet Union, new regulations and obstacles to international migration have been adopted, particularly in high-income countries. However, this has not stopped the flow of migrants who are contributing significantly to the supply of labor in receiving countries. Economic crises, poverty, unemployment and underemployment in developing countries have reinforced this trend, which has also converted traditionally immigrant countries (such as many in Latin America) into net exporters of labor.

Neoliberal globalization has generated opportunities for economic growth and an unprecedented accumulation of resources in many areas and sectors. However, it has also created gaps and imbalances and a tendency toward growing inequalities within and between countries; this is at the root of the global tensions that are the subject of this collection. From a development perspective the last two decades have been discouraging. Many developing countries have witnessed a deterioration of living conditions for a large majority of their population, with increased financial instability, economic insecurity, and sociopolitical tensions. In Latin America, for example, the historically high degree of income concentration has continued and in many cases inequalities have increased, even in those countries that achieved some growth. For example, in Mexico—a country that has been viewed as a leader in Latin American trends—a recent study shows that economic liberalization has led to an increasing "economic, social and territorial polarization" (Dussel-Peters, 2000). Most indicators show that Mexico is not a unique case.

At the global level, the United Nations Development Programme (UNDP) estimates for 1998 showed that the assets of the three richest people were more than the combined gross national product (GNP) of all least developed countries, and the assets of the 200 richest people were more than the combined income of 41 percent of the world's population (UNDP, 1999). Similarly, capital has become increasingly concentrated through mergers and acquisitions of corporations, raising questions about the dangers in the corresponding concentration of power and the process and meaning of democracy. In addition, the autonomy and sovereignty of nation-states are challenged and eroded as independence in policy-making, through democratic parliamentary procedures, are eroded by neoliberal policies that promote economic liberalization and privatization and are mainly formulated in the capitals of the G7 countries.

Since the East Asian financial crisis of 1997, the initial triumphalism that accompanied hegemonic discourses of globalization has been more subdued and tamed by the vociferous protests and demonstrations—from Seattle in '99, Prague in '00, Quebec in '01, and Genoa in '02, to many others in Latin America, such as in Argentina. Against the backdrop of these demonstrations, the growing resistances to free trade and current global trends have drawn thousands of participants to events such as the Porto Alegre World Social Forum, with parallels worldwide at the regional, country, and local levels. These events express the growing conviction from citizens of the world that the market needs interventions and forms of regulation to curb and stop erosion of the well-being of the majority of the world's people. As a *Financial Times* editorial (January 18–19, 2003) noted with reference to the 2003 World Economic Forum's Davos meeting: "Chief executives who were acclaimed [in previous meetings] as new masters of the universe, lofted upwards on buoyant markets and visions of endless growth, have been brought abruptly down to earth. [. . .] Growth is faltering almost everywhere."

The chapters in this volume present critical evaluations of the dynamics of this model of globalization, the tensions therein, and the practical problems to be addressed. Themes explored include challenges, risks, and opportunities of global governance in the twenty-first century; financial instability and economic crises in developing countries; trade liberalization and the WTO trading regime; gendered dimensions of development and trade; and effects of increasing urbanization and the growth of global cities. The chapters discuss some of the ways in which corporate power undermines the capacity of governments to promote, protect, and fulfill basic rights. It is our contention that there is an urgent need for the re-examination of the neoliberal thinking that currently informs economic and development policies.

This collection is the result of a conference that took place at Cornell University on March 8–9, 2000. Organized under the auspices of the Gender and Global Change Program, the meeting honored the work of the late Danish economist Ester Boserup, a pioneer in the field of gender and development and author of the book *Woman's Role in Economic Development* (1970). Some of these chapters are inspired by her vision and challenge to researchers and policy-makers to more completely analyze and reveal the complexities of socio-economic realities by prioritizing gender issues. In particular, Part 4 focuses on new and emerging research within the gender-development-globalization nexus, including some reflections on Boserup's life and work and significance for further research. The volume is divided into five sections.

The chapters in Part 1, Globalization and Global Governance, explore the roles of multilateral institutions in facilitating global governance while rejecting the notion that it results in the demise of the nation-state. In Chapter 1, Toward a Stark Utopia?: New Constitutionalism and the Politics of Globalization, Stephen Gill argues that the dominant juridical and political dimension of global governance is "the new constitutionalism of disciplinary neoliberalism." According to Gill, this new constitutionalism is intended to reconstitute relations of the state, the economy, and society, positing that much of contemporary political struggle has been between those that attempt to "extend and lock-in" the rights of capital and those that seek to "democratize, socialize, and politically control capital."

In the contemporary period the actors who seek the former are attempting to impose legal frameworks that facilitate the rights of capital and reconstitute the state on its behalf. To this end the institutionalization of private property rights and economic liberalization have been central. Gill develops this point through an exploration of the formulation and implementation of the multilateral trading rules. He notes that they are attempts to create a set of "long-term economic and political reforms that gain constitutional status," and promote the rights of capital worldwide.

In Chapter 2, Tax Distortion in the Global Economy, Howard Wachtel focuses on taxation to argue that in the contemporary movement the concept of elasticity of response translates into political power that in effect "venerates the mobile and denigrates the stationary." He expands this argument by contrasting the high degree of capital mobility with the rootedness of labor. This difference, Wachtel posits, results in companies challenging tax policy by threatening to move to lower tax areas and creates a tension between the "unbounded global reach of commerce and a bounded national government." The shrinking tax base that results from this tension is further intensified by the current trends to liberalize and privatize. The share of total taxes from labor has been increasing while the share from capital has been declining. In the context of globalization, the challenge therein centers around the question: "What can be done to restore a degree of tax proportionality between the mobile and immobile, capital and labor, the fast and the slow?" This is a question Wachtel explores in some detail, providing interesting and useful insights into theoretical and practical paths for taxation.

In her chapter on Human Rights and Corporate Profits: The UN Global Compact—Part of the Solution or Part of the Problem?, Diane Elson interrogates the recent formation of the United Nations (UN) Global Compact. This alliance between the UN and the corporate world is an attempt to harness the power of the latter to promote the realization of human rights, including labor rights and the improvement of environmental standards.

Elson argues that the Compact deserves attention because it is "emblematic of 'Third Way' politics at the beginning of the 21st century." This politics, she argues, sees no fundamental contradictions between the hope of human rights and the exigencies of competitive capital accumulation." She critically examines this alliance focusing on its immediate modalities, and on its positioning between the processes of commodification and decommodification of human life.

In Chapter 4, Cross-Border Externalities and International Public Goods: Implications for Aid Agencies, Ravi Kanbur prioritizes the question: "What does the supply of international public goods imply for the organization of aid delivery, and especially for aid agencies?" He argues that the intersections between cross-border externalities, international public goods, and development assistance will present key challenges for aid agencies. Kanbur notes that there is general consensus that the aid delivery mechanisms of the past four decades have failed to adequately contribute to development and poverty reduction. Mechanisms for managing global externalities like atmospheric pollution are international public goods that need resources that, Kabur argues, could be funded by rich countries. This could be beneficial to poor countries. He concludes that current contestations within the aid community imply that the regime will have to ensure that mechanisms for managing global externalities benefit poorer countries and peoples.

Part 2 addresses specific issues relating to North-South Tensions: the fallout of financial crises, and the architecture of the present international financial system, including the international financial institutions (IFIs). In terms of the latter, there is much agreement that the present system is flawed; however, the questions of how to proceed in terms of reform and adjustment to current needs are still open. Given the severity of the damage to the "Asian Tigers" after the 1992 financial crisis, in Chapter 5, Financial Sector Liberalization and the Asian Financial Crisis: The IFIs Got It Wrong Twice, Iwan J. Azis grapples with the complex issues surrounding the corresponding response from the International Monetary Fund.

Linking this crisis with the drive for economic liberalization, he analyzes the policies related to banking reforms and governance in the affected countries, and he interprets the dynamics of achieving joint policy responses. Reinforcing some of the criticisms made by Stiglitz (2002), Aziz argues that in some cases the "Fund's policies were ineffective" and "counterproductive," and may, in fact, have "aggravated the situation" by exacerbating the loss in market confidence. He states that economic restructuring policies must be implemented in a gradual manner. The chapter enhances our knowledge of the background of policy responses to financial crises and reveals why, in the case of South East Asia, the IMF policies resulted in limited effectiveness.

In Chapter 6, Developing Countries and the New Financial Architecture, Stephany Griffith-Jones continues on the theme of international financial instability and notes that the wave of currency and banking crises of the 1990s have generated a consensus that fundamental reforms are required in the international financial system. This is increasingly important given the growing integration of capital and credit markets across countries and regions. More specifically, the current financial architecture is insufficient in a context characterized by very large, extremely volatile, and highly concentrated private capital flows. Griffith-Jones argues that two elements of a new architecture that would both "support and not undermine development" are: the prevention and better management of currency and banking crises; and the need to ensure that sufficient net private and public flows go to developing countries.

Guy Standing's chapter (7) focuses on key issues regarding labor, economic insecurity, and social welfare. In Globalization: Eight Crises of Social Protection, he argues that unlike the twentieth century, which was dominated by two laborist models, state socialism, and welfare state capitalism, through which states attempted to shape the economy, the twenty-first century faces the challenging task of developing new forms of social protection. Rejecting the market regulation model associated with neoliberalism, he discusses the different forms of labor market insecurity it has generated, and develops the concepts of social income and the possibility of providing new forms of social support systems. Finally, Standing presents selected policy options to explore the elements of socio-economic security in a "Good Society of the twenty-first century."

The chapters in Part 3, The Politics of International Trade, explore the roles of the World Trade Organization in regulating and promoting international trade in goods and services. The contributors engage with both the discursive and material effects of trade liberalization policies, as well as new arrangements emerging out of the multilateral trading system. In Chapter 8, Biotechnology and Food Security: Profiting on Insecurity?, Philip McMichael notes that the food security debate will dominate the international agenda in the twenty-first century, arguing that the emphasis will be on whether, and to what extent, food security can and will be guaranteed by the market. Questioning the assumption that it can, he emphasizes that in a market-based system, considerations about "what food is grown, where, and who can afford it" are driven by the desire for profits rather than concerns for food security. Within this context, McMichael posits that the WTO's Agreement on Agriculture attempts to open agricultural markets for northern products. Thus, the linkages between globalization, biotechnology, and food security serve to detract attention from current causes of poverty and hunger and foreclose alternatives to transgenic crops.

In Chapter 9, The WTO, GATS, and TPRM: Servicing Liberalization and Eroding Equity Goals?, Savitri Bisnath argues that the ideology of free trade is a discursive formation that involves specific regulatory and disciplinary processes. At the multilateral level, GATS and the Trade Policy Review Mechanism are regulatory devices that bring the imperatives of the multilateral trading system into national domains. Within this policy context WTO member-states are challenged to both facilitate an enabling environment for international trade in services, and address social and development needs. Bisnath explores emerging tensions therein. She argues that the deployment of global trade rules within national borders will undermine democratic decision-making and compromise the ability of governments to address issues of equity and development. To accomplish this Bisnath analyzes ways in which the GATS, as written, specifically intrudes upon domestic regulatory regimes in those service sectors traditionally prone to government intervention.

In Chapter 10, Labor Standards, Women's Rights, Basic Needs: Challenges to Collective Action in a Globalizing World, Naila Kabeer highlights two specific and interrelated aspects of globalization, namely, the ongoing globalization of production and the attempted globalization of labor standards. In particular, she documents the changes in the international division of labor and their implications for North-South trade. Kabeer analyzes the discourse and growing demand for linking labor standards to international trade agreements. To accomplish this she asks a key question: "Are globally enforced labor standards in the interests of all workers?" Kabeer contextualizes this debate by discussing the case of women workers in the garment industry in Bangladesh. She presents a nuanced, balanced, and differentiated account of the realities in Bangladesh and inspires us to do the same in other spatial contexts. Kabeer argues that without some "attention to basic needs, the campaign for global labor standards may end up eroding, rather than promoting, the rights of women workers in the poorer regions of the world's economy."

In Chapter 11, Contesting Global Trade Rules: Social Movements and the World Trade Organization, Marc Williams explores social movement activism directed at the WTO. He charts the ways in which the creation of this multilateral institution transformed the politics of international trade and, as a consequence, provided a site of contestation for competing groups and perspectives. Williams argues that the shift in global trade policy-making from "bargaining over products to negotiation over policies that shape the conditions of competition" partially result from the legitimacy the new trade rules derive from the neoliberal regime. Further, he analyzes activism against this regime. To this end Williams notes that social movement actors have challenged the liberalization project at the heart of the WTO as well as its democratic credentials. In addition, he discusses criticisms of the World Trade Organization, focusing on demands for procedural reform made by social movement activists.

Part 4, Gender, Globalization, and Development, focuses on Ester Boserup, her influence on the field of gender and development, as well as on related emerging issues. In Chapter 12, Utilizing Interdisciplinarity to Analyze Global Socio-Economic Change: A Tribute to Ester Boserup, Irene Tinker traces the evolution of Boserup's thought and discusses the critical importance of her work to the development field. In particular, Tinker emphasizes, Boserup provided intellectual credibility to this field by challenging the economistic approach to development thought and practice of her time. Tinker contextualizes Boserup's writings from an historical perspective. She argues that Boserup's interdisciplinary approach, which enables an examination of agricultural, technological, and population issues within "a unified model," provides insights into current trends, therefore anticipating contemporary debates.

In Chapter 13, Development and Productive Deprivation: Male Patriarchal Relations in Business Families and Their Implications for Women in South India, Barbara Harriss-White models the family firm and reveals the operation of patriarchy in its original sense: the control of younger men by older men. A number of paradoxes for economic and human development, in particular women's well-being, posed by these gendered governance relations are also explored. She builds on Boserup's method of stylized descriptive modeling to analyze the consequences of gender dynamics of family businesses. Her analysis goes beyond growth to include well-being, a dimension of development neglected by Boserup.

In a rigorous, detailed, and rich analysis, Harriss-White argues that family businesses provide employment that marginalizes women. Further, she argues that "relations of control of men over men," neglected by most theorists in feminist economics, are of paramount importance for a more complete understanding of the effects of development and globalization. In addition, she illuminates the contradictory effects of development through a discussion of the ways in which women of material standing are often complicit in the oppression of girls and women. Her case material is drawn from a study of the reproduction of elite businesses in South India; it reinforces the notion that economic development and household accumulation of resources do not necessarily translate into increased gender equality but might, in fact, do the opposite.

In Chapter 14, Promoting Women's Capabilities, Martha Nussbaum argues that many women lack support for "fundamental functions of a human life," a basic objective of the human development approach to development. She elaborates on this approach, focusing on the attainment of gender equality. Thus, Nussbaum brings a feminist perspective to the capabilities approach developed by Nobel laureate and economist Amartya Sen. The best way to hold concerns about diversity, pluralism, and personal freedom together, she argues, is to formulate norms as a "set of capabilities for full human functioning, emphasizing the fact that capabilities protect, and do not foreclose, spheres of human freedom." To this end, she advances a set of universal norms in connection with gender equality, arguing that the capabilities approach goes beyond the rights-based approach to development and is particularly useful for contextualizing women's issues because it focuses on what women are "actually able to do and be." Nussbaum notes that the capabilities approach has the potential to guide both governments in establishing basic constitutional principles and international agencies in assessing the quality of life.

The chapters in Part 5, Urban and Global Linkages, explore tensions and connections between the processes of globalization, economic restructuring, changing demographics, and urbanization. These contributions analyze tensions associated with urban poverty and social polarization, and argue that they are largely the product of the globalization of capital, labor, and culture, as well as the worldwide diffusion of large-scale urbanization. As the urban landscape becomes increasingly filled with a dense multiplicity of cultural and economic cleavages, it becomes the arena not just for struggles over resources but also for many other conflicts and confrontations that arise in the global geopolitical economy.

In Chapter 15, The Global City: Strategic Site/New Frontier, Saskia Sassen argues that the global city of today emerges as a strategic site for new types of operations. It is a location from which new claims materialize and assume concrete forms. She states that this is in part because the loss of power at the national level produces the possibility for new forms of power and politics at the subnational level. In her words: "The national as container of social processes and power is cracked and this opens up possibilities for a geography of politics that links subnational spaces." Sassen argues that cities are foremost in this new spatiality. Within this context, she explores whether, and the ways in which, new types of transnational politics are localizing in global cities.

In Chapter 16, Urban Tensions: Globalization, Economic Restructuring, and the Postmetropolitan Transition, Edward W. Soja discusses ways in which urban tensions arise from and are increasingly caused by contemporary urban conditions, including the social and spatial processes that generate them. As such, urban tensions must be addressed in ways that recognize the distinctive properties of contemporary urban transformations and the imprints of new and different urbanization processes that have been reshaping cities and urban life over the past three decades.

Grounded empirically on the city of Los Angeles, his starting point is the deepening and widening poverty and related conditions of urban deterioration for a large proportion of the population. Accompanied with growing social polarization, Soja argues that the urban condition is becoming increasingly similar among major metropolitan areas worldwide. He sees as a key factor "the increasing cultural heterogeneity of urban populations, arising primarily from extraordinary increases in transnational migration." Finally, he shows ways in which this has been transforming urban politics in Los Angeles.

In Chapter 17, Urban Transport and Tensions in Developing Countries, Eduardo Alcântara de Vasconcellos summarizes the structural factors that challenge the transportation needs of urban areas in developing countries. Providing rich empirical information, he argues that a social analysis of urban transport must evolve around actual mobility and accessibility conditions, as well as distribution among social groups. Based on an analysis of the ways in which economic changes in developing countries have transformed the "geography of power," Vasconcellos looks at the ways in which this process has affected urban transport. He critically analyzes the increasing use of private transportation and the appropriation of public spaces for such use, on the basis that it privileges the middle- and upper-classes and urban elites. As a result, he argues, the poor and those who rely on public means of transportation are penalized, including a larger proportion of women. The chapter explores current policy prioritizes and offers alternatives regarding mobility and accessibility.

Taken together, this collection provides rich insights into key issues, questions, and tensions generated by neoliberal policies. Driven by a sense of social and economic justice, the analyses often anticipate future deepening of specific tensions—for example—those that pertain to national and global governance, immigration, urbanization, and well-being, as inequalities both between and within countries are intensified. Further, the authors provide several important avenues through which to rethink the current processes of globalization, and they provide suggestions for the design of transformative policies and actions.

References

Boserup, Ester. 1970. *Women's Role in Economic Development.* London: Earthscan.

Dussel-Peters, Enrique. 2000. *Polarizing Mexico: the Impact of Liberalisation Strategy.* London: Lynne Rienner Publication.

Financial Times. 2003. "Business in an Alpine Retreat: Grim Challenges Cloud Next Week's Davos Meeting." January 18–19, 2003.

Stiglitz, Joseph. 2002. *Globalization and its Discontents.* New York: W.W. Norton & Co.

United Nation Development Programme (UNDP). 1999. *Human Development Report.* Oxford University Press.

PART 1

Globalization and Global Governance

CHAPTER 1

Toward a Stark Utopia?

New Constitutionalism and the Politics of Globalization

STEPHEN GILL

Introduction

The dominant juridical and political dimensions of governance in the present-day global political economy is "the new constitutionalism of disciplinary neoliberalism." It corresponds to an attempt to create a "stark utopia" on a world scale: a political project to institutionalize the self-regulating market system undertaken in the nineteenth century and carried out by the capitalist ruling classes in England (Polanyi 1975). At the turn of the millennium there is a similar moment involving a type of counterrevolution of the powerful against the weak, intended to reconstitute the state and capital to reorder social relations on a world scale. A re-extension of the rights of private property and its prerogatives in processes of commodification is occurring, leading to intensifications in the discipline of capital in social relations (what I call *disciplinary neoliberalism*). This also involves imposition of constitutional and quasiconstitutional legal frameworks that reconstitute the state (*new constitutionalism*). New constitutional frameworks also shape the operation of strategic, macroeconomic, microeconomic, and social policies. These frameworks are central constitutive mechanisms of the dominant political project of globalization.

The wider context is therefore a global political project combining the old and the radically new. However, the new stark utopia, or dystopia, is in practice unachievable since it has in-built contradictions. On the one hand it is a process central to the intensification and extension of alienation, exploitation, and commodification of human life and nature—processes intensifying in the era of capitalist globalization. These processes atomize human communities and contribute to destruction of ecological structures that support all life forms. The stark utopia is unsustainable politically, not least because different social movements and classes resist the destruction of their livelihoods and the intensified discipline of capital central to neoliberal globalization. Thus the central contradiction of globalization is not between capital and democracy as such, although this is crucial to new constitutionalism. It is much broader and it concerns the degree to which neoliberal globalization is serving to generate a crisis of social reproduction on a world scale, a crisis that is ecological as well as social. The wide-ranging nature of this crisis links diverse forces across and within nations that oppose neoliberal globalization in new forms of political struggle that will shape the future of global politics.

New Constitutionalism and the Rule of Law

New constitutionalism can be understood historically as part of the *longue durée* of liberal state formation, as well as a political project to "lock in" the power gains of capital on a world scale: it combines the old and the radically new. Many of its political precepts are regressive and link rights of representation to ownership of private property, and as such hark back to the predemocratic age of the great bourgeois revolutions. Of course, today formal democracy has extended with relatively universal suffrage—citizenship rights are not formally premised on private property, and the politics of new constitutionalism also involves the need to attenuate or incorporate and co-opt democratic forces and potential opposition to globalization.[1]

However, the main point is that the liberal conception of the state is a limited one, constrained by, and ultimately subordinate to, interests within civil society. The state has limited legal competence because the constitutional framework of a liberal state is pluralist, with formal decentralization of power, or put differently, the subordination of the state to civil society. This framework of power is the corollary of the sovereignty of private property rights and freedom of contract written into, and protected by, constitutional forms. Thus freedom of enterprise appears as a constitutive element of the Rule of Law. In turn, the Rule of Law formally defines the actions of the state in terms of a separation of state and civil society, of public and private, and of statute and contract. Of course, pluralism in the modern context needs to be related to a world in which there are large concentrations of private power with vast corporations operating in oligopolistic and monopolistic markets. Nevertheless, in a liberal constitution the state is subordinated to civil society and thus, by definition, the state cannot monopolize power and authority, which is in principle decentralized partly by concentrations of privately controlled capital that serve to define the distribution of power.

Within this context, the bourgeois state gave rise to a specific legal form—drawn from Roman Civil Law—that constituted the property-owning legal subject as the bearer of rights (Anderson 1974). The subject of the law is understood as a possessive individual who has full ownership of him-/herself and has formal equality before the law. He/she is assumed to have freewill and thus the freedom to enter into contracts (as a citizen). This of course allows for the labor contract—as well as other contractual relations—to take place *as if* they involved free exchange between individuals exercising their will. Thus this legal form underpins the commodification of labor and things, or more precisely the power to control the disposition of people relative to things (Edelman, 1979).

What this might mean in the context of a stark, commodified dystopia was illustrated as early as the sixteenth century in Shakespeare's comedy *The Merchant of Venice* (c. 1596). Here Shakespeare interrogated the potential legal basis of an order based on the principle of the absolute sovereignty of property rights:

> Go with me to a notary, seal me there
> Your single bond; and, in a merry sport,
> If you repay me not on such a day,
> In such a place, such sum or sums as are,
> Express'd in the condition, let the forfeit
> Be nominated for an equal pound
> Of your fair flesh, to be cut off and taken
> In what part of your body pleaseth me.[2]

Were such private property rights to assume an absolute, sovereign quality, it implied the right to privatize control over life itself through contract (e.g., Shylock's claims over Antonio's pound of flesh to be taken from wherever he chooses). When later faced with Antonio's plea of mercy, Shylock argues that contract right is supreme and that the property holder holds this right as a "sovereign" power, if need be over the life of Antonio. So what was at issue was how far private property rights included the right to treat people as if they are commodities and as such, the question of the legal underpinning of the emerging modern state. Resistance to absolute property rights was embodied in Portia, in the guise of Justice, who proposes constraints on, and if necessary confiscation of, property rights.

Seen in this way we can suggest that much of modern political struggle has involved the effort to extend and lock in rights of capital (insofar as these tend toward sovereign rights of property) on the one hand, and those that seek to democratize, socialize, and politically control capital on the other (the socialist project). This is why the law has usually placed limits on the scope of contractual relations, for example, forbidding an individual from selling parts of his/her body or genetic code, although these limits are increasingly transgressed.

Such issues become not simply issues of individual choice and morality under conditions of modernity. They are social and political issues since legal discourse transforms social relations insofar as both human beings and social entities change and, in particular, corporations become legal subjects that bear rights and duties and form primary constituents of law. In this respect the law can be said to *actively constitute* the very subject to which it refers, such as corporations and the parties to contracts—including labor contracts. In Althusserian terms, the law *interpolates* individuals as subjects with certain attributes, powers, and freedoms within the practice of law. Thus law is not merely an external mechanism of regulation but a constituent way in which social relations are lived and experienced. In this way the form of the subject constitutes a basic grounding for the rights of property (and of political representation) in global capitalism (Hunt, 1993).[3]

This is why Marx contrasted the formal freedoms of the law with the substantive inequality generated in the processes of production and exploitation. In this way, the law facilitates the capitalist form of the relationship between labor and capital, granting employers rights to not only control and exploit labor, but also over hiring and firing. The most important relations within capitalist society are molded into the form of contractual relations: They rest ultimately on the separation of public and private, or state and civil society in the constitutional and political structures of the state.

For example, it was the post-revolutionary French *Code Civil* that marked the advent of liberalism in France. Drawing on a range of sources in French jurisprudence, Georges Robé notes that the texts of the *Code Civil* still constitute the framework in which property rights are used in France. These are summarized as follows: The owner (and today this principally means the corporation) is sovereign in his specific field of action—whatever the limited, constitutionally valid application of the state's legislative and regulatory powers may entail (Robé 1996).

Robé concludes that full acknowledgement of private property rights is a decentralization of sovereignty for the legal order acknowledging. This allows individuals to enjoy their property however they choose, unless expressly prohibited. Indeed not everything can be prohibited. Thus power is decentralized in a liberal society principally through property. This explains the high degree of autonomy of the corporation (and large property owners) relative to the state and the rest of civil society: the citizens. The Rule of Law allows the corporation autonomy to make decisions concerning the disposition of its private property rights.

The enterprise also commands the individuals under its jurisdiction as a consequence of the labor or employment contract they sign. Contracts constitute the foundations of the corporation in positive law. Thus with regard to employment contracts, the employer has authority over employees. Employees have freely entered into the employment contract, creating a necessarily unequal relationship based on the command of the employer over the employee since the employer controls the property rights of the enterprise. Thus the existence and power of the enterprise derives from fundamental legal principles that guarantee private property rights as a part of liberal constitutions. The power of the enterprise is therefore built on positive constitutional foundations by which the *Liberal* State *must* abide (Robé, 1996: 60, his emphasis).

Robé goes on to argue that the Liberal State opens up the possibility for the employer to create special "private" laws, the existence of which is accepted by the state since they derive from overriding legal principles that guarantee private property rights, and as such, set the context for an erosion or transformation of social or collective property rights. The enterprise forms part of the constitutional structure of the exercise of power, ultimately sanctioned by liberal constitutions. Enterprises, therefore, to a certain extent, constitute a form of private government since some of the legal rules they create are final and may not be reviewed by any public body. When defining property, the French Civil Code speaks of "the right to enjoy and dispose of *things*, not *people*."

Robé (1996: 60) notes that property is not so much a right "over the thing itself as much as a right over the behaviour of others (including the state's agents and judges) in connection with the thing." Indeed, as the American scholar and judge James Oakes (1981) points out, drawing on sources in American jurisprudence, property is a broad set of legal *relations*: it is a subset of social relations and it encompasses a range of rights and freedoms, as well as certain limitations therein. The legal relations associated with property are thus connected to the behavior of people relative to things, in the present and in the future, as well as to control overflows of income deriving from control over a commodity (an asset or investment).

When we think of these issues in global politics, contemporary trade and investment rules and procedures can be viewed as a counterpart to the liberal Rule of Law on a multilateral basis. Quintessential new constitutional frameworks include multilateral investment agreements and bilateral investment treaties, or forward-looking "commitment mechanisms" or "disciplines" (Schneiderman, 1997). These agreements have quasiconstitutional status at the global level in key aspects of economic and political life—in ways that subordinate the state to elements in civil society—in this case, investors and private corporations. Thus new constitutionalism is a liberal global political project *par excellence*, indeed the primary political project of globalization today.

The World Trade Organization and other organizations of governance such as the international financial institutions are attempting to create a set of long-term economic and political reforms that gain constitutional status, thus underpinning the extension of the disciplinary power of capital on a world scale. In the case of the World Bank this also relates to an effort to reshape the internal and external structures of states in the Third World. The goal is to create what the Bank calls an "enabling state," one that will deliver an improved *long-term* investment climate, better protection of private property rights, and among other things, higher levels of profit flows in the future. A central goal of new constitutionalism is to secure protection for property rights and investor freedoms on a world scale, although the precise form that such initiatives will produce varies in and across different states and civil societies.

Many of these changes are related to an American-led G7 project to institutionalize disciplinary neoliberalism on a world scale, although what is striking is the degree to which the United States government itself refuses to accept the constraints and limitations on its sovereignty that it advocates for other states: unlike Ulysses before the Sirens it refuses to be tied to the mast of neoliberal economic globalization, and unlike other countries, it enjoys the relatively unique privilege of paying its debts in its own currency. Nevertheless, the American government has been strongly associated with the promotion of economic liberalization and a particular form of limited, electoral type of democratization defined in terms of free, periodic elections and party competition for votes as a means to strengthen American leadership in global politics (Robinson, 1996).

Some of what this means in a strategic sense was spelled out by the former U.S. Treasury Secretary for the Clinton Administration, Robert Rubin, who joined the world's biggest financial conglomerate, Citicorp (on October 27, 1999). Rubin explained that the geostrategic aim of American policy toward Russia and the Former East Bloc was not to create a liberal democracy in Russia as such, but rather to build what he called a "market democracy." He noted that unlike other countries in Central Europe, seventy years of communism meant that Russians had "no memory of a functioning market economy." He then outlined, in an odd use of the future conditional, the basic components of new constitutionalist strategy as applied to the reform effort in Russia:

Contract law and property rights would have to be created from scratch. Institutions to develop and enforce market regulations would have to be established. Judges to interpret the laws and regulations would have to be trained. [. . .] The rule of law is not established overnight. Nor is a market democracy. These are long-term objectives.[4]

The modern origins of this process can be found in the post-war occupation settlements in Germany and Japan under the Marshall Plan Administration, where the writing of new constitutions was part of the effort at political and economic reconstruction.

Three Dimensions of New Constitutionalism

Some of the present emphasis on new constitutionalism can be gleaned from a reading of three "texts." In late 1997 the globalization theorist Saskia Sassen, based on her attendance at the predominantly white, male, and plutocratic World Economic Forum (WEF) in Davos, Switzerland, reported on a shift in policy emphasis amongst the leaders of corporate capital. Sassen noted that the WEF participants previously stressed "market, market, market" as the focus of reform efforts worldwide. Now what was emerging was a concern to reinforce a "global economic governance" project, with more conscious emphasis on actively molding and reinforcing the state to provide a more stable political environment for capital.[5] The WEF participants' concerns were also reflected in the World Bank's *World Development Report* (1997), a document that in many ways exemplifies the project to create a constitution *for* global capitalism. Finally, the general nature of this project was reflected in the comment by Renato Ruggiero, former Director General of the World Trade Organization, who stated, "we are writing the constitution of a single global economy."[6]

So how does new constitutionalism relate to the extension of capitalist markets and free enterprise? From the viewpoint of the owners of capital, its freedoms—for example, the freedom to acquire, exchange, or move property rights—require not only constitutional guarantees against expropriation but also the imposition, internally and externally, of *binding constraints* on states' macroeconomic, trade, investment, and industrial policies. For example, devaluation or inflation may affect the capital value of an asset or investment; state industrial strategies may imply that domestic capital gains preferential treatment over foreign capital; national laws may have the same effect.

Some of the goals of new constitutionalism were spelled out by Michel Camdessus (1999), the former Managing Director of the International Monetary Fund (IMF), in a speech to the Institute of International

Bankers in Washington in March 1999. He saw the overarching method to realize the IMF utopia in the twenty-first century as the "universal promotion of free-market mechanisms strengthened by a set of standards and principles of good conduct." Specifically, Camdessus called for "open and integrated capital markets, achieved through a gradual process of liberalization supported by good macroeconomic policies and sound financial institutions." Second, he imagined a world where the discipline of capital ("the private sector") would operate along hyperrationalist principles based on full access to relevant public and private information, with databases constructed according to uniform accounting and financial standards so that risks can be calculated more effectively—this is a process of normalization and surveillance or transparency that we call "panopticism" (Gill, 1995).

Third, Camdessus noted that compensatory measures are needed to deal with marginalization and dislocations associated with the globalization (i.e., the spread of the commodity form). Using arguments similar to the World Bank (1997) he foresaw a utopia where "no countries are marginalized . . . with social policies [to insure] equitable access to opportunities in education, health, livelihood, and social protection in times of crisis" (Camdessus, 1999: 2). New constitutionalism involves more than simply "locking in" forms of market discipline. It encompasses three sets of interrelated "productive constraints."

Measures to Reconfigure State Apparatuses

A central purpose of new constitutionalism is to make states operate under greater market discipline. One method is to institutionalize or lock in free entry and exit options for mobile capital. Associated with this type of initiative is promotion of an ideology of "best practice," promulgated by the international financial institutions that involves application of new systems of incentives and surveillance (panopticism). In addition to privatization, state agencies are made to compete with the private sector in, for example, service provision, and behave, at least in theory, as if they were marketplace actors. These reforms are justified in the name of *credibility* and provision of political conditions to guarantee full security to the rights of property and thus encourage private investment (World Bank, 1997). However, what neither the World Bank nor the IMF emphasize is that these measures involve limiting mass popular-democratic and indeed parliamentary influence over central aspects of economic policy. These measures institutionalize protections for corporations and investors from democratic accountability and control. In effect, both constitutional and institutional measures are involved.

Measures to Construct and Extend Liberal Capitalist Markets

New constitutionalism serves to institutionalize liberalization of markets for capital, goods, and labor. Some of this is linked to primitive accumulation—for example—privatization of state assets or alienation of common lands and resources in a new enclosure movement (e.g., in the Amazon and Chiapas). Other forms of market development relate to the new frontiers of alienated property—for example, the extension and institutionalization of (intellectual) property rights and contract law into diverse areas such as computer software and the output of life science corporations, and the centralization of ownership of patents over seeds or parts of the human genetic structure. Such measures are institutionalized in the new international agreements such as trade-related intellectual property rights of the WTO, measures that have been challenged by much of the Third World for monopolizing cultural and technological knowledge and transforming it into a commodity (e.g., the disputes over AIDS drugs between developing countries and the giant pharmaceutical firms). What is at issue here is, on the one hand, the gradual acceleration and universalization of a social and biological monoculture in ways that reduce cultural and biological diversity and, on the other, how this tends to intensify social and political hierarchies at the local and global levels. This deprives working class and peasant women and men of access to resources.

Extreme examples of market extension referring mainly to the USA—the epicenter and the vanguard of the liberalization trend—are as follows: The first example relates to the genetic engineering of animal forms: a process that has been called "unnatural selection." This is connected to the rapid destruction of biodiversity, for example in seeds, crops, and in the ever-reducing gene pools for animals such as cattle. The economic conditions for the intensification of this trend are largely related to a combination of market power and legal protections. Such processes rest politically and legally on control of intellectual property rights over life forms by giant life sciences and agro-corporations. These corporations, as well as farmers who use their products under competitive conditions fostered by liberalization of trade and agriculture, search for ways to maximize crop and profit yields. The effect of their actions is to narrow gene pools; farmers argue that the greatest genetic dangers herein probably lie in animal breeding, especially in pigs and poultry that, at the level of the farm, offer the fastest turnover of capital.[7]

Geneticists use computer programs to select the desirable traits from "a small number of apparently ideal animals and get results more quickly than ever before." It appears, however, that what are being reproduced are animals who "may have incredible performance potential and quality characteristics but cannot stand, will not breed, and tend to lie down and die."[8] Dairy farmers worldwide, seeking greater milk yields, use the "best bulls in the world" to inseminate the cows that, through superovulation, can produce twenty–thirty eggs. The eggs are fertilized in test tubes and inserted in wombs of host cows. Thus virtually universal use of artificial insemination today means that one bull can father tens of thousands of "perfect" calves in his lifetime:

> The danger is, however, that most of the calves in the world may soon be related to just a few dozen superior bull families as breeders select from an ever-reducing gene pool . . . [Yet] Suppose one of these elite bulls had a congenital defect that did not show itself for a generation or two? Such is the potential influence of a single animal of these days that the result could be catastrophic on a world scale.[9]

Another related set of examples relate to commercialization of genetic discourse and the new eugenics, linked to the commodification of the human body. For example, in recent years there has been a broad emergence of commercial surrogacy, sex selection, and the sale of sperm, eggs, and human tissue. The forces pushing back the frontiers, at least in North America, are grounded in a perspective linked to the American liberal discourse of the Rule of Law and doctrines of individual legal rights. Human beings have ownership of the self (they are self-possessive) and as such they have the right to sell their ova, sperm, or even body parts as their private property. American courts have therefore begun to declare property rights over the genetically engineered products made from human bodies—for example—genes and cell lines. It is expected that genetically altered human "embryos" may soon be offered for sale. Soon almost any part of the body—the kidneys, the pancreas, the heart, and other vital organs—may be replaced with implants engineered from living cells and synthetic materials: the bionic age has arrived.

Measures for Dealing with Dislocations and Contradictions

This section relates to the political dialectic associated with these developments. Because "new" constitutionalism requires the restructuring of social relations and the exposure of individuals and communities to the nakedness of the cash nexus, it is resisted. This is not least because it entails significant dismantling of certain types of protection for industry, agriculture, and workers, as well as the privatization of the state or primitive accumulation. However, disciplinary neoliberalism cannot simply proceed by coercive means alone: it requires at least passive consent. Thus compensatory measures are associated with the new disciplines—that is, to prevent social atomization and limit political consequences of intensified exploitation of human beings and nature. More broadly, what is involved is an effort to co-opt political opposition in a process that Gramsci called *trasformismo*. This is intended to constrain political tendencies that might generate a broad-based political backlash against neoliberal globalization, such as occurred from left and right in the 1930s (Gramsci, 1971). Put differently, the politics of neoliberal globalization involves a dialectic between the strengthening/disciplining of the state (through new constitutionalism) to intensify the power of capital while simultaneously seeking to widen the social basis of support for the state through incorporation of opposition (e.g., adopting arguments from the feminist and postmodern discourses of empowerment and linking these to material concessions).

A general example of this today would be in much of the former Soviet Bloc, after the collapse of communist rule, its gradual incorporation into the institutional and constitutional forms associated with Western capitalist hegemony, and gradually during the 1990s with European integration. The reform programs that have been introduced by external forces drawn from Western Europe within the broader framework of the institutional complexes of transnational capitalism are also linked to the leadership of the United States in the G7 and the international financial institutions. The process of transformation from state socialism and Soviet communism to liberal capitalism is a classic example of the introduction of new constitutional and political forms from above and the outside—in order to advance capitalism in the absence of a domestic capitalist class that has attained hegemony.

Trasformismo also relates to the capillary aspects of power in society. An example is the way the World Bank discourse on participation by the agents of civil society (NGOs, business associations) seeks to legitimate a hierarchical and unequal system of representation in the making of state policy—policy, for example, in Africa and Latin America that is linked to the expansion of an externally prescribed model of capitalist development. In this process the key areas of policy—relative to the remaining "commanding heights" of the economy that have not already been privatized— are separated from real democratic participation and accountability. Thus the World Bank develops its notion of "participation," for example, the participation of women in shaping social programs, partly as a means to make policies work at lower cost and to incorporate opposition. Put differently, the bank is seeking to offset limitations imposed on mass democracy in the economic realm by increasing democratic participation in other safely channeled areas.

One way that this is legitimated is by a strategy of targeting the very poorest in the urban centers with real material concessions, so that they can aspire to enter the world of market civilization. At the same time this is intended to help contain mass-based resistance. Of course in some nations, such as Mexico, compensatory measures in the context of globalization and liberalization are notable by their absence, so if World Bank policies were actually followed this would result in real gains for the poorest.

More generally, in a world of increasing inequality and instability associated with globalization, a key role of the international financial institutions and governments is not only to restructure the state and the patterns of economic regulation, but also to deal with the dislocations associated with the transformation process. This is reflected partly through the rhetoric of poverty alleviation, the new discourse of participation, and the "enabling state" that is now central to the contemporary role of the World Bank.

So whereas the "locking-in" measures with respect to macroeconomics and property rights may be a coercive way of preventing a backlash against neoliberal globalization (i.e., by insulating states from popular demands), measures dealing with dislocations are, in a sense, the consensual counterparts in that they seek to reduce the demands for other types of reform in the first place. Thus it can be argued that the World Bank and other agencies associated with the development of world capitalism are now attempting systematically to co-opt and channel forces of civil society. The tactic seems to be to legitimate the attenuation of democracy in economic policy by increasing participation in safely channeled areas, away from the "commanding heights" of macroeconomic and strategic policy.

Conclusion

New constitutionalism is economistic and involves a form of rule narrowly based on the primacy, indeed sovereignty of holders of large private property. It prescribes measures to restructure states and their civil societies based on the primacy of free enterprise and the discipline of capital operating broadly within the constraints of classical liberal notions of the Rule of Law. However, if constitutional order and Rule of Law is to constitute a positive form of freedom, it cannot be simply and narrowly viewed as an economic mechanism that guarantees private property rights. It must be linked to more fundamental questions of democracy. A democratic Rule of Law thus might involve basic human rights (including political rights to freedom of conscience, expression, and association); human security (freedom from all forms of violence, discrimination, and intolerance); and human development (for example, rights to education, health, livelihood, and nonalienating work). This would involve a very different program of moral and social reform to that proposed by neoliberals; indeed it would point toward a new form of state that would not be imposed from above, since it would correspond to basic democratic and universal aspirations of people throughout the world, and to a historical process that has been called "reflexive democratization" (Sakamoto 1994). Indeed, this democratic potential is linked to a historical process and normative project that seek to unify the particular with the universal. By contrast, the rules and disciplines of global constitutionalism operate in ways that seek to subordinate the universal to the particular interests of large capital—that is, its discipline operates hierarchically (in terms of social classes, gender, race, and national power) within and across different nations, regions, and in the global political economy. Possessive individualism and rights of private property, of individual, particular, or private appropriation are increasingly subordinating social reproduction and engendering dislocations in global production as the latter has become progressively universal and socialized.

Many changes associated with new constitutionalism have been linked to a pragmatic discourse of political economy called disciplinary neoliberalism. However, such reforms are largely imposed *from above and often from outside* on populations, and are largely premised on the subordination of democracy to the pursuit of profit. As such, they lack substantive legitimacy and hegemonic appeal. This is one reason why the new constitutional reform project is not complete, since it contains political and economic contradictions, and it provokes resistance from across the political spectrum: resistance to the projects of new constitutionalism and neoliberal globalization. Thus whether new constitutionalism can succeed in institutionalizing the new stark utopia seems open to doubt at the beginning of the new millennium.

References

Anderson, Perry. 1974. *Lineages of the Absolutist State*. London: N.L.B.

Camdessus, Michel. 1999. "Capital Flows, Crises, and the Private Sector." Washington D.C.: Institute of International Bankers.

Edelman, Bernard. 1979. *Ownership of the Image: Elements for a Marxist Theory of Law*. Translated by E. Kingdom. London: Routledge.

Gill, Stephen. 1995. "The Global Panopticon? The Neo-liberal State, Economic Life and Democratic Surveillance." *Alternatives*, 20(1): 1–49.

Gramsci, Antonio. 1971. *Selections from the Prison Notebooks of Antonio Gramsci*. Translated by Q. Hoare and G. Nowell-Smith, 1st ed. New York: International Publishers.

Hunt, Alan. 1993. "Explorations in Law and Society: Toward a Constitutive Theory of Law," in J. Brigham and C. B. Harrington eds, *After the Law*. New York: Routledge.

Oakes, James L. 1981. "'Property Rights in Constitutional Analysis Today." *Washington Law Review*, 56(3): 583–626.

Polanyi, Karl. 1975. *The Great Transformation: Political and Economic Origins of Our Times*. New York: Octagon Books.

Robé, Jean-Phillipe. 1996. "Multinational Enterprises: The Constitution of a Pluralistic Legal Order," in *Global Law without a State*, G. Teubner ed. Aldershot: Dartmouth Publishing.

Robinson, W. I. 1996. *Promoting Polyarchy: Globalisation, US Intervention and Hegemony*. Cambridge: Cambridge University Press.

Sakamoto, Y. 1994. *Global Transformation: Challenges to the State System*. Tokyo: United Nations University Press.

Schneiderman, D. 1997. "Investment Rules and New Constitutionalism: Interlinkages and Disciplinary Effects." Consortium on Globalisation, Law and Social Science (CONGLASS III). New York University.

Shakespeare, William. 1980. "The Merchant of Venice," in *The Complete Works of Shakespeare*. 3rd ed., David Bevington, ed. London: Scott, Foresman and Company.

World Bank. 1997. *The State in a Changing World. World Development Report, 1997*. Washington DC and New York: World Bank and Oxford University Press.

Notes

1. See the section on *trasformismo*, p. 23.
2. Shylock to Antonio in Act 1, Scene 3 of the *Merchant of Venice*. I am grateful to Gibin Hong for reminding me of this early Shakespearean example of critical social theory.
3. At the same time, the bourgeois forms of state have become democratized so that the "legal-subject-as-citizen" is arrived at and whose significance is that "right no longer remains exclusively tied to property relations," and the culmination of this process was the emergence of welfare states after World War I, with their distinct social rights. For the purpose of clarity in the context of our specific argument in this chapter, we will leave this aspect of rights to one side and focus on economic rights, powers, and freedoms in liberal capitalist states.
4. Robert E. Rubin, "Don't Give Up on Russia," *New York Times*, September 21, 1999.
5. Remarks at the opening session of the conference, Non-State Actors and Authority in the Global System, Warwick University, UK, 31 October 1997.
6. Renato Ruggiero, "The High Stakes of World Trade," in *Wall Street Journal*, interactive edition, February 28, 1997.
7. David Richardson, "Unnatural Selection: Care Is Needed to Ensure the Survival of Crop and Livestock Varieties," in *Financial Times*, January 3, 1996.
8. Ibid.
9. Ibid.

CHAPTER 2

Tax Distortion in the Global Economy

HOWARD M. WACHTEL*

As globalization challenges national borders, governments are discovering that their tax base is eroding, especially their ability to tax corporate profits. The share of total taxes from labor has been increasing while the share on capital has been declining.[1] In the European Union half of all tax receipts were derived from capital in 1980; by the mid-1990s it had fallen to 35 percent. At the same time, the share of taxes collected from labor rose from 35 percent to over 40 percent. In the United States, which has historically had a lower capital share, there is a similar pattern: the capital share of 27 percent in 1965 has fallen to only 15 percent in 1999. It is important to note that this minimal corporate share occurred at a moment of historical records in corporate profits.[2]

The source of this change can be partially explained by globalization. Capital is more mobile than labor and can escape taxes by moving to low tax Third World countries. By manipulating their books through transfer pricing, corporations are able to show high profits in low tax jurisdictions, and avoid the high tax jurisdictions of Europe and the United States. In developed countries (DCs), financial and tangible forms of capital roam the

*Many of the ideas for this chapter were developed at the American Academy in Berlin, where I was a Distinguished Visiting Scholar in Fall 1999. I am grateful for comments from the members of American University's Inter-Disciplinary Council on the Global Economy, where this paper was presented in Fall 2000.

globe, rendering it difficult either to define profits for tax purposes or decide in which country the taxable profit is earned. Less-developed countries (LDCs) find themselves under such pressure to grant tax holidays, tax abatements, and generous land giveaways, that they cede their tax base in an obsessive competition for foreign investment. Corporations have then used these concessions to leverage tax reductions in their home countries, in what is by now a well-tuned orchestration of political pressure. "Tax degradation," is the way the International Monetary Fund's former Director of Fiscal Affairs characterizes this general phenomenon, ". . . whereby some countries change their tax systems to raid the world tax base and export their tax burden" (Tanzi, 1996: 3).

A different spatial alignment defines the new global era. Capital operates both within and beyond states while labor is rooted in the specific space of nation states. A tension arises therefore, between the unbounded global reach of commerce and a bounded national government. The economic concept of elasticity is relevant here: a higher elasticity of response of capital to taxes, as compared to labor, affords corporations greater power in leveraging their influence against governments. If capital is taxed, it can move and tax receipts from corporations decline. This yields a high response elasticity. The contrary is true for labor. Simply put, companies can challenge government tax policy by threatening to move to lower taxed jurisdictions, a tactic that is not credible for labor. Thus, the technical economic concept of elasticity translates into political power in a global era that venerates the mobile and denigrates the stationary.

The French social critic Susan George (1999: 179) describes this distinction between the mobile and the stationary as the "fast castes . . . the owners of capital and skilled professionals, [who] are at the top of the global pyramid," echoing Jacques Attali's apt characterization of them as "elite nomads." "Below them," she continues, "is a vast pool of stationary, 'slow people,' whose chief common characteristic is their substitutability, whether the substitution takes place North-North, North-South, or South-South." This has changed relative bargaining power and the terrain within which negotiations over a social contract once took place. George argues that previously the "negotiating table was geographically grounded. People had to negotiate because they were going to have to go on living with each other in . . . the same space." This is not this case any longer because of the spatial alterations associated with globalization, in which the "key words are speed and mobility," says George. Power relations now slice through capital and labor into a new division between the fast, mobile people and the slow, stationary ones.

The fast and the mobile stay a step ahead of the tax collector, something the slow and the rooted cannot do. Existing tax policy was designed for defined borders and tax jurisdictions that coincided with nation-states. Indeed, that was one of the raison d'etre for states in the first instance when they were formed a half millennium ago. The current global era has changed this. Differing mobilities and elasticities of capital and labor reconfigure power relations in the United States and Europe and expose developing economies to a competitive race to the bottom. The route to an analysis of tax distortion and its consequences runs through a discussion of the conceptualization of globalization and the confusions surrounding this buzz word.

Defining Globalization

Globalization began as an economic phenomenon in the mid-1970s following the collapse of the regulation of international money in what was known as the Bretton Woods system. Following this event, the profusion of definitions that attempt to describe globalization has focused primarily on the purely quantitative, especially in conventional economic circles, international organizations, and governments. It is conventionally defined as more money moving around the world, more trade, more investment, more people, more information, and all at a dizzying faster pace. Interdependence is the catchword that encapsulates these phenomena. To this is added the observation that some activities, such as trade and the movement of people, were as large or larger before World War I than they were at any time up to the 1990s. David Hale (Hale, 1999: 6) a journalist, is representative of this group when he points out that the "process called globalization was well under way in the closing decades of the nineteenth century," but then was halted "in much of the world for nearly eight decades because of World War I" as well as, one could add, the Great Depression and World War II. For example, British overseas assets rivaled those of the United States today (adjusted for inflation) and the movement of people from the mid-nineteenth century until World War I was similar to today.

In an otherwise sharply etched report on how the new globalization has exposed the failures of European social democracy, the Organization for Economic Cooperation and Development (OECD) offers this numbingly tepid definition, typical of this international organization genre:

> Globalization refers to an evolving pattern of cross-border activities of firms, involving international investment, trade and collaboration for the purposes of product development, production and sourcing, and marketing. [...] These strategies are shaped by declining communication and transport costs, and rising R&D costs; macroeconomic trends and exchange rate fluctuations; and liberalization of trade, investment and capital movements.
>
> (OECD, 1994: 28)

Few academic economists go beyond these characterizations of globalization, especially in international economics' textbooks.

An exception is the text of two Canadian economists, Brown and Hogendorn, who have attempted a synthesis between traditional international economics and the economics of globalization. They acknowledge that "globalization is the increasing economic integration of the world [which] began a century and a half ago," and then go on to point out that it "reduces the power of governments to control their economies" (Brown and Hogendorn, 2000: 16). More typical is the definition that appears in the most comprehensive and interdisciplinary anthology as of this writing and published in the U.S., where the new global economy is represented simply as the first epoch in which the "international economic system has become truly *interdependent*. A web of interconnections between, within, and above states have tied together formerly disparate forces" (O'Meara, Mehlinger, and Krain, 2000: 215). By way of contrast, an earlier anthology with a distinctly European perspective highlights the "rapid expansion of financial markets worldwide, the competitive struggle of nations for exports, the radical uncertainty of future investment opportunities and the failure of existing government strategies" to address globalization and its tensions (Boyer and Drache, 1996: 9).

There is no mistaking the fact that quantitative changes and their pace are important defining characteristics of globalization. What is missing from these definitions, however, is the *qualitative* dimension of globalization. At some point quantitative change translates into qualitative change. Further, the single most important aspect of the qualitative change wrought by globalization is the challenge to the sovereignty of the nation-state, its independence in making policy through democratic parliamentary procedures; and the emergence of policy as a "tradable commodity," its export and import and convergence toward uniformity—the "single price" associated with the trajectory of all tradable commodities.

Nowhere is this clearer than in the contrast between the World Trade Organization (WTO) and its predecessor, the General Agreement on Tariffs and Trade (GATT). The birth of the WTO in the mid-1990s distinguished it from the GATT, which had been in existence since 1948, precisely along globalizing lines. GATT was a regulatory regime that stopped at the borders of countries. It encouraged countries to lower tariff and nontariff barriers to trade, allowing outside products to enter countries on equal terms with those produced inside.

In contrast, the WTO inserted itself inside borders to open up trade, challenging policies that interfered with the commercial principle of the free movement of goods and services, whether it be intellectual property statutes, environmental regulations, or standards that controlled such services as insurance or banking safeguards. It sets up mechanisms for changing internal policies within countries that interfered with the entry of products and services, thereby establishing itself as a regulator of domestic policies that affect trade. This has been most clearly identified with patents, trademarks, and copyrights—aspects of intellectual property—that countries such as India have been required to alter to conform to WTO requirements. But the unidimensional commercial principle has also been applied to environmental regulations in the U.S. and Europe.

The WTO received vastly enhanced rule-making authority over an extended jurisdiction, superceding national governmental policy. At the core of the conflict between the WTO, as representative of the new globalism, and the nation-state is the monochromatic quality of the WTO's commercial principle, its *pensee unique* as the French call it, as against the multiple prisms of the state where the commercial principle is juggled against health and safety objectives, environmental standards, rights of labor, and so on.

The imagery erected in the half millennium since the advent of the nation-state was one of verticality: a series of vertical borders that figuratively separated one country from another in which a blend of free access across borders and national regulation of borders coexisted. The essence of globalization is a set of horizontal functional intrusions that cut swaths through borders in a regime where free access trumps national regulation: First financial markets penetrated "vertical" borders; then trade increased—fostered by a radical reduction in transportation costs; then foreign investment increased. Outside the economic realm culture was next and crime, the movement of larger numbers of people through legal and illegal immigration, and changes in telecommunications followed. In each of these realms the assault on national borders was nothing new.

As Fernand Braudel and the *Annales* school argue, all of this had been going on since the beginning of history. But what was new was the scale, the scope, the rapidity of movement, the shrinkage of time and space. It is as if a block of Swiss cheese stood in for the nation-state and small holes previously had permeated its mass. The functional incursion of globalization makes the holes ever bigger so that at the end they are much larger than the mass, threatening the stability and structural soundness of the mass itself; a metaphorical way of describing the translation of quantitative change into qualitative transformation. When that happens a threat of collapse and implosion is imminent. This is the fear that has motivated an ill-formed language of dissent, one that has tried to find a voice for saying enough. A pause is needed to take stock of where we are, and what can be done to absorb and assimilate change.

> A different conceptual premise from the conventional views capital as a constantly "revolutionizing" process. Because capital needs an "expanding market" for its products [it] chases over the whole surface of the globe . . . settle[s] everywhere, establish[es] connections everywhere . . . give[s] a cosmopolitan character to production and consumption in every country. . . . In place of the old local and national seclusion, . . . we have intercourse in every direction, a universal interdependence of nations [and] . . . a world after its own image.
>
> (Marx and Engels, 1998: 38–40)

This contemporary-sounding language is actually a prescient piece of writing from *The Communist Manifesto*.

To bring this forward to the present, globalization alters the space in which individuals, institutions, and governments comport themselves. It both expands and contracts space. Vistas are enlarged through modern telecommunications, information delivery, travel, and institutional changes that allow corporations to produce and market instantaneously across the globe. Space, however, also constricts. Corporate space encroaches upon private space. Individual privacy contracts and the room for the fabrication of spontaneous space are crowded out by corporate constructions, in which individuals follow a "script" for their behavior within a public space written by corporate planners.

One need only compare the spontaneous space in the café culture of the typical French café with that of corporate constructed space in a Starbucks, notwithstanding the positive accomplishment of that company in bringing better coffee to the United States, within a peculiarly American-style homogeneous coffee-drinking experience. Or take the case of being a spectator at a sports event that has been transformed into a theater of corporate entertainment in the new arenas built specifically for that purpose, in which higher profits are made on the ancillary expenditures than on the admission ticket. This connects with taxes in that government space for the collection of taxes has shrunk at the same time as the corporate universe has broadened for the deployment of accounting devices to select where it wants to pay taxes. Corporations are able to globalize their tax burdens, to minimize these obligations, and allocate them so as to enhance their worldwide profits, while government is constrained to a more restricted territorial boundary.

Pulling these observations together points to a definition of globalization that captures both the quantitative and the qualitative, its spatial transformation, and power structures. One example is from *The Economist*: "a minimum definition would include a diminishing role for national borders and a gradual fusing of separate national markets into a single global market."[3] To this should be added the import and export not only of tangibles but also intangibles, such as policy ideas, culminating in the single policy formula, the *pensee unique*, replacing a matrix of varying policies in various settings. Broadening this, my colleague at American University Colin Bradford (n.d.: 16–17), has delved into literature and art to find a means to capture the essence of globalization. Inspired by the work of the Mexican Nobel Prize winner Octavio Paz, he borrows this writer's literary symbolism of "roots and wings," the tension between national identity (roots) and universality (wings), between the concrete space where life is lived and the abstract space of the cyberworld, the stationary and the mobile, the slow and the fast, or in Paz's words the separation of writers into those "air-borne and those deeply rooted,"[4] to describe this complex phenomenon.

Taxation and Factor Mobility

"The heart of the problem" of tax distortion, according to *The Economist*, derives from the fact that "modern tax systems were developed after the second world war when cross-border movements in goods, capital and labor were relatively small. Now, firms and people are more mobile—and can exploit tax differences between countries."[5] To firms and people, factors of production in economics, a third is added: land. Historically, tax systems were developed with the creation of the nation-state. Indeed, one of the motivations for state creation and defined geographical jurisdiction was the desire of authorities to capture the tax base that was originally land. Land is the most reliable and predictable tax base because it cannot be moved to another tax entity. It is virtually inelastic with respect to any tax rate.

A government's ability to tax depends on its ability to maintain its tax jurisdiction. Factor mobility erodes this. Governments can more effectively tax factors of production if there is a high degree of inelasticity with respect to the tax base following on an increase in tax rates. The taxed factor cannot escape by fleeing the tax jurisdiction if there is immobility and inelasticity. This explains the declining proportion of tax revenues emanating from capital and the increasing proportion on labor. The mobile factor of production—capital—can more readily jettison an unfavorable tax jurisdiction and seek refuge in a Third World tax haven. A government can raise the tax *rate* on capital but discover its tax receipts have declined because the *base* on which the tax is calculated drops proportionally more than the rate has risen. Capital flees the high tax jurisdiction; the tax on capital is more elastic. This is the principal reason for the decline in corporate tax receipts in the face of record profits.

Capital flight is more easily accomplished by owners of financial capital, but it is increasingly attained with physical capital. However, inelastic labor remains confined to the tax jurisdiction in which it resides. Profits are a moving target; labor is stationary and more readily targeted for taxation. Even if labor wanted to move to another tax entity, it cannot easily do so. Immigration laws restrict labor mobility, but fewer restrictions are placed on capital movements. For example, the proposals for a Multilateral Agreement on Investment (MAI) aimed to further increase the ease of fixed and financial capital movements.[6] In addition, language, culture, the costs of moving and reversing the move, and risk, all influence the limited mobility of labor. Picking up and relocating halfway around the world is not as easy for humans as it is for stateless and rootless capital, which is specifically aided by the modern marvels of information technology. The difference in opportunities for the movement of capital as opposed to labor therefore, accounts for the shifting of taxes onto labor and away from capital, with consequences for unemployment, equity, and efficiency.

A corporate "underground economy" avoids taxes but absorbs benefits from other's tax payments. The OECD seemed to surrender to this reality in 1997 when, in a staff paper, it observed that "with growing international mobility of both fixed investment and financial investment there may be a need to reduce taxes on income from capital. Thus, most of the tax burden will have to fall on labor as this is the less mobile factor.[7] Four years later, however, the same OECD had reversed itself having found what it calls "tax competition" to be harmful when countries can develop tax policies:

> aimed at diverting financial and other geographically mobile capital [...] shifting part of the tax burden from mobile to relatively immobile factors and from income to consumption, [creating] "free riders" who benefit from public spending in their home country and yet avoid contributing to its financing.
> (OECD, 1998: 14[8])

At first glance it may appear to be a wise policy for a developing country to compete for foreign direct investment (FDI) by offering a low tax rate on profits. However, it can be a trap: a *cul de sac* that pits one poor country against another in an inevitable race to the bottom. In other words, a "prisoner's dilemma" in which each Third World government would prosper by not giving away its tax-collecting potential but cannot do so without a collaboration that is precluded by the character of competition for direct foreign investment. Foreign direct investment to Third World economies stood at $190 billion in 2000, the same as it was in 1999. This represents a trend reversal following on the 1997 Asian financial crisis and its spread to Latin America. Before 1997, FDI had been growing rapidly in the Third World, its share of total FDI growing from around 17 percent in 1990, to a peak of 40 percent by 1994, and 17 percent in 1999. At least one-third of total FDI in emerging markets has gone to China.[9] Through the prism of neutral parties in the advanced countries it becomes a form of poaching on taxes from profits, shifting internal tax burdens, and producing free riders in the most productive sectors.

Transfer Pricing and Tax Distortion

Transfer pricing is the device corporations use to locate their profits worldwide so as to minimize their global tax payments. It was first discovered by analysts in the early 1970s, applicable to only a slice of corporate activity that had become multinationalized.[10] Today, however, transfer pricing is so widespread that it has caused the erosion of the profits tax base.[11] A corporation operating globally has considerable transactions internal to the company, where the cost and price of those transactions are not set on an external market, but established by the corporation itself. A company can, therefore, manipulate these internal prices so as to show high profits in low-tax jurisdictions and low profits in high-tax jurisdictions. The typical template yields high prices for headquarter activities, normally conducted in high-tax jurisdictions, such as marketing, research and development, production and inventory management, legal, intellectual property, accounting and financial services, some of which is used to manage the internal transfer pricing mechanism. Low market prices are placed on those direct production activities conducted in low-tax developing countries. External markets will dictate these basic price differentials.

However, when a multinational corporation (MNC) "imports and exports" products and services within its worldwide affiliates, it flips these differentials. It charges a lower internal price than that on the external market for headquarter activity "exports" in order to show high profits in low-tax developing countries. Higher internal "import" prices are charged than those in the external market for the direct production undertaken in Third World affiliates to show lower profits in the high-tax country. Through this method of pricing its internal imports and exports, underinvoicing headquarter prices and overinvoicing foreign costs, the MNC establishes transfer prices that allow it to conduct a profit location strategy to minimize its global tax liability. Transfer prices for exports and imports internal to the company permit the MNC to optimize its placement of profits with the goal of minimizing tax payments, constrained by a band of price differentials that does not invite the suspicion of the tax collector in the high-tax country (Tanzi, 1995).

The problem for taxing authorities arises from the nature of profits, the base on which taxes are levied on corporations and financial institutions. Profits represent the difference between revenues and costs, but the questions raised by transfer pricing in a global theater are: what are costs, and which institution defines them—the external and tax-neutral market or the biased internal transfer-pricing "market" of the tax-paying entity itself? Moreover, in which country taxing jurisdiction do profits originate? Although governments attempt to audit the transfer-pricing mechanism of tax avoidance, the problems are acute and the costs of enforcement high.

In theory MNCs are supposed to use the external market price test, called arm's-length pricing, when they price internally for tax purposes, but disputes inevitably arise and the ability of tax auditors to challenge prices is constrained by enforcement costs.[12]

When the profits tax was introduced as a major revenue source for national governments during and after World War II, the corporate entity was more or less geographically bound and coincident with the nation-state. Globalization, by definition, changes this. Although legally based in a country, corporate economic activities are now so globalized that pursuing a moving profit target becomes an almost impossible task for the state. This is revealed by the statistics on intra-firm trade in international markets.[13] Of the nearly $700 billion in imports of products and services in the U.S. in 1994, 43 percent were "sales" within a company.[14]

This intra-firm trade reflects worldwide production and the movements of products and services internal to companies. For example, when General Electric (GE) produces a toaster in China and sells it in the U.S., it appears as an import to the United States. The same applies to intra-firm exports when GE supplies China with whatever it needs from the U.S. to produce the toaster. Intra-firm exports from U.S. MNCs to their affiliates around the world amounted to 36 percent of total U.S. exports, approximately $272 billion in 1994. The $301 billion in intra-firm imports and $272 billion in exports represent the magnitude of what the MNCs have to play with when they establish costs and the location of profits. Based on 1992 data, 43 percent of intra-firm exports went to LDCs (less-developed countries) and 49 percent of imports were intra-firm from LDCs (Zeile, 1997: 32–33).

The problem arises from unidimensional and dated definition of profits. Computing profits as revenue minus cost in a country was an effective tax base for several decades after World War II; corporate taxes on profits produced a fair share of revenues for governments. Globalization, however, has rendered this form of profit taxes increasingly difficult for governments to capture because of the mobility of capital and the ability of MNCs to escape high-tax jurisdictions through transfer pricing: buying and selling to itself with more or less fictive prices. Key to this is the nature of profit, an elusive concept and a slippery accounting category for tax purposes, because it involves both revenues and costs; the size of costs can be shown to originate in the corporation's country of choice. What results is tax arbitrage, an opportunity that no rational company should pass up, playing one country's tax rate against another to minimize tax responsibilities worldwide.

A body of literature starting in 1971 affirms the successful use of transfer pricing in allocating profits so as to minimize tax responsibilities. In a

1998 econometric study, building on earlier research, Clausing concludes that "intra-firm trade may be different from international trade conducted at arm's-length. Intra-firm trade flows are influenced by the tax minimization strategy of multinational firms."[15] In another cross-section study of thirty-three countries using 1982 data, Grubert and Mutti (1991: 285–290) find that a reduction in the profit tax rate from 20 to 10 percent increases the net capital stock of a U.S. foreign affiliate by 65 percent, and more than doubles after-tax profits on sales. This leads them to conclude that "taxes and tariffs play an important role in determining the allocation of capital internationally by U.S. multinational corporations."

In another review of the empirical literature on taxes and transfer pricing, Hines (1999: 312) concludes that the "econometric work of the last 15 years provides ample evidence of the sensitivity of the level and location of FDI to its tax treatment," with a typical estimate indicating that a lower tax rate of 10 percent results in an FDI increase of 6 percent, after controlling for other influences on the location of FDI. Other research focuses on the impact of lower taxes on expanded internal trade within a MNC, affirming the appeal of transfer pricing for a global tax strategy. A tax differential of 10 percent is associated with an increase of net internal trade of 4.4 percent (Clausing, 1998: 15).

Evidence that FDI shifts investment from the home country to the foreign country comes from a summary of several empirical studies in which Hines (1996: 20) concludes that for each dollar of FDI there is a transfer of investment from the domestic to the foreign economy of 20 to 40 cents. In another study examining shifts of FDI from high- to low-tax countries, Hines and Rice (1994: 151) found that the forty-one identified tax havens account for about one-fifth of all FDI and 30 percent of foreign source income. The fundamental problem, concludes one of the principal researchers in this field, is that the "basic structure of federal income taxation was in place before the American economy acquired the kind of international position it has in the last few decades; as a consequence, international considerations are afterthoughts in its design" (Hines, 1996: 1). It is precisely these "afterthoughts" that explain the decline in the profit component of taxes. Investment moves transnationally in response to lower tax rates, intra-company trade increases, and tax bases thin. This emerges from the ability of a company to execute a global tax-minimization strategy by using the device of transfer pricing.

Fixing Tax Distortion

What are governments to do in the face of a globalization that has sundered their profits tax base? The answer is found in a variant of unitary taxes that has been used in some dozen states in the United States, where each state has attempted to define profits originating in its taxing jurisdiction based on a formula that apportions total company profits by sales occurring in the state. Elevated to a global arena, here is how it works.

The unitary tax starts with accounting categories that are known and cannot easily be fudged: aggregate worldwide profits, total global revenues received, and revenues earned in a particular tax jurisdiction.[16] To discover the profit base for tax purposes, a calculation would be made as follows: Divide revenues acquired through sales in a country by total worldwide revenues. To identify profits earned in the country's tax jurisdiction, apply this percentage to global profits. This becomes the profits base on which a national tax is levied (Wachtel, 2000: 349).

For example, assume Nike makes worldwide profits of $500 million. It receives 40 percent of its worldwide revenues from sales in the United States. The profit earned in the U.S. is then $200 million and the corporate profit tax rate is applied to that base. The advantage of this unitary tax is that the problem of transfer pricing disappears. The three statistics—worldwide profits, sales revenue worldwide, and sales revenues in the country tax jurisdiction—are known or can readily be obtained by tax authorities. Opportunities for evasion are few. The unitary tax system is an option for the headquarters country; the recipient of FDI can continue to tax local profits as it has been doing. Tax collections, therefore, need not change in developing countries, and a destructive zero-sum-game tax competition is also mitigated.

For a successful tax reform, this one has multiple merits. It is easy to administer and has clear purposes. A political constituency could be mobilized on the grounds of tax fairness, especially after examples of transfer-pricing fiddles were publicly exposed. It collects large sums of money that today escape taxation by any government, the headquarter where foreign direct investment originates, and the Third World tax haven. It does not involve any new tax, only a new way to identify and administer an old tax. It engages the North and the South and reduces the pressures on Third World countries to offer tax havens, because there are no longer ways to avoid profit taxes.

As to the argument that this will discourage foreign investment and tax collections in Third World countries, this may happen to some extent in the short run. Companies will continue to engage in direct investment with developing countries, based on organic comparative advantages that reflect market-based variances in wages, capacities to effectively absorb FDI, and regulatory differentials. This promotes a "high road" form of competition among countries to provide the most educated labor force, the most efficient governmental institutions, and reliable receptacles for production. The unintended consequences of removing tax abatements from the table may be salutary for poor countries in a way not presently capable of being understood because of the way tax competition now works.

It will encourage them to create comparative advantages that are growth enhancing and elevating of life for their poorest, rather than engage in an unproductive competition over which country can be poorest.[17]

For the headquarters countries, typically the EU and the United States, the unitary global tax will restore a modicum of fairness to tax proportions between capital and labor, one that prevailed for nearly half a century before globalization magnified and transformed a wedge into a large chasm. It corrects a distortion so widely accepted in economics literature that one of the principal empirical studies concludes by lamenting the fact that the "international mobility of economic activity now looms over any attempt to tax domestic income-producing activity too heavily. Indeed, the importance of this consideration raises the very real question of whether there any longer exists such a thing as purely domestic tax policy" (Hines, 1999: 319). By removing costs and their ambiguity from the taxing equation, transfer pricing is rendered ineffective in setting profits.

There are precedents for the unitary tax. California introduced this in the 1970s. After congressional action that outlawed the practice and a subsequent reversal by a Supreme Court ruling in favor of California, the tax was reinstated, and it has been introduced in about ten other states. An altered ideological and political climate in the 1980s elevated corporate dominance over economic policy, and essentially rendered the unitary tax mute. States either gave corporations the option of using a unitary tax computation or the standard profits tax basis for choosing which method they want to employ. At the national level, the unitary tax was seriously considered in the form presented here in 1962. It was supported by the Kennedy administration but it ultimately failed to gain approval (Bergsten, Horst, and Moran, 1978: 172–173). Today a corner of the corporate tax system partially uses the unitary tax principle: since the tax changes of 1986, a portion of research and development costs must be allocated in a complicated formula that uses fractions of sales and assets located in the U.S. (Hines, 1996: 36).

Tax Distortion and Financial Corporations

Financial corporations do not use transfer pricing to avoid tax obligations in headquarter countries because they have an easier way to accomplish the same objective: they simply site loans as originating in an offshore tax haven and assign interest income offshore emanating from that loan. Since there is no "production" in the sense of a tangible product being fabricated, the intangibles of banking activity can be located anywhere to take advantage of the tax arbitrage. Globalization's telecommunications and information technology revolutions conveniently came on-line at this historical moment to reinforce the accounting and legal devices that made the banking and financial sectors the innovator, trendsetter, and definer of globalization.

These forces began to come together in the 1970s, and bank methods of tax avoidance were perfected to such an extent that the Federal Reserve effectively duplicated the offshore tax haven onshore in what is called an International Banking Facility (IBF). Starting on October 1, 1981 the Federal Reserve permitted states to establish "enterprise zones" for banks, where the international activities of banks are exempt from taxation, reserve requirements on deposits, and deposit insurance. Restricted to so-called "nonresident" activity, deposits can be received from U.S. or foreign individuals and corporations if they are initiated outside the U.S. Loans are treated in the same way; so long as they are received outside the U.S. they can be made to American MNCs, U.S. citizens, or foreign nationals and companies (Wachtel, 1986: 116–117).

In the mid-1970s when skeptical New York state legislators challenged the Federal Reserve's plan to allow a tax-free international zone, they were told by supporters of the scheme, the major New York banks, that "neither the state nor the city would lose any tax money since the foreign loan activities that would be exempted from taxation have already moved out of New York." The lost taxes to New York in 1976 from offshore tax havens converted into tax-free onshore IBFs were estimated to be $12.6 billion.[18] Just twenty-one months after establishing the IBF, there were over 400 created by individual banks in seventeen states and the District of Columbia. New York accounted for about half of all IBFs.

Concluding Remarks: The Long Cycle in Ideas

That there has been tax distortion directly derived from the essence of globalization is not in doubt. The only question is what can be done to restore a degree of tax proportionality between the mobile and immobile, capital and labor, the fast and the slow, the winged and the rooted. The solution is more political and ideological than technical. For the past quarter century, and with increasing intensity, the fundamentalism of the market has overtaken the secular appeals of regulating, reordering, and restoring through political economy. Market fundamentalism is an evangelical faith that has been sold to its converts as a doctrine from which straying is as close to a mortal sin as we have in life today. But ideologies and belief systems do not endure forever. A twenty-five-year run of hegemony is about its limit before a new period of testing and challenge begins, followed by political tension, and a new policy envelope.[19]

Looking back historically, there are long cycles in the development of ideas that typically lag technological and structural changes by perhaps as much as a quarter century. Technological and organizational changes that emerged in the second half of the nineteenth century, for example, only found their ideological construction at the turn of the century. Economies became dominated by large-scale enterprises, trusts in the United States, and cartels in Europe that organized capital markets on a national basis when they had previously been limited to localities and regions of a country. The railroad, telephone, and telegraph integrated financial and product markets, border to border, stretching to the limits of the territory enclosed by a nation-state.

Institutionally a new corporate form, the trust in the United States and the cartel in Europe, was created to organize the technological and the capital accumulation processes. The very word "trust" is interesting in that it connotes a private profit-seeking enterprise, acting as trustee over national assets that travel over largely unoccupied space belonging to the state. This was the case with the U.S. land, over which the railroads, telephone, and telegraph moved information and products. There were ideological, political, and policy lags in catching up with these transformations. It took about a half century for the evolution of the twentieth century's economic and social theories to be framed and subsequently challenged.

The last quarter of the nineteenth century saw the preeminence of the trust and the cartel as organizing entities, receiving accolades not unlike those emanating from today's celebrants of the Washington Consensus. From the turn of the century onward, almost another twenty-five years was dominated by these ideas until effective contention appeared: one that began to establish political and policy strategies to address the tensions emanating from capital organized on a national plane. This period began to produce the development of the social contract that accommodated and absorbed the fin de siècle's transformations, attaining its apogee from around 1950 to 1975—a half century after the structural changes occurred that brought on the tensions in the first instance.

After 1975 the social contract of the mid-twentieth century began to atrophy in the face of a contest from a new set of organizing principles and ideas, following on the current stage of globalization that began around the same time. We are currently witnessing another evolution of ideas. They are in the earliest phase of challenge and response. It would be a mistake to misread this moment as one of market fundamentalist hegemony at a time when its tensions have produced an opening for a new debate about globalization and its discontents.

References

Bergsten, Fred C., Thomas Horst, and Theodore H. Moran. 1978. *American Multinationals and American Interests.* Washington, D.C.: The Brookings Institution.

Boyer, Robert and Daniel Drache. 1996. *States Against Markets: The Limits of Globalization.* London: Routledge.

Bradford, Colin I., Jr. "Being and Becoming Bound: The Nexus between Globalization, Culture and Economics," unpublished paper.

Brown, Wilson B. and Jan S. Hogendorn. 2000. *International Economics in the Age of Globalization.* Peterborough, Canada: Broadview Press.

Clausing, Kimberly A. 1998. "The Impact of Transfer Pricing on Intrafirm Trade," in James R. Heines, Jr., ed. International Trade and Multinational Activity. Chicago: University of Chicago Press.

George, Susan. 1999. *The Lugano Report.* London: Pluto Press.

Grubert, Harry and John Mutti. 1991. "Taxes, Tariffs and Transfer Pricing in Multinational Corporate Decision Making," *Review of Economics and Statistics,* VLXXIII, 12. May.

Hale, David D. 1999. "Back Now to Globalization After a Turbulent Century," *International Herald Tribune,* December 30, p. 6.

Hines, James R. Jr. 1999. "Lessons from Behavioral Responses to International Taxation," *National Tax Journal,* 52(2). June.

———. 1996. "Tax Policy and the Activities of Multinational Corporations," NBER Working Paper 5589. May.

Hines James R. Jr. and Eric M. Rice. 1994. "Fiscal Paradise: Foreign Tax Havens and American Business," *Quarterly Journal of Economics,* CIX, 1: 151. February.

Marx, Karl and Frederick Engels. 1998. *The Communist Manifesto.* London: Verso.

OECD. 1998. *Harmful Tax Competition: An Emerging Global Issue.* Paris: OECD.

———. 1997. "Taxation and Economic Performance." (unpublished paper).

———. 1994. *The OECD Jobs Study: Facts, Analysis, Strategies.* Paris: OECD.

O'Meara, Patrick, Howard D. Mehlinger, and Matthew Krain. 2000. *Globalization and the Challenges of a New Century.* Bloomington: Indiana University Press.

Tanzi, Vito. 1996. "Globalization, Tax Competition and the Future of Tax Systems," IMF Working Paper. Washington DC: International Monetary Fund.

———. 1995. "Taxation in an Integrating World." Washington DC: The Brookings Institution.

Wachtel, Howard M. 2000. "Tobin and other Global Taxes," *Review of International Political Economy,* 7(2). Summer.

———. 1986. *The Money Mandarins: The Making of a Supranational Economic Order.* New York: Pantheon Books.

Zeile, William J. 1997. "U.S. Intrafirm Trade in Goods," *Survey of Current Business,* 77(2): 32–33. February.

Notes

1. This is the case after social security taxes are removed from the calculation.
2. "Taxing Matters," in *The Economist,* April 5, 1997, p. 33; and U. S. Council of Economic Advisers, *Economic Report of the President 2001,* Washington: Government Printing Office, 2001, p. 369.
3. "Globalization and Tax: The Mystery of the Vanishing Taxpayer," *The Economist,* January 29, 2000, p. 2.
4. The reference to Octavio Paz is from *Convergences. Essays on Art and Literature,* London: Bloomsbury, 1987, p. 221.
5. "Disappearing Taxes," in *The Economist,* May 31, 1997, p. 21.
6. A documentary record of the MAI controversy can be found on the Web site of the Transnational Institute: tni-news@tni.org
7. In this chapter, the OECD reviewed the empirical research on capital mobility and conducted its own econometric study. It concluded that "capital mobility is substantially higher than suggested [by other research] and [. . .] has increased over time" (p.22).
8. This report is directed at the financial sector, but it notes that similar conclusions apply to direct foreign investment. In a survey on "Globalization and Tax," *The Economist* echoes the OECD's sentiment: "Footloose capital is free-riding on less mobile taxpayers, getting the benefit of services provided by governments in higher-taxing countries while paying taxes in low-tax jurisdictions, if at all" (January 29, 2000, p.5).
9. World Trade Organization, "Trade and Foreign Direct Investment" (unpublished, 1996, pp. 2–8); and United Nations, *World Economic Situation and Prospects 2001,* New York: United Nations, 2001, pp. 23 and 51.

10. One of the earliest theoretical studies of transfer pricing and taxes is: Thomas Horst, 1971, "The Theory of the Multinational Firm: Optimal Behavior Under Different Tariff and Tax Rates," in *Journal of Political Economy*, 79(5): 1059–1072.
11. A different mechanism is used by financial institutions and this will be described later in this chapter.
12. Technically, foreign income is taxed in the U.S. when the profits are repatriated. However, legal and accounting loopholes allow corporations to avoid this obligation.
13. Exports and imports among affiliates within a multinational.
14. U. S. Council of Economic Advisers, *Economic Report of the President 2001*, p. 392; and Kimberly A. Clausing, "The Impact of Transfer Pricing in Intrafirm Trade," NBER Working Paper 6688, August, 1998, p. 1.
15. The statistical work is based on the years 1982–1994. The 1971 study is by Horst.
16. The reference to sales as the basis for the formula is illustrative. It is simple to understand and calculate: instead of sales, value added may be a more precise indicator of the origins of profits; however, it is a bit more complicated to calculate and subject to more valuation challenges.
17. I discuss the "criteria" for a successful tax in: Howard M. Wachtel, "Trois Taxes Globales pour Maitriser la Speculation," in *Le Monde Diplomatique,* October, 1998, pp. 20–21.
18. E. J. Dionne, "Tax Breaks on Overseas Loans Pushed for New York City Banks," in *New York Times,* February 13, 1978, p. D6; and Ann Crittenden, "Citibank Found to Lead in Shift to Tax Havens," in *New York Times,* March 4, 1977, p. D5.
19. I discuss this further in Howard M. Wachtel, "World Trade Order and the Beginning of the Decline of the Washington Consensus," in *Politik und Gesellschaft,* 3, 2000, pp. 247–253.

CHAPTER 3

Human Rights and Corporate Profits

The UN Global Compact—Part of the Solution or Part of the Problem?

DIANE ELSON[1]

Introduction

The idea of globilization is now giving way to the idea of global tensions as protest mounts at the gross inequalities within and between countries. One important tension is between the global system, organized through the United Nations (UN) for the realization of human rights, and the global system, organized through business corporations and business associations for the realization of corporate profits. The human-rights system treats people as ends in themselves, valued simply because they are human beings. The corporate profits system treats people as instruments for making money, valued through a financial calculus of profit and loss.

The last half of the twentieth century saw the development of both systems on an unprecedented global scale. However, they have not been equally successful in achieving their aims. The actual enjoyment of human rights—social, economic, cultural, civil, and political—lags far behind the norms laid down in the Universal Declaration of Human Rights and subsequent human-rights declarations, conventions, and covenants. Alternatively, the scope and reach of the corporate system have vastly expanded, and the majority of people in most regions of the world are now dependent for a living on selling their ability to work (United Nations, 2000: 115). At the apex of the corporate system stand the large multinational corporations whose domination of production, trade, and finance has expanded rapidly since the mid-1970s. After reviewing a large amount of empirical evidence, a recent book on spatiotemporal patterns of globalization finds that at the end of the twentieth century "the balance of power between labor and multinational capital, under conditions of globalization, is undoubtedly shifting to the latter" (Held, McGrew, Goldblatt, and Perraton, 1999: 280).

The UN Global Compact, devised by the Office of the UN Secretary General, is presented as an attempt to harness the power of the corporate system to promote the realization of human rights, including labor rights and to improve environmental standards. It deserves attention because it is emblematic of "third-way" politics at the beginning of the twenty-first century, politics that see no fundamental contradictions between the hope of human rights and the exigencies of competitive capital accumulation. This chapter critically examines the compact, focusing both on its immediate modalities and on its positioning on an important global fault line between processes of commodification and decommodification of human life.

The Challenge of the Global Compact

The idea of the Global Compact was first put forward by the secretary-general at the meeting of the World Economic Forum at Davos in January 1999, where he spoke of "a global compact of shared values and principles, which will give a human face to the global market." It was then formally launched at a meeting in New York on July 26, 2000. This meeting was convened by the UN Secretary General Kofi Annan and attended by the heads of the International Labor Organization (ILO), the Office of the High Commissioner for Human Rights (OHCHR), the United Nations Environment Programme (UNEP), and the United Nations Development Programme (UNDP). It brought together in support of the compact, the secretariat of the International Chamber of Commerce, representatives of forty-four major corporations, six business associations, and fourteen nongovernmental and trade union organizations (Utting, 2000: 3).[2] The International Chamber of Commerce, the key association representing international big business, is thought to have played a key role in developing the compact (Kelly, 2001; Judge, 2000). Representatives of the member states of the UN played no formal role in its development. Of the companies participating in the launch of the compact, four were American, twenty-seven Western European, and the other thirteen from developing countries.

According to the Executive Summary of the meeting:[3]

> The compact challenges business leaders to promote and apply within their corporate domains nine principles in the field of human rights, labor standards, and the environment. The aim is to help strengthen the social pillars within which any market, including the global market, must be embedded if it is to survive and thrive. The Principles derive from the Declaration of Human Rights, the International Labor Organization's Fundamental Principles on Rights at Work, and the Rio Principles on Environment and Development.

The secretary-general asked world business to:

1. Support and respect the protection of international human rights within their sphere of influence.
2. Make sure their own corporations are not complicit in human-rights abuses.
3. Uphold freedom of association and the effective recognition of the rights to collective bargaining.
4. Uphold the elimination of all forms of forced and compulsory labor.
5. Uphold effective abolition of child labor.
6. Uphold the elimination of discrimination in respect to employment and occupation.
7. Support a precautionary approach to environmental challenges.
8. Undertake initiatives to promote greater environmental responsibility.
9. Encourage the diffusion of environmentally friendly technologies.

These are very broad principles and much depends on how they are interpreted. No company is going to say that it believes in disrespect for human rights, unlimited exploitation of labor, and disregard for the environment. Furthermore, there is nothing explicit in the principles to draw attention to one of the most important aspects of corporate power: the way in which it is so often wielded so as to undermine democratic governance. Research has charted the ways in which powerful companies operate behind the scenes to shape, in their own interests, the operation of domestic and international laws, and the policies of governments and intergovernmental bodies (Hertz, 2001; Panitch and Leys, 1999; and van der Stichele, 1998).

Corporate power is frequently used in ways that undermine rather than enhance the capacity of governments to promote, protect, and fulfill human rights. Of course it would be rare to find a company directly lobbying governments to abuse human rights, exploit labor, and degrade the environment. Instead a persuasive rhetoric of "efficiency," "productivity," and "competitiveness" is used in ways that obscure what is often the primary purpose: strengthening the rights of companies to use people and natural resources as instruments for profit-making.

Sometimes companies push the logic of financial calculations to lengths that are widely seen as illegitimate and absurd. For example, the U.S. tobacco company Philip Morris commissioned a report from the consulting firm Arthur D. Little International on the advantages to the Czech government of a high incidence of smoking among the Czech population. It claimed that as well as raising money through taxation of cigarettes, there were savings for governments on pensions, health care, and housing for the elderly as a result of early deaths of smokers. It was calculated that the Czech government had a net gain of 103m in 1999. This survey was widely criticized and the chief executive officer of Philip Morris was forced to apologize, saying that the survey "exhibited terrible judgment as well as a complete and unacceptable disregard of basic human values." Similar surveys in other parts of Eastern Europe were canceled (*The Guardian*, 8/27/01).

But most often the clash of values is less apparent because companies do not make their reasoning so explicit, or because inhuman practices (such as disregard for adverse impacts on the health of employees and surrounding communities) that result in financial savings are seen by public opinion as inadvertent by-products of company policy, not as stemming from its core purpose. Moreover, companies that want to respect human values and human rights are often under competitive pressure from those that do not, if disrespect saves money in the short run. Only a strong international statutory regulatory framework can modify this pressure and ensure that increases in efficiency and productivity are genuine, rather than false economies that shift costs to where they do not show up in account books.

This is not to say that the goals of making money and respecting human rights are always at odds. It may be possible to introduce practices that both increase profits and deepen the realization of human rights. This kind of interaction has been emphasised by the director general of the ILO in some of his comments of the Global Compact:

> Well-corroborated evidence shows, for instance, that safer jobs are more productive jobs; that child labor undermines longer-term economic capacity; that effective policies for gender equality lead to more dynamic business growth.
> (Somavia, 2000)

But often there is a problem of short-run costs versus long-run gains. To introduce such practices requires some immediate outlays, and the profits take time to emerge. Meanwhile, there are competitive pressures from firms that have not made these investments, and the "good-practice" firms may be outcompeted. This is a particular problem if shareholders want results in the short run and are not prepared to wait.

The tension between human-rights principles and financial values has been highlighted in a comment on the Global Compact by the secretary-general of the ICC. Pointing to economic responsibilities as well as human-rights responsibilities he notes that:

> Business accepts the challenge and is eager to cooperate with the UN and other public-sector bodies to enhance [the nine principles]. Alongside them however, we must place a fourth value—the economic responsibility incumbent upon any company to its customers, to its employees, and to its shareholders.
> (Cattaui, 1999)

So what kind of challenge does the compact offer to business leaders? In what way does it seek to strengthen the social foundations of markets? Companies are asked to give three commitments:

1. Advocate the Global Compact and its nine principles in mission statements, annual reports, and similar public venues.
2. Post on to the compact's Web site at least once a year the concrete steps they are taking to act on the nine principles—discussing lessons learned, both positive and negative.
3. Join with the UN in partnership projects of benefit to developing countries, including policy dialogues (e.g., the role of corporations in zones of conflict) and operational activities (e.g., the Health InterNetwork, or Ericssons First on the Ground Initiative).

The third commitment makes it clear that the compact is not only about good practice in observing human rights and other principles. It is also about mobilizing private resources to support the work of the UN. As such it is part of a growing trend involving many UN agencies.[4]

In order to participate in the compact, a company simply needs to send a letter from its chief executive officer to the secretary-general saying that it supports the compact. It has been made clear that the secretary-general does not envisage the compact as in any way constituting an international code of conduct for business. In May 1999 he stated that "the Global Compact is not a code of conduct [. . .] It is a compact to help markets deliver what they are best at while at the same time contributing to a more humane world" (UN Press Release SG/SM/7004, May 25, 1999).

If the compact is not a code of conduct, what is it? A further source of clarification is remarks made by Assistant Secretary General John Ruggie, who presented the compact as:

> An issue-based network that brings together all the relevant social actors: governments, which defined the principles on which the initiative is based; companies whose practices we are seeking to shape through the power of good example, in whose hands the concrete work of global production takes place; NGOs, representing the wider community of stakeholders; and the United Nations, the world's only truly global political entity.
>
> (*International Herald Tribune*, special supplement on the Global Compact, January 25, 2001)

This was not sufficient for the U.S. Council for International Business, which submitted twenty questions on what companies need to know. The answers are posted on the Global Compact Web site. This organization makes it clear that the letter from the CEO is seen as a first step toward "full engagement" with the Global Compact and "not a binding commitment associated with specific performance criteria." Reporting and auditing of participating companies will not be introduced into the compact; mention is made of reserving the right to not accept participants, but no criteria for acceptance or exclusion have been elaborated.

The compact is far less demanding than private-sector ethical investment funds and share indexes, which screen companies against stated ethical criteria and typically exclude many companies, especially tobacco and arms companies.[5] Some leading NGOs not represented at the meeting to launch the Global Compact immediately criticized the participation of Nike, Shell, BP Amoco, Rio Tinto, and Novartis, arguing that these companies' activities "run counter to the spirit and the letter of the compact itself."[6] The compact has already been dismissed as "blue-wash" by many members of the NGO community (Bruno and Karliner, 2000).

Defenders of the compact argue that there are advantages to a policy of inclusion of more or less any company that wishes to join. By joining the network they will be exposed to international scrutiny of their claim to support the nine principles. In a speech in Geneva to the international NGO community, many members of which are intensely critical of the compact, Ruggie argued that the compact:

> Seeks to utilize the power of transparency and dialogue as its chief tools. And it is a collaborative effort involving not only the United Nations and corporations, but also international labor and NGOs as core participants.
>
> (www.unglobalcompact.org/gc/unweb.nsf/content/Ruggiengo.htm)

Speaking more informally to NGOs gathered in New York for the Millennium Summit in September 2000, he urged that "[t]he transparency and the dialogue are powerful tools. If I were a company and I wanted to pull the wool over anybody's eyes, I wouldn't do it in this fishbowl."[7]

The challenge of the compact thus seems to rest on how transparent the Global Compact is, and what kind of role can be played by civil society and trade union members. It is clearly a challenge that bypasses the regulatory mechanisms of the member-states of the UN, some of whom are far from happy with the compact. References to the compact were deleted from an official UN declaration at the Copenhagen Plus 5 Social Summit in Geneva in July 2000. Apparently a substantial number of developing country governments opposed its voluntary, nonbinding character (Bruno and Karliner, 2000).

One test of the transparency of the compact is how easy it is to find out which companies have committed to it. A second is the extent to which it is possible for NGOs and trade unions to evaluate the "good practices" posted on its Web site. An examination of the Global Compact Web site in July 2001, one year after the launch, reveals only a list of companies present at the inauguration. There are claims that the number of companies publicly supporting the compact has substantially increased to "several hundred very diverse participants" but they are not listed.

Some examples of "good practice" have been posted, but they are anonymous: "a bank in Germany," "a Norwegian energy company," "a Swiss financial services company," "a UK telecommunications company," and so forth. The only place where companies are named is in a section on awards, where we can learn the names of the twelve companies that have received the Millennium Business Award for Environmental Achievement, which is presented by the ICC in collaboration with UNEP. The Global Compact Web site was dismissed as "toothless" by the Corporate Europe Observatory when it was launched, and it does not seem to have acquired much bite since.

Role of Civil Society and Labor Organizations in the Compact

Some civil society and labor organizations are members of the compact, though the nonbusiness members are very much in a minority.[8] They appear to have a variety of views on the compact, ranging from the enthusiastic to the pragmatic to the guarded. The World Conservation Union "greatly welcomes the invitation to join" and commends Kofi Annan for "launching this initiative to strengthen the mutually beneficial relationships between markets and society." The ICFTU welcomes the compact as a contribution toward building an "effective framework of multilateral rules for a world economy."

Some of the International Trade Secretariats associated with the ICFTU are now negotiating with international companies to include compact principles in framework labor agreements. For instance, in March 2001 the International Federation of Chemical, Energy, Mine and General Workers Unions (ICEM) signed an agreement incorporating the compact principles with Statoil, a Norwegian–based multinational (which is scheduled for partial privatization). ICEM reports a high level of interest among companies in Europe and South Africa in signing comparable agreements and will insist that all such agreements incorporate the Global Compact Principles. The ICFTU's Web site has a positive presentation of the Global Compact—but unlike the Global Compact Web site, it also makes information available on the anti-union behavior of companies.[9]

While Amnesty International has welcomed the initiative, it also encourages companies to adopt independently verifiable codes of conduct. Pierre Sane, head of Amnesty International, warned at the launch that only independent monitoring and strong enforcement mechanisms would give the Global Compact credibility.[10] Human Rights Watch believes that the compact is a positive but limited first step and hopes the end result will be a "binding legal regime for corporate conduct," backed by an effective enforcement mechanism. It emphasises that NGOs do not have enough resources to assume an enforcement role and argues that this should be the province of governments and the UN.

It is clear that some of the business members of the compact do not view nonbusiness members as equal partners. The secretary-general of the ICC has warned that:

> [a]s long as the Global Compact remains true to the original concept of a voluntary two-way partnership as set out by Kofi Annan, it will continue to command business support. [...] the danger is that too many players will be brought in, and we have seen hints that that might happen in some of the rhetoric coming out of the UN. If labor unions and so-called civil society nongovernmental organizations are seen as full partners in the Global Compact, its nature will certainly be different from the concept that a group of CEOs—all of them ICC members—welcomed wholeheartedly when they pledged their support in July 1999.
>
> (*International Herald Tribune*, 25 January, 2001)

Many NGOs have been very critical of the compact, and an international coalition of NGOs who are not party to the compact has been formed to promote an alternative Citizens Compact on the United Nations and Corporations. This is supported by more than seventy organizations on six continents and calls for a complete reassessment of the relations between the UN and business corporations, and for a legally enforceable framework for corporate behavior.[11]

The Privatization of Relations between the UN and Corporations

The Citizens Compact wants to roll back what we might call the ongoing privatization of relations between the UN and big corporations. By privatization I mean a process wherein UN agencies no longer see it as their role to strengthen member-states in their dealings with corporations, but rather facilitate the self-regulation of corporations and promote bilateral deals between UN agencies and corporations that bypass member-states. Judge (2000) suggests that

> This effectively commenced at the Earth Summit in 1992 when the UN refused to circulate the recommendations of its Center on Transnational Corporations. The UN decided instead to adopt the proposals of the World Business Council for Sustainable Development that recommended corporate self-regulation. The center was dissolved in 1992.

The Center on International Corporations was established in 1974 in the context of the demand from Southern governments for a New International Economic Order that would be regulated to promote international development. Its aim was to enable developing countries to obtain a greater share of the benefits from TNCs. The center monitored the activities of TNCs and provided developing countries with advice on how to deal with them. In an effort to support and supplement national regulation, it also developed a Draft Code of Conduct on TNCs, which set out an international framework for their regulation.

However, the debt crisis and recession of the early 1980s changed the balance of power between governments of the North and South, and between corporations, governments, and citizens. The Draft Code of Conduct was never put into operation and in 1993 the UNTNC was absorbed into a division of the United Nations Conference on Trade and Development (UNCTAD), which then concentrated on giving advice on how to attract foreign investment through reducing regulations and taxation (Jenkins, 2001). Instead of a global regime for regulating companies, what emerged in 1995 was a global regime for regulating governments, in the form of the WTO rules on trade and trade-related policies, and the powerful, legally binding, dispute settlement mechanism.

The Earth Summit in 1992 marked not only the fatal weakening of the UNTNC, but also the beginning of a new kind of "partnership" between UN agencies and private business. The secretary-general of the summit created an "Eco Fund" to help finance the summit, and the Earth Summit logo was franchised to corporations like ARCO, ICI, and Asahi Glass (Bruno and Karliner, 2000). These partnerships with big business gathered strength in the latter part of the 1990s, within the context of a severe shortage of funds in the UN system itself. The U.S. government ran up arrears of $1 billion in its dues to the UN.[12] The Funds and Programmes, which are dependent on funds from the aid programs of wealthy countries, found themselves competing for a shrinking flow, as OECD development funding also declined from $61 million in 1992 to $48 million in 1997. There was talk of closing down some agencies and downsizing others (Utting, 2000: 7).

A major new partnership, initiated in 1997, was the creation by Ted Turner (founder of CNN) of the $1 billion United Nations Foundation. This foundation is set up to support projects on environment, children's health, women and population, peace, security, and human rights. Another was the formation of the Global Alliance for Vaccines and Immunization, with substantial funding from the Bill and Melinda Gates Foundation (derived from the profits of Microsoft). Other members of the alliance include the International Federation of Pharmaceutical Manufacturers Associations, the Rockefeller Foundation, and UNICEF.

An overall framework for such partnerships was finally produced in July 2000, with the publication of the "Secretary-General's Guidelines on Cooperation Between the United Nations and the Business Community." The forms of cooperation include advocacy, fund-raising, policy dialogue, humanitarian aid, and development. The guidelines state that companies that violate human rights "are not eligible for partnership"; and that "private enterprises should have demonstrated a commitment to meeting or exceeding the principles of the compact by translating them into operational corporate practice." Controversially, the guidelines do envisage business use of the UN logo:

> The use of the name and emblem by a business entity may be authorized, even if it involves the making of profit, so long as the principle purpose of such use is to show support for the purpose and activities of the UN, including raising funds for the organization, and the generation of profit is only incidental.

Many NGOs have been very critical of this, arguing that:

> Hypothetically we could see a clinic funded by Rio Tinto, operated by WHO, with Rio Tinto and UN logos side by side. For activists fighting Rio Tinto to save their own environment and health, that would be quite a slap in the face. For Rio Tinto it could be a PR bonanza—for example, if it were to publicize this collaboration with the UN in a television commercial.
>
> (Bruno and Karliner, 2000)

The advantages to corporations keen to improve their reputations are clear. The problem remains that most UN agencies do not have the capacity to thoroughly evaluate operational corporate practice, and there seem to be no plans to create such capacity.

Current Tensions within the UN

The UN system is complex and diverse, encompassing a range of semiautonomous agencies and programs as well as the secretariat headed by the secretary-general. A variety of views have been expressed by UN organizations outside the secretariat on the appropriate way to deal with multinational corporations, some of which are very different from the views incorporated in the Global Compact. One example is the United Nations Research Institute for Social Development (UNRISD). The director of the UNRISD project on Business Responsibility for Sustainable Development has commented critically on the developing partnerships between the UN and the private sector (Utting, 2000). He questions the ability of the partnership approach to fulfil the UN mandates on development and human rights and suggests that the UN should instead become an ally of the movement for corporate accountability. However, UNRISD is a small research institute not closely linked to any of the operational divisions of the UN. Thus its impact on the UN secretariat is limited.

The movement for corporate accountability is also highlighted in a new report on women's progress from UNIFEM (the United Nations Development Fund for Women). It explains how women have been active, as consumers, workers, and shareholders in campaigns to hold corporations to account. The report recommends that transnational corporations must be held to stringent, independently monitored codes of conduct, and argues that such codes should include the application of all core ILO labor standards, action programs to combat sexual harassment, and reproductive-rights protection clauses (UNIFEM, 2000: 128). However, though UNIFEM is very dynamic and innovative, its budget is minuscule compared to other operational UN agencies.

The widely influential UNDP *Human Development Report* focused in 1999 on globalization and noted critically that "[t]here are no mechanisms for making ethical standards and human rights binding for corporations and individuals, not just governments" (UNDP, 1999: 8). The report recommended that:

> [a] multilateral code of conduct needs to be developed for multinational corporations. Today, they are held to codes of conduct only for what national legislation requires on the social and environmental impact of their operations. True, they have in recent years taken up voluntary codes of ethical conduct. But multinationals are too important to be left to voluntary and self-generated standards.
> (UNDP, 1999: 12)

However, it should be noted that this report is a report *to* UNDP by a group of independent consultants and advisers, including unorthodox economists such as Nobel Prize winner Amartya Sen. Although it is coordinated by the UNDP Human Development Report Office, its conclusions are not necessarily fully endorsed by UNDP.

Mary Robinson, at the time the UN High Commissioner for Human Rights, called on participants at the conference to inaugurate the Global Compact to recognize that:

> there is a price to be paid for participating in the Global Compact [...] We must be working toward independent monitoring of the application of the

principles; there must be public reporting of how the principles are implemented [. . .] and we must identify measures to be taken against those who have subscribed to the Global Compact but are clearly not adhering to the principles. It is quite clear that you can't just sign on and think there will be a free ride.

(Quoted in Utting, 2000: 8)

Statements like this have given rise to some concern among corporations, especially U.S. corporations. The ICC has made it known that companies need reassurance that the agreement will remain as originally presented by Kofi Annan and are concerned that statements by some heads of UN agencies are:

at odds with what had been presented by the secretary-general, particularly on external monitoring and verification [. . .] Companies need to receive the same consistent message from all the UN officials involved.

(*International Herald Tribune*, January 25, 2001)

The issue of a legally binding international code of conduct for transnational corporations is under consideration by the UN Sub-Commission on the Promotion and Protection of Human Rights. In 2000 it discussed a set of draft principles relating to the human rights conduct of companies and identified three key aims:

(1) To help Governments identify what types of legislation they should enact and what types of enforcement mechanisms they should implement to ensure the principles had a positive influence; (2) to encourage companies to implement the draft principles; (3) to lay the groundwork for the binding international standard setting process.

(Commission on Human Rights, 2000: 33)

In contrast to the Global Compact, these principles put states at the center of efforts to ensure that TNCs respect human rights, and emphasize regulation rather than voluntary codes of conduct. However, it is necessary to bear in mind that the sub-commission has very limited resources and its mandate is confined to undertaking studies and making recommendations. Moreover, the U.S. government is opposed to the work of the sub-commission on corporations and has backed proposals to cut back its capacity (Karliner, 1999). Without a process to build wider support for the draft principles, there is a strong risk that the final recommendations of the sub-commission will not lead to any action.

The ILO produced a Tripartite Declaration of Principles concerning Multinational Enterprises and Social Policy in 1977. However, there are no related legal instruments to make this binding. Disputes about its application can be referred to the ILO Committee on Multinational Enterprises for "interpretation." But as Jenkins (2001) points out, this is not a procedure for dispute settlement over compliance, and during its first decade of operation the committee only issued two such declarations. Regular surveys are undertaken on the impact of MNEs on the enjoyment of human rights on the basis of information from governments and employers and workers organizations. The ILO has constructed an on-line business and social initiatives database,[13] which can be searched for named companies. It permits some comparison of what companies are saying about themselves and what is being said about them by a wide range of organizations that are monitoring their ethical behavior. At the time of writing, this database offers a more effective tool for holding companies accountable for their impact on human rights than does the Global Compact Web site.

Alternative Approaches to Human Rights and Corporate Profits

The director of the UNRISD project on Business Responsibility for Sustainable Development poses the alternatives thus:

> The UN has a choice. Either it can be a party to corporate strategies of reputation management, or it can be an ally of the global corporate accountability movement.
>
> (Utting, 2000: 14)

By the "global corporate accountability movement," Utting means a diverse, international web of NGOs that investigate and monitor the behavior of large corporations, and hold them accountable for the environmental and social impacts of their operations. It includes organizations such as Amnesty International and Corporate Watch, as well as many others. Many of the best known and most well-resourced are Northern NGOs. Their activities are well represented in the ILO database on Business and Social Initiatives, and they constitute what some researchers call "civil regulation" (Murphy and Bendell, 1999; and Newell, 2001).

The UNIFEM report *Progress of the World's Women 2000,* provides examples of several forms of "civil regulation," including consumer action focusing on fair trade and ethical trade, investor action focusing on ethical investment and shareholder activism, and the independent design and monitoring of codes of conduct with which, it argues, companies should comply (UNIFEM, 2000; Newell, 2001). However, these civil society codes have not been adopted by many firms (Jenkins, 2000: 27). A recent survey of the strengths and weaknesses of civil regulation recognizes that NGO actions have created some important checks and balances on corporations, though they are limited in scope, both geographically and in terms of the corporations covered. It concludes its careful examination by suggesting that:

> civil regulation does not amount to an adequate or appropriate replacement for regulation at the state or the international level. The NGOs engaging with

the corporate sector in this way have neither the mandate nor the legitimacy to represent broader publics.

(Newall, n.d.: 10)

In addition, companies and business associations have been producing their own voluntary codes of conduct. A recent OECD inventory suggests that almost 300 corporations are covered by such codes; with the extractive, petroleum, and chemical industries focusing on environmental issues, and those in footwear and retail on labor rights in textiles (OECD, 2000). An analysis by Jenkins (2000: 25) suggests that just over 10 percent of the codes included in the inventory had provision for independent, external monitoring. Another survey of 132 voluntary company codes of conduct came to a similar conclusion. Provision for independent monitoring was made in less than 10 percent of codes set up by companies and in 5 percent set up by business associations (Kolk et.al., 1999: 168). The Global Compact can be seen as an extension of this kind of self-regulation, with a stronger emphasis on human rights. As Jenkins notes,

> The reluctance of many firms to include independent monitoring as an integral part of their code of conduct gives rise to some suspicion that they may be used as a public relations exercise rather than a genuine attempt at improving conditions and performance.
>
> (Jenkins, 2000: 27)

Even where there is independent monitoring, concerns have been expressed about the quality of the monitoring. A new business called "social auditing" has emerged, much of it done by conventional international accounting firms that often lack expertise in environmental and labor standards, and have no links with local communities that may be adversely affected.[14]

The challenge is to make stronger connections between the global accountability movement, local social movements (including the trade union movement), and bodies responsible for statutory regulation. Representatives of the people most directly affected by a corporation's activities (as employees, or as users of local resources) need to be involved in the formulation of appropriate laws, and in their implementation. The aim would be to create a new synthesis of statutory and civil regulation, which might be called something like "participatory statutory regulation." One example, which points the way, is recounted in the UNIFEM (2000) Report.

A Nicaraguan women's organization, Maria Elena Cuadra Movement of Working and Unemployed Women, helped women workers to develop a code of conduct for firms operating in free trade zones in that country. In 1998 they successfully lobbied the government to introduce the code, which emphasizes both compliance with existing national law and issues of particular importance to women, including the safeguard of pregnant women from dismissal and physical, psychological, or verbal abuse. It also includes the right of workers to negotiate collective agreements. Compliance with the code will be monitored by those most affected by it, the women who work in the zones, with the support of a Central American regional NGO, Central American Network in Solidarity with Women Workers in the Maquilas.

The UN system could throw its weight behind this kind of public "participatory statutory regulation" of companies that works from the bottom-up, rather than the private self-regulation of companies that work from the top-down. It would be important to link this kind of initiative to the development of an international framework, such as that which might emerge from the Sub-Commission on Human Rights.

Competitive Markets and Human Rights

It is important to recognize that business corporations are subject to market forces that may constrain the efforts of individual corporations to adhere to the nine principles of the Global Compact. The pressure is likely to be most intense for companies that lack any company-specific assets, such as a global brand name or a unique technology, and are forced to compete by short-run cost cutting. Large corporations from rich countries are more likely to have such assets, and are therefore more likely to be able to resist short-term pressures and comply with the principles. But even they will face pressure from economic recessions or financial crises, which will make it difficult to fully uphold human rights, such as the right to an adequate standard of living. Several of the companies that were present at the inauguration of the Global Compact have since deprived thousands of their employees of that right by retrenching their jobs.

These competitive pressures result from the specific way in which markets are currently socially constructed and managed. Thus, in considering corporate power and human rights, some attention has to be given to the characteristics of the system of markets in which corporations operate. The UN secretary-general hopes that the Global Compact will "give a human face to the global market," yet at the same time he argues that the compact is necessary to head off threats to the existing market regime:

> I fear that, if we do not act, there may be a threat to the open global market, and especially to the multilateral trade regime.[15]

Ironically, the current multilateral trade regime is far from being one of open markets. As many have argued, whatever the rhetoric about "free trade," this regime in practice is a mercantilism of the rich, promoting open markets where they benefit multinational corporations and preserve barriers to trade where this benefits important domestic business sectors in rich countries. As such it has selectively raised the incomes of some poor people in some poor countries (especially in East Asia and China), while plunging other poor people and countries into greater poverty (especially in sub-Saharan Africa). As the 1999 *Human Development Report* notes, income inequality has vastly increased both within and between countries (UNDP, 1999). Even if the regime did promote free trade, in current conditions this would translate into a free-for-all competitive struggle in which advantage would be with those who already have the greatest strength in terms of globally transferable assets.

To give markets a human face, to enable them to support rather than undermine the realization of human rights, fragmented, voluntary actions by progressive corporations are not enough. What is necessary is to transform the market system itself. As Karl Polanyi argued, we need to "transcend the self-regulating market by consciously subordinating it to a democratic society" (Polanyi, 1957). This will require creating market institutions that enable us to relate to one another as human beings possessing human rights, rather than as opportunities for profit.[16]

It will certainly mean enabling people to lessen their dependency on markets by strengthening other ways of accessing resources (e.g., through taxation and public expenditures) and the reciprocal exchange of gifts, especially the gift of personal care. It will also mean fostering and protecting new kinds of buying and selling networks, linking businesses of a different kind, not-for-profit enterprises, individually, cooperatively, or municipally owned. Unfortunately, the Global Compact has no vision of opening up new kinds of market institutions. The "openness" it promotes closes off many avenues for exploring how to forge better links between the realization of human rights and the business of producing, buying, and selling.

Conclusion

The Global Compact doubtless encompasses many good intentions, both in the UN Secretariat and in company boardrooms. But at the time of this writing, the lack of transparency in the way it operates does not inspire confidence. It appears to be one more example of the privatization of relations between the UN and big corporations, as well as the promotion by business of the practice of self-regulation. Perhaps it will garner more corporate contributions to UN operations, but without provisions for independent monitoring, it seems unlikely to make much difference to the realization of human rights. There is clearly a diversity of opinion within the UN system on the best way to engage with corporate power. An alternative approach for UN agencies would be one of strengthening the links between the corporate accountability movement and government regulatory bodies, to create a new species of "participatory statutory regulation." This could be supplemented by abandoning the mantra of open markets, and exploring the creation and protection of new kinds of market institutions—in which respect for human rights does not have to be refracted through the calculation of corporate profits.

Appendix 3.1

List of Corporations and Organizations Supporting Global Compact Corporations (issued by UN Headquarters, 26 July, 2000)

ABB Ltd	Sweden/Switzerland
Aluminium Bahrain	Bahrain
Aracruz Celulose SA	Brazil
Aventis	France/Germany
Bayer Corporation	Germany
BP Amoco Corporation	UK/USA
BASF	Germany
British Telecom	UK
Charoen Phokpand Group	Thailand
Concord	Mexico
Credit Suisse Group	Switzerland
Dupont	USA
Daimler Chrysler	Germany/USA
Deloitte Touche Tohmatsu	France/UK
Deutsche Bank AG	Germany
Deutsche Telekom AG	Germany
Eskom	South Africa
Esquel Group	Hong Kong
France Telecom	France
Gerling Group	Germany
Organizacoes Globo	Brazil
Group Suez Lyonnaise	France
International Service System	Denmark
LM Ericsson	Sweden
Martina Berto Group	Thailand
Minas Buenaventura	Brazil
Natura Cosmeticos	Brazil
Nike Inc	USA
Norsk Hydro ASA	Norway
Novartis	Switzerland
Pearson plc	UK

List of Corporations and Organizations Supporting Global Compact Corporations (*continued*)

Power Finance Corporation	India
Rio Tinto plc	UK
Royal Dutch Shell Group	UK/Netherlands
SAP	Germany
Seri Sugar Mills Ltd	Pakistan
ST Microelectronics	France
Statoil	Norway
Tata Iron and Steel Company Ltd	India
3 Suisses France	France
UBS AG	Switzerland
Volvo Car Corporation	Sweden
WebMD	USA

Labor and Civil Society Organizations

ICFTU	International Confederation of Free Trade Unions
AI	Amnesty International
LCHR	Lawyers Committee for Human Rights
HRW	Human Rights Watch
IUCN	World Conservation Union
WWF	World Wide Fund for Nature
WRI	World Resource Institute
IIED	International Institute for Environment and Development
RING	Regional International Networking Group

Business Associations

ICC	International Chamber of Commerce
IOE	International Organization for Employers
WBSCD	World Business Council on Sustainable Development
PWBLF	Prince of Wales Business Leaders Forum
BSR	Business for Social Responsibility

Source: www.corpwatch.org/un/background/2000/corplist.html

References

Benería, L. 1999. "Global Markets, Gender and Davos Man," *Feminist Economics*, 5(3): 61–83.
Bello, W. 2001. "The Global Conjuncture: Characteristics and Challenges," *Focus on Trade*, No. 60.
Bruno, K. and J. Karliner, 2000. *Tangled Up in Blue: Corporate Partnerships at the United Nations*. Transnational Resource and Action Center: www.igc.org/trac/globalization/un/tangled.html

Cattaui, M. L. 1999. "Business Takes up Kofi Annan's Challenge," ICC Press Release, March 15.

Commission on Human Rights. 2000. "The Realization of Economic, Social and Cultural Rights—The Question of Transnational Corporations," Sub-Commission on the Promotion and Protection of Human Rights, E/CN.4/Sub.2/2000/12.

Elson, D. 2000. "Socializing Markets, not Market Socialism," in L. Panitch and C. Leys eds. *Necessary and Unnecessary Utopias: Socialist Register 2000* Rendlesham: Merlin Press.

———. 1988. "Market Socialism or Socialization of the Market?" *New Left Review*, No. 172, 3–44.

Held, D., A. McGrew, D. Goldblatt, and J. Perraton. 1999. *Global Transformation*. Cambridge: Polity Press.

Hertz, N. 2001. *The Silent Takeover*. London: Heinemann.

Jenkins, R. 2001. "Corporate Codes of Conduct: Self-Regulation in a Global Economy," Technology, Business and Society Programme, Paper No. 2. Geneva: UNRISD.

Judge, A. 2000. "Globalization: the UN's 'Safe Haven' for the World's Marginalized: the Global Compact with Multinational Corporations as the UN's 'Final Solution,' " *Transnational Associations*, 6: 295–313.

Karliner, J. 1999. "A Perilous Partnership." Transnational Resources and Action Center, San Francisco.

Kelly, D. 2001. "Markets for a Better World?: Implications of the Public-Private Partnership Between the International Chamber of Commerce and the United Nations," Paper presented at annual conference of International Studies Association, Chicago.

Kolk, A., R. van Tulder and C. Welters. 1999. "International Codes of Conduct and Corporate Social Responsibility: Can Transnational Corporations Regulate Themselves?" *Transnational Corporations*, 8(1).

Murphy, D. and J. Bendell. 1997. *In the Company of Partners*. Bristol: Policy Press.

Newell, P. 2001. "Environmental NGOs, TNCs and the question of governance," in D. Stevis and V. Assetto, eds. *The International Political Economy of the Environment: Critical Perspectives*. Boulder: Lynne Riener.

Newall, P. (n.d.) *Race to the Bottom? Strategies for Fostering Corporate Accountability*. Institute of Development Studies, Sussex: mimeo.

O'Rourke, D. 2000. *Monitoring the Monitors: A Critique of PriceWaterhouseCooper's (PwC) Labor Monitoring*. Cambridge, Mass: MIT, mimeo.

OECD. 2000. "Codes of Conduct—An Expanded Review of Their Contents," OECD Working Party of the Trade Committee, TD/TC/WP(99)56/Final. Paris: OECD.

Panitch, L. and C. Leys eds. 1999. *Global Capitalism versus Democracy*. Rendlesham: Merlin Press.

Polanyi, K. 1957. *The Great Transformation*. Boston: Beacon Press.

Somavia, J. 2000. "Weaving the Global Compact: Business—Its Direct Stake in Putting Human Needs First." United Nations Chronicle Vol XXXVII No 2.

Standing, G. 1999. *Global Labor Flexibility*. London: Macmillan Press.

TRAC—Transnational Resource and Action Centre. 1999. "TRAC Facts—the UN and TNCs: Perilous Partnerships." www.igc.org/trac/globalization/un/unfacts.html

UNDP. 1999. *Human Development Report 1999*. New York: Oxford University Press.

UNIFEM. 2000. *Progress of the World's Women 2000*. New York: UNIFEM.

United Nations. 2000. *The World's Women—Trends and Statistics*. New York: United Nations.

Utting, P. 2000. "UN-Business Partnerships: Whose Agenda Counts?" Paper presented at Seminar on Partnerships for Development or Privatization of the Multilateral System: Oslo.

van der Stichele, M. 1998. "Towards a World Transnational Organisation?" Amsterdam: Transnational Institute.

Notes

1. I would like to thank the editors for their helpful comments, and Paul Steedman for his efficient research assistance.
2. See Appendix 3.1 for a list, pp. 61–62.
3. It is posted on the Global Compact Web site: www.unglobalcompact.org
4. This point is further discussed.
5. See, for instance, the criteria used to create the new "ethical" *Financial Times* share index FTSE4Good at www.ftse4good.com

6. Letter to Kofi Annan, July 25, 2000, reproduced at www.corpwatch.org/un/updates/2000/letter.html
7. www.villagevoice.com/issues/0036/todaro.shtml
8. This is apparent from the list of participants in the inaugural meeting. See Appendix 3.1.
9. www.icftu.org
10. www.igc.org/trac/globalization/un/gccc.html
11. More details are available on www.corpwatch.org/un
12. Such dues finance the core activities of the secretariat.
13. www.oracle02.ilo.org/vpi
14. For a critique of one prominent social auditor see O'Rourke (2000).
15. www.un.org/partnets/business/davos.htm
16. For further discussion see Elson (1988 and 2000); Beneria (1999); Standing (1999); and Bello (2001).

CHAPTER 4

Cross-Border Externalities and International Public Goods
*Implications for Aid Agencies**

RAVI KANBUR

Introduction

Cross-border externalities and international public goods have come to the fore in the development debate and in the debate on global governance like never before. This is because there is greater awareness of these issues, and also because advances in technology and trade have made them more important. At the same time, there is considerable soul-searching on development assistance and on the issue of "aid effectiveness." There is a strong feeling that the aid-delivery mechanisms of the past three or four decades have not contributed as much to development and poverty reduction as they might have done. Relatedly, there is dwindling political support among rich country taxpayers for continuing traditional patterns of aid (aid fatigue), although there seems to be general support for helping those in need.

Given this conjuncture of aid assessment, and the emergence of the issue of cross-border externalities and international public goods, several questions arise: What are the implications of the latter for the former, and vice versa? What does the presence of cross-border externalities do to the

*Paper presented to the Conference on Global Tensions, in honor of Ester Boserup, Cornell University, March 9–10, 2001.

case for aid? Do international public goods provide an additional modality for the delivery of aid? What does the supply of international public goods imply for the organization of aid delivery, and especially for aid agencies? The interplay between cross-border externalities, international public goods and development assistance, and the relationship between this interplay and the conventional rationales for development assistance, will be a key problematic facing aid agencies in the next decade. This chapter sets out a conceptual framework for thinking through the problematic, and draws some tentative implications for the major actors in global governance.[1]

Concepts and Definitions

A cross-border externality[2] occurs when actions of one country have consequences for another, unmediated by classically competitive markets. Examples of negative cross-border externalities are: water use in countries that share rivers and water tables; atmospheric pollution; infectious disease control; financial contagion; and the spillover effects of civil war. A pure international public good is one whose benefits are nonrival and nonexcludable. Nonrivalry means that one country benefiting does not preclude another from doing so, should it wish to. Nonexcludability means that no country can, in fact, be excluded from benefiting. Most international public goods are not pure; however, they all have significant elements of nonrivalry and nonexcludability.

This chapter considers three types of international public goods: (a) country-specific development (growth, poverty reduction, and improvement in social indicators) which mitigates negative cross-border externalities; (b) intercountry mechanisms for managing cross-border negative externalities (such as water-management agreements or an international lender of last resort); and (c) noncountry-specific investments in basic scientific research (e.g., development of a vaccine for malaria).

A key point to be made is that whereas the property of nonrivalry may be technologically determined, the property of excludability is determined by technology and policy. The benefits of International Telecommunications Satellite INTELSAT for example are nonrival, but only potentially nonexcludable. With some investment in scrambling technology, it can be turned into a private good for the benefit of those who pay. The findings of basic genetic research have the capacity to benefit many simultaneously because of their inherent nature, but whether they will, in fact, be made available to many is a matter of choice.

Aid is the unrequited transfer of resources, financial or nonfinancial, from rich to poor countries. Thus, a financial transfer that results from paying market price for a commodity is not aid. Paying a higher than market price, or selling at below market price, would be aid. As of now, lending at below market rates is a significant form of aid, of the same order of magnitude as pure grants. Aid agencies are governmental national or multilateral organizations that manage the flow of aid resources from donor to recipient governments. There are a large number of these agencies. In a typical African country for example, there would be at least a dozen or more such agencies: the IMF, the World Bank, the AFDB, the European Union, UNDP, FAO, IFAD, WHO, USAID, DFID, KFW/GTZ, Caisse Francaise, OECF/JICA, CIDA, SIDA, DANIDA, NORAD, and so forth. These agencies also contribute directly or indirectly to the supply of international public goods.

Aid and Country-Specific Development as an International Public Good

If country-specific aid flows lead to country-specific development, which in turn mitigate negative cross-border externalities, then aid could be seen as an international public good. If assistance to a domestic vaccination program in a poor country helps prevent the spread of infectious disease across borders, or if the assistance leads to infrastructure investment, an increase in incomes, and thus a reduction in cross-border illegal migration, then aid is an international public good. Apart from benefiting the direct recipients, it benefits others, including perhaps the donors themselves.

Indeed, this line of argument has increasingly been used by aid advocates in rich countries to persuade an aid-fatigued public to keep up support for aid. "By helping the poor we help ourselves," so the argument goes. There are two issues that arise: one philosophical and one pragmatic. The philosophical question is: if the donor gets back direct and tangible benefits from the giving (over and above the "warm glow" of altruism or the satisfaction of a duty performed), to what extent is the initial transfer unrequited? Is this not simply "purchasing" less-infectious disease or fewer illegal migrants? There are those who believe that the case for aid must be made on its own terms—in terms of duty to a common humanity, rather than slipping into the rationale of getting something back in return.

The pragmatic question is whether aid, in fact, leads to development. There is extensive literature on the effectiveness, or otherwise, of country-specific aid in engendering country-specific poverty reduction, development, and growth.[3] Suffice it to say that the current assessment of aid is not very encouraging. Considerable theoretical and empirical work have gone into understanding the failures of aid and conditionality. The discussion on the latter has led to the conclusion that unless the domestic political economy of a country leads to it, there is very little that external pressure can do to induce a sustainable change in policy. At the same time, aid flows have been greatly influenced by the political economy of donors, especially during the cold war era. No wonder the record of aid appears so bad.

It is partly this failure of country-specific aid that has raised the question of whether aid flows could be better used to deliver international public goods, and hence development and growth to poor countries. Let us therefore turn to the management of cross-border externalities and non-country-specific investments in basic research.

Managing Cross-Border Externalities

The central characteristic of a cross-border externality is the number of borders involved. Thus the mechanism for managing an externality, and the role of aid in this management, depends on the nature and spread of the externality. Conceptually, we can distinguish between two levels of spread: across poor countries only, and across rich and poor countries.

If the relevant externality—say water use—is restricted to a given number of poor countries, what role can aid play? Externalities give rise to a coordination problem. Each country following its own interest leads to actions that make all countries worse off than if they had coordinated their actions. In the case of water use, coordination might involve lower short-run water consumption in each country to preserve the water table for the long run. But if coordination were easy, it would have already happened. Managing this externality requires at least three types of interrelated inputs: bringing the countries together to discuss and agree upon the problem and the coordinated actions; monitoring the coordinated actions; and compensation for the short-run costs that result from the coordinated actions, relative to the option of breaking ranks.

The role of aid—resource transfers from rich to poor countries—should now be clear. The institutional setting for discussing and arriving at an agreement, and then monitoring and enforcing it, is not costless. To the extent that poor countries have to pay for this themselves, at least initially, coordination is less likely to happen. But the institutional resources are only part of the narrative. Financial resources to meet the short-term costs of sticking to, rather than breaking, the agreement are the key to an agreement holding, and these could be large—think of the agricultural demand for water and the sociopolitical consequences of restricting supply in the wake of a multicountry water conservation agreement. In fact, if there are no resources for compensation up front, there will probably not be an agreement. Both the institutional and short-term financial compensation costs of an agreement are central to achieving coordination, and hence management of the externality. Further, since coordination makes poor countries better off than they otherwise would be, this activity has a claim on aid resources.

Consider the case where the externality is across rich countries as a group and poor countries as a group. Mechanisms for managing global externalities like atmospheric pollution or financial contagion are international public goods. However, these mechanisms need resources: institutional resources for arriving at and monitoring agreements, and financial resources for compensation to short-term losers from the agreement. It would be understandable if the bulk of these resources came from rich countries. In the short run therefore, rich countries would most likely finance the provision of these international public goods. If the entire package is beneficial to poor countries, at least some of the resources expended can be seen as aid. Indeed, there might be an argument for diverting some conventional aid resources to this channel.

The central questions with these global arrangements are whether they are, in fact, beneficial to poor countries, or whether they are agreements between rich countries that are then imposed upon poorer countries to their detriment. These are the pivotal issues, for example, in managing the "race to the bottom" in labor and environmental standards through the ILO or WTO, in managing atmospheric pollution through the Kyoto or Montreal accords, or in managing international financial instability through a new international financial architecture with varying roles for the IMF. A key indicator of the extent to which these arrangements are likely to be beneficial to poor countries, and hence a key indicator in deciding whether resources expended in these arrangements could count as "aid," is the extent to which poor countries have a voice in decision-making and management.

Investment in Basic Research

The findings of basic research satisfy a criterion of a pure public good: nonrivalry. The use of knowledge by one party does not diminish the knowledge available to another party. Thus, the central question is excludability, and as noted earlier, this is not just a technological construct, it is deeply tied to policy. In the early days of radio no one could be excluded from receiving signals because the technology was not there to do so. With technological developments, first jamming and then scrambling, exclusion became possible. However, whether or not exclusion was permitted were policy questions. Similarly today, the findings of basic genetic research satisfy the nonrivalry property but not the property of nonexcludability. In fact, we have a peculiar state of affairs where public-sector researchers make available their findings to all, whereas private-sector researchers have a right to keep them private.

A related issue is, research on what? Basic knowledge may be nonrival but its benefits could differ greatly from person to person. Basic knowledge on temperate crops or on temperate diseases is no use in the tropics, and vice versa. These two issues, excludability and the type of research, bring us to a dynamic new area in discussions of aid: the encouragement and dissemination of basic research into issues of concern to poor countries. This presents exciting possibilities, but is not without its problems. I illustrate with two examples, vaccine and crop research on the one hand, and social science research on the other.

It is now well known that some vaccines could save millions of lives in poor countries and yet do not constitute sufficient of a market for the big pharmaceutical firms to invest in their development. The same is true of basic research into crop varieties in the tropics. In the past, public sector or nonprofit sector entities conducted this basic research and made the findings freely available to poor countries. This is brilliantly exemplified by the work that led to the Green Revolution. The role of these entities has been declining over the last two decades, and basic scientific research is now concentrated in large Northern private-sector companies.

Even if we accept that the private sector overcomes some of the incentive problems of large public-sector organizations, the issue of how to use the sharper incentives of the private sector to generate basic research of benefit to poor countries remains. One suggestion on how to do this is the celebrated proposal for a Vaccine Purchase Fund, where private-sector companies would be guaranteed purchases of the vaccine at a given price and quantity, if it were to be developed to pre-agreed standards. This is an ingenious device to overcome the excludability restrictions that go with private-sector research. It facilitates the conversion of research findings into nonexcludable benefits, and supplies a truly international public good that will benefit the poorest countries. This clearly qualifies as aid, and is a candidate for channeling aid resources.

Scientific research attention must be drawn to a global issue where formerly public goods are being converted into private goods, through the social and policy construct of intellectual property rights. The genetic properties of wild plants and grasses in poor countries are being privatized through the global system of intellectual property rights. Many of these are now owned by private companies and this could represent a substantial resource transfer from poor to rich. Modifying the current legal regime to keep these public goods public could be as important a mechanism of (preventing negative) resource transfer to the poor as anything we have discussed so far.

Now consider social science research. It is often argued by some international agencies, such as the World Bank in presenting itself as the Knowledge Bank, that one of their main contributions to development is the research that they do and the knowledge that they transfer about the success or otherwise of different development projects and strategies. This argument is made analogously to scientific research, only more so. Unlike the work of private-sector pharmaceutical companies, international agency research is disseminated actively, to the extent possible and no one is excluded from these findings. The last point is clearly true. For example, World Bank output is widely available; it has one of the most accessed Web sites, its publications form the basis of courses at universities in rich and poor countries, and so on.

There are, however, two issues. The first is straightforward: Does an agency like the World Bank, in fact, do enough to gather together all the experience that its myriad operations generate? The second issue is trickier, and relates to the nature of social science research as well as research by an operational institution. The analogy with scientific research breaks down because social science research is often on contested terrain, across disciplines that do not necessarily share methodological precepts or criteria for empirical verification. Some would deny entirely the objectivity of social science research, preferring instead to examine the assumptions and motivations that researchers bring to the questions they ask and answers they provide. These concerns are multiplied when that research takes place in an operational organization whose operations can be controversial, and where it is felt by outsiders that preset positions are being supported through the research process.

Whether this is true or not is in a sense beside the point. The central questions are: how credible is the research, and credible to whom? Here the dangers of doing research in an aid-giving organization become apparent. Whether justified or not, critical responses to research on a country by a policy-maker may be conditioned by the aid resources in play. All this to say that for social science research in aid agencies to lay claim to the mantle of an international public good, and hence to the resources that might flow from this association, extra efforts have to be made to ensure credibility and independence of research as seen by those it is meant to benefit: the poor countries.

The Organization of International Public-Goods Supply: Basic Principles

There are two basic tensions in conceptualizing the organization of international public-goods supply. The first is the tension between organizing supply as close as possible to the beneficiaries, versus taking advantage of economies of scale. The second is between organizing supply along narrowly defined sectoral lines, versus taking advantage of the economies of scope. Consider each of these in turn.

If there were no other considerations, the institution for management of a cross-border externality should be closest to the borders across which there is the externality. If there is a three-country riparian rights issue in Africa, there is no reason why there should be a global institution set up to manage it. The principle of subsidiarity suggests this should be a three-country setup. But of course, if there is another three-country problem, as well as other combinations of borders, there could be some gains from economies of scale in having an institution set up to deal with cross-border problems in general, no matter where they occur. It is difficult to know a priori at what level of aggregation the costs and benefits will balance out. However, a good start is to think of regional institutions as primarily dealing with cross-border problems in their regions, and truly global institutions being brought in for problems that cross regional borders.

Similarly, it makes sense to have one institution deal with all cross-border problems of a narrowly defined type. Economies of scope might be reaped by grouping all health issues into one institution, all water issues into another, financial contagion issues into yet another, and so on. There may still be cross linkages (e.g., between water and health), but there is a happy medium defined by broad sectoral categories. Investment in basic scientific research does not have a cross-border aspect to its organization, only a sectoral one. Thus, similar considerations apply here, although it can be argued that in the case of social science research, an integrative function across sectoral research may be needed.

Arguments from first principles would thus suggest an organizational structure for the provision of international public goods that is clustered around broad sectors, with groupings by regions within each sector.

Implications for Aid Agencies

In reality we have myriad agencies built up and added through accretion over half a century, some of whose original rationales are now lost in the mists of time, but survive as expressions of one political interest or another in the realpolitik of aid-delivery mechanisms. Even though there are periodic attempts to start a discussion of rationalization of the current mess of agencies, and the recent spate of discussions of the international financial architecture exemplifies this, it is highly unlikely that there will be any clean slate from which to start. Rather, reform will have to focus on the agencies as they currently exist. What, then, are the implications of the conceptualization and discussion in this chapter for the operation of aid agencies?

The first and most important is that there will have to be a relative shift of resources from conventional country-specific aid to international public goods as defined herein. This is natural. When a new opportunity to deploy resources to reduce poverty comes along, it should lead to some diversification from older methods. This is particularly so when the older mechanisms do not seem to be delivering, even though efforts may be under way to improve them.

But there is a caveat to this conclusion. It is, in turn, based on the assumption that international public goods will, in fact, benefit the poor. For those that deal with cross-border externalities among poor nations, this is more likely. For those that deal with externalities across rich and poor countries, this is more open to question. This leads us to focus, on global management of trade through the WTO, or global mechanisms for containing financial contagion, or global social science research at the World Bank, to ensure that they do indeed benefit poor nations. A key indicator is the extent to which poor nations have a voice in the management of these arrangements.

The argument developed in this chapter suggests a division of resources more heavily skewed toward sectoral agencies in sectors that have clear international public-goods implications. The World Health Organization (WHO) is a leading example, and the conceptualization speaks to a debate that has been going on in the proper focus for this agency. There has been an argument that WHO has been too much involved in country-specific health programs and not enough on programs with clear cross-border and international public-goods dimensions. The WHO should clearly be given the resources to manage such issues as infectious disease control, or to encourage basic vaccine research. The principles developed here support this position.

My argument also suggests a division of resources more heavily skewed toward regional institutions. Global institutions will be needed to manage truly global issues, but the principle of subsidiarity leads to a balance that would build up regional institutions to deal with regional cross-border issues. The fact that some regional institutions, such as in Africa, may not be fully ready to take over tasks, is important and relevant in designing a pragmatic strategy. However, this constraint serves to further emphasize the task of building the capacities of regional institutions.[4]

Conclusion

This chapter posed the problem of aid resources deployment in the context of cross-border externalities and international public goods, framed by doubts about the effectiveness of country-specific aid. It developed a conceptual framework for thinking through the interactions, derived principles for organizing the supply of international public goods, and arrived at implications for the system of aid agencies as it actually is, not as we might wish to design it de novo.

Of course, aid agencies will both continue to respond to their specific political mandates and deliver country-specific aid. However, the new realities mean that the aid system will have to: allocate a greater share of aid resources to cross-border externalities and international public goods; ensure that mechanisms for managing global externalities have adequate poor country voice and actually do benefit poorer countries; skew resources more in favor of sectoral agencies in sectors with major international public goods; and build capacities of regional institutions to deal with region-specific cross-border externalities.

References

Arce, M., G. Daniel, and Todd Sandler. 2002. *Regional Public Goods: Typologies, Provision, Financing and Development Assistance.* Stockholm: Almkvist and Wiksell International.

Burnside, Craig and David Dollar. 2000. "Aid, Policies and Growth," *American Economic Review,* September, pp. 847–868.

Cornes, Richard and Todd Sandler. 1996. *The Theory of Externalities, Public Goods and Club Goods,* 2nd Ed., Cambridge: Cambridge University Press.

Ferroni, Marco and Ashoka Mody, eds. 2002. *International Public Goods: Incentives, Measurement and Financing.* Norwell, MA: Kluwer Academic Publishers.

Gerrard, Christopher D., Marco Ferroni, and Ashoka Mody, eds. 2001. *Global Public Policies and Programs: Implications for Financing and Evaluation.* Washington D.C.: The World Bank.

Jayaraman, Rajshri and Ravi Kanbur. 1999. "International Public Goods and the Case for Foreign Aid," in I. Kaul, I. Grunberg, and M.A. Stern, eds. *Global Public Goods: International Cooperation in the 21st Century.* New York: Oxford University Press.

Kanbur, Ravi. 2000. "Aid, Conditionality and Debt in Africa," in Finn Tarp ed. *Foreign Aid and Development: Lessons Learnt and Directions for the Future.* London: Routledge.

Kanbur, Ravi. 2002. "IFI's and IPG's: Operational Implications for the World Bank," Cornell University working paper, http://www.arts.cornell.edu/poverty/kanbur/IFI-IPG.pdf

Kanbur, Ravi, Todd Sandler, and Kevin Morrison. 1999. *The Future of Development Assistance: Common Pools and International Public Goods.* Washington, D.C.: Johns Hopkins Press for the Overseas Development Council.

Kaul, I, I. Grunberg, and M. A. Stern, eds. 1999. *Global Public Goods: International Cooperation in the 21st Century.* New York: Oxford University Press.

Sagasti, Francisco and Keith Bezanson. 2001. *Financing and Providing Global Public Goods: Expectations and Prospects.* Stockholm: Fritzes Kundservice.

Tarp, Finn, ed. 2000. *Foreign Aid and Development: Lessons Learnt and Directions for the Future.* London: Routledge.

Notes

1. There is a rapidly growing literature on international public goods and development assistance, with new books and papers appearing even since the first version of this chapter was

written in early 2001. Some of the relevant writings include: Kaul, Grunberg, and Stern (1999); Kanbur and Jayaraman (1999); Kanbur, Sandler, and Morrison (1999); Gerrard, Ferroni, and Mody (2001); Sagasti and Bezanson (2001); Arce and Sandler (2002); Ferroni and Mody (2002); and Kanbur (2002).

2. For a good discussion of these concepts, see Cornes and Sandler (1996).

3. For example, see Burnside and Dollar (2000); Kanbur (2000); and Tarp (2000).

4. For a discussion of Regional Public Goods and Regional Institutions, see Arce and Sandler (2002); and Ferroni and Mody (2002).

PART 2

North-South Tensions

CHAPTER 5

Financial-Sector Liberalization and the Asian Financial Crisis
The IFIs Got It Wrong Twice[1]

IWAN J. AZIS

Introduction

A large body of literature has been written about what caused the Asian Financial Crisis (AFC). Attention is usually given to structural weaknesses in the affected countries that led to self-fulfilling expectations and speculative attacks. One of the structural weaknesses is located in the region's banking sector; it became more severe and visible after the financial-sector liberalization. The equally frequent claim of "crony capitalism" is given as the main explanation for the crisis.

Under pressures from the international financial institutions (IFIs), all Asian-crisis countries liberalized their financial sector in the 1980s. Both deposit and lending rates were freed, so were credit allocations. Despite the higher growth following liberalization, the economy became much more vulnerable to external shocks, raising the likelihood of a crisis (Bekaert, Harvey, and Lundblad, 2001). In the aftermath of the shock, many analysts argued that the banking sector's vulnerability and the corresponding instability was closely associated with financial-sector liberalization policy (Kaminsky and Reinhart, 1999). Expressing it in a less forceful way, the International Monetary Fund (IMF) also admitted this through its attempts to stress the importance of the long-standing issue of sequencing (Johnston, Darbar, and Echeverria, 1997).

By most accounts, the AFC has been more severe than originally predicted, even after a set of proposed policies was adopted—in line with IMF conditionality. This raises questions about the effectiveness of those policies: What exactly are the IMFS's policies in the AFC, and how are they expected to help the region recover? Why have they failed, and what are the alternatives? This chapter explores these issues. First, a critical evaluation of the financial-sector liberalization policy is provided, a policy fervently advocated by the IFIs during the 1980s. Second, its inconsistency related to the preconditions required to insure net benefits is pointed out. It is argued that much of the ingredients of the AFC in 1997–'98 was the result of such a liberalization policy. Second, the subsequent discussion centers around the policies advocated by the IMF in response to the crisis. I compare those policies with the alternatives in order to understand why some of the intended outcomes could not be attained, indirectly suggesting that the alternative policies would have produced more favorable outcomes.

Financial-Sector Liberalization

An increasing body of literature has focused on why some countries in the region survived from the 1997 AFC. An often-quoted example is China. Most, if not all analyses, point to the relatively closed capital account as the key explanation.[2] In distinguishing countries that managed to survive the crisis and those that did not, John Williamson (1998), a proponent of the Washington Consensus, admitted that: "The one dimension in which there is systematic difference between the two groups is with respect to whether or not they had liberalized their capital accounts."

In all Asian-crisis countries, full current-account convertibility (trade liberalization) had been in place since the mid-1980s. They all accepted the IMF's Article VIII obligations. But liberalizing the trade and financial sectors are fundamentally different. The policy implications are not the same. Consensus on the postulate that trade liberalization brings significant economic gains has, by and large, been reached. It is not so with financial-sector and capital-account liberalization. Theoretically, one should distinguish between the welfare impacts of financial markets and those of other markets. The most critical difference is the role and presence of *asymmetric information*. In a financial market, providing information is central, yet it is precisely on this market that failures and asymmetric information abound, for example, moral hazards and adverse selection (Stiglitz, 1994).

One should contrast the potential short-term gains of the policy with the instability that the policy can create. Such instability could be a fertile ground for a financial crisis. Kamisky and Reinhart (1999) show that based on the episodes of seventy-six currency crises, of which twenty-six are also characterized by banking crises, financial-sector liberalization appears to activate a boom-bust cycle—causing instability—by providing easy access to financing. Proponents of liberalization would argue that in order to reduce the risks of instability, several requirements and preconditions need to be met. In essence, they suggest some sort of microsequencing. The commonly suggested sequence is: improve the quality of regulation; make sure they are enforced; and improve the supervisory mechanisms. Once the markets are liberalized, the level of the bank's minimum capital requirements can be brought closer to what the Basle Accord suggests. There are variations to this, but basically that is the essence: Meet the "pre-conditions prior to liberalization."

However, when the Asian-crisis countries liberalized the financial sector in the 1980s, the aforementioned preconditions (assumptions) were not in place. Yet, they were rushed to liberalize by the IFIs. Ironically, when at the early stage the policy showed favorable impacts (higher economic growth and greater access to financial services), the IFIs applauded. But when the crisis hit, the very same countries previously praised were swiftly placed into the category of those with misplaced development strategies. All of a sudden, nothing was right with these countries. When confronted with such an embarrassing contradiction, the international institutions were quick to claim that they actually *saw* the faults, and had *already reminded* the governments about the existing flaws, such as the weak banking system, the unsustainable exchange rate system, and widespread corruption.

One of the common features to emerge after the financial-sector liberalization was the surge of interest rates. This occurred in all Asian-crisis countries. This trend significantly altered the incentive system and prompted nonprudent behaviors from within the banking sector (Hellman, Murdock, and Stiglitz, 2000). Under these circumstances the amount of investment credits going to risky sectors rose (adverse selection), the incidence of bailout in the absence of free-exit schemes increased (moral hazard), and the subsequent banks' franchise values (expected returns) declined. All these are precisely what the "preconditions prior to liberalization" are expected to avoid. Thus, the implicit logic is inherently self-conflicting: expect bank's prudent behavior while allowing franchise value to fall. The suggested preconditions, although seemingly logical, simply do not match with the prevailing institutional conditions.

The IMF persistently argued for simultaneously liberalizing the sector and meeting the preconditions. A study by the fund on the sequencing of capital-account liberalization using the case of Chile, Korea, Indonesia, and Thailand stresses the importance of proper sequencing if benefits from liberalization are to be achieved and risks minimized. This study also argues that financial-sector liberalization, especially in capital accounts, should be a part of a coordinated and comprehensive approach in which the sequencing of regulatory and institutional reforms are critical. The design of macroeconomic and exchange-rate policies should also play a vital role (Johnston, Darbar, and Echeverria, 1997). Although intuitively making sense, such conclusions are too broad and are far from practical. No one would argue against the importance of making liberalization policy (or any policy for that matter) consistent with the prevailing macroeconomic policy. But *how to do it* remains unanswered. The information contained in this study is of limited value to policy-makers. Even though many countries still had problems meeting the stated preconditions, they were pushed to accelerate liberalization by recommending one or two new measures to safeguard. More often than not, these measures are based on the practice of developed countries that have different institutional conditions.

The removal of credit controls under the liberalization policy in all Asian-crisis countries resulted in a surge of credits, including those allocated to the speculative real-estate sector. This occurred even at very high interest rates because some investors continued to borrow with such rates (adverse selection). Hence, a "bubble" was born—someone was able to sell something at a price well beyond the realm of making reasonable profits. The bubbles were also fully blown in the pay scales of executives and those who worked in finance, securities, and other firms, tremendously increasing their excessive purchasing power to create other bubbles in the prices of durable goods, including cars, houses, and luxury items. As a result income and consumption surged. Foreign investors were attracted to join the "party." They flocked into the Asian equity markets. Those who sought equity funds at high share prices found no difficulty in obtaining them. With the booming stock market, many industries expanded well beyond their means. Hence, the economy was growing like a bubble with a fragile foundation. A bursting of it was just waiting to happen.

Financial-sector liberalization was also responsible for the appreciation of the precrisis real-exchange rate in most Asian-crisis countries. Under perfect foresight (myopic assumption), the opening of capital markets to foreign investors increased the demand for, and prices of, domestic assets (Azis, 2002a; and Berg and Taylor, 2000). This pressured the real exchange rate to appreciate. Faced with such a challenge, governments in the region attempted to intervene in the foreign exchange market, followed subsequently by sterilization (sterilized intervention). The sterilization came in the form of either raising reserve requirements or through open-market-operations (OMO) by selling bonds or securities. This typically requires an increase in interest rate, which stimulates raised capital inflows, and results in increased pressure on the real exchange rate. As a result, an unfavorable combination of high interest rates and appreciating real exchange rate was produced. With uncompetitive rates, the trade sector suffered, causing the current account deficits (CAD) to increase.

Hence, the liberalization of the financial sector throughout the region consistently caused the standard "fundamentals" to be weak. In other words, it resulted in the appreciation of real exchange rates, credit booms, and high interest rates (Sachs, Tornell, and Velasco, 1996). Moreover, there is another factor that distinguishes the AFC from other crisis episodes: A considerable portion of CAD was financed by short-term foreign debts. Most of this debt was unhedged, made by either the private banking sector (e.g., Korea) or by the private nonbank corporate sector, as in Thailand and Indonesia. While domestic credits expanded significantly (credit boom) following the liberalization, the sheer size of short-term private foreign debts was much more serious than domestic credits. Measured in terms of its ratio to foreign exchange reserves, countries with the worst economic situation were precisely those that had short-term debt (STD) greater than their reserves [e.g., Indonesia (1.7), Thailand (1.5), and Korea (>2)]; see Table 5.1.

With large short-term debts denominated in foreign currency, the exchange rate risk increased. In such circumstances currency and maturity mismatch abound, and a relatively small shock is sufficient to cause the system to fall into debt and exchange-rate crises (Chang and Velasco, 1998). Looking at the debtors' balance sheet, when the exchange rate depreciated, greater pressures on the liability side significantly constrained their capacity to expand. When the debtors are mostly banks, as in Korea, the depreciation adversely affected credit expansion. Where most debtors are members of the corporate sector, such as in Indonesia and Thailand, the capacity to invest became severely constrained. Hence, the positive relation between depreciating exchange rate and increased output in a standard macroeconomic model breaks down. The AFC that was originally characterized by only an exchange-rate crisis turned into a widespread economic crisis (recession).

Thus, the composition of capital flows matters. The sudden reversals of capital flows during 1997 and 1998 led many to believe that most capital flows in the region were of portfolio investment type. Reversals of such capital can strain the region's financial system sufficiently to cause or exacerbate its collapse (Reisen, 1999; Rodrik and Velasco, 1999). However, though it is true that portfolio investment was on the rise, data indicate that foreign direct investment (FDI) remained the largest in all Asian-crisis countries.

What is more critical to observe is the capital flows category of "others," in which loans and debts are the major components. As revealed in Table 5.1, in all Asian-crisis countries, foreign debts increased persistently until

Table 5.1. Foreign Debts (billion dollars, except the last row)

| | Indonesia | | | Korea | | | Malaysia | | | Philippines | | | Thailand | |
	End 1995	End 1996	June '97	End 1995	End 1996	June '97	End 1995	End 1996	June '97	End 1995	End 1996	June '97	End 1995	End 1996
Borrowers														
Banks	8.9	11.7	12.4	50	65.9	97.3	4.4	6.5	10.5	2.2	5.2	5.5	25.8	25.9
Public sector	6.7	6.9	6.5	6.2	5.7	4.4	2.1	2	1.9	2.7	2.7	1.9	2.3	2.3
Nonbank	28.8	36.8	39.7	21.4	28.3	31.7	10.1	13.7	16.5	3.4	5.3	6.8	34.7	41.9
Total	44.4	55.4	58.6	77.6	99.9	103.4	16.6	22.2	28.9	8.3	13.2	14.2	62.8	70.1
Lending Banks														
Japan	21	22	23.2	21.5	24.3	23.7	7.3	8.2	10.5	1	1.6	2.1	36.9	37.5
USA	2.8	5.3	4.6	7.6	9.4	10	1.5	2.3	2.4	2.9	3.9	2.8	4.1	5
Germany	3.9	5.5	5.6	7.3	10	10.8	2.2	3.9	5.7	0.7	1.8	2	5	6.9
Others	16.8	22.7	25.3	41.1	56.3	58.9	5.8	7.8	10.2	3.7	6	7.2	16.8	20.8
Maturity														
Short-term debt (STD)	27.6	34.2	34.7	54.3	67.5	70.2	7.9	11.2	16.3	4.1	7.7	8.3	43.6	45.7
Long-term debt (LTD)	16.8	21.2	23.9	23.3	32.4	33.2	8.7	11	12.6	4.2	5.5	5.9	19.2	24.4
STD and Forex														
Foreign reserves (forex)	14.7	19.3	20.3	32.7	34.1	34.1	23.9	27.1	26.6	7.8	11.7	9.8	37	38.7
STD/Forex	1.88	1.77	1.71	1.66	1.98	2.06	0.33	0.41	0.61	0.53	0.66	0.85	1.18	1.18

Source: Azis 2002a, Fig. 2.

the onset of the crisis. These are debts made by the private sector. At the time no one saw the trend as worrisome, let alone alarming. Not even the IFIs, probably because it was considered consistent with and to some extent expected as a result of the privatization strategy also advocated by them. Yet, financial and balance-of-payments crises become interlinked precisely because of the existence of foreign-currency-denominated liabilities (foreign debt) in the domestic financial system (Krueger, 2000).

The trend of rising foreign debts, especially short-term and unhedged, clearly aggravated the region's vulnerability to a shock, suggesting that it should be added to the list of "fundamentals" (Azis, 1999). Interestingly, there seems to be a close correlation between increased debts and crony capitalism. A relatively large proportion of loans or debts is generally found in a system where the degree of corruption and crony capitalism is high. This type of flow is also much more volatile and fragile when compared to FDI or portfolio investments. Based on a sample of a large number of countries, a study has found that corrupt countries tend to receive substantially less FDI and more foreign bank loans. The study also shows that such a result is robust across different measures of corruption and econometric specifications (Wei and Wu, 2001). Even though some of the assumptions used are subject to verification, this kind of study integrates two rival explanations for the AFC: vulnerability due to large foreign debts that led to speculative attacks, and crony capitalism that was indeed present in the region.

It is clear that financial-sector liberalization in the Asian-crisis countries have significantly contributed to the vulnerability of the region's financial sector. At the very least, liberalization increased the likelihood of a crisis. Yet, the IFIs vehemently and persistently advocated that these countries proceed with such a policy in the 1980s. The rival explanation for the AFC, crony capitalism and corruption, also holds some truth. These two explanations are interlinked through the composition of capital flows that tilts toward foreign debt. This type of flow has been found to be most volatile, and it clearly increased the region's vulnerability to crisis.

IMF Policy Response and Alternatives

A traditional policy mix of monetary tightening and fiscal restraints was imposed as part of the IMF funding conditions. Their "success" with the handling of the Mexican crisis in 1995 convinced the fund that such a policy mix would also be appropriate for Asia, despite the fact that the precrisis conditions in Asia were different.[3] Further, the IMF insisted on a rather drastic and fundamental change in the countries' institutional structures. The experience with policy adjustments of this kind in Eastern Europe and the former Soviet Union (from communism to market economy) had inspired the fund to do the same thing in Asia.

The first two columns of Table 5.2 summarize what the IMF believes to be the causes of the crisis and their corresponding policies. A weak banking system (labeled WEAKBANK in the first column) was among the most serious sources of economic vulnerability. This was reflected, among others, through the high growth of bank credits. Yet, before both the Mexican and Asian crises, the growth of bank credits in Asia has never been higher than that in Mexico and some countries in Latin America.

The IMF was also of the opinion that the fixed exchange-rate system prior to the crisis (labeled FIXEDER) had put the region in a susceptible position.[4] Again, the appreciation of the real exchange rate (RER) in the region was never higher than in Mexico, Brazil, and Argentina. Chinn (1998) revealed a similar finding. Depending on how one measures the RER, in one scenario using the consumer price index as deflator, the precrisis RER even depreciated, not appreciated (Azis, 2001). Ironically, in many instances during the 1990s the IMF praised the fixed rate system for its ability to propel a robust economic growth with stability. It is indeed too common to fault a financial crisis on the fixed-exchange rate system. When things go wrong, the rate tends to be overvalued. While the nominal rates may be fixed, the RER is likely to appreciate, hurting exports and the overall balance of payment.

Poor governance in the corporate, banking, and government sectors (labeled GOVANCE) is another source of vulnerability (Summers, 2000). The IMF believes that this has featured heavily in Asia, exacerbating the region's vulnerability. The prescribed policies are consequently based on the foregoing perspectives. The weak banking system needs to be resolved by systematic banking reform. When necessary it should also include the closure of nonviable banks. At the same time, the problems of poor governance had to be resolved by major reforms that allowed drastic and fundamental changes in microeconomic and institutional structures.

To the extent that a real appreciation of the exchange rate and the overall market confidence are determined by the inflation rate and government signals to the market (its seriousness to respond to the shock), at the early stage the IMF also requested the recipient countries to tighten their budgets.[5] This policy is fairly standard in the fund's conditionality.[6] According to the argument, a tighter budget would help reduce the inflation rate and simultaneously assure the market that government is dealing seriously with the problem.[7] Further, a more important and controversial policy prescribed by the IMF was to tighten the monetary sector by increasing the interest rates (labeled TMP).

In addition to curbing the inflation caused by currency depreciation, such a policy was also expected to prevent further capital outflows and/or

Table 5.2. Sources of Vulnerability and Policy Response: IMF Perspectives and Alternative Views

	IMF Views				Alternative Views	
Sources	**Policy**	**Expected Outcome**	**Unintended Outcomes**		**Sources**	**Policy**
Weak banking system (WEAKBANK)	Budget, bank rest, fundamental reforms (CLM)	Resume bank lending (BLENDING)	High cost and ineffective restructuring (ECCOST)		Massive inflows and corporate debts (CORPDEBT)	Debt rescheduling and capital control (LBDH)
Fixed EXR system & RER appreciation (FIXEDER)	Tight money policy (TMP)	Positive net capital flows (CPFLOWS)	No real improvement in the balance sheet (NOBS)		Contagion (CGION)	Moderately tight net financial policy and gradual bank and corporate rest (MPBC)
Poor governance (GOVANCE)	Liquidity support and open cap. acc (LIQ)	Low inflation to avoid RER appreciation (RERAP)	No capital inflows and big windfall to savers (SAVERS)		Weak prudential enforcement (PRUDBANK)	
		Improved governance and improved BOP (GOVT)	High social cost (SOCCOST)			

attract new capital inflows, both of which would help strengthen the local currency. Only with CLM and TMP in place could the IMF's role as a lender of last resort to provide liquidity supports (labeled LIQ) could be carried out. However, according to the IMF's original mandate, such financial help should be directed only to support the country's balance of payment. Despite the IMF's frequent requests for budget consolidation and bank restructuring, no IMF resources could be used for those purposes.

Each of the foregoing policies has its specific rationale and objective. Bank restructuring and fundamental microeconomic reforms were meant to clean up the financial and real sectors, and enhance the quality of governance (labeled GOVT in the third column of Table 5.2). The corresponding improvements in the banks' balance sheets would allow banks to resume their intermediation function by extending loans (labeled BLENDING). A strict government budget together with tight monetary policy would help remove any inflationary pressures that might be fueled by exchange-rate depreciation. If successful, the real exchange rate could be prevented from appreciating (labeled RERAP). In turn, this would help increase the country's exports and improve the balance of payment position. The tightening of monetary policy by increasing the interest rates was also expected to generate positive net capital flows (labeled CPFLOWS).[8]

In reality, some of these intended outcomes did not materialize. Worse, several unintended outcomes emerged. In some instances the latter neutralized the positive results. The following is a list of such unintended outcomes. In restructuring the banking sector a huge amount of resources, mostly public money, had to be spent for the main component of the program: bank recapitalization. Indeed, a most notable sign of vulnerability prior to the crisis was the sheer size of private-sector debt, largely short-term and unhedged. The proportion of short-term debt in total foreign reserves reached more than 100 percent in those countries that were severely hit by the crisis, namely Korea, Indonesia, and Thailand.

As the exchange rate began to depreciate, the local currency value of the debts surged, hurting the balance sheet position of most corporate and banking sectors throughout the region. Hence, a recapitalization program was inevitable. In practice, however, the amount of resources used for the program went beyond what the countries could actually afford. The costs of bank recapitalization range from 30 to 60 percent of GDP. Yet, by 2000, well over two years after the program was implemented, the intended objective of resuming banks' intermediation function has not been met, implying that the program is cost ineffective (labeled ECCOST in Table 5.2).

In all Asian-crisis countries bank recapitalization had been financed largely by public money. Although each country has different formats and mechanisms, they all used some sort of government bonds. The value of bonds appear in the asset side of the banks' balance sheets, removing the prevailing banks' negative net worth. However, the actual financial position of the banks did not really improve. With a considerable amount of bonds in their assets, most banks still have liquidity problems (flooded with nonliquid assets). As a result, many recapitalized banks are not in a position to lend.[9] Hence, no real improvement in banks' balance sheets (labeled NOBS) is one of the unintended outcomes listed in Table 5.2. Worse, the regulatory policy imposed during the bank recapitalization program resulted in a substantial decline in the banks' small business lending, in part because their lending behaviors became excessively cautious, as clearly found in the case of Korea (Kim, 1999; Domac and Ferri, 1998).

Further, expected capital inflows did not occur, suggesting that the costs of setting high interest rates—credit crunch, exacerbating firms' balance sheets—are likely to exceed benefits. There is yet another kind of "cost" to the economy. The high interest rates provide huge windfalls to savers, mostly of the medium and high-income groups.[10] This has worsened the income disparity (Azis, 2000).[11] Another unintended outcome is related to the tightening of government budgets. It is often the case that this would mean massive expenditure cuts, including those items related to social overhead capital. In Thailand and Indonesia many subsidies (e.g., for fuel and food) had to be either drastically slashed or completely removed from the budget, causing prices of some basic necessities to increase. This led to further deterioration of the social conditions (labeled SOCCOST).[12]

From many discussions with policy-makers, analysts, and observers throughout the region, I found that most hold an opinion not necessarily in line with the IMF's.[13] In fact, at the early stage of the crisis Thailand, the country where the AFC began, clearly tried to avoid the involvement of the IMF. Blustein (2001) described the episode in great details, showing that the IMF was eager to jump into policy design in Thailand. At one point the Fund's first deputy managing director ordered a mission to depart for Bangkok, although not invited. His subordinate protested the order since it would clearly breach the protocol.[14] The director replied: "Just go, and in the time it takes for you to get there, I'll persuade them." At the end of course we know that, with the exception of Malaysia, all Asian-crisis countries came under the IMF program. The Fund has immense power to force governments to accept its policy advice since it can both withhold financial supports (IMF loans) and declare whether a country has been "Seal Approved" to be eligible for funds from other multilateral institutions and foreign countries.

The list of what I perceive as alternative views is shown in the last two columns of Table 5.2. For example, unlike the IMF, many hold an alternative view that massive amounts of inflows of private debts is the major source of vulnerability (labeled CORPDEBT). In some countries, policy-makers had detected the surge in such debts as early as 1992. But at the time the trend was considered normal, even expected as a consequence of increased private-sector role in the economy.[15] Many also believed that contagion (labeled CGION) played an important role in precipitating the crisis and intensifying its depth.[16] On the banking sector the alternative view agreed with the IMF assessments that this sector was weak. But most policy-makers and analysts are also of the opinion that financial sector's weaknesses actually began to appear right after the financial-sector liberalization in the 1980s. The key problem rests on the lack of enforcement of prudential regulations (labeled PRUDBANK), not the lack of regulation itself.

The alternative views tend to opine that any restructuring policy, be it for the banking or corporate sectors, had to be conducted in a gradual manner allowing agents to adjust to the new environment. A drastic measure can destabilize a system that needs to be rescued in the first place.[17] Since deteriorating market confidence precipitated capital outflows, some control measures in the financial policies (monetary and budgetary) were needed. However, unlike what was proposed by the IMF, the tightening of the financial policy should have been moderate so that it would not aggravate the already damaged balance sheets of many banks and corporate firms.[18]

Similarly, budget retrenchments ought to be done moderately. Some even argued that under the distress situation the budget should have been made more expansionary—in order to avoid the so-called "bad" equilibrium (Sachs and Woo, 2000; and Krugman, 1999). Notwithstanding the question of whether a gradual or moderate measure is more effective than a drastic one, the above policies alone were not likely to help strengthen the exchange rate. As long as indebted banks and the corporate sector could not resolve the debt mismatch, it would be difficult to avoid pressures on the exchange rate. Hence, the opinion expressed tends to opt for some sort of a debt rescheduling.[19]

Elsewhere I have explored, in greater detail, the conflicting nature of the two sets of policies, as well as how the "compromised" policies could be arrived at (Azis, 2002b). The scenario that is closer to what really happened is a combination of a tight monetary policy, with government budgets slightly slashed but with the restructuring of the banking and corporate sectors conducted in a gradual manner (in terms of Table 5.2 it is a joint-policy TMP-MPBC). Such a joint-policy scenario failed to produce a robust and sustainable recovery. Consequently, the IMF pushed for more drastic restructuring. The alternative views point to the damaging effects of high interest rates on the economy. On this issue, unless counterfactual policy simulations are conducted, any conclusions would be premature.

As I have shown elsewhere (Azis 2001; and 2002a) such counterfactual simulations by using a dynamic financial model applied to one of the Asian-crisis countries. It is revealed that by not adopting a high interest-rate policy the country's socioeconomic conditions would have been more favorable. Interestingly, the results of the counterfactual simulations are highly dependent on the effectiveness of debt rescheduling (LBDH in Table 5.2).[20] Further, I argued that the IMF's tight monetary policy not only failed to restore the exchange rate, it also exacerbated the loss of market confidence by pushing the country into a recession.[21] The ineffectiveness of interest-rate policy to strengthen the exchange rate is consistent with the conclusions of other studies (Turongpun, 2001; Gould and Kamin, 1999; Ohno et.al, 1999; Goldfajn and Baig, 1998). Moreover, the model simulations indicate that income distribution and poverty conditions would have been more favorable had the country not been stuck too rigidly with the IMF-style policy. In addition, the combination of nonhigh interest rates and partial debt resolution at the early stage of the crisis is found to be most favorable from the social indicators perspective.

By now it is widely accepted that the AFC is very different from a standard crisis caused by unsustainable current account deficits. The AFC is a capital account crisis featured by sudden withdrawals of foreign money due to panic and other reasons. The weak spot seen by investors is in neither the standard macroeconomic fundamentals nor the size of current account deficits. Rather, it is in the composition of capital flows to finance the deficits—that is—the currency and maturity mismatch of the country's debts. The phenomenon occurred because most of the financial sector in the region had already been liberalized (pushed by the IFIs), and capital was globally mobile more than ever. The IMF was ill-equipped to combat this new type of crisis, as confessed by the IMF's highest official:

> A lot is related to financial-sector issues, where the IMF staff did not have necessary expertise at all [. . .] we find ourselves making standard policy prescriptions [. . .] very seldom would you go wrong if you said "raise interest rates and tighten fiscal policy" [. . .] I thought the teams in Asia were sort of conditioned by the framework they had in mind.[22]

Conclusions

There are formidable risks involved when a country embarks on financial-sector liberalization. The IFIs, the proponents of such a policy, often undermine the risks of instability it can create. The pressure by the IFIs on the Asian-crisis countries to pursue this policy during the 1980s, and their standard suggestion to provide necessary preconditions prior to liberalization (such as good quality regulation, legal frameworks, and supervisory mechanisms), are inherently self-conflicting. Given the region's existing institutional conditions, the liberalization policy encouraged imprudent behaviors (reducing the "franchise value") of the banking sector, something that the preconditions tried to avoid. By the mid-1990s, all Asian-crisis countries had liberalized the financial sector, making this sector much more vulnerable to external shocks. When the shock came in the summer of 1997, they all fell into crisis. The push by the IFIs for liberalization, which overlooked the prevailing institutional conditions, clearly raised the likelihood of a crisis.

After the crisis burst, the policy response advocated by the IMF also contained several faults. The Fund's insistence on severely tightening the monetary policy by raising the interest rates proved to be counterproductive. Its arguments for drastic and fundamental microeconomic adjustments seemingly make sense; who would not agree with ending corruption, curtailing special business privileges, and imposing the practice of good governance? But in addition to the fact that this is outside the IMF's mandate, such adjustments severely undermine the source of stability. The Fund's involvement in issues that go beyond its mandate during the AFC was eloquently expressed by former staff member Morris Goldstein: "Both the scope and the depth of the Fund's conditions were excessive. [. . .] They clearly strayed outside their area of expertise. [. . .] If a nation is so plagued with problems that it needs to make 140 changes before it can borrow, then maybe the fund should not lend" (*New York Times*, October 21, 2000). Some analysts went further by comparing the IMF with a heart surgeon who, in the middle of an operation, decided to do some works on the lungs and kidneys too.

Demanding sweeping changes in the region's institutional structures is not really needed for the return of capital, nor is it required to restore market confidence. On the other hand, to make such a drastic change in the midst of a currency crisis could be more disastrous than helpful. Changes would have been more effective when conducted gradually, such that only few shocks would be created in the system. While acknowledging the importance of institutional reforms, many policy-makers are fully aware that comprehensive and fundamental reforms, especially when conducted rather drastically, are difficult to implement. Not even OECD countries could execute the programs with such great detail and comprehensiveness as the IMF prescribed. Because of these differences, wrangles and disputes over program implementation often characterized the process, even after the official letter of intent (LOI) had been signed.

Both the advocated financial-sector liberalization and the policy response to the AFC proved to be unsuitable to the prevailing conditions in the region. The IFIs got it wrong twice. Liberalization increased the likelihood of a crisis, and the broad structural reforms failed to restore confidence. The tightening of the monetary sectors skewed the relative income distribution by disproportionately benefiting the high-income savers, worsened the financial positions of many sectors, particularly the medium and small industries, and dampened investment that resulted in a major recession. This further damaged market confidence, something that the IMF intended to restore in the first place. The social repercussions of economic contraction have been serious. No wonder international criticism of the Fund's role in the recent Argentine's fallout is currently being echoed throughout Asia.

References

Azis, Iwan J. 1999. "Do We Know the Real Causes of the Asian Crisis?," *Global Financial Turmoil and Reform: A United Nations Perspective.* Tokyo: The United Nations University Press.

———. 2000. "Modeling the Transition From Financial Crisis to Social Crisis" in *Asian Economic Journal,* 14(4).

———. 2001. "Modeling Crisis Evolution and Counterfactual Policy Simulations: A Country Case Study." ADB Institute Working paper, no. 23, Tokyo.

———. 2002a. "What Would Have Happened in Indonesia if Different Economic Policies Had Been Implemented When the Crisis Started?" *The Asian Economic Papers.* MIT Press.

———. 2002b. "IMF Perspectives and Alternative Views on the Asian Crisis: An Application of Analytic Hierarchy Process and Game Theory Approach," in Partha Gangopadhyay and Manas Chatterji, eds. *Globalization and Economic Reform.* Cheltenham: Edward Elgar Publishing.

Azis, Iwan J. and Willem Thorbecke. 2002. "The Effects of Exchange Rate and Interest Rate Shocks on Bank Lending," Research report for the Asian Development Bank Institute, Tokyo, January.

Bekaert, Geert, Campbell R. Harvey and Christian Lundblad. 2001. "Does Financial Liberalization Spur Growth?" NBER Working paper, no. 8245.

Berg, Janine and Lance Taylor. 2000. "External Liberalization, Economic Performance, and Social Policy." Working paper, no. 12, Center for Economic Policy Analysis (CEPA), New York.

Blustein, Paul. 2001. *The Chastening: Inside the Crisis that Rocked the Global Financial System and Humbled the IMF.* Public Affairs, New York.

Chang, Roberto and Andres Velasco. 1998. "The Asian Liquidity Crisis." NBER Working paper, no. W6796, November.

Chinn, Menzie D. 1998. "Before the Fall: Were East Asian Currencies Overvalued?" NBER Working paper no. W6491, April.

Domac, Ilker and Giovanni Ferri. 1998. "The Real Impact of Financial Shocks: Evidence from Korea." unpublished manuscript. Washington, D.C.: World Bank.

Fischer, Stanley. 2000. "Strengthening Crisis Prevention: The Role of Contingent Credit Lines." Speech delivered at the 75th Anniversary of the Banco de Mexico, Mexico City, November 15.

Goldfajn, Illan and Taimur Baig. 1999. "Monetary Policy in the Aftermath of Currency Crises: The Case of Asia." IMF Working paper, WP/98/170. Washington, D.C.: International Monetary Fund.

Gould, David M. and Steven B. Kamin. 1999. "The Impact of Monetary Policy on Exchange Rates During Financial Crisis." Paper presented at the 1999 Pacific Basin Conference, San Francisco, September.

Hellman, Thomas F., Kevin C. Murdock, and Joseph E. Stiglitz. 2000. "Liberalization, Moral Hazard in Banking, and Prudential Regulation: Are Capital Requirements Enough?" *American Economic Review,* 90(1), March.

Johnston, Barry R., Salim M. Darbar, and Claudia Echeverria. 1997. "Sequencing Capital Account Liberalization—Lessons from the Experiences in Chile, Indonesia, Korea, and Thailand." IMF Working paper WP/97/157. Washington, D.C.: International Monetary Fund.

Kaminsky, Graciela L. and Carmen M. Reinhart. 1999. "The Twin Crises: The Causes of Banking and Balance-of-Payments Problems," *American Economic Review,* 89(3): 473–500.

Kashyap, Anil K. and Jeremy C. Stein. 2000. "What Do a Million Observations on Banks Say about the Transmission of Monetary Policy," *American Economic Review*, 90(3), June.

Kim, Hyun E. 1999. "Was Credit Channel a Key Monetary Transmission Mechanism Following the Recent Financial Crisis in the Republic of Korea?" Policy Research working paper no. 3003. Washington D.C.: World Bank.

Krueger, Anne O. 2000. "Conflicting Demands on the International Monetary Fund," in *American Economic Review*, 90(2), May.

Krugman, Paul. 1999. "Analytical Afterthoughts on the Asian Crisis," mimeo. MIT.

Lane, Timothy, A. Gosh, J. Hamman, S. Phillips, M. Schulze-Ghattas, and Tsidi Tsikata. 1999. *IMF-Supported Programs in Indonesia, Korea and Thailand: A Preliminary Assessment.* Washington, D.C.: IMF.

Ohno, Kenichi, Kazuko Shirono, and Elif Sisli. 1999. "Can High Interest Rates Stop Regional Currency Falls?" Working paper, Asian Development Bank Institute (ADBI), no. 6, December.

Reisen, Helmut. 1999. "After The Great Asian Slump: Towards a Coherent Approach of Global Capital Flows." OECD Development Center, Policy Brief, no. 16.

Rodrik, Dani and Andes Velasco. 1999. "Short-Term Capital Flows: The Consequences and Causes Thereof." Annual World Bank Conference on Development Economics, May.

Sachs, Jeffrey D., A. Tornell., and A. Velasco. 1996. "Financial Crises in Emerging Markets: The Lessons From 1995." Brookings Papers on Economic Activity, no. 1.

Sachs, Jeffrey D., and Wing Thye Woo. 2000. "Understanding the Asian Financial Crisis," in Woo Wing Thye, Jeffrey D. Sachs, and Klaus Schwab, eds., *The Asian Financial Crisis: Lessons for a Resilient Asia.* Cambridge: MIT Press.

Stiglitz, Joseph E. 1994. "The Role of the State in Financial Markets." Proceedings of the World Bank Conference on Development Economics 1993. Washington D.C: World Bank.

Summers, Lawrence H. 2000. "International Financial Crises: Causes, Prevention, and Cures," in *American Economic Review*, 90(2).

Tobin, James, and Gustav Ranis. 1998. "The IMF's Misplaced Priorities: Flawed Funds," in *The New Republic:* http://www.thenewrepublic.com/archive/0398/030998/tobin030998.html

Turongpun, Wichai. 2001. "On Exchange Rates, Interest Rates, and External Effects." PhD dissertation, Cornell University, Ithaca, NY. March.

Wei, Shang Jin and Yi Wu. 2001. "Negative Alchemy: Corruption, Composition of Capital Flows and Currency Crises." NBER working paper no. 8187, March.

Williamson, John. 1998. "Whither Financial Liberalization?" Keynote address for the Second Annual Indian Derivatives Conference, Mumbai, India, November 12.

Notes

1. I have benefited from the comments and suggestions of participants in the following meetings: (1) Conference on "Social Implications of the Asian Financial Crisis," jointly organized by the UNDP and Korean Development Institute (KDI), Seoul, 1998; (2) Carnegie Endowment for International Peace conference on "The Politics of Economic Reform in Asia," Bangkok, June 4–5, 1999; (3) IMF meeting on the fund's approach in Indonesia, Washington, D.C., September 5, 2000; (4) NBER project meeting on "Exchange Rate Crises in Emerging Markets" Cambridge, MA, September 15, 2000; (5) Internal seminar at the Asian Development Bank Institute, Tokyo, December 19, 2000; and (6) the "Asia Panel," Center for International Studies (CID), Harvard University, Cambridge, MA, April 20–21, 2001. Exchanges of views with Walter Isard, Masahiro Yoshitomi, Takatoshi Ito, Sudradjad Djiwandono, Wing Thye Woo, Kanit Sangsubhanand, and Jae-ha Park on the subject are also highly appreciated. The usual disclaimer applies.

2. China's financial sector remained controlled throughout the 1990s. Further, a large size of foreign reserves ($140 billion in 1997), and the Yuan's devaluation in 1994 are important factors that enabled China to escape from the shock.

3. Nobel laureate James Tobin and Gustav Ranis (1998) are among those who believe that the IMF programs in Asia were based on the Fund's experiences with Mexico in 1994: "The IMF's Asian packages are based on its experiences with Latin America, in particular with Mexico in 1994."

4. For example, on an IMF mission to Thailand in early 1997 Stanley Fischer wrote a letter to Thai Finance Minister Amnuay Viravan stating: "We continue to believe that the introduction of a more flexible exchange rate arrangement is a policy priority."

5. In the second column of Table 5.2, bank restructuring, fundamental changes, microeconomic reforms, and tightening of government budget are combined in a policy item labeled CLM.

6. Lawrence Summers, the then U.S. Treasury Secretary, once joked that IMF stands for "It's Mainly Fiscal."

7. In the case of Thailand, the IMF demanded a substantial budget surplus, including raising the value-added tax from 7 to 10 percent and cutting expenditures by 3 percent of GDP. Putting the figures into perspective, Blustein (2001) compared it with what would have happened if the cut applied to Americans, i.e., as if the U.S. raised taxes or cut government benefits by $300 billion each year, or over $1,000 for each person.

8. For more detailed explanations of the IMF policies, see Timothy Lane et. al (1999).

9. The constraint on banks' supply of loanable funds (the "credit channel effect") was more significant than the decline in the demand for credits during the crisis. For a conceptual analysis see Kashyap and Stein (2000), for empirical proof in one of the Asian crisis countries, see Azis and Thorbecke (2002).

10. This unintended outcome is labeled SAVERS in Table 5.2.

11. Using a price endogenous model applied to one of the Asian crisis countries, it has been shown that a high interest rate policy deteriorates inequality (see Azis, 2001).

12. One could argue, however, that the IMF did not have sufficient time to analyze the costs and benefits of each policy. They were expected to produce a policy package when the economy was already in crisis. Though this is reasonable, it remains the fact that some of the fund's policies were ineffective. In some cases, they even aggravated the undesirable outcomes.

13. Obviously the views are not identical in all countries. I found differing opinions among analysts and policymakers within the same country. But what is more interesting is that in almost all cases the differences are more on the priority (ranking of importance) rather than about the substance or types of policies.

14. Unless invited or requested the IMF should not interfere with domestic policies. Each year, IMF staff missions visit member countries to conduct an assessment of the country's economy and to consult with policymakers in relation to what is known as "Article IV." The director's order to go was clearly outside such a mission.

15. When reminded about it, a senior minister once told this author that "the private sector knows better than the government in deciding how much, and under what terms they have to borrow." Although they might know precisely what they did, they were also surely aware that without incorporating the standard risks (in interest and exchange rates), the short term and unhedged foreign borrowing could potentially create a financial disaster.

16. The IMF also believes that a process of contagion could play a role. In the words of the then Fund's managing director Stanley Fischer (2000): "contagion or weaknesses in the affected economy? The answer is both. Establishing the presence of excess volatility and contagion in the system is complicated by the fact that a crisis of confidence can push a country from a good to a bad equilibrium."

17. This gradual approach is not to the liking of the IMF. The following statements of Ann Krueger, the Fund's managing director, when commenting on the rescue program in Indonesia sets an example: "Market sentiment has been adversely affected by conflicting signals in some key areas, such as privatization, and continued concerns about progress of the broader reform agenda." She further remarked that "structural performance criteria" of the program had not been met. Accelerated restructuring of corporate, state-owned enterprises and banking sectors are among the disputed issues (IMF News Brief no. 02/7, January 29, 2002).

18. The combination of gradual restructuring and moderate financial policy is denoted by MPBC in Table 5.2.

19. This policy measure is labeled LBDH in Table 5.2.

20. Actually, the Brady Bonds scheme introduced in the 1980s to resolve the debt crisis in Latin America, in which some debts were swapped for government-guaranteed bonds with lower interest rates (some also with reduced principal), is an alternative form of debt rescheduling. There are no compelling reasons why such a scheme will not work in Asia. In early

1998, when I asked Stanley Fischer why in Asia the IMF did not do what it did in Latin America, he indicated that it is much more difficult to organize effective meetings between a large number of private debtors and lending banks, most of which are not syndicated banks. In Latin America, most debtors are governments, and most lenders are syndicated banks.

21. Not to mention that raising the interest rate would also further weaken the already weak banking system. Krueger (2000) clearly states that "raising the interest rate addresses the balance-of-payments crisis at the costs of weakening the financial system still further."

22. Remarks by the IMF Institute's director Mohsin Khan, as quoted in Blustein (2001).

CHAPTER 6

Developing Countries and the New Financial Architecture

STEPHANY GRIFFITH-JONES

What Progress on International Financial Reform?

The wave of currency and banking crises that began in 1997 in East Asia, then spread to many other emerging markets, and even threatened to spill over to the U.S., generated a broad consensus that fundamental reforms were required in the international financial system. International financial instability was widely seen as a global public good (Griffith-Jones, 2001), and the existing institutions and arrangements were largely viewed as inadequate for dealing with very large and extremely volatile capital flows, in which an important part of the volatility was caused by large imperfections in the financial markets themselves.

The seriousness of the situation is underlined by the fact that in the 1990s, 40 out of 120 months (33 percent of the time) important crises occurred. This is particularly problematic for two reasons. First, currency and banking crises, which have recently occurred mainly in emerging markets, have extremely high development and social costs (Wade, 1998). Indeed, deep and frequent crises in developing countries could undermine achievement of the United Nations target to half world poverty by 2015. Second, there is always the very small, but unacceptable, risk that contagion and spillover in an increasingly interdependent international financial system could lead to global problems. Both these problems implied the need for urgent action to overcome the risk of important benefits that globalization offers in other fields. These could be seriously undermined by international financial developments.

Besides the objective of achieving international financial stability, an equally important objective (which has been stressed less often) is the provision of sufficient, and sufficiently stable, private and public capital flows to different categories of developing countries. These flows could complement domestic savings as well as transfer technology and management know-how, thus allowing for higher levels of growth. This latter objective has emerged as particularly urgent in recent years, given that net private capital flows, both to emerging economies and low-income countries, have fallen sharply since 1997. Indeed, net private flows to emerging markets were practically zero in 2000 and 2001, and net private flows to low-income countries had fallen dramatically in all categories, including foreign direct investment. A particular source of concern is that an important part of this decline may be due to structural reasons, and not just to cyclical ones (IMF, 2001). This would imply that net private flows to developing countries could remain very low for a fairly significant period of time, and would thus not contribute much foreign exchange or external savings, essential for their growth and development.

The two challenges for a new international financial architecture that would both support and not undermine development are twofold: (*a*) to prevent and better manage (if they occur) currency and banking crises; and (*b*) to ensure that sufficient net private and public flows go to developing countries, including emerging and low-income ones. Some progress has been made, but it is clearly insufficient. The fact that deep crises have continued to happen, most recently in Turkey and Argentina, indicates that the current international financial system needs further changes.

Important changes have been implemented. For example, IMF lending facilities for both crisis prevention and management have been usefully expanded and adapted, and the Fund's total resources were increased. Adaptations are continuously made. For example, a week before the Prague Annual Meetings, the Fund's Contingency Credit Line (CCL)—a new facility that would help countries fight crises spilling over from other countries—was modified. The changes to the CCL include greater automaticity in disbursing such loans once a country is in a crisis resulting from contagion and lower cost of the facility. Such modifications were clearly necessary since the CCL, created over a year ago, had not yet been used. This was like having new fire-fighting equipment, but not having made the crucial connections to the water supply!

Important institutional innovations have been introduced, such as the creation of the Financial Stability Forum (FSF), to identify vulnerabilities and sources of systemic risk, to fill gaps in regulations, and to develop consistent financial regulations across all types of financial institutions. As capital and credit markets become increasingly integrated, both amongst each other and between countries, it is essential for regulation to be efficient such that the domain of the regulator is the same as the domain of the market that is regulated. Given that regulation is still national and sectoral, an institution like the FSF is valuable to help coordinate regulation globally and across sectors. The creation of the G20, a body to discuss international financial reform that includes both developed and developing countries, is also a positive development.

Developing countries have been asked to take a number of important measures to make their countries less vulnerable to crises; these include the introduction of a large number of codes and standards. Though introducing standards is very positive, there are concerns in developing countries that the number of standards (at more than sixty) is too large. Developing countries are also worried that standards are too uniform, in the assumption that "one size fits all." At a recent conference held at the Commonwealth Secretariat, senior policy-makers from developing countries called for greater selectivity and flexibility in the standards they are asked to implement (Griffith-Jones, 1999).

A more inclusive process is also necessary whereby developing countries could participate in the development of standards and codes, which at present, they are asked to implement without having been involved in their design. In addition, the recent Argentinean experience suggests that codes and standards are not enough to guarantee financial stability. Paradoxically, the Argentinean authorities were by far the most enthusiastic supporters of codes and standards. One of the main reasons was that Argentinean economic authorities thought it would help attract private flows. Clearly, codes and standards are not successful at supporting financial stability when other macroeconomic problems are more serious.

A recent important proposal is the new approach to complement smaller lending packages with an international framework, both for standstills—in case of liquidity crises—and for orderly debt workouts in cases of solvency crises, being increasingly suggested by developed countries (Krueger, 2001). Such an international framework would be desirable, though it could have some negative impact on the capacity of developing countries to attract private flows. However, the main problem (and drama) for a country like Argentina is that such an international framework for standstills and debt restructuring is not yet in place. At the same time, there is less willingness than in the past to make large IMF packages. To a certain extent, it could be argued that the international community abandoned its old strategy of large IMF packages for crises countries, without having in place an alternative one. For example, in December 2001 Argentina (though having many problems generated domestically) fell into a semivacuum of international financial architecture.

Even though there has been quite significant progress on reform of the financial architecture, it has suffered from four serious problems. First, it has been insufficient, given the magnitude of the changes required to create a financial system that supports and does not undermine growth and development in the dramatically changed context of the twenty-first century—a context characterized by very large, but extremely volatile and highly concentrated, private capital flows. It is essential to develop a clear vision of an appropriate financial architecture in the new circumstances. Drawing parallels from the institutional mechanisms developed nationally as domestic credit and capital markets grew, a new international architecture requires: (*a*) appropriate transparency and regulation of international financial loan and capital markets; (*b*) provision of sufficient international official liquidity in distress conditions; and (*c*) standstill and orderly debt workout procedures at an international level. However, the mechanisms that exist and the adaptations made until now do not fully meet the new requirements.

Second, progress made has been asymmetrical in three key aspects. A first asymmetry in the reform process is that far more progress has been made on important measures taken by developing countries, which are being asked to introduce a large number of codes and standards, so as to make them less vulnerable to crises. However, far less progress is being made on equally important and complementary international measures. As many leading economists such as Furman and Stiglitz (1998), Radelet and Sachs (1998), and Rodrik (1998) have stressed, crises (such as in Asia) were not just caused by country problems but also by imperfections in international capital markets, such as herding, that led to rapid surges and reversals of massive private flows. To deal with the problems in the international financial markets, it is essential that international measures both for crisis prevention and management are also taken.

As the G24, which represents developing countries, pointed out recently, standards in the area of transparency are being pressed upon developing countries to improve information for markets, without equal corresponding obligations for disclosure by financial institutions, including highly leveraged ones such as hedge funds who have no reporting obligation. Better information on financial markets would be of great value to policymakers, especially in developing countries. Transparency should not be a one-way street. Furthermore, there is painfully slow progress in filling important gaps in international regulation of institutions, such as mutual and hedge funds, or of modifying regulations of banks where current regulations may have contributed, rather than prevented, greater short-termism of flows.[1] In the context of international regulation, valuable studies have been carried out, particularly by the Financial Stability Forum Working Parties, but recommendations made are yet to be implemented.

Passing from crisis prevention to crisis management, it is important that the IMF's resources are large enough to meet the financing needs of a systemic crisis involving several economies simultaneously, while also retaining sufficient liquidity to meet normal demands on the fund's resources. Michel Camdessus and others, including the influential U.S. Council of Foreign Affairs, have suggested that this expansion of official emergency financing could be funded in part by temporary and self-liquidating issues of special drawing rights (SDRs). Such a mechanism would not add to total world liquidity, except in a temporary manner during a crisis situation when it would be compensating for reductions or reversal of private flows. In addition, faster progress on orderly debt workouts is urgent.

A second source of asymmetry in the reform process that needs to be urgently overcome is the insufficient participation of developing countries in key fora and institutions. Regarding the international financial institutions, more representative governance needs to be discussed in parallel with a redefinition of their functions. It is particularly urgent that developing countries (which are now only represented in a very limited way in the FSF working parties) are fully represented in the Financial Stability Forum, as the issues discussed there have profound effects on their economies, and their insights can make an important contributions to the forum's valuable work. The inclusion of major developing countries in the G20 is clearly a welcome step, but it might be of value to include some smaller developing nations to reflect their specific concerns. Above all, it would be helpful if the agenda of the G20 could be broadened, to include more explicitly the key issues of international financial reform.

A third asymmetry that has emerged in discussions on reform of the system is that we have all placed excessive focus on crisis prevention and management for middle-income countries. Important as this is, it may have led us to neglect the equally, if not more important, issues of appropriate liquidity and development finance for low-income countries. Regarding liquidity, it is important that existing IMF facilities for low-income countries, such as the Compensatory Financing Facility and the Poverty Reduction and Growth Facility, be made more flexible, in case the present level of oil prices are sustained or if other terms of trade shocks affect such countries. More generally, the role of the IMF in providing liquidity to low-income countries is crucial.

Regarding development finance, low-income countries need sufficient multilateral lending and official flows, as well as speedy debt relief. It is a source of concern that multilateral lending to low-income countries, especially via IDA, has fallen sharply. Furthermore, in a world of rapidly increasing private flows it is important that low-income countries, donors, and international organizations collaborate to attract more significant private flows. Mobilizing sufficient and stable development finance, both private and official, to low-income countries is an essential precondition to help ensure growth and poverty reduction in the poorest countries.

A third serious problem with progress on the international financial architecture is that recently there has been a risk of reversal in progress. There is currently growing reluctance by developed countries, especially the U.S., to support large IMF lending (or to contribute bilateral short-term lending) to better manage crises. The main argument given has been that these large packages lead to excessive moral hazard, which implies that both borrowers and lenders behave more irresponsibly, knowing that they will be "bailed out." This argument is vastly overstated, and insufficient weight has been given to the tremendous costs (financial, economic, and human) that crises cause in developing countries, as well as the possible threat they pose for global financial stability.

A fourth problem is that the focus has been on preventing and managing crises, with emphasis on curbing excessive and excessively volatile private-capital inflows in recipient countries, and to some extent in source countries. The discussion on national capital controls, on regulations in source countries, and the weight attached to curbing excessive "moral hazard" via smaller IMF and other lending are, from different ideological and analytical perspectives, all aimed at reducing excessive private flows, especially of a short-term and reversible nature. This will be crucial in the future to help prevent a new wave of crises. But currently, as we have seen, the problem is of insufficient private flows. Therefore, an important task is to design measures that will both encourage higher levels of private flows (especially long-term ones) and provide country-cyclical official flows (both for liquidity and development finance purposes) during the periods when private flows are insufficient.

Better International Information and Financial Regulation

Additional Information on Markets to Developing Countries

Information on developing countries to markets has to be complemented with the provision of, and access to, increased and better information on international financial markets to policy-makers, especially (but not only) in developing countries. Particularly during the crisis that started in Asia, emerging country policy-makers have found important limitations in the essential information available on the functioning of international capital and banking markets.

The IMF has led the way in improving information on emerging markets economies, and its dissemination, which is of particular use to markets. A parallel symmetric effort needs to be done to gather and provide timely information on market evolution to emerging markets' policy-makers. This task should perhaps be led by the BIS (Bank for International Settlements), and coordinated by the Financial Stability Forum. Inputs from other institutions would be valuable, such as the IMF and the private sector (e.g., the Institute of International Finance). Suggestions in the October 1998 G22 Report of the Working Group on Transparency and Accountability provided important elements for this task. They relate not just to better statistics on international banks' exposures, but also on compiling data on international exposures of investment banks, hedge funds, and other institutional investors.

Given the speed with which markets move, it seems particularly important that the frequency with which relevant data is produced be high (and possibly higher in times of market turbulence, when it becomes particularly crucial), and that dissemination is instantaneous to the central banks of all countries. Indeed, a special additional service could be provided by the BIS in which it would play the role of clearinghouse for information. To this end it could draw not just on information from markets, but could collect and centralize information from each country. This could include both quantitative and qualitative information; via the internet, the BIS could standardize information requirements, collect aggregate, and disseminate data to all central banks and other relevant institutions. Such a service would be of the greatest use to developing country policy-makers, especially immediately before and during crises. In addition, it would be valuable to developed country policy-makers and international institutions in handling crisis prevention and management.

Improved International Financial Regulation

The Case for Regulation   A strong case can be made that international financial regulation is welfare increasing. This is particularly true if such regulation has explicit countercyclical elements to compensate for inherent procyclical behavior by financial actors. Indeed, there is growing support for the view that the process of international financial intermediation has a second-best element in which welfare for both source and recipient countries can be increased by regulatory changes (through measures in source and/or recipient countries) that would reduce excessive lending or investing. It is noteworthy that in the case of interbank lending, Chairman Alan Greenspan (1998) proposed that it could be appropriate for either borrowing or lending countries to impose reserve requirements to

> deter aberrant borrowing: sovereigns could charge an explicit premium, or could impose reserve requirements, earning low or even zero interest rates, on

interbank liabilities. Increasing the capital charge on lending banks, instead of on borrowing banks, might also be effective.

There is growing recognition that it may often be desirable to regulate excessive surges of potentially reversible capital flows in recipient countries. Indeed, an important part of the responsibility with discouraging excessive reversible inflows, as well as managing them, lies with recipient countries. However, the experience of the 1990s with very large scales of international funds compared to the small size of developing country markets, leads to the question of whether measures to discourage excessive short-term flows by recipient countries are sufficient to deal with capital surges and the risk of their reversals.

Aizenman and Turnovsky (1999) have formalized such an analysis by developing a rigorous model that analyzes the impact, via externalities of reserve requirements on international loans (both in lending and recipient countries), on the welfare of both categories of countries. They thus evaluate the macroeconomic impact of reserve requirements in a second-best world, where there is moral hazard due to likely bailouts on the lender's side and sovereign risk on the borrower's side. Both generate large negative externalities on welfare. The general conclusion of their model is that the introduction of a reserve requirement in either source or recipient country reduces the risk of default and raises the welfare in both countries.

The aim of such regulatory changes is to help smooth capital flows to emerging markets without excessively discouraging them. This is in contrast with views based on a belief that crises in emerging markets are due only to moral hazard, and that the appropriate way to combat such moral hazard is by scaling down the role of the IMF in providing financial packages before and during crises. The latter view has acquired some prominence in developed countries, particularly but not only in the U.S. (Meltzer et al., 2000). The Meltzer Report to the U.S. Congress took such views to the extreme.

A reduction of the role of the IMF could either make crises even more costly, and/or lead to a sharp reduction in private flows to developing countries. These are both highly undesirable effects that could significantly diminish welfare, particularly but not only in developing economies, as well as undermine support for open economies and market-based economic policies. Therefore, an approach based on better regulation is clearly more acceptable and more welfare-enhancing than one that cuts back the IMF.

Filling Gaps The broad welfare case for applying reserve requirements in both source and recipient countries can also be applied to institutional investors, such as mutual funds. The growing importance of mutual funds occurred in the 1990s within developed countries, particularly the U.S.— where mutual funds receive more than 50 percent of total deposits in the financial system—and in capital flows from developed to developing countries (d'Arista and Griffith-Jones, 2001). The narrowing of differences between banks and institutional investors like mutual funds, and the fact that securities markets and mutual funds also have access to the lender of last resort (due to the rescue packages put together by the IMF in recent serious currency crises), point to the importance of improving prudential standards for institutional investors.

Regarding portfolio flows to emerging markets, there is an important regulatory gap at present since there is no international regulatory framework for taking account of market or credit risks on flows originating from institutional investors, such as mutual funds (and more broadly for flows originating from nonbank institutions). This important regulatory gap needs to be filled to protect retail investors in developed countries, and to protect developing countries from the negative effects of excessively large and potentially reversible portfolio flows.

Institutional investors (e.g., mutual funds), given the liquid nature of their investments, can play an important role in contributing to developing country currency crises.[2] It seems important, therefore, to introduce some countercyclical regulation to discourage excessive surges of portfolio flows. This could perhaps best be achieved by a variable risk-weighted cash requirement for institutional investors. These cash requirements would be placed as interest-bearing deposits in commercial banks. Introducing a dynamic risk-weighted cash requirement for mutual funds (and perhaps other institutional investors) is in the mainstream of current regulatory thinking and would require that standards be provided by relevant regulatory authorities and/or agreed internationally. The guidelines for macroeconomic risk, which would determine the cash requirement, would take into account vulnerability variables as defined by the IMF and BIS.[3]

The September 1998 Emerging Markets IOSCO Report on "Causes, Effects, and Regulatory Implications of Financial and Economic Turbulence in Emerging Markets" describes in some detail, and evaluates rather positively, the foregoing proposal. This report emphasised that "there appears to be scope—and an urgent need for further work. This is very likely to require a multilateral effort—i.e., by regulators from both source and recipient countries in collaboration with industry."

Regarding Highly Leveraged Institutions (HLIs), the FSF working group on HLIs rightly focused on two problems: systemic risk linked to high leverage and reduction of market; and economic impact of collapse of unregulated HLIs. Particular emphasis was placed on HLI activities in small- and medium-size open economies where the potential damage that can be caused by large and concentrated positions can seriously amplify market pressures. The FSF Working Group considered formal direct regulation of currently unregulated institutions. This would include a licensing system, minimum capital and liquidity standards, large exposure limits, minimum standards for risk management, and an enforcement regime with fines for transgressions.

Such regulation was seen to have several desirable effects, such as regular oversight of HLIs and the reduced likelihood of disruptive market events. However, because of what was seen as both philosophical and practical problems, the working group did not recommend applying a system of direct regulation to currently unregulated HLIs, though it did not reject the possibility of establishing such a regime at a later stage. It emphasized that the failure to carry through their recommended measures would prompt such reconsideration.

The philosophical objection relates to the fact that direct regulation would not be aimed at investor protection (as investors are sufficiently wealthy or sophisticated to do their own due diligence), but on the mitigation of systemic risk. However, it could be argued that mitigation of systemic risk is also an increasingly valid regulatory aim. There were also practical objections, including how to avoid leakage through offshore centers. However, current efforts to improve and complete regulation in offshore centers should help overcome those problems.[4]

Other practical issues are more technical, including the need to adapt capital adequacy and large exposure rules to the specific risk profile of HLIs. This should be done in ways that any regulatory capital requirement did not adversely affect the efficiency and liquidity of markets in which HLIs are significant participants. It is particularly important in a context when several large hedge funds have been wound down, which may diminish some of the negative impacts they had in recent crises but could, according to some observers, deprive markets of countrarian actors with useful roles to play in stopping the deepening crises.

Removing Regulatory Distortions and Dampening Exuberance of Bank Lending Regarding bank lending, there has first been concern that the 1988 Basle Capital Accord, due to its significantly lower capital adequacy requirements for short-term lending, contributed to the buildup of short-term bank lending and its reversal in East Asia and elsewhere. The new proposal, published in June 1999, attempts to address this distortion by reducing (though perhaps not sufficiently) the differential between capital adequacy for short-term and other lending. Though they include many positive elements (Cailloux and Griffith-Jones, 1999), they are widely seen as problematic (Griffith-Jones and Spratt, 2001).

The first problematic aspect is that the proposed IRB approach would most probably further reduce international bank lending and significantly increase costs of such lending to most developing countries, particularly those (the large majority) that do not have investment grades.[5] Low-income countries would be especially badly hit. Both effects would be particularly negative for developing countries especially given the new trend (since 1997/98) for bank lending to developing countries to be negative, and more broadly, private flows to be very low. The new Basle Accord could further discourage new lending, as well as institutionalize increased perceived risk.

Second and equally serious, the proposed IRB approach would exacerbate procyclical tendencies within the banking systems. The drive for risk-weights to more accurately reflect probability of default (PD) is inherently procyclical. During an upturn, average PD falls and the IRB approach, based on banks' internal risk model, would reflect lower capital requirements. During a downturn or recession, average PD will increase as deteriorating economic conditions cause existing loans to "migrate" to higher risk categories, therefore raising overall capital requirements. As it is difficult to raise capital in a recession, this may lead to a credit crunch, which would further deepen the downturn. The concerns with increased procyclicality of the proposed new Capital Accord are widespread (Goodhart, 2002).

Increasing inherent procyclicality in regulation, as would result from the current Basle Accord, goes against what is increasingly accepted as best practice in regulation, which is to introduce neutral or countercyclical elements into regulation so as to counteract the natural tendency of procyclicality in banking and capital markets (BIS, 2001; Borio et al. 2001; Ocampo 2001). For developing countries, increased procyclicality of bank lending is particularly damaging given that it contributes to the increased likelihood of crisis, as well as their development and financial costs.

These problems should not, however, question the need for reforming the 1988 Accord. A new Basle Capital Accord proposal that would overcome some of the problems listed should include some of the following elements: (*a*) possible postponement of the IRB approach for further research and improvement of internal bank models; (*b*) if the IRB approach is to be implemented, capital requirements should be lowered for low-rated borrowers, which include most developing countries, to the levels suggested by banks' own models. This would imply significant flattening of the IRB curve; (*c*) a special curve for SMEs is being considered by the Basle Committee. If it is implemented the possibility of a separate curve for developing countries should be seriously studied to avoid excess discouragement of bank lending to developing countries, and to more accurately reflect risk of lending to them (which seems presently to be overestimated by current bank models); and (*d*) serious attention should be given to countercyclical elements in order to mitigate inherent procyclicality of the IRB approach.

Countercyclical Elements in Regulation   The answer may lie in the implementation of an explicit countercyclical mechanism that would, in boom periods and in contrast to ratings, dampen excess bank lending. Counter-cyclical elements can also be introduced in regulating other actors, such as mutual funds. In periods of slowdown and scarcity of finance, the new mechanism should not further accentuate the decline in lending as exemplified by the 1997–1998 Asian crisis, but rather encourage it.

There would be two linked objectives for introducing elements of countercyclical regulation. One would be to help smooth capital flows and the other would be to smooth the domestic impact of volatile capital flows on the domestic financial system and therefore on the real economy. Introducing countercyclical elements into regulation would help build a link between the more microeconomic risks on which regulators have tended to focus until recently and the macroeconomic risks that are becoming increasingly important, both nationally and internationally.[6] Countercyclical elements in regulation related to bank lending could be applied, either internationally, nationally, or at both levels.

Several mechanisms could be used to introduce a countercyclical element into bank lending regulation. One mechanism would be to get the required capital ratio higher in times of boom and allow banks to use the additional cushion provided by the higher capital ratio so they could sustain lending in times of recession at a lower capital asset ratio (when increased bad loans are likely to be reducing their capital). Some practical difficulties may arise in implementing such a mechanism, of which the most serious may be getting international agreement on a general formula for cyclically adjusted capital asset ratios.

A second mechanism for introducing countercyclical elements in bank lending regulation is for regulators to encourage higher general provisions for possible loan losses (i.e., subtracted from equity capital in the books of the bank) to cover normal cyclical risks (Turner, 2000). This would allow for provisions built up in good times to be used in bad times, without affecting reported capital. The way to ensure this would be to maintain higher general provisioning that applies to all loans. The main problem for this mechanism, according to Turner, may be that tax laws often limit the tax deductibility of precautionary provisioning. However, it is possible to change such tax laws, as indeed was done in the late 1980s in the UK.

A third mechanism particularly relevant for domestic bank lending is for regulators to place caps on the value of assets (such as real estate, or stocks and shares) acceptable as collateral, when the value of such assets has risen sharply in a boom and is at risk of sharply declining in a recession. Rules could be used, such as averaging values for the last five years or accepting only 50 percent of current prices in the peak period of a boom. The latter mechanism seems to have the least problems of implementation (indeed, it is already applied in some jurisdictions, e.g., Hong Kong). A fourth possible countercyclical mechanism is that monetary authorities could monitor and limit or discourage lending for property, construction, and personal consumption, as these items tend to increase substantially, and often even be a major factor in booms (McKinnon and Pill, 1998). A possible implementation problem would be the difficulty in verifying final use of credit, and such measures could be partially evaded.

Furthermore, regulators should be flexible, particularly in allowing banks to easily use cushions in times of recession, for example, of capital or provisioning. It may even be advisable if a recession is very serious, to allow ratios to fall below normally required levels so as to help sustain lending, with the understanding that they will be rebuilt as soon as the economy starts recovering. A tension may arise here between the regulatory concerns about individual bank liquidity and solvency and the macroeconomic externalities of their actions, particularly in recessions.

Specific issues seem to require further study. How best can the distinction between a temporary boom and a permanent increase in growth be made? After what period of "boom," should regulatory changes be introduced? How large should such changes be? What are the best mechanisms through which countercyclical measures should be introduced: flexible capital adequacy ratios; higher provisioning against losses; more realistic pricing of collateral? Should such measures be introduced for both international and domestic lending, or for one of them?

References

Aizenman, J. and S. J. Turnovsky. 1999. "Reserve Requirements on Sovereign Debt in the Presence of Moral Hazard—on Debtors or Creditors?" National Bureau of Economic Research working paper, no. 7004. March.

Bank for International Settlements. 2001. Annual Report. BIS.

Borio, C., C. Furfine, and P. Lowe. 2001. "Procyclicality of the Financial System and Financial Stability: Issues and Policy Options." BIS Paper, no 1. March.

Cailloux, J. and S. Griffith-Jones. 1999. "Encouraging the Longer Term: Institutional Investors and Emerging Markets: a Research Agenda." UNDP/Office of Development Studies. Discussion paper series, no. 16.

d'Arista and S. Griffith-Jones. 2001. "The Boom of Portfolio Flows to Emerging Markets and their Implications," in S. Griffith-Jones, M. Montes, and Nasution, eds. *Short-Term Capital Flows and Economic Crises*. Oxford: Oxford University Press.

Financial Stability Forum (FSF). 2000. "Report of the Working Group on Offshore Financial Centres." http://www.fsforum.org/Reports/RepOFC.pdf

Furman, J. and J. Stiglitz. 1998. "Economic Crises: Evidence and Insights from East Asia." Brookings Papers on Economic Activity, no. 2.

Goodhart, C. 2002. "The Inter-Temporal Nature of Risk." London: Financial Markets Group, London School of Economics.

Greenspan. A. 1998. Remarks before the 34th Annual Conference of the Federal Reserve Bank of Chicago, May 7.

———. 1999. "A New Financial Architecture for Reducing Risks and Severity of Crises." Sussex: Institute of Development Studies.

Griffith-Jones, S. 2001. "New Financial Architecture as a Global Public Good." Paper prepared for UNDP.

Griffith-Jones, S. and S. Spratt. 2001. "The Pro-Cyclical Effects of the New Basel Accord," in J .J. Teunissen, ed. *New Challenges of Crisis Prevention*. FONDAD: The Hague.

International Monetary Fund. 2001. *World Economic Outlook*. Washington D.C.: International Monetary Fund.

Kaminsky, G., S. Schmukler, and Lyon. 2000. "Economic Fragility, Liquidity and Risk: The Behaviour of Mutual Funds During Crisis." Mimeo, preliminary draft.

Krueger, A. 2001. "A New Approach to Sovereign Debt Restructuring." Address given at the Indian Council for Research on International Economic Relations, Delhi, India, December 20.

McKinnon, R. and H. Pill. 1998. "International Overborrowing: A Decomposition of Credit and Currency Risks," in *World Development* 26(7): 1267–82. July.

Meltzer, A. H., et al. 2000. "Report to the U.S. Congress of the International Financial Advisory Commission." Washington, D.C. March.

Ocampo, J. A. 2001. "Counter-Cyclical Policies in the Developing World," in J. J. Teunissen, eds. *New Challenges of Crisis Prevention*. The Hague: FONDAD.

Powell, A. 2001. "A New Capital Accord for Emerging Economies?" Universidad Torcuato di Tella.

Radelet, S. and J. Sachs. 1998. "The East Asian Financial Crisis: Diagnosis, Remedies, Prospects." Brookings Papers on Economic Activity, no. 1.

Reisen, H. 2001. "Will Basel II Contribute to Convergence in International Capital Flows?" Mimeo, Paris: OECD Development Centre.

Rodrik, D. 1998. "Who Needs Capital Account Convertibility?" Cambridge, MA: Harvard University.

Turner, P. 2000. "Pro-Cyclicality of Regulatory Ratios." CEPA Working Paper Series III on International Capital Markets and the Future of Economic Policy, no. 13, Jan. New York.

Wade, R. 1998. "The Asian Debt and Development Crisis of 1997: Causes and Consequences," *World Development*, 26(8).

Notes

1. This point will be discussed in greater detail.
2. For evidence see Kaminsky, Schmukler, and Lyon (2000).
3. For a more detailed discussion of this proposal see d'Arista and Griffith-Jones (2001).
4. See discussion of FSF Working Group Report on Offshore Centres (FSF, 2000).
5. For different estimates of potential cost increases see Powell (2001) and Reisen (2001).
6. I thank Andrew Crockett for his suggestive remarks on this point.

CHAPTER 7

Globalization
Eight Crises of Social Protection

GUY STANDING

Introduction

Like size, definitions matter. Around the world there is widespread unease about the growth of social and economic insecurity and inequality. Whatever the causes, people look to systems of social protection to overcome the worst effects, whether the system is the informal network of family relationships or a complex web of state policies. They look to institutions to enhance their security and that of their families and communities. Thus, in analyzing globalization and changes in socioeconomic inequality, we need to be clear about changing patterns of social protection, social security, and socioeconomic security.

Social security is best defined as a combination of social insurance and social assistance. It is the system by which state transfers are provided, usually but not always in cash form, supposedly related to specific *contingency risks* such as sickness, invalidity, old age, unemployment, and motherhood. Defining what is a risk and specifying which risks should be covered and which should not, are among the difficulties of social security.

Social protection is a broader concept. It covers state-based schemes of income transfers based on social insurance or means-testing or other conditionality tests or universal or citizenship rights. It also covers social *services*; community initiatives; private, commercial, or voluntary schemes; and self-help arrangements such as "friendly societies." If social security is about "social risk management by or for the individual," then social protection, which includes social security, may be said to be also about protection of the social: civility, fraternity, and social solidarity. Any social protection system may give a large role to social security or a minimal one, as is the case in most low-income developing countries.

Socioeconomic security is broader still. Besides encompassing protection of the social sphere of transfers and services, it is also about economic protection of the social—embedding the economy in the society through structures of systems of regulation, protection, and distribution that limit social and economic insecurity, reduce inequalities, and provide patterns of opportunity. This chapter addresses the development of social protection policy in the context of recent economic and political changes. These changes have induced eight crises in social protection, which can only be resolved by a profound but eminently feasible change in direction.

Restructuring Social Income

Social protection is fundamentally about providing income security. For this we need a reasonable idea of what counts as income and security. Accordingly, we should think in terms of what we might call *social income*. In any society every individual has to have some source of income or they cannot survive. Perhaps the most important negative results of globalization have been the erosion of informal social-support systems, particularly in developing and "transition" countries, and the removal or loss of entitlement to enterprise and state benefits.

There are other ways that are often harder to evaluate. Suppose a man was receiving $100 as a wage and had a long-term secure employment contract, guaranteed health care, subsidized canteen food, and of a group pension plan. The total value might be $200. How do we measure the value to the worker of the employment guarantee? One imagines many people would be prepared to sacrifice 10 percent of their income to retain such a guarantee. If an employer takes the guarantee away and gives the worker a 10 percent pay raise, our statistics would show income rising by 10 percent, which is misleading because all that has happened is that the structure of social income has changed.

Although there is good data to demonstrate it, something like this seems to have been happening all over the world—except that for many there has been no compensation for loss of security, or the hope that they could obtain it has diminished. We may hypothesize that under the impact of economic liberalization and globalization, the structure of social income has been changing. In most parts of the world there has been a shift to money wages and a shrinkage in the share provided by state benefits and services. Perhaps most significantly there is increasing reliance on private provision (personal investment and saving) and community support (voluntary provision), or an increased need for those sources to fill voids opened by diminishing public provision.

The New Global Stratification

It is of limited use to consider social protection and socioeconomic security as if there were no social groups or classes. Conventional labor statistics are not very helpful. For instance, there are no peasants in international statistics. Further, we have no information on classifications based on the range of income sources and controls by which patterns of economic security or insecurity are reproduced or undermined.[1]

It may be useful to consider the following image of social fragmentation taking place internationally. The point of any such exercise is to identify groups that have distinctive sets of entitlements and patterns of social protection and security, and as a result, are likely to have a particular attitude to various forms of social protection. A feature of stratification is that growing numbers of people are detaching themselves, or being detached from, mainstream national regulatory and protective systems. It is presented in descending order based on average social income.

The Elite

At the zenith of the globalizing economy is an *elite*, consisting of a tiny minority of absurdly rich and high-earning people whose impact on social and economic policies and political developments is out of all proportion to their number. Some of these individuals have long since reached the stage of seeing their incomes rising almost exponentially. They are global citizens. With their billions or many millions of dollars, they are detached from national regulatory and social security systems, neither needing nor contributing to them either psychologically—not feeling committed to their maintenance or improvement—or politically. The elite has strong income security and whatever they need of other forms of security. Their biggest danger is hubris and being caught in criminality. Their winner-takes-all existence sets patterns of social risk and sickness.

Proficians

These are the new craftsmen of the global flexible economy. As the name implies, they are a mix of professionals and technicians, mostly working as consultants or in short-term employment contracts. They operate in a climate of insecurity but are well compensated. Perhaps their main form of insecurity is work insecurity, epitomized by the frenzied pace of their erratic work schedules, stress, and burnout. They are often able to evade or avoid taxation, and are at least partially detached from state-based social protection systems.

The Salariat

This consists of salaried employees, including those working in civil services, large corporations, parastatals, and other bureaucracies. They have a high degree of labor security, but probably suffer from some job and skill reproduction insecurity because they may be moved around and/or gain promotion in their enterprises by leaving technical skills behind them. Because of their reasonably high incomes and a tendency to identify with managements, employers, and the elite and profician strata, members of the salariat typically feel detached from the state social protection system, seeing their future and income security mainly in terms of private insurance benefits and earnings from judicious investment.

Core Workers

These are the bulwark of what those of us with long memories used to call the working class. Welfare states were created to serve the needs of core workers: those in full-time, regular, typically unionized jobs, usually with manual skills. In the post-1945 era of statutory regulation, it was implicitly presumed in industrialized countries that these workers represented the norm and that a majority of workers in all countries would eventually belong to this stratum. The larger the proportion of people belonging to it, the more people would be in a position to support and benefit from the mainstream, insurance-based social protection and regulatory systems.

However, although the legitimacy of a redistributive welfare state depended on core workers, they never comprised a majority of the workforce in most countries, and since the 1970s, have been shrinking almost everywhere. This is not just a reflection of "de-industrialization" and the dispersion of manufacturing wage labor around the world. It is also because of various forms of labor-market flexibility. Core workers traditionally benefited from most forms of labor security, but with the growth of wage system flexibility a growing proportion of their income has come in insecure forms. They also suffer from increasing job and employment insecurity while their unions have been weakened almost everywhere. With core workers dwindling in numbers and not expected to grow, their agenda has lacked *legitimacy*.

Flexiworkers

These comprise a disparate group in nonregular work statuses, including casual workers, outworkers, contract labor, and agency and domestic workers. Their common characteristic is labor insecurity in most respects. In the era of statutory regulation and welfare-state capitalism it was presumed that these informal forms of employment would decline as economies developed. More recently they have appeared to be the future. Not only have the number of people trapped in petty activities in rural and peri-urban areas grown, but flexible labor processes have boosted other forms. Among the associated trends, growing proportions of labor forces have lacked entitlement to statutory protection and have been disentitled to social transfers.

The Unemployed

The number has risen extraordinarily in the era of market regulation. They suffer from labor-market insecurity, risk unemployment and income insecurity more than in the past, because the level of benefits has been cut, duration of entitlement has been shortened, and conditions for entitlement have been tightened.

The Detached

This is a growing minority of the population in many countries: cut off from mainstream state benefits, lingering in poverty, anomic, and threatening those above them in the income spectrum simply because others fear falling into their ranks. In recent years politicians have been inclined to treat these, many of whom are victims of economic liberalization, as in need of "re-integration." They linger on the streets, and in bus and train stations and city parks. They make those above them in the social order feel uncomfortable or smug, depending on where they fit. The detached represent fear, and it is fear that induces concessions from the near poor— the ultimate tool of inequality.

If one divides societies (and the international economy) into these seven fragments, one sees that the top three strata are increasingly detaching themselves from state-based social protection while the bottom three are increasingly being detached by explicit and implicit disentitlement to its benefits and services. Although one may choose a different way of stratification, the analytical device may also help us to picture the growing inequality of social income and deterioration of economic security.

Socioeconomic fragmentation has produced a situation in which those in, or identifying with, the top three strata feel increasingly *detached* from the mainstream state-based social protection system. They are less inclined to defend its principles of social *solidarity* while the bottom three feel deprived, detached by disentitlement to the benefits long offered to core workers to whose ranks they had aspired. To them there is no solidarity on offer, and for them to talk about social solidarity would sound like a sick joke. Pervasive detachment and lack of social solidarity have contributed to the loss of *legitimation* of the welfare state. An image of fragmentation, coupled informal activities and forms of flexibility, may be useful for assessing the relevance of social protection and security policies, as well as the limitations and apparent lack of general appeal for social protection systems promoted in the twentieth century.

The Eight Crises of Social Protection[2]

Given the developments associated with globalization—notably the privatization of economic activity and social policy, informalization, the spread of flexible labor practices, and the new globalized socioeconomic stratification—it is no exaggeration to describe the emerging tensions and dilemmas in social policy as crises. The point to bear in mind is that crisis, in the ancient Greek sense of the word, means a *threat* and an *opportunity*, so that to depict a crisis does not imply pessimism or an inability to turn the situation to advantage. A crisis could be a good thing to have, because it induces action to make improvements. What is perhaps generally the case is that a crisis requires a change in direction if an adverse trend is to be reversed. Although not in any order of implied significance, social protection systems face the following eight crises:

A Linguistic Crisis

In the sixteenth century Francis Bacon recognized the tendency to mislead by the clever use of words, which he described as the "idols of the marketplace." Social thinking has always been afflicted by the misuse of words and phrases. Images conveyed by simple terms are taken as reality, and words are increasingly loaded with ideological symbolism and political correctness. The reason is that the terms we use help to shape the policy agenda. Take just two examples. Perhaps the most influential terms in the sphere of social protection in this era have been *the social safety net* and *active labor market policy*. In both cases the images conveyed to the unwary are quite different from what they usually mean in reality. Who could possibly be against having a social safety net to catch all those poor victims falling off the globalizing economy? The reality is that this is a disembedded notion that amounts to giving conditional crumbs to the poor. Instead of a safety net, which suggests something broad and comforting, what is meant is a highly targeted, selective scheme, usually based on means-testing. The notion of *targeting* may sound sensible—directing scarce resources at the poorest of the poor—but, in fact, empirical evidence show that means-tested and other selective benefits rarely reach those most in need, due to low take-up rates, stigma, administrative inefficiencies, and so on.

The notion of *active labor market policy* is equally disingenuous. Active policy is little more than having the state tell people what they must do in order to receive some moderate state benefit directing them to training or job schemes. By contrast, the much derided *passive* policy entails giving funds to individuals or families with minimal or no conditions, leaving them to make choices about how to conduct their lives and allocate their resources. It could, more fairly, be described as liberating. Perceptions influence policy-makers and inform the "focus groups" that increasingly determine policy.

A Fiscal Crisis

A fiscal crisis arises if the revenue required to pay for social transfers and services falls relative to the income required, which may arise because raising income is becoming harder or because the need for benefits is rising. For several reasons, in both developing and industrialized countries, both trends have been operating. Both are due to the combined effects of globalization, flexible labor markets, and economic informalization.

In industrialized countries, the main problem is that with higher unemployment and labor-market flexibility, contributions tend to fall while demand and need for income transfers rise. This is compounded by demographic pressures, mainly due to aging, so that pensions and "old-age dependency" require rising state expenditure. In recent years high labor-force participation rates reflect growing levels of part-time employment and the spread of what has been called "the working poor": a large and growing number of people earning less than enough from jobs to pull them out of poverty or to give them economic security.

Consequently, contributions to social insurance have tended to shrink while the need for income transfers has risen. Indeed, governments have extended "in-work" benefits, designed to raise earnings as a policy of labor "commodification." States that have increased contribution rates have merely worsened the situation by raising labor costs and contributed to wage demands, which, in turn, have contributed to sluggish employment growth and a higher NAIRU (the level of unemployment compatible with an acceptable level of inflation). In the U.S., social security contributions have comprised 12.4 percent of wages; in Germany the corresponding figure is 19.1 percent, and in Italy it is an extraordinary 33 percent.[3] Most governments have tried to hold down contribution rates, but in doing so, have allowed the share of revenue required to pay for social protection coming from general taxation to rise.

However, the main response to fiscal pressures has been a curtailment of state benefits. This has taken four forms: cuts in the levels of benefits, restrictions in entitlements through tighter conditions, privatization, and decentralization. There has been a tendency to lower gross and net income-replacement rates, cut the duration of benefit entitlement, and increase the duration of contributory employment required to obtain full or even partial entitlement. The IMF, among others, has called for governments to "reduce the generosity of benefits," as if they were a gift rather than income derived from "insurance."[4] The range of benefits may also be reduced. There has been a drift to means-testing, categorical testing (only providing benefits to narrowly defined groups), and behavior testing (requiring claimants to act in certain ways). By these means, governments have curbed the number of people receiving benefits, either by blocking people who are qualified for them or by creating situations in which the "take-up rate" is low. In most countries, large proportions of those entitled to means-tested benefits do not obtain them, often because they do not apply due to stigma, ignorance, or incapacity to do so.

Means and behavior testing also tend to worsen fiscal pressures because they require high administrative and monitoring costs, while encouraging both moral and immoral hazards, which, in turn, encourage the evasion and avoidance of legal tax-paying employment. With means tests, there are poverty and unemployment traps because taking a job results in a loss of benefits, implying a high marginal tax rate. Thus, the response to fiscal pressures can intensify those pressures because people can react to poverty traps by resorting to tax-evading hidden employment or own-account work.

Second, governments have decentralized and delegated responsibility for public social protection to regional and local authorities, which may result in lower and more discretionary benefits because the state can divert political pressure by claiming that providing such protection is not their responsibility. Third, governments have responded to fiscal pressures by privatizing social protection. Some have given incentives to people to take up private insurance for a growing number of contingency risks. Others have indulged in what one early advocate called the micropolitics of privatization by allowing public benefits and services to decline so as to induce people to opt out of the public sector. Others have contracted out the administration of benefits and services to commercial firms, allowing them to be responsible for cost-cutting methods. Finally, others have turned to nongovernmental organizations to act as lower-cost providers. Although this raises alarming questions, which I will consider in relation to other crises of social protection, they have appealed to governments keen to cut public social spending.

Many of these issues are marginal in developing countries where fiscal crisis has been more dramatic and drastic: coverage rates are low and only a minority of the population have contributed, or are entitled, to the main forms of social protection. Further, the need for transfers is enormous. There is also the pressure to cut social spending under the dictate of globalization's economic orthodoxy. Governments believe that it is hard to raise money by taxation, particularly on relatively mobile capital and flexible labor. Globalization has also hindered the ability of developing country governments to raise taxes from tariffs. By contrast, not many years ago, trade taxes provided about one-third of all tax revenue in developing countries.

A Legitimation Crisis

The welfare states that developed in the middle decades of the twentieth century were based on the notion of *social solidarity* in which social insurance and other transfers were based, in theory, on a pooling of risks, so that the fortunate effectively subsidized the unfortunate, and so that consumption and incomes were smoothed over the life cycle. A presumption of the model, and its several variants, was that the working class accounted for the overwhelming majority of the population, or was expected to become a majority. The norm was the man, as "breadwinner" in regular, full-time employment. When women were perceived as part of the labor force, they were implicitly or explicitly expected to become regular, contributory workers.

For various reasons the social solidarity basis of the welfare state has been eroded. The working class is no longer expected to be that majority and the *core* stratum has been shrinking in industrialized countries. In terms of the new global stratification, the three groups above the core have been detached by fortune whereas the three groups below have been detached by misfortune. At the upper end of the spectrum more people feel they have little or nothing to gain from a system that pools risks because they believe that either they have a much lower risk of being in need than those below them, or that they can obtain more-effective insurance coverage from private sources.

These sentiments are put into effect via political democracy, since changes in the relative numbers in the various strata, and more important the financial power of the top strata, have persuaded politicians to shift social protection systems away from a social solidarity structure. There is a literature that has postulated a *median voter model*, by which there is a tendency to vote for politicians and parties that promise systems and policies that benefit those with something close to the median income. A modification of this is that actually the median voter has an income *above* the median because the poor are least likely to vote.

The changing socioeconomic stratification structure neglects the interests of the bottom two social strata, any small group in need, and any group that does not vote as a group. The elite, proficians, and salariat are also likely to favor the privatization of social protection. Differential risks can be taken into account in determining contributory rates and individual choice can be focused on the specific risks faced rather than those faced by the core or those in the strata below. Those linked to major pension funds or health-care corporations have also promoted the privatization of social protection. These funds are powerful, are able to set the tone of debate, and have become enmeshed in the process of "conditionality" for aid, foreign loans, and capital flows. In some countries pension funds have assets that are greater than the GNP, and in others they are approaching that level.[5]

Privatization of social protection creates new mechanisms of inequality, accentuating the growth of "winners-take-all losers-lose-all" markets and income patterns. It leads to worries about *accountability*, since private providers can collude or alter their strategies as they see fit, or may become so financially powerful that they become oligopolistic. However, it may be a long time before an adequate regulatory regime exists to enforce appropriate codes of practice. Private providers also prompt concerns about *equity*, in light of the exclusion of the relatively noninsurable and higher premiums for high-risk people, such as those living in depressed regions or working in high-risk jobs. As the latter tend to be relatively low-income earners, the impact on social income inequality is significant. Unless private schemes are mandatory, *adverse selection* (providing benefits to those less in need of them rather than to those in most need) is likely to become endemic.

An outcome of the "social safety net" political agenda, coupled with partial privatization of pensions, health care, schooling, and other social services, including employment and unemployment services, has been *multitierism*. For pensions this includes a "best practice" minimal state-based (means-tested) model, a privately funded second tier, a social insurance tier, an enterprise-based tier (occupational welfare), and a voluntary, private tier. Governments and international bodies are considering how each of these tiers could be regulated and how the middle tiers could be made mandatory for all or most workers. In terms of legitimacy, any such system will imply that individuals will look primarily to one or some of the tiers but not all of them. In particular, the elite, proficians, and salariat will favor the upper tiers and will be disinterested, if not hostile, to the means-tested, bottom-tier benefits and services. The trend to multitierism intensifies the legitimation crisis by creating a series of zero-sum situations where one group's loss is perceived as another's gain, potentially if not actually.

Further, in developing countries, to the extent that there is a tendency for the World Bank, the IMF, and foreign-aid donors to concentrate funds on targeted schemes intended for the poor, it could paradoxically result in a worsening of social protection because targeting could undermine any sense of social solidarity among the elites and middle class. In rationalizing policies impeding the development of social solidarity, they can press for mechanisms that enable them to opt out of socially redistributive schemes.

Ironically, if the progressive populist position was upheld (i.e., there should be no conditionality in international aid), this tendency would be accentuated. An absence of conditionality may not be neutral or one of noninterference; it is interference because it helps to empower elites and the middle class.

Globalization has tended to *raise expectations* among middle-class groups in industrializing countries, whose members look enviously at benefits and services in industrialized countries, while allowing critics of social protection in the latter to argue for reductions in state benefits by reference to international "competitiveness." Moreover, in developing countries where support for national politicians and parties comes mainly from their ranks, the urban middle classes are likely to vote for politicians without a strong orientation to pro-poor social policies. In general, a stable and comprehensive social protection system requires a reasonably strong sense of social solidarity. The legitimation crisis in the twenty-first century arises because it is unclear that modern "political democracy" is conducive to such a system.[6]

A Moral Crisis

The fiscal pressures that built up in the 1980s and '90s, and the policy responses by governments, fed into a *moral crisis*. Initially encouraged by libertarians and the political "right," a sentiment spread that state benefits encouraged behavior and situations they were actually supposed to overcome, creating what is known as *moral hazards* and *adverse selection*. Some claims were fanciful and offensive, such as the assertion that teenagers were rushing to have babies so as to claim food stamps or child support. The selective schemes may, to a minor extent, have facilitated what was happening in any case: a decline in the conventional nuclear family. However, the reforms that the critics and defenders of state benefits were inclined to adopt accentuated the moral criticisms, putting defenders of the laborist welfare state further on the defensive.

Contributing to the moral dilemmas are three claims, which Charles Murray (1984: 212–216) characteristically described as laws, derived from his analyzis of U.S. experience from 1950 to 1980:

- *The Law of Imperfect Selection*: Any rule defining eligibility for a transfer irrationally excludes some people, policy-makers broaden target populations.
- *The Law of Unintended Rewards*: Any transfer increases the value of being in the condition that prompted the transfer.
- *The Law of Net Harm*: The less likely the unwanted behavior will change voluntarily, the more likely a scheme to induce change will cause net harm.

Murray and his fellow libertarians want radical cuts in state benefits and belong to a tradition of thinkers favoring insecurity. However, this perspective highlights something that is lost on a generation that has championed *active policy:* Scarcely any policy is *passive.* They condition and regulate in one way or another. The perceived moral crisis initially led in the direction favored by those who worried about a fiscal crisis: to greater selectivity and conditionality based on moving in the direction of deciding who was *deserving* and who was *undeserving.*

Moral hazards may be cited as reasons for increased selectivity and conditionality, but other hazards are generated by the reactions. For instance, new conditions of entitlement create new hazards as well as poverty, unemployment, and other behavioral traps. Suppose a policy is made more conditional by stipulating that benefits will only be paid to those who *lose* their job, not to those who quit a job, on the grounds that that policy should not encourage "voluntary unemployment." This condition will deter labor mobility as well as encourage claimants to lie, scarcely the intention but hardly irrational in the circumstances.

The moral crisis is epitomized by the willingness for policy-makers and commentators to divide potential recipients of social protection into three categories:

1. *The deserving poor:* Offered a residual social safety net through means-tested basic benefits (including basic first-tier pensions).
2. *The undeserving poor:* Offered the carrot and stick of "workfare" and/or conditional low-level transfers.
3. *The transgressing poor:* Those who fail and are undeserving, but are also silly enough to break the rules, resorting to unsociable behavior, offered the stern state prepared to uphold the law in keeping public order.

This is slightly more sophisticated than the nineteenth-century dichotomy of the deserving and undeserving poor. However, the modern tendency suffers from the same shortcomings as the old. Categorizing people in this way is arbitrary, unnecessarily judgmental, and inequitable. Nevertheless, it has resulted in greater income insecurity for those on the margins of society.[7] The most striking outcome of the trichotomy is that those perceived as deserving are offered conditional assistance that smacks of charity rather than seen as a right. Those who are undeserving are offered a route to social decency and "inclusion," and those who transgress are offered social "exclusion," through prison, hard labor, stigmatization, summary justice, and the prospect of social tagging.

The moral crisis reflects many years of steady reform. One can trace the way the state abandoned the pretense of *social insurance,* or an income/need approach to social protection in liberal welfare states, as a "moving the goalposts" approach to social protection. For instance, the age of retirement, or age for full pension has been raised, the number of years of employment required for full pension has increased, the duration of past employment for entitlement has been lengthened, registration procedures have been tightened, and willingness-to-move tests have been introduced. Dozens of new rules have been rationalized into existence. The means-tested, asset-tested, behavior-tested schemes breed moral dilemmas. The *moral hazards*, whereby it pays to stay in selective schemes because one is penalized by moving out of them, are compounded by the less-mentioned *immoral hazards*, whereby unfair poverty traps means that it pays to be dishonest.

A Social Dumping Crisis

With globalization there has been a tendency, whether justified or not, for policy-makers to indulge in social-policy competitiveness. Intent on attracting or retaining foreign capital, they are resorting to *social dumping*. There are reasons for dismissing wilder fancies such as "a race to the bottom," because most interests recognize that if social protection or labor standards were dismantled, social cohesion and productivity would suffer. However, competitive pressures are likely to lead to an international convergence around a hegemonic model, so that countries and communities with high shares of state benefits in social income are likely to cut back state benefits and the social protection share of national income.[8] They will also shift the cost for social protection from capital to labor, thus raising the share of the costs borne by workers through higher contribution rates, rather than employers. For similar reasons they will support partial privatization and greater selectivity of state benefits.

The social dumping crisis is revealed when governments justify cuts in social protection in order to promote competitiveness. They tend to cut benefits and services for the unemployed, thus the tendency to indulge in social dumping most hurts the unemployed and detached strata in the emerging stratification system. At the same time, and also in the pursuit of competitiveness and job creation, governments are stepping up their subsidies for low-wage labor. If paid to firms, subsidies will depress incomes of low-paid workers; if paid to workers as "in-work benefits," they will encourage firms to keep wages down and put the workers in a low-wage trap—losing benefits if they raise their wages and leaving them with little or no advantage.[9] The tendency to indulge in social dumping has weakened the state benefit share of social income and contributed to income insecurity.

A Governance Crisis

Social protection rests on some sense of social solidarity: a perception that the system is accountable, transparent, and democratic, or at least that it is not arbitrary and that ordinary people have a voice in its design, implementation, evaluation, and modification. In the twentieth century, welfare states "workers," in the form of trade unions, and "employers," in the form of bureaucratic employer associations, were part of the governance of social protection. This no longer continues to be the case. The emerging governance crisis arises from the fact that increasingly, as a result of privatization of various social protection policies, countries are finding that there are oligopolistic, if not monopolistic, private providers of services that scarcely bother to conceal their tendency to indulge in opportunistic profiteering. Thus, there is a growing need for regulatory instruments, which are not easy to construct if the country is economically weak or small.

There are several alternative governance systems for social protection. The system may be direct (without intermediaries); bipartite (through the state and employers); tripartite (through arrangements overseen by government agencies, employer bodies, and trade union confederations); or what might be called civil governance (where government agencies oversee the policy in partnership with nongovernmental organizations, with or without the involvement of other bodies). The system may also be centralized, decentralized, or multitiered. Governance changes reflect a desire to make systems more accountable, equitable, or efficient. One tendency is the policy of integrating public employment services with social protection in one ministry. There may be cost reasons, but it risks making social protection more regulatory in character or less concerned with the simple task of supplementing the incomes of the poor or vulnerable in society.

However, the strongest governance tendencies of recent years are what could be called *decentralization* and the erosion of *tripartism*. The loss of bargaining strength of *core* workers and de-unionization have contributed to the fading of tripartism and variants in which workers had a strong voice in governing social security institutions and policy formulation. Unions have retained a central role in a few countries, but even so, concessions have been made by unions. The loss of voice by the core has, in turn, contributed to the loss of state benefits and services in social income.

Decentralization refers to the shifting of governance away from national level, upward to supranational levels and downward to regional or local levels. Shifting part of rule-making to the international level has unclear implications for the structure or level of social protection. Decentralization of functions and responsibilities may have inegalitarian effects, unless countered by national policies. It tends to mean that more affluent regions can provide their residents with higher levels of benefits and better services. So, unless interregional subsidies are boosted, interregional social income inequalities are likely to grow. For similar reasons, lower-income groups are likely to suffer because they tend to be concentrated in lower-income regions with limited fiscal resources.

Decentralization historically fosters *clientelism*, in which localized interests can influence or control local officials and the pattern of social protection. Unless adequate national checks and balances are implemented, the greater the degree of decentralization, the more likely it is that social protection will be discretionary in character, selective, prone to "creaming" in allocating benefits and services, and inclined to support commercial interests and the most vociferous organizations of civil society, which may or may not be representing groups most in need.

Efficiency claims have also triggered changes in governance systems. In some countries, the desire to make services more efficient has led to the use of more market mechanisms by public agencies, turning citizens needing help into "customers" expected to buy a service. This has led to the contracting-out of social services, which in the U.S. has become a sphere of big business, and is spreading elsewhere.

In particular, the privatization of w*elfare delivery services* is taking bizarre directions, and has implications for governance. In the U.S. some states have contracted out their entire social-protection system. Texas put out its services to tender and the three short-listed bidders were the world's largest defense contractor (Lockheed Martin) and two other corporations with no prior involvement in social policy. There and elsewhere, private firms have been awarded contracts to place welfare recipients into jobs, and are paid according to results. Such practices lead to "creaming," with better treatment given to some groups, with others facing discrimination, and with a proliferation of paternalistic and other control functions, without any pretense at accountability. It can also lead to local monopolistic or oligopolistic structures working against the interests of "clients" or low-income groups in general. Prices of services will rise or, more likely, quality of the services for supplicants will decline relative to the quality of the service delivered to the funders or employers.

Partial privatization has given a growing role to the vast array of non-governmental organizations (NGOs). They have filled gaps left by the receding role of government as provider of state benefits and services. Governments have encouraged them by providing subsidies and contracts. The model of *civil society* being fostered is complex and reliance on NGOs represents part of the restructuring of *social income*, with implications for the income security of those who need services and financial assistance.

A Work Crisis

The desire of policy-makers to roll back state-based social protection, make it more selective and conditional, privatize benefits and services, and

tie entitlements more to the performance of labor, has created a fundamental dilemma, which could become the most subversive "crisis" of all.
What should count as "work" to gain entitlement? The point here is that
policy-makers have an awkward dilemma: Do they narrow the definition
so as to limit fiscal pressures and steer people in laudable directions? Or do
they broaden the definition because some of the work excluded by narrow
definitions is valued, particularly given that rolling back state provision
leaves various welfare deficits, most notably in the sphere of care work—
caring for children, the sick, disabled, and elderly?

Welfare state capitalism led to a substantial growth of state-provided
social services, particularly in northern Europe, where priority was given
to tax-financed universalistic services rather than monetary transfers. This
is part of social income. Their availability reduces dependency on private
care, which has to be paid for either directly or by reciprocity arrangements. However, in the era of market regulation, selectivity, multitierism,
individualization, and partial privatization have also affected social services. Two models of state provision have emerged: the *client model,* in
which a person can obtain a service if satisfying basic conditions, but can
obtain only modest assistance; and the *conditionality model,* where a person can obtain more than basic assistance *if* prepared to satisfy more conditions and go through more bureaucratic procedures. Some have
described Australia and the Netherlands as operating the former model,
Sweden the latter. The UK went in the latter direction with its Social Fund,
since a shortage of money obliged officials to ration by discouragement.

The provision of *care* has been partially privatized, with a renewed expectation that the elderly, children, and others would be cared for by relatives or voluntary organizations. Parental care has spread, as has subsidized
parental care of children, cash transfers for care, income entitlement protection for those providing care, and insurance for care. In some countries,
subsidies have been introduced to encourage people to care for the elderly,
chronically ill, and incapacitated.

The spread of payments to caregivers, or those receiving care, has commodified this type of work, with a shift from directly provided state benefits and services to community provision and wages. Indeed, care work has
become pivotal in the reorientation of welfare states, the restructuring of
social income, and the evolution of work. There is a growing "care deficit"
in much of the world due to aging, rising divorce rates, single parenting,
AIDS, and a weakening of intergenerational reciprocities. This puts pressure on state services and encourages governments to shift to more selective schemes and private services. Multitierism is emerging, a mix of cash
transfers from government coupled with payment or services from chari-

ties, paid or unpaid voluntary care, and a subsidy in the form of the unpaid time of caregivers.

A Social Justice Crisis

The biggest global challenge to social protection systems is that, quite simply, they do not offer the prospect of income security and social protection for the poor and near-poor. There are a few rich countries where effective coverage is high but they are a shrinking minority. At one extreme are most African and Asian countries where a tiny percentage of the population is *covered* by state-based schemes of any sort. In the middle are the "transition" countries where often a majority is denied any realistic prospect of decent coverage. In welfare states a growing minority are either not covered or fear that they are not. A survey in the U.S. found that more young people believed in UFOs (unidentified flying objects) than that they would be covered by social security later in life. Diminishing coverage and fear of uncertain coverage are global phenomena.

Besides the global problem of lack of coverage, changes in social protection systems have thrown up awkward questions about social justice. For instance, a shift in priority from horizontal to vertical and administrative efficiency has implications for the equity of social policy, since it is a matter of judgment whether it is more equitable that 90 percent of those who receive benefits are in need, than if only 80 percent of those in need receive benefits. Many policy-makers seem more keen to prevent the "undeserving" from receiving benefits than to make sure that all the "deserving" receive them.

In the rush to selectivity, a conflict emerges between vertical efficiency and other forms of efficiency. The more you target, the more you design criteria for selectivity, the more conditions that are applied, then the more complex the necessary procedures of identification, implementation, monitoring, and auditing. In most countries, it is cynical or naive to advise governments to adopt finely tuned targeting, given poor administrative structures, lack of information, fear and lack of knowledge among potential beneficiaries, poorly trained, inadequately paid, and overburdened officials, and pervasive distrust between applicants and officials. The system will end up being highly discretionary, prone to corruption, and demoralizing for all concerned.

The problems are no different in industrialized countries. Targeting implies selecting those who you think are deserving. The narrower or more tightly defined the target, the greater the difficulty of identifying people correctly and the harder the legal, administrative, and practical tasks of maintaining equitable boundaries. Perversely, selectivity almost inevitably

leads to arbitrariness and this further erodes the legitimacy of state benefits and services in general, and worsens moral dilemmas. Selective, conditional schemes lead to a proliferation of local rules and judgments and the
quiet spread of *discretion* as the underlying "principle" of social policy.
This is not a sound basis. Some discretion may be benign and well-
intended, some judgments will flow from laziness, some will be opportunistic to benefit local officials or politicians, some will be blatantly
corrupt. Yet selective social policy is always discretionary and the more active the policy, the more discretionary its implementation.

Social services are the most prone to *discretionary failure*: They allow officials to decide whom they will meet, whom they will help, what form of
help to offer, what form of monitoring, what form of evaluation, and so
on. Individual case treatment is often required because laws cannot be specific enough to cover all circumstances. Further, means- and behavior-
tested transfers allow discretionary control by local authorities, in terms of
interpreting, applying, monitoring, and sanctioning rules, and selective
oversight. The right to appeal may not always exist and where it does, it
may be curtailed, costly, and time-consuming. Means-tested benefits targeted on the poor are impoverishing and stigmatizing, and are likely to be
eroded because they are for the voiceless or weak groups. As Titmuss
tersely concluded long ago, benefits specifically for the poor will be poor
benefits.

Even in the spheres of *unemployment protection* and employment services a private market has been emerging. There can be little doubt about
the impact on social income inequality of privatization. Even where a private market is beginning, high-income groups are gaining. For instance, in
the spheres of *unemployment protection* and employment services, the proficians and salariat have been taking out employment insurance or have it
taken out for them by their employers, and large firms have been offering
core employees and managers generous redundancy benefit packages,
capped by golden parachute clauses for directors and senior managers.
This is part of the fragmentation of enterprise benefits, but it also helps
erode the legitimacy of state benefits, on which such workers do not rely.

Privatization also has implications for the social justice qualities of social
protection. Privatization results in the *individualization* of benefits, which
favor the relatively insurable, increases inequality, and makes economic insecurity more inegalitarian. For instance, people with chronic illnesses or
disabilities often pay more or cannot obtain private health insurance, and
those in insecure jobs or living in low-income areas typically find they have
similar problems. Insurance companies can screen out above-average risks
or refuse to insure them or demand such high premiums that they cannot
afford to insure themselves. Finally, privatization of insurable risks and

benefits is likely to create an *underclass of the uninsurable,* unless subsidies are provided for those at the bottom of society, which would prompt new moral hazards. The shift from state to private benefits adds to the income insecurity of people who are economically disadvantaged.

Toward an Alternative to Third Wayism[10]

The celebrated social policy thinker of the middle period of the twentieth century, T. H. Marshall, pointed out that the eighteenth century was when *civil rights* became established as the legitimate goal of social reform, the nineteenth century was when *political rights* became legitimized, and the twentieth century was when *social rights* became recognized. One may predict that the twenty-first century will be the century of *economic rights.* In this spirit, consider again the question posed at the outset of this chapter: What is it that should be equalized in the Good Society of the twenty-first century? All theories of distributive justice believe in the equality of something. Third wayism believes in equality of merit: those who do their duty earn or merit social rights, which are fundamentally based on labor. We see in this the resurrection of the Puritan ethic. Libertarians and to some extent *compassionate conservatives* (who like a potpourri of third wayism and libertarianism) are less squeamish. They believe in procedural and contractual justice and the equality of due process. As long as procedures are followed correctly and equally, unequal outcomes are not just acceptable but socially just. Dealing with the losers is left to charity, philanthropy, and good neighbors (even in the global village that they seem to envisage, with billionaires disbursing their marginal millions to the causes they consider most worthy).

In contrast to the third wayists and libertarians, we may assert that the answer is what might be called *complex egalitarianism:* the fundamental economic right is, or should be, the right to *equal basic security.* This requires basic income security. However, in order to enable the vulnerable and less well-endowed to retain basic security, there must also be equal *voice representation security* at the collective and individual levels. Cconsider the Polanyian idea of *embeddedness:* All socioeconomic systems depend on systems of *protection, regulation,* and *distribution*—to embed the economy in society. Social thinkers are struggling to redefine these three in the new global world (dis)order. I believe that complex egalitarianism, or distributive justice, requires respect and adherence to the following policy rules:

> **The Security Difference Principle:** A policy or institutional change is just if and only if it improves the security of the least secure groups

in society. This is derived from John Rawls's famous Difference Principle, but the emphasis is on *security*. The complementary rule is also essential.

The Paternalism Test Principle: A policy or institutional change is just if and only if it does not impose controls on some groups that are not imposed on the most free groups in society.

With these policy decision rules in mind, we must ask about social protection. This must shift away from *risk compensation* to extending and enhancing individual and collective rights, based not on labor as in the twentieth century, but on citizenship in its broadest sense. It is important to emphasize that protection is not equivalent to any social safety-net notion; it is to *liberate*. We should play on the Kennedy aphorism: Ask not what social protection must protect you *against*, ask what social protection can protect you *for*.

In this context basic security requires an unconditional basic income, or a solidarity or security income.[11] Real freedom requires a system of social protection that allows people of all backgrounds to be able to make choices. Social protection, regulatory, and distributive policies must be integrated in a way that facilitates and extends *occupational security*. How can *redistribution* be achieved in the emerging global context? Although this is not the place to develop a detailed response, suffice it to assert that we need new mechanisms.

The returns to capital and technological innovation have risen relative to those of labor, and the functional distribution of income may well have become more skewed in favor of capital. Further, the use of progressive direct taxation may have become more problematical because of pressures of "competitiveness." Thus, re-embedding the economy requires policies and institutions to raise the aggregative capital market participation rate (CMPR) toward the labor force participation rate (LFPR) so that all of us have a broad portfolio of forms and sources of income. This may mean reviving ideas of *stakeholder capitalism* within firms and local communities, as well as social investment funds and community profit-sharing plans. Trends in these directions are happening, gradually and inequitably for the most part.

How can effective and equitable *regulation* be achieved? Regulations should become progressively less paternalistic, and the use of fiscal regulation of individual behavior should be reduced and subject to the two policy decision rules stated previously. In fiscal policy, the principle of *behavioral neutrality* should be developed. In other words, fiscal policy should not be designed to be a vehicle of social engineering, and where it impinges on individual behavior, it should adhere to the decision rules.

Reliance on old-style statutory regulations cannot be envisaged. Although they are useful in setting standards and guidelines, they veer between bureaucratic rigidities and lax gestures depending on the administrative effort put into them. The priority should be to reinvigorate *voice regulation*, which means rethinking issues of tripartism, neocorporatism, and the new euphemisms of *governance* and *social capital* (sic). Any agenda that sees the extension of rights or freedoms without collective voice representation security could mean only that the vulnerable would remain vulnerable. But in thinking about voice we must admit that old-style trade unions are weak, have lost or are losing their legitimacy, and are tied atavistically to the twentieth-century laborist agenda. They have tended to look after the needs of core workers, the old working class.

Although unions have been a force for social progress, we need to move forward. There is a need to respect the idea that we need as many types of representative association as there are *interests* to represent. This means, among other things, there is a need for strong independent organizations to bargain on behalf of *flexiworkers*, so-called "informal workers," voluntary workers in civil society organizations, care workers, the unemployed, and so on. At the other end of the spectrum there is a need for legitimate *occupational associations*, that is, bodies that can defend and enhance standards and practices but that must also avoid the danger of being monopolistic rent-seeking devices, as has been the case with many professional bodies. We can see positive and negative signs in the spread of social clubs based on ethnic background, gender, type of work, and so on. To complement group-based and occupational associations there is also a need to strengthen *community associations*.

All of this is happening, but globally, nationally, and locally it is happening in a haphazard and often opportunistic, inegalitarian manner. This is why there is a need for a *Charter for Interest Associations*. This charter should establish the governance principles of *democracy, accountability, transparency,* and *equity*. Such interest associations must become instruments of representation, not control mechanisms or the means of securing monopoly rents for their members.

Finally, the policies and institutions of social protection, regulation, and redistribution must be based on the legitimation of *all* forms of work, not just labor. This is essential to give meaning to the *right to work* mouthed by radicals over the centuries. We must not let paternalists of any kind—third wayists, religious groups, Leninists, populists—turn that right into a duty. An exclusive focus on labor or paid work marginalizes other forms of work and workers. In so doing, one would perpetuate an ethos of competitive individualism, rather than social individualism based on a recognition and celebration of mutual interdependencies. Policies must ensure that equal protection is given to those doing "jobs" and other forms of work, such as care, voluntary, community, ecological, and civil society work. This means rethinking how to provide basic income security, voice and social protection. This means delinking income security from the mere performance of, or willingness to perform, *labor*.

A key example is the work of care or caring, which straddles the uneasy division between a gift and a market exchange relationship. If we think of development as freedom, then our emphasis on basic security and voice, as the two pillars of the Good Society, means that we should want basic income security for caregivers, surrogates of carers, and those needing care. There should also be equally strong voice for both sides of the relationship. Rethinking care work in the context of aging and the fragmentation of old-style norms of family and household, leads to an answer to the question posed at the outset of this chapter. It is a vision of diversity. Basic security should be what is equalized, where security is defined in terms of freedom from morbidity and controls that fail the paternalism test, and equal opportunity to pursue our individual sense of occupation.

Concluding Thoughts

The eight crises of social protection are unlikely to be resolved in the near future. We will have to learn to live with the linguistic crisis, and learn to respond to the deluge of euphemisms that threatens to take the place of objective analyzis. The fiscal crisis reflects a failure of nerve, since there is no evidence to show that societies cannot afford a comprehensive system of social protection, albeit at *levels* of support compatible with the income level of the country. The legitimation crisis is a political challenge, and can surely be met by seeking a rationale for a new universalism and sense of social solidarity. The moral crisis must be countered with scorn and an appeal to renew the march to freedom; paternalism will not be accepted for long. The social dumping crisis will almost certainly run up against the pressure to extend the international trading system.

The governance crisis is already moving in a positive direction, in that the associational revolution taking place around the world is creating institutions and interest organizations that are demanding to be part of the system of governance. The work crisis is also moving in a very positive direction. It has become manifestly absurd to link entitlements to social protection only to the performance of labor, and in that governments are trying to reduce social spending, so that they are expecting citizens to undertake more of the social services that for many decades had been presumed to be the responsibility of the state. If citizens are to do citizenship work, they will need the same protections afforded to those doing labor.

Finally, the social justice crisis is fueling the sense of social anger spreading around the world, and forcing politicians and social-policy analysts to look to first principles. As they do so, they may find that to make progress toward complex egalitarianism, they should put on their walls the equivalent of Bill Clinton's famous message to himself as he campaigned to become President of the United States: "It is distribution, stupid!" Unless the structural inequalities are addressed, there will never be social protection worthy of the name.

References

Murray, Charles. 1984. *Losing Ground: American Social Policy, 1950–1980*. New York: Basic Books.

Notes

1. Note the recent revision in "occupational classes" for UK statistics. This is an improvement, although it does not cover the issues raised in this chapter. For a theoretical approach see G. Standing. 2001 "Modes of Control and Insecurity: An Approach to 'Decent Work,'" in SES Paper, ILO.
2. The notion of crisis is overused and it is used in this chapter with some unease.
3. G. Standing, *Beyond the New Paternalism: Basic Security as Equality* London: Verso, 2002.
4. International Monetary Fund, *World Economic Outlook 1999* (Washington, D.C., 1999). References to high replacement rates can be misleading: if those who lose jobs are low-income earners, even modest benefits may comprise a high proportion of past income; a benefit that is 75 percent of a low wage may be quite inadequate for bare survival.
5. Standing, 2002, op.cit., ch.3.
6. This is a major sphere of debate and research.
7. For a review of evidence, see Standing, 2002, op.cit.
8. For a set of international studies, see the Special Issue of the *Journal of European Social Policy*, March 2000.
9. Lower social protection standards and subsidies for low-wage labor are issues that should creep up the international trade regime agenda as aspects of unfair trading practices.
10. Points made in this section are developed at length in my book, *Beyond the New Paternalism: Basic Security as Equality*, London: Verso, 2002.
11. This has had many distinguished advocates over the centuries, probably most notably of all, Tom Paine. In 1986, a group formed BIEN (Basic Income European Network) to consider the desirability and feasibility of moving in that direction. Membership is open to all those interested, and in recent years has included members from all over the world, with pressure to change the *E* to *Earth*.

PART 3

The Politics of International Trade

CHAPTER 8

Biotechnology and Food Security
Profiting on Insecurity?

PHILIP MCMICHAEL

Introduction[1]

The global debate on food security will dominate the international agenda in the twenty-first century. It is currently being framed in terms of whether, and to what extent, food security can be guaranteed by market solutions. There are two parts to the argument: first, that comparative advantage allows for an optimal solution on a global scale via "free trade" in food; and second, that free trade in food is most efficiently organized by the crop-development industry. The premise, that food consumption is a market act, is so deeply entwined with the faith in global markets that critics of this conception of food security are cast as misguided, even immoral, folks who would let people starve before allowing multinational corporations to get on with their business. This global tension has intensified as the industry and its supporters present biotechnology as a solution to global hunger. For example, Nigeria's former minister of agriculture and rural development recently castigated biotech opponents in *The Washington Post*: "To deny desperately hungry people the means to control their futures by presuming to know what is best for them is not only paternalistic but morally wrong."[2]

In this chapter, I do not wish to debate the virtues or vices of biotechnology as such; rather, I call into question the premise that food security requires market solutions. There are two related issues at stake here: first, to impose market solutions across a culturally and ecologically diverse world is questionable in ethical and sustainable terms; and second, the world market is a political construct in which exchanges between unequal societies and/or incommensurable cultures privilege powerful states and institutions.

The content of world market exchanges—what food is grown, where, and who can afford it—is driven by profit rather than food-security considerations. Regulations and subsidies may be deployed to modify this drive but there are far more powerful forces working in the opposite direction: the WTO and its commitment to free trade, and Northern agricultural protectionism from import restrictions to farm and export subsidies. Although these forces are opposed in principle, in practice they combine to dump food surpluses on to the world market at the expense of Southern peasantries. The market is evidently not working in textbook fashion. To evaluate the debate over food security, it is necessary to consider the market as an institutional and discursive construct.

Constructing Food Security

At the most basic level, the debate on food security rests on historically informed definitions. For example, the United Nations Food and Agriculture Organization (FAO) defines food security at the individual level as "access to adequate safe and nutritious food to maintain a healthy life . . . without undue risk of losing such access." The FAO observes that "people take hypercautious decisions that forfeit their chances to escape from chronic hunger."[3] The FAO's annual report argues that the key lies in expanding small-farm staples production, since food-staples production is a labor-intensive means of generating income, and "for food-insecure low-income populations higher yields (per hectare and per liter) for food staples, and therefore extra employment and self-employment income in growing them, will be the main source of enhanced food security, at least until 2020."[4] Although chronic hunger is left unexamined as an historical condition, the report notes that: "For most of the undernourished, extra employment income from local staples production has been the key to enhanced food entitlements in the period from 1950 to 2000."[5] The FAO report continues:

> This will remain so until 2025, given the continued rapid growth of workforces and the need to restrain and stabilize local staples prices [. . .] The slowdown in food staples yield growth since the 1970s, and in its employment impact, offers new challenges. The experience of the green revolution shows how to address them in ways that enhance food entitlements and household food security. *So far, however, the promising new tools of biotechnology have not been applied for the purpose of raising staples yields for poor smallholders.*[6]

Arguably the FAO perspective, as sensitive as it is to the importance of land redistribution to stabilize staples production and reduce undernutrition as the first stage of development,[7] remains wedded to a market epistemology. This is evident in the unproblematic use of chronic hunger, the assumption that development is stagelike (shifting away from food self-sufficiency via staples production toward industrial employment, exports, and net staples imports), and its implicit invitation to a biotechnological solution.

Market epistemology reached its highest form in the neoliberal formulation of food security as a global arrangement. This formulation framed the GATT Uruguay Round, laying the groundwork for the 1994 WTO Agreement on Agriculture (AoA). It was articulated by the U.S. representative thus: "The U.S. has always maintained that self-sufficiency and food security are not one and the same. Food security—the ability to acquire the food you need when you need it—is best provided through a smooth-functioning world market."[8] The coincidence of the U.S. prescription with the FAO formulation is striking. One could say that the U.S. position proposed a separation between self-sufficiency and security in food that the FAO perceived as a developmentalist outcome. The conceptual convergence is clear. However, the convergence ends there: the FAO is not a dominant state, it is not in a position to declare, as did the U.S. Secretary of Agriculture at the opening of the Uruguay Round in 1986: "[The] idea that developing countries should feed themselves is an anachronism from a bygone era. They could better ensure their food security by relying on U.S. agricultural products, which are available, in most cases at much lower cost."[9] On the basis of that declaration the U.S. sought to institutionalize a role of "breadbasket to the world" via the GATT negotiations.

The 1986 Uruguay Round initiated the liberalization of agriculture when the Cairns Group of agri-exporters and a powerful U.S.-centered agribusiness lobby pressed for agricultural reforms in the GATT.[10] Reforms included reductions in trade protection, farm subsidies, and government intervention. Free trade was the ostensible demand, but the underlying agenda was an informal mercantilism of constructing a comparative advantage through deregulating a highly unequal world market.[11] The AoA was designed to open agricultural markets by adopting minimum import requirements and tariff and producer subsidy reductions. The effect was to open markets for Northern products, strengthening the position of the OECD countries in the international division of labor in agriculture. From 1970–1996 the OECD share in the volume of world cereal exports rose from 73 percent to 82 percent; the U.S. remained the world's major exporter of such commercial crops as maize, soya bean, and wheat; and the share of world cereal imports in Africa, Latin America, and Asia increased to nearly 60 percent.[12]

To all intents and purposes the Northern breadbasket function appears to be in place, with Northern farm exports provisioning the world. Arguably this global food regime is accelerating the expulsion of Southern rural populations from agriculture, via cheap food exports from the North. Conservative estimates are that between 20 and 30 million people have recently lost their land as a result of the impact of trade liberalization.[13] As Oxfam asks: "How can a farmer earning $230 a year (average per capita income in LDCs) compete with a farmer who enjoys a subsidy of $20,000 a year (average subsidy in OECD countries)?"[14]

The resulting structure of agriculture (concentration of land and generation of rural labor forces) creates the eventual conditions for a wholesale relocation of industrial, and increasingly transgenic, agriculture to a cheap-labor South. Whether and to what extent the latter outcome materializes depends on the acceptance of transgenic foods, and on how the debate about biotechnology's role in solving global hunger is resolved. At present, the reluctance of Northern consumers to embrace transgenic foods unnerves the biotechnology industry on the one hand, but arguably shifts its gaze toward the South as a potential market, in much the same way as the tobacco industry has shifted its market focus southward.

Food Insecurity and Biotechnology

In the post-WWII world the principal condition legitimizing the development project was combating Third World poverty, one nation at a time.[15] Similarly, projections today of deepening global hunger serve to legitimize the crop-development industry's claims to resolving food security on a world scale. In promoting its European campaign in 1998, Monsanto corporation's Web site proclaimed: "Guess Who's Coming to Dinner? 10 billion by 2030." It warned that low-tech agriculture "will not produce sufficient crop yield increases and improvements to feed the world's burgeoning population," declaring that "biotechnology innovations will triple crop yields without requiring any additional farmland, saving valuable rainforests, and animal habitats" and that "biotechnology can feed the world . . . let the harvest begin."[16] Such rhetoric counterpoises hunger and biotechnology as if they constitute alternatives within the framework of a single choice.

Similarly, Jennifer Thomson wrote in the *Christian Science Monitor* (November 13, 2000):

> In developing countries, the case for biotechnology can be made very easily: It is needs-based. Rich countries may engage in lengthy disputes about real or imagined risks. We suggest that is largely a luxury debate. Meanwhile, the rest of the world needs to focus on a rigorous risk-benefit analysis. From the perspective of many developing and newly industrialized countries, agricultural

biotechnology's benefits are very real. They are urgently needed today and indispensable tomorrow.

These appeals involve a crusade to offer a simplistic interpretation of the world designed to recruit public opinion via the ethics of guilt. The dualism of hunger/biotechnology obfuscates the range of alternatives to transgenic crops, some of which would involve more democratic use of farmland and natural resources, as well as more diverse farming styles, crop systems, and diets likely to be more appropriate to local ecological and community sustainability. It is ironic that while much of the scientific community considers social, economic, and political relationships to be beyond their brief, the role of biotechnology in agriculture is routinely justified in social and economic terms.[17]

But such terms are quite simplistic. Not only do they homogenize the world as a single-market culture with a one-dimensional juxtaposition of wealth and poverty, but they also obscure complex landed relations, and assume an unproblematic market access by the target peasantries. As Linda Cayanan, a farmer in Pampanga in the Philippines, observes:

> I don't even have land. I am renting some land together with my husband where we are planting rice. Sometimes I work as a farmworker for other farmers. What can I do with these new seeds? I'm sure they are expensive [. . .] Who will pay for them? We cannot. And even if we would be able to plant them, any surplus they would create would go to the landlord and to the traders. We would still be as poor as ever. Poor farmers need land in the first place so they can reap the fruits of their own work.[18]

Behind the ethics of guilt lies a more troubling authoritarianism based on corporate control of technology and markets, the reduction of global biodiversity to transgenic monocultures, and the rejection of the diversity of local knowledge embedded in the cultures of the world's remaining 3 billion peasant farmers. Anuradha Mittal, codirector of Food First, notes that biotech firms "don't really want to get to the crux of the matter, which is about control of the food system."[19]

In an article entitled "We Need Biotech to Feed the World" in the *Wall Street Journal* (December 6, 2000), green revolution scientist Norman Borlaug, arguing for biotechnology as a solution to geometric rates of population growth, touted the record yields of the green revolution in South Asia and dismissed activists' concerns about bioengineered foods. He remarked:

> The citizens of affluent nations may be able to pay more for food produced by "natural" or "organic" methods. The chronically undernourished people of impoverished nations cannot. They also cannot afford to have the promise of new agricultural technology nipped in the bud, as many antibiotechnology activists wish. The latter have been agitating about the supposed threats to human health engendered by bioengineered foods. But such foods pose no

greater threat to health than foods by conventional methods—probably even less. While activists inveigh against introducing a gene from one plant or one species into another, they fail to note that conventional breeders have been doing just that for many years. Today we do it better [. . .] Conventional plant breeding is crude in comparison to the methods being used in genetic engineering, where we move one or a few genes that we know are useful. We must do a better job of explaining such complexities to the general public, so people will not be vulnerable to antibiotech distortions.

Food First codirectors, Anuradha Mittal and Peter Rosset, responded that future projections of the promises of biotechnology distract policy-makers from current conditions of poverty and hunger. In a food-abundant world, as we have now,

> the problem is not one of production but of access and distribution: 78 percent of countries reporting child malnourishment export food. Mr. Borlaug refers to India [. . .] where 800 million hungry live. While he talks of green revolution successes and biotech potentials, he fails to mention that the number of the hungry and malnourished has been steadily rising, though India is faced with an unmanageable food glut [. . .] Instead of distributing the surplus among those who desperately need it, the government either wants to find an export market or release it in the open market.[20]

In addition to this question of control of food systems, there is the question of public dialogue about biotechnology and the importance of avoiding distortion. One distortion routinely made by biotech promoters such as Norman Borlaug, is that there is no significant difference between transgenic and plant-breeding science. Moving isolated genes among organisms that would not otherwise exchange genetic material (e.g., bacteria and corn, or strawberries and fish) is substantially different from cross-breeding *within* a species across centuries. In addition to crossing species boundaries, transgenic technology is not yet proven to be stable, nor can the short time scale of laboratory and greenhouse experiments compare to the natural time of traditional processes of selection and evolution.[21]

More recently the crusade shifted gears, symbolized in the development of vitamin A or golden rice as an answer to micronutrient deficiency. Golden rice, which contains a nutrient (beta-carotene) derived from bacterial and daffodil genes and converted by the body to vitamin A, has become the "poster crop" in the hunger debate.[22] Vitamin A deficiency is widespread in the South, and golden rice was viewed as an answer to the 1 million annual deaths of children weakened by this micronutrient deficiency, and to the other 350,000 who go blind. Gordon Conway, director of the Rockefeller Foundation, which initiated golden rice research, remarked on biotechnology's role in the fight against hunger: "contrary to public perception, those who have the least to lose and the most to gain are not well-fed Americans and Europeans but the hollow-bellied citizens of the developing world."[23]

Syngenta, owner of many of the ninety-odd patents on golden rice, claimed that one month's delay in bringing the rice to market would cause blindness in 50,000 children.[24] Ingo Potrykus, the Swiss scientist who developed the technology to combat hunger, claimed "it would be irresponsible, not to say immoral, *not* to use biotechnology to try to solve this problem!"[25] He charges that the opposition to golden rice "has to be held responsible for the foreseeable unnecessary deaths and blindness of millions of poor every year."[26] In fact, an average daily intake of golden rice would provide less than 10 percent of the daily requirements. Charles Kronick of Greenpeace remarked: "It is clear that the GM industry has been making false claims about golden rice. It is nonsense to think anyone would or could eat [9 kg of cooked] rice, and there is still no proof that it can provide any significant vitamin benefits anyway."[27]

Golden rice promotion leaves unaddressed the social context in which nutritional deficiency occurs. Golden rice attempts to correct for the removal of beta-carotene from unpolished rice. Critics have pointed out that because of the green revolution's focus on improving macronutrients through cultivation of high-yielding rice varieties, micronutrient deficiencies, through polishing rice and eliminating the traditional leafy greens redefined as weeds in a monoculture regime, are actually a product of early genetic modification of food crops.[28] In fact, Gordon Conway publicly agreed with Vandana Shiva's report on golden rice, declaring:

> We do not consider golden rice to be the solution to the vitamin A deficiency problem. Rather it provides an excellent complement to fruits, vegetables, and animal products in diets, and to various fortified foods and vitamin supplements. [. . .] I agree with Dr. Shiva that the public relations uses of golden rice have gone too far.[29]

Biotechnology's Urgency: Time Is Money

The urgency of biotechnology's public relations stems from the industry's mixed success in convincing consumers, and therefore farmers, to accept a food system based in transgenic seeds and products. It is a simple legitimacy problem, which has taken on a life of its own.

Within the biotech industry, there are two related dynamics. First, the progressive concentration of agribusiness, agrochemical, and pharmaceutical firms via market expansion. The five largest "gene giants" (AstraZeneca, DuPont, Monsanto/Pharmacia, Novartis, and Aventis) account for 60 percent of the global pesticide market, 23 percent of the global seed market, and almost 100 percent of the transgenic seed market.[30] In 1999 four crops—soya, maize, canola, and cotton—accounted for 99 percent of all transgenic crops worldwide.[31] The transgenic seed market is a new market frontier. There is intensive and unstable merger activity as conglomerates have attempted to position themselves on this frontier:

> Access to and control of complex genomic information is now perceived as the cornerstone for the future development of transgenic plants, and the leaders of the agro-industrial genetic complex have entered a race for being the first to identify—and hopefully own—the genes involved in the regulation of commercially interesting traits and their interactions.[32]

The second dynamic is an emerging, but speculative, interest in developing Generation 3 "functional foods." The genealogy of agbiotechnology begins with Generation 1, involving "input trait-control systems most profitable for the seed/agrochemical industry," such as genetic engineering of crops to tolerate herbicides or to express insecticidal genes. Herbicide-tolerant crops accounted for 71 percent of total GM area in 1999, with insect resistance accounting for 22 percent, and the remaining 7 percent combining both. Generation 1 incorporated farmers into "a regime of input suppliers and output buyers." Generation 2 involved reducing food/feed processing costs by modifying crops for increased oil, protein levels, or starch content—such as Calgene's unsuccessful slow-rotting tomato engineered to extend its shelf life.

As the Rural Advancement Foundation International (RAFI) observes: "biotech's first and second generation GM products were rushed to market and the biotech industry failed to consider the fact that none of their products had any basic appeal to consumers: GM foods were not cheaper, better tasting, safer or more nutritious."[33] Monsanto, for example, has been busy backpedaling publicly ever since to acknowledge what its CEO admitted in 1999 as "condescension or indeed arrogance"; and Novartis pledged in August 2000 to stop using GM ingredients in its food products (especially Gerber baby foods), even though this meant not buying seeds from its own seed subsidiary, Syngenta.[34]

In 2001, Sergey Vasnetsov, a leading chemical industry analyst with Lehman Brothers, noted: "The outlook is less certain than it was three years ago. The euphoria has gone. Growth has fallen significantly. The industry has overstated the rate of progress and underestimated the resistance of consumers." He went on to say: "Let's stop pretending we *face* food shortages. There is hunger, but not food shortages. GM food is for the rich world. The money for GM is in developed countries. The battle is in Europe."[35] Credit Suisse First Boston claimed in 1999 that the biotech industry was experiencing "negative momentum," that food manufacturers were wary of GMO crops and "if anyone is in control it appears to be environment and consumer groups. However, most analysts assume the market for GMO crops will revive in the long-term when output traits (e.g., vitamin or vaccine enhancements engineered into the crops) come onto the market."[36]

Generation 3 is a futuristic transgenic technology going beyond production via the food chain, and beyond rudimentary functional foods such as calcium-fortified orange juice or cholesterol-reducing margarines, to nutraceuticals geared to addressing health concerns ranging from obesity, growth and development, cancers, diabetes, and gastrointestinal functions. The recent United Nations announcement that the global population of overfed and underfed people is now equivalent, at 1.2 billion, gives credence to a financial journalist's observation that: "If cancer and brain disease are the two most exciting areas of medical research, a third El Dorado is opening up for the pharmaceutical disease: obesity."[37] Globally, 300 companies are engaged in research into functional foods, which Novartis estimated will be worth between $10 and $37 billion by 2010. RAFI suggests the Generation 3 strategy "is not merely to come up with something consumers will be prepared to pay for, but to redefine the consumers' concept of food in order to gain total control of the food system."[38]

The target for these foods is clearly affluent consumers. The counterpart is the world's hungry, for whom vitamin A rice was developed. Combining PR with expectations for the future of the Generation 3 products in the North, AstraZeneca offered to give golden rice seeds away in the South so long as it could sell the technology in the North. The connection is important because the South represents an alternative commercial frontier, especially in the event that Generation 3 transgenic products do not take off in the North. In the context of an unstable market riddled with consumer ambivalence, the gene giants use merger strategies to maximize flexibility, including investing in Southern cropping.

Whereas in 1999 most of the 34 million hectares of GM crops were grown in the North, 550 million hectares out of a world total of 900 million hectares were estimated to be growing in the South in 2002.[39] Of the four crops (soybean, cotton, canola, and corn) that dominate transgenic cropping, two-thirds of their combined total area are in the South where, according to ISAAA board member Clive James, "yields are lower, constraints are greater, and the need for improved production of food, feed, and fiber crops is the greatest."[40] Under these circumstances firms are pursuing two avenues of penetration. On the one hand, they are introducing transgenic crops tested in the North and "imported by the developers of the technology to get approval to market transgenics within the country."[41] On the other hand, firms are purchasing local seed companies in the South, assuming growing dominance in national seed markets. Monsanto, for example, now controls 60 percent of the Brazilian seed market.[42] It is positioning itself to capitalize on the likelihood that Brazil will legalize transgenic technology. As the world's second largest producer of soybeans, this country is the global pivot for GM crops: either Brazil retains a comparative advantage in GM-free soybeans for the large European GM-free market, or it embraces biotechnology and its output tips the balance in favor of GM food everywhere.[43]

The biotech/seed company merger allows the gene giants to form strategic alliances with agribusiness firms, allowing firms with transgenic interests access to production.[44] Such crop development conglomerates consist of networks of enterprises interested in specific genetic crop development:

> Typically, a crop-development conglomerate is organized around one OECD-based transnational enterprise (TNE), rooted in the chemical, pharmaceutical, or food-processing industry. This TNE maintains a network of linkages with one or more plant-breeding firms, new biology firms, genomics and software firms, and also with public research institutes. The nature of the linkages is diverse and varies from temporary research collaboration to complete takeovers.[45]

Crop development, as distinct from plant breeding or crop improvement, refers to the structuring of decisions regarding the future of world agriculture.[46] Structuring of decisions involves the politics of market construction, where the promotion of genetic patenting and genetic engineering privileges a certain kind of world agriculture. It is expressed in discursive struggles centering on proposals for global food security and an intellectual property-rights regime.

As Farshad Araghi has pointed out, today "hunger has assumed a uniquely global character. 'Hunger amidst scarcity' has given way to 'hunger amidst abundance.' "[47] This movement is perhaps mirrored in the reformulated conceptions of food security. World market–based food security combined the spatial metaphor of "breadbasket of the world" with the capacity of the grain traders to provide or supplement food requirements globally. This form of food-security arrangement corresponded to the national dimensions of the "development project,"[48] when U.S. food aid and green revolution technologies addressed the problem of scarcity via bilateral relations.

Bioengineered food security replaces the spatial relationship with a temporal relationship within the context of the "globalization project."[49] The obsession with time *appears* to stem from neo-Malthusian projections of population growth outstripping food production, leading firms like Monsanto, gene giants like Novartis and AgrEvosay, and agricultural research institutes like IRRI, to propose biotechnical solutions *now*. As Klaus Leisinger, head of Novartis Foundation for Sustainable Development stated: "To turn a blind eye to 40,000 people starving to death every day is a moral outrage [. . .] we have an ethical commitment not to lose time."[50]

Since we know there is a global food surplus, the sense of urgency for the biotech industry stems not from solving present and future hunger needs, but from solving immediate financial needs. These needs are threefold: first, the future of genetic engineering is uncertain; second, the window of opportunity for investments in transgenics is short because transgenic patents last only twenty years; and third, capturing the advantage on the transgenic frontier rewards the pioneering firm. These needs do not address the real solution to hunger in a global redistribution of food.

While uncertainty prevails, investments in genomics remain risky. Thus biotech spokespeople recycle the scenarios of poverty that legitimized the development project in the post-WWII decades as a strategy to institutionalize transgenic crop development, sanctioned by the TRIPs protocols in the WTO. This definition of food security forecloses the future in the interest of resolving the investment horizon of biotechnology in the present. Should transgenic technology prevail, its genetic reductionism forecloses the future by denying the potential of existing food cultures, or reformed land relations to resolve poverty and hunger via forms of agro-ecology. Urgency pervades the politics of bioengineering, leading one commentator to observe: "Before we embrace genetic engineering as the saviour of the world's poor, it seems wise to sort out what problem is being solved here. Is it the crisis of malnutrition, or is it the crisis of credibility plaguing biotech?"[51]

The South: the Agro-Industrial Frontier

The war on the credibility front may be stalled, but the war on the hunger front continues. Under the pretext of heading off a future of unfed populations, the crop-development industry is positioning itself in the South to inherit the commercial momentum triggered by the green revolution. Crop-development firms operate with a compelling logic in two senses: first, in the biological sense, insofar as the monocultures of the green revolution exacerbated problems of plant disease, soil depletion, and pest infestation—and GM is presented as the solution; and second, in the socioeconomic sense, insofar as commercial cropping privileges wealthier farmers, centralized upstream suppliers, and downstream processors and retailers.

Thus, DuPont's recent global joint venture—RiceCo—not only sells agrochemicals and seeds but plans to promote contract farming and "market the rice through partnerships with millers and maybe even with retailers."[52] The bottom line is that the market for seed has huge commercial potential if an intellectual property rights regime is installed. As Monsanto, the second largest seed company in the world, observed: "With the advent of adequate intellectual property protection in several countries, private-sector investment in rice has dramatically increased, particularly in the seed industry."[53]

The first step is hybridization, a recent development in rice, the self-pollinating plant that Asian farmers selectively reproduced over the centuries. Hybridization of rice applies the model of corn hybridization from North America to a crop that has leveled off in terms of yields from the high-yielding varieties developed in the green revolution. It is noteworthy that the hybrid corn model encouraged land concentration in North America and spawned an oligopoly in which Monsanto and Dupont (through Pioneer) control 90 percent of the American seed corn market. IRRI admitted that: "The cost of hybrid seed, being 10–15 times higher than that of ordinary seeds of rice, discourages poor farmers from taking advantage of hybrid technology."[54] Hybrid rice is highly susceptible to disease and holds great commercial potential for those agrochemical firms with hybrid rice subsidiaries in Asia.[55]

In the Philippines the International Rice Research Institute, which works closely with Novartis and AgroEvosay on transgenic rice, planned to conduct the first open-field test in Southeast Asia of transgenic BB-rice in 2001. BB-rice is genetically engineered to resist bacterial blight using a gene (Xa21) from a wild African rice "found" in Mali. Like golden rice this transgenic rice was developed to redress a problem created by the green revolution. Golden rice is designed to restore vitamin A deficiency that stems in part from the reductionism of high-yielding variety monocultures that systematically displaced leafy vegetables and dietary diversity.

BB-rice is designed to address the problem of bacterial blight, a water-borne disease exacerbated by the nitrogen fertilizer used with the IR8 rice variety introduced by IRRI in 1959. Within a decade, bacterial blight proliferated alongside the use of IR8 and farmers lost up to 80 percent of their harvests. Despite local farmer and NGO recommendations of six cultural management practices that control bacterial blight, and IRRI's discovery of bacterial blight races in the Philippines that resist the gene Xa 21, IRRI proceeds under a neo-Malthusian projection that rice demand by 2020 will reach 820 million tons, 700 million of which will be from Asia. IRRI argues: "To ensure food security and to continue the advancement against poverty in rice-consuming countries of the world, farmers will have to produce 40 to 50 percent more rice to meet the consumer demand in 2025."[56] IRRI's prognosis appears to foreclose the future and the possibility of stabilizing and developing alternative agro-ecologies.

In Southeast Asia about 40 percent of the corn area is planted in farmers' varieties where the seed replacement rate is as low as 4 percent, as is the case in Indonesia. Small farmers typically intercrop corn with other crops such as groundnut, mungbean, cowpea, soybean, other pulses, cassava, sweet potatoes, and vegetables—constituting 69 percent of Indonesia's corn area and about 50 percent of the upland corn areas of the Philippines. Nevertheless, the promotion of hybrids by governments and firms since the green revolution encroaches on farmer varieties: 60 percent of Thailand's corn area in 1997 was occupied by hybrids; this figure is expected to increase to 70–75 percent by 2000. In Vietnam, hybrid corn is expected to soon double to reach 80–90 percent of the corn area.[57]

This commercial push will accelerate with the application of GM crops. Between 1980–1994, commercial seed demand increased by more than 30 percent in Asia.[58] In this region, three companies, Cargill, Pioneer, and DeKalb, control almost 70 percent of the seed market, supplying hybrid seed for 25 percent of the total corn area (although DeKalb and Cargill Seeds have recently been acquired by Monsanto). Further, Novartis is entering the corn seed business and establishing alliances with local Filipino companies such as Cornworld.[59]

One of the emergent areas of crop development, Bt corn,[60] is likely to be the first transgenic corn to enter the Southeast Asian market. Monsanto is conducting Bt corn tests in Thailand, Indonesia (along with Pioneer), and the Philippines. Its current R&D portfolio focuses on the feed and processing industries, rather than promoting corn as a staple. Because the seed suppliers and grain processors are the same corporate complex, commercial farmers will have no control over prices and will bear the risks.[61] Through market and environmental relations, the introduction of Bt corn threatens to prejudice a staple crop that has fed Asians for 400 years, and continues to do so in those areas untouched by the hybrid corn introduced by the green revolution.

The combined effect of market liberalization flooding the South with cheap grains, coupled with the integration of crop-development conglomerates, pose a long-term threat to both the biodiverse system of intercropping of farmer varieties, and farmers who will either lose their land or enter into "bioserfdom." The most fundamental implication of the crop-development industry is its movement to own and control the world's seeds. Recent research discloses a total of 132 genetic patents on crops that evolved in the South but which are now grown worldwide—68 for maize genes, 17 for potato, 25 for soybean, and 22 for wheat—indicating that staple foods (and feeds) are increasingly targeted for corporate patenting.[62]

Conclusion

This chapter questioned the apparent self-evident and reinforcing association between globalization, biotechnology, and food security in the new millennium, arguing that this association is based on a simplifying view of the world as a homogeneous and ultimately self-regulating market. Food security is viewed as an outcome of market development, which includes a future role for transgenic foods. In relation to this, U.S. Secretary of Agriculture Dan Glickman recently encouraged agribusinesses to donate transgenic food through food-aid programs, arguing: "If they took the longer view they might see the benefit of focusing on the developing world not just as a gesture of corporate citizenship, but because such an investment will ultimately pay dividends as development countries mature into reliable customers."[63]

Continuing the developmentalist mantra of using technology to solve hunger, the 2001 *Human Development Report* of the United Nations Development Program (UNDP) advocates biotechnological solutions to food insecurity in the South, accusing Northern opponents of transgenic crops of ignoring Southern food needs. As Anuradha Mittal retorts, the UNDP ignores widespread Southern civil society opposition to GM seeds and food, as well as the coexistence of overproduction of food and 36 million hungry in the U.S., concluding:

> Over 60 million tons of excess food grain—unsold—because the hungry are too poor to buy it—rotted in India last year, while farmers in desperation burnt the crops they could not sell, and resorted to selling their body parts like kidneys and committing suicide, to end the cycle of poverty. A higher, genetically engineered crop yield would have done nothing for them. And if the poor in India cannot buy two meals a day, how will they purchase nutritionally rich crops such as rice engineered to contain Vitamin A? No technological fix can help change the situation.[64]

Food security remains an elusive goal in a world market constructed around unsustainable breadbaskets, elimination of local ecological knowledges, and the appropriation of the world's seed resources by a handful of crop-development conglomerates privileged by a set of irregular trade rules. The economic, political, and cultural, not to mention environmental implications, are profound. They go to the heart of the historic North/South relationship rooted in colonialism. As Shiva notes:

> The seed is, for the farmer, not merely the source of future plants and food; it is the storage place of culture and history. Seed is the first link in the food chain. Seed is the ultimate symbol of food security.[65]

Because of the social relations embedded in the seed, the corporate bid for its control—in the name of global food security—is generating increasing, consequential resistance to the imposition of a market monoculture on a world of cultural and biological diversity.

Globalization may be represented as inevitable and self-evident, but the reality is profoundly ambiguous. Not only are global and industrial agricultures experiencing crisis in terms of mad cow and foot-and-mouth diseases, genetic erosion, disease susceptibility, and environmental stresses, small farming continues to offer more productive, stable, biodiverse, and place-based culinary alternatives to the abstractions of global monoculture. It is on the basis of these alternatives that food sovereignty movements, led by the transnational Via Campesina, are mushrooming across the world.

Notes

1. I wish to acknowledge Dia Mohan and Anna Zalik's assistance in data gathering, and helpful comments by Doreen Stabinsky on an earlier draft of this paper.
2. Quoted in Andrew Pollack, "A Food Fight for High Stakes," *New York Times*, Feb. 4, This Week in Review, p. 6.
3. Food and Agricultural Organization, *The State of Food and Agriculture, 2000*, Rome: FAO, 2000, p. 2.
4. Ibid., p. 22.
5. Ibid., p. 3.
6. Idem. (emphasis added).
7. Ibid., p. 26.
8. Quoted in Mark Ritchie's *Breaking the Deadlock: The United States and Agricultural Policy in the Uruguay Round*, Minneapolis: Institute for Agriculture and Trade Policy, 1993, fn 25.
9. Quoted in Walden Bello's "Does World Trade Need World Trade Organization?" in *Businessworld*, January 11, 2000.
10. The U.S. proposal was drafted by the former senior vice-president of Cargill, which shares 50 percent of U.S. grain exports with Continental.
11. Philip McMichael's "Global Food Politics" in *Hungry for Profit. The Agribusiness Threat to Farmers, Food and the Environment*, Fred Magdoff, John Bellamy Foster, and Frederick H. Buttel eds., New York: Monthly Review, 2000.
12. R. Pistorius and J. van Wijk's *The Exploitation of Plant Genetic Information. Political Strategies in Crop Development*, Oxon: CABI Publishing, 1999, pp. 110–111.
13. John Madeley's *Hungry for Trade*, London & New York: Zed, 2000, p. 75.
14. John Bailey's "Agricultural Trade and the Livelihoods of Small Farmers," Oxfam GB Discussion Paper 3/00, 2000. www.oxfam.org.uk/policy/papers/agric.htm
15. Arturo Escobar's *Encountering Development*, Princeton: Princeton University Press, 1995; and Philip McMichael's *Development and Social Change: A Global Perspective*, Thousand Oaks: Pine Forge Press, 2000.
16. Quoted in Andrew Kimbrell's "Why Biotechnology and High-Tech Agriculture Cannot Feed the World," *The Ecologist*, 28(5): 294, 1998.
17. Wendy Russell's "What's the Good of Gene Technology in Agriculture?" (Presentation to Agri-Food Research Network conference, Tumbarumba, New South Wales), 2000.
18. Quoted in Devlin Kuyek's "ISAAA in Asia. Promoting corporate profits in the name of the poor," 2000a. www.grain.org/publications/reports/isaaa.htm
19. Quoted in Pollack, op. cit.
20. *Wall Street Journal*, December 21, 2000.
21. Katherine Barrett and Gabriela Flora's "Genetic Engineering and the Precautionary Principle: Information for Extension," 2000. www.sustain.org/biotech/lib
22. Pollack, op. cit.
23. Cited in Madeleine Nash's "Grains of Hope," in *Time*, July 31, p. 42, 2000.
24. Paul Brown's "GM Rice Promoters' Claims 'Have Gone Too Far'," in *Guardian Weekly*, February 15–21, p. 5, 2001.
25. Nash, op.cit., p. 45.
26. Quoted in Pollack, op. cit.
27. Quoted in Brown, op. cit.
28. GRAIN. 2000a. "Engineering Solutions to Malnutrition," www.grain.org/publications/reports/malnutrition/

29. Quoted in Brown, op. cit.
30. ActionAid. 2000. "Crops and robbers. Biopiracy and the Patenting of Staple Food Crops." www.actionaid.org/resources/publications/foodrights. S. Gorelick's "Facing the Farm Crisis," in *The Ecologist*, 30(4): 30, 2000.
31. Hugh Warwick's "Syngenta. Switching off Farmers' Rights?" 2000. www.oneworld.org/nbar2.cgi
32. GRAIN, op. cit., p. 25.
33. RAFI. 2000. "Biotech's Generation 3," RAFI Communique #67. www.rafi.org
34. Warwick, op. cit.
35. John Vidal's "Global GM Market Shows Signs of Wilting," in *Guardian Weekly*, September 20–26, p. 26, 2001.
36. Charlie Cray's "The View from Wall Street," in *Multinational Monitor*, 21, 1&2, 2000.
37. Quoted in Tim Lang, M. Heasman, and J. Pitt's "Food, Globalization and a New Public Health Agenda," International Forum on Globalization, San Francisco, p. 77, 1999.
38. RAFI, op. cit.
39. ActionAid, op. cit., p. 4.
40. Clive James' "Global Status of Commercialized Transgenic Crops: 2000." ISAAA Briefs, 21, 2000. www.isaaa.org/publications
41. Mary Arends-Kuenning and Flora Makundi's "Agricultural Biotechnology for Developing Countries: Prospects and Policies," unpublished paper, University of Illinois, Urbana-Champaign, 2000.
42. Warwick, op. cit., p. 7.
43. Anthony DePalma's "Brazil: Latin America's Next Biotech Market?" *Corporate Watch*, 2000. www.igc.org/trac/headlines/2000/178.html
44. Bill Heffernan's "Consolidation in the Food and Agriculture System," Report to the National Farmers' Union, 1999.
45. Pistorius and van Wijk, op. cit., p. 118.
46. Ibid., p. 4.
47. Farshad Araghi's "The Great Global Enclosure of Our Times: Peasants and the Agrarian Question at the End of the Twentieth Century," in *Hungry for Profit. The Agribusiness Threat to Farmers, Food and the Environment*, Fred Magdoff, John Bellamy Foster, and Frederick Buttel eds., New York: Monthly Review Press, p. 155, 2000.
48. Philip McMichael's *Development and Social Change: A Global Perspective*, Thousand Oaks: Pine Forge Press, 2000.
49. Idem.
50. Quoted in M.W. Fox's "More help or more harm? Genetically engineered crops and world hunger," 2000. Bioethics@hsus.org
51. Naomi Klein's "There's Nothing Like a Feel-Good Bowl of Golden Rice. Or Not," in *Toronto Globe-Mail*, August 2, 2000.
52. Devlin Kuyek. 2000b. "Hybrid Rice in Asia: an Unfolding Threat." www.grain.org/publications/reports/hybrid.htm
53. Quoted in Devlin Kuyek's "Blast, Biotech and Big Business. Implications of Corporate Strategies on Rice Research in Asia," 2000c. www.grain.org/publications/reports/blast.htm.
54. Kuyek, 2000b.
55. They are Ring Around Products (a joint venture of Syngenta with Mitsui), Hybrid Rice International of India (Aventis), Agroseed/Cargill Seeds of the Philippines and Mahyco & Maharashtra Hybrid Seed Company of India (Monsanto), and SPIC-PHI of India (DuPont). Idem.
56. Quoted in Michael A. Bengwayan's, "Entry of GMO BB-Rice Stirs Hornet's Nest," in *The Philippine Post*, October, 2000. Released by Masipag News & Views masipag@mozcom.com
57. BIOTHAI, GRAIN, MASIPAG AND PAN Indonesia. 1999. "Whose Agenda? The Corporate Take Over of Corn in SE Asia."
58. Pistorius and van Wijk, op. cit., p. 111.
59. BIOTHAI, GRAIN, MASIPAG AND PAN Indonesia. 1999. "Whose Agenda? The Corporate Take Over of Corn in SE Asia."
60. A genetically modified corn with a gene for an insect killing toxin isolated from the soil microbe *Bacillus thuringiensis*.

61. Idem.
62. ActionAid, op. cit. p. 9.
63. Quoted in Food First's "Fact Sheet: Food Aid in the Millennium—Genetically Engineered Food and Foreign Assistance", 2000. www.foodfirst.org/pubs/factsheet/2000/biotechfs.1.html
64. Anuradha Mittal's "UN Dead Wrong About Engineered Crops," Knight-Ridder/Progressive Media Services, July 16, 2001.
65. Vandana Shiva's *Stolen Harvest. The Hijacking of the Global Food Supply*, Cambridge: South End Press, p. 8, 2000.

CHAPTER 9

The WTO, GATS, and TPRM
Servicing Liberalization and Eroding Equity Goals?

SAVITRI BISNATH[1]

Introduction

> Trade agreements in the contemporary period require governments to not
> only live up to the traditional disciplines by reducing trade barriers at the bor-
> der, but also to *adopt and implement specific policies, practices, and procedures*
> *that reach well behind national borders.* This new focus of trade rules consti-
> tutes a major paradigm shift *with profound implications in the relationship be-*
> *tween trade rules and domestic regulations and governance.*
>
> > Ruggiero, 1998 (emphasis added)

At the end of the twentieth century, trade in services increased and accelerated partially because of advances in electronic communication and information technology. Services encompass numerous activities, including
those related to national administration, health, education, information
processing, and manufacturing. Thus, services facilitate many aspects of
economic, political, and social life. The formulation and implementation
of the General Agreement on Trade in Services (GATS) reflect the services
sector's growing commercial importance, as well as the influence of multinational corporations on the multilateral trading system.[2]

At the multilateral level, GATS and the Trade Policy Review Mechanism
(TPRM) are regulatory devices that bring the imperatives of the multilateral trading system into national domains. As such, they facilitate certain
liberalizing actions and foreclose those rules and regulations that the

world trading system deems as restrictive to the conduct of "free trade" in services. In particular, GATS propels trade liberalization policy beyond tariffs into domestic legislation and national governance. The TPRM secures the preferred policies of the multilateral trading system at the national level. As former director-general of the World Trade Organization (WTO), Ruggiero notes, this seeping of global trade policy rules and norms into national governance structures has profound implications for the extent to which member-states are able to determine domestic policies. For many countries the new governance requirements of the multilateral trade regime, coupled with growing internationalization and commercialization of services, present both opportunities and challenges.

In particular, governments must both facilitate an enabling environment for international trade in services and address social and development needs. This chapter explores tensions between these objectives. It argues that the deployment of global trade rules within national borders will potentially erode state sovereignty and autonomy, undermine democratic decision-making and human rights,[3] and compromise the ability of WTO members to address issues of equity and development.

More specifically, it traces the central role of private-sector interest in the formulation of GATS. Second, it describes the scope and objectives of this multilateral agreement on services. Third, it analyzes how the trade policy review process reinforces the adoption of trade liberalization policies. Fourth, it explores ways in which the GATS as written specifically intrudes upon domestic regulatory regimes in those service sectors traditionally prone to government intervention. Finally, the chapter briefly uses the examples of the water and health-care subsectors to argue that GATS can limit access to basic services and erode equity and development goals while formally integrating member-states in the global economy.

GATS: Policing Trade in Services

> An increasing complaint from business is that governments have too many different approaches to regulations and policies that affect a company's ability to do business internationally.
>
> (Feketekuty, 1998: 83)

Trade in services is a highly regulated economic activity, with a significant degree of government involvement in the ownership and provision of specific services. In the past, and to a lesser degree at present, national monopolies controlled the supply of health care, water and sanitation, postal, energy, and telecommunications services. Proponents of services liberalization argue that current levels of domestic regulatory control create barriers to international competition (Sauve and Stern, 2000; Stephenson,

2000 and 1999; Low and Mattoo, 1998; Aharoni, 1997; Kostecki, 1994). The negotiations of the General Agreement on Trade in Services are attempts to erode most of these barriers. As written, GATS will reduce regulatory constraints, including such legal barriers to entry as local content requirements that restrict foreign direct investment, obligations for joint ventures, and limitations on foreign personnel.

In the late 1970s, private-sector service companies in the United States (the Coalition of Service Industries) and the United Kingdom (British Invisibles) began to lobby their governments for a "more level playing field" in accessing foreign markets.[4] In a Brookings-Wharton (2000) paper, Harry Freeman[5] states that in 1979, while working in strategic planning and acquisitions for the American Express Company, he noticed that American Express was experiencing "market access problems" in approximately forty countries.[6] American Express could not seek remedy under the General Agreement on Tariffs and Trade (GATT), so they decided "to change that, which meant starting a new round of trade negotiations including services."

Freeman notes that his boss, Jim Robinson, the chief executive officer of American Express, asked him "to start a new trade round as soon as possible."

> We put a person in Brussels, a person in Tokyo, two or three people in Washington, three people in New York, and so forth. We enlisted the aid, which was really important, of Citicorp and also AIG. [. . .] We went to the ministerial meeting in 1980, 1982, 1984, and 1986, and the Uruguay Round started.
> (Brookings-Wharton, 2000: 456)

He notes that had the Uruguay Round ended on time there would be no multilateral agreement on services: "The round almost collapsed in 1990, and we finally got services in right before 1993, at the end of the Uruguay Round" (Brookings-Wharton, 2000: 456). Freeman states that the "U.S. private sector on trade in services is probably the most powerful trade lobby, not only in the United States but also in the world." At the close of the Uruguay Round they had approximately 400 people working on increasing market access in the services sector (Brookings-Wharton, 2000: 458).[7]

During this historic negotiation, attention centered on conceptual and architectural issues, such as defining trade in services. For example, in the context of financial services Freeman notes that,

> . . . we had to deal with [. . .] the meaning of financial services. The first thing we did in 1979 was to coin the phrase. You will not see the term "financial services" before 1979. We did that by asking everybody in the company to talk about financial services particularly with the media, and in about two years the term financial services was part of the lexicon.
> (Brookings-Wharton, 2000: 457)

Further, the trade diplomats tried to construct a framework through which to pursue future liberalization (Brookings-Wharton, 2000; Hoekman, 1999).[8] The results of the GATS negotiations included attempts to stop restrictions through standstill commitments,[9] and to liberalize specific sectors through the built-in agenda.[10]

As a result, the General Agreement on Trade in Services became the first set of multilateral, legally enforceable rules regulating international trade in services. The member-states of the World Trade Organization note in the preamble of GATS that they wish

> . . . to establish a multilateral framework of principles and rules for trade in services with a view to the expansion of such trade under conditions of transparency and progressive liberalization.
>
> (GATT, 1994)

GATS operates on three levels: first, its main text outlines general concepts, principles, and rules that apply to all measures affecting trade in services; second, its annexes delineate rules for specific sectors; and third, its national schedules define each member's commitments on market access and national treatment in those sectors and subsectors that are listed in members' schedules (GATT, 1994). It is important to note that GATS covers *all government measures affecting* services. A "measure," according to Article XXVIII (*a*) of GATS, can be "a law, regulation, rule, procedure, decision, administrative action, or any other form" that is used to regulate services (GATT, 1994).

Multilateral rules regulating services are based on the following key principles: first, members must engage in negotiations to further liberalize services trade five years after entry into force of the agreement and periodically thereafter;[11] second, the results of such negotiations should be bound in national schedules;[12] third, commitments should apply equally to services and service providers from all member countries, except for those provided in the exercise of "governmental authority";[13] and fourth, national regulations should not restrict foreign services or service providers, or discriminate against them, in a manner that is inconsistent with the commitments[14] (GATT, 1994). Given the final principle, member-states are required to list their reservations on market access and national treatment.[15] In cases where members decline to make commitments in a subsector, the presumption is *not* that the member has no obligations in that domain. In fact all subsectors are covered by Articles II and XVII.[16]

The twenty-nine articles of GATS cover all service sectors. The agreement also applies to all manners of providing services[17] including: (*a*) services supplied from one country to another, for example, telephone calls, officially known as "cross-border supply" (Mode 1); (*b*) consumers or firms making use of a service in another country, such as, a French student attending graduate school at a U.S. university, referred to as "consumption abroad" (Mode 2); (c) a foreign company setting up subsidiaries to provide services in another country, for example, a Spanish telecommunications company providing its services through a subsidiary to a Latin American country, officially known as "commercial presence" (Mode 3); and (d) individuals traveling from one country to supply services in another, such as fashion models or consultants, officially known as the "presence of natural persons" (Mode 4)[18] (World Trade Organization, 1998).

The commitments of the member-states cover approximately 160 types of services activity, some of which can be supplied through all four modes. The use of "modes" is significant in that they both reflect and address the production and distribution needs of multinational corporations (MNCs). As many have noted (Brookings-Wharton, 2000; Fuchs and Koch, 1996), MNCs view domestic regulation as the most significant barrier to market access in the services sector. In addition, negotiations through the four modes will facilitate deeper and broader economic integration (Ostry, 1997), and further erode national regulation in the services sector.

The Trade Policy Review process makes transparent to the international financial institutions, trading partners, and MNCs the extent to which WTO members are constructing an enabling environment for the conduct of free trade in services. As a complementary policing instrument to GATS, the Trade Policy Review Mechanism further solidifies this agreement. The following section elaborates this element of the multilateral trading system.

The Trade Policy Review Mechanism: Tightening Liberalization and Coherence at Whose Expense?

The Trade Policy Review Mechanism was established at the end of the Uruguay Round to ensure that member-states adhere to multilateral trade rules. Through formal reviews of members' trade environments, the TPRM's review committee makes recommendations with the aim of constructing more coherent and integrated frameworks for economic policy-making in general, and trade liberalization in particular. According to the WTO (1998), the TPRM aims to: increase transparency and understanding of the trade policies and practices of member-states through regular monitoring; improve the quality of public and intergovernmental debate on issues of relevance to the trading system; and enable a multilateral assessment of the effects of specific policies on the world trading system.

The reviews take account of the requirements of the multilateral trading system and focus attention on domestic economic policies that constrain and/or enhance free trade. To this end, reports of the trade policy reviews describe the national macroeconomic environment of the country under review, outline changes in laws and regulations deemed necessary to facilitate openness, and discuss those rules and regulations under consideration for change.

Specific issues covered during the review include: national trade-policy objectives; domestic laws and regulations governing the application of trade policies; trade-policy measures in use, such as tariffs, qualitative restrictions, rules of origin, government procurement, technical barriers, and antidumping actions; and trade liberalization programs.[19] In effect, the review facilitates "an internal coordination of trade policy and practice" (Qureshi, 1996). However, this is done with little regard for development challenges and social needs of member-states.

Further, and in an effort to ensure that members do not deploy "unnecessary barriers to trade in services," the WTO's Council for Trade in Services (CTS) formed the subsidiary Working Party on Domestic Regulations (WPDR). The WPDR is mandated to ensure that nondiscriminatory domestic measures deployed by members, including those related to licencing, technical standards, and qualifications, are not more trade restrictive than necessary. It also enables the WTO to "examine whether an individual measure is actually *necessary* to achieve the specified legitimate objective" (World Trade Organization, 1999, emphasis added).

This level of scrutiny raises several important questions: Who decides what is "necessary"; what is a "legitimate objective"; and what criteria are the defining ones? According to World Trade Organization (1999, emphasis added), the

> . . . necessity test—especially the requirement that regulatory measures be no more trade restrictive than necessary—is the means by which an effort is made to balance between two potentially conflicting priorities: *promoting trade expansion versus protecting the regulatory rights of governments.*

These conflicting priorities become evident within the context of the public-services sector: through the implementation of their commitments, including the national treatment obligation, members could be challenged to liberalize public services.

This is important because the tension goes beyond capital and national governance to include issues of equity and democratic legitimacy. The necessity test has the potential—given the varying levels of infrastructural development among member-states—to constrain members, particularly developing countries, from building infrastructure and human capacities in specific subsectors because it would be economically inefficient and against the trade rules. Moreover, a member's stated responsibility to supply basic services to those citizens who cannot afford them at market prices may make such subsectors vulnerable to liberalization under GATS. This, in turn, can affect equity goals and run counter to democratic will when popular sentiment calls on states to deprioritize what the WPDR deems "necessary" for private capital.

GATS: Servicing Profits at the Expense of Equity?

> New constitutionalism involves law (both public and private), regulation and standardization, and a series of formal and informal practices. [. . .] New constitutionalism operates at several jurisdictional scales: subnational, national, regional, and international.
>
> (Gill, 2001: 9)

> Liberalization in many services sectors cannot be achieved without substantial domestic regulatory reforms.
>
> (Feketekuty, 2000: 90)

> A business-oriented approach tends to treat national public policy only as an obstacle to be overcome.
>
> (Fuchs and Koch, 1996: 164)

This section analyzes tensions between markets, nation-states, and peoples within the global economy. It positions international trade as part of an historically constituted formation—namely globalization[20]—that is embedded in neoliberalism and supported by the multilateral trading system (Bisnath, 2002). So positioned, it is clear that international trade reaches beyond the economic, and that the multilateral trade regime is a political formation that operates within a regime of unequal power relations.

The multilateral trading system's emphasis on market access in trade negotiations and policy-making partially results from the legitimacy it derives from neoliberal ideology. Neoliberalism promotes as "rights" the interests of capital and encourages actions and policies at the national level that address the needs of private enterprise. Coherent within the neoliberal framework, multilateral trade arrangements such as GATS and the TPRM promote such actions and policies. Additionally, neoliberalism obscures asymmetry between member-states within its analyses of the merits of trade liberalization.

Herein, Gill's (2001) elaboration of "new constitutionalism" provides further insight into global economic governance and trade liberalization. For Gill, multilateral trade agreements and trade liberalization mechanisms function as elements of the new constitutionalism that frame the policy, political, and economic environments in the current moment. Gill defines new constitutionalism as "the political-juridical" complement to disciplinary neoliberalism. For him, new constitutionalism requires the adoption of those rules, norms, and standards that are presumed to increase market access to foreign services and goods. Because these regulations tend to focus on "the economic"[21] and reflect the needs of capital, they often lack appreciation for social needs, national development constraints, and uneven development within and between member-states. As such, they have the potential to undermine local objectives that aim to promote and preserve equity.

Thus, new constitutionalism can also be interpreted as "an effort to define the limits of the possible for political agents" (Gill, 2001: 1). In effect, it facilitates a redefinition of the formal relationships between the political and the economic and between states and corporations. For example, the implementation of GATS has the potential to stifle the growth of small- and medium-size enterprises that are unable to compete effectively with cheaper imports of foreign-service suppliers. Further, the livelihood possibilities for citizens of certain member-states, specifically those with underdeveloped service industries, will be constrained. Infrastructural development within the services sector will also be discouraged, thereby further limiting the development possibilities of specific WTO members.

In the public-services sector, given the centrality of public services to development and equity goals, governments often hesitate to devolve all their ownership and control. However, the deployment of the General Agreement on Trade in Services will require a shift from this position. As written, GATS requires governments to open up their service sectors to foreign competition. In particular, two articles embody this requirement: Articles I and XVII. In Article I—which sets out the scope for and defines the agreement—members agree that "all measures by members affecting trade in services" are covered. In other words, GATS extends to measures implemented by: central, regional, and/or local governments and authorities; and nongovernmental bodies in the "exercise of powers delegated by central, regional, or local governments or authorities" (GATT, 1994).

The services covered "include any service in any sector except services supplied in the exercise of governmental authority" (GATT, 1994). This means any service that is supplied either on a commercial basis, or in competition with one or more service suppliers. Further, the National Treatment Commitment (Article XVII) obliges each member to treat "services and service suppliers" of other members "in respect of all measures affecting the supply of services, no less favorable than that it accords to its own like services and service suppliers." The WTO defines less-favorable treatment as that which "modifies the conditions of competition in favor of services or service suppliers of the member compared to like services or service suppliers of any other member" (GATT, 1994; emphasis added).

Article I poses a challenge to the suppliers of public services because such services are often provided, and increasingly so because of World Bank and IMF conditionalities, by both governmental and private-service providers. The conflict of interest between the multilateral trading system and the supply of public services is further intensified by the aim of the WTO to facilitate regulatory reforms that "aim, directly or indirectly, on the establishment of a more uniform system of intervention" (Hoekman and Messerlin, 2000: 12). Thus, WTO suggested regulatory changes often deprioritize the differences in national development, market structures, infrastructure, and human resources, as well as the social needs of member-states.

Herein lies the tension between the development and equity imperatives of nation-states and the needs of the free market. This tension is worth exploring because of the rules-based nature of the multilateral trading system: Being rules-based translates into the expectation that the results of the negotiations, once ratified by national parliaments, will be legally binding.[22] Further, and in order to ensure and facilitate compliance, the trade-policy review acknowledges and recommends changes of state policies, regulations, and legislation as appropriate. The following section explores this tension by looking at the case of public services.

GATS and Public Services

> ... the right of establishment, and the obligation to treat foreign suppliers fairly and objectively in *all relevant areas of domestic regulation,* extend the reach of the [services] agreement into areas *never before recognized as trade policy.* I suspect that neither governments nor industries have yet appreciated the full scope of these guarantees.
>
> Ruggiero, 1998 (emphasis added)

To date, domestic regulations are the most significant means through which governments are able to exercise influence and control over services trade. For World Trade Organization members, however, the deployment of GATS and the TPRM require examination of all aspects of domestic regulation, and reform of those measures deemed to be barriers to market access for foreign-service suppliers. According to Hoekman (1994), the four broad categories of regulatory measures states often use are: those that explicitly restrict the volume and/or value of transactions; price-based regulation through imposition of monetary fees or taxes on foreign suppliers seeking market access; regulations specific to an industry;[23] and generalized broad-based government policies.

The requirements of the GATS and the TPRM enforcement procedure therefore intrude upon domestic regulatory regimes in those public-service areas traditionally most prone to government intervention. This

intrusion into domestic governance, coupled with transparency requirements, will likely shift states roles from direct ownership and management
of certain basic services toward more harmonized and generalized subsector policy and regulation. Such a shift will be felt in those subsectors traditionally regulated without regard to their trade effects because they serve
other objectives, namely those that pertain to equity and redistribution
goals, and individual rights.

Most governments view basic services, such as health care, water, and
education, as both nontradeable and as serving intersecting developmental, distributional, economic, and social functions. Consequently, these
services are mainly provided by public institutions. As such, they historically depend on regulations, institutions, and funding arrangements that
restrict access to private industry and prohibit competition. The public
funding and delivery of basic services have been specifically critical to
poverty-reduction efforts and equity goals in WTO member-states. However, for many members these goals are in jeopardy. With the implementation of GATS as currently written, the regulatory arrangements
governing public services in many member-states are vulnerable to policy
shifts.

As several nongovernmental organizations are beginning to argue,[24]
GATS will potentially threaten and erode the autonomy of governments to
manage and provide public services to disadvantaged groups.[25] This will
specifically result with implementation of GATS Article I and the National
Treatment Commitment. According to Article I, only fully public services
will be exempt from liberalization. Thus, members will be mandated to
liberalize those subsectors that supply services through both commercial
and governmental enterprises.

Institutional arrangements governing the provision of public services
vary. Government regulation ranges from full ownership and control to
moderate oversight of private suppliers. In some countries, hospitals and
schools provide services free of charge through government funding. In
other countries these services are provided by private enterprises, who
experience no access controls, at free market prices. In the latter case governments only assume the role of regulator, setting quality- and qualifica-
tion-related controls. However, and increasingly since the 1980s, the
arrangement in many countries is private-sector provision of basic services, with government intervention through targeted subsidies. Many developing countries have adopted this semipublic form of arrangement in
an effort to both conform to the conditionalities of the international financial institutions and supply basic services such as health care, water,
and education to the poor.

In the case of semiprivatized subsectors, the implementation of GATS raises potential challenges. It will be both possible and logical for the World Trade Organization to require its members to extend the same arrangements to both foreign and domestic suppliers for the purposes of facilitating market access and enabling competition. Analyzed from a rigid economic point of view this appears to be fair. However, this approach erases an important function of semiprivatized arrangements for the provision of public services. These arrangements enable access by low-income and poor communities to services they would otherwise be unable to afford. The erosion of state support in these subsectors will limit access by low-income and poor communities. Thus, in addition to promoting liberalization in services trade, GATS Articles I and XVII have the potential to limit access to basic services and erode equity and development goals.

With the implementation of GATS, those public-service institutions that are subsidized will be increasingly challenged to transform themselves into private enterprises while simultaneously facing competition from multinational corporations.[26] For example, GATS as written regulates the supply of water[27] and health care.[28] Water is used in agricultural production, manufacturing, power generation, primary resource extraction, and residential use. According to UNCTAD (1998), many governments partially provide "infrastructure for drinking water, waste water treatment, waste management and decontamination, and resource management." Given this arrangement, GATS may subject this subsector to liberalization, privatization and competition, which can result in access problems for the poor.[29]

A brief survey of the literature on water indicates that there is growing private interest in this sector. During their 2nd World Water Forum in March, 2000 a key message of the Global Water Partnership (GWP), a network of private companies, multilateral institutions and government agencies, was that "Water is Everybody's Business."[30] Accompanying this interest is a preoccupation with the impending scarcity of water. Interestingly, privatization advocates frame this crisis within a discourse of the "crisis of governance" (Global Water Partnership, 2002). To quote from the GWP (2002), the "water crisis is mainly a crisis of governance" which, if left unsolved, will lead to water scarcity.

"Water governance," for the Global Water Partnership (2002), refers to the range of political, social, economic and administrative systems that are in place to regulate the development and management of water resources and provision of water services at different levels of society. The Partnership would like to more effectively manage the provision of water by streamlining its governance arrangements within the GATS framework.

According to a GWP background paper, elements of the regulatory regime (Rees, 1998, emphasis added) include:

> *The general framework of laws*, constitutional rules, policies and administrative structures within an economy, *which while not developed with the water sector in mind*, nevertheless impinge on its activities and affect the willingness of the private sector to participate in service provision. These include labor law, company taxation rules, currency controls, and the constitutional division of responsibilities between national, regional, and local government.

This statement reveals a lack of appreciation for, and an attack on, state decisions and regulatory measures designed to prioritize and protect the rights and access of citizens *before* the rights of the private sector.

The semipublic nature of the health-care sector in many WTO member-states also makes this sector vulnerable to GATS. The provision of health services in many countries comprise both government- and privately owned enterprises that operate on commercial bases. In such arrangements patients pay for services, but in an effort to ensure access, governments also provide subsidies for those patients who are unable to pay market rates. Under GATS, however, this arrangement is subject to reregulation. According to a World Trade Organization background paper (1998b),

> [t]he co-existence of private and public hospitals may raise questions [. . .] concerning their competitive relationship and the applicability of GATS: in particular, can public hospitals [. . .] be deemed to fall under Article I:3?

In other words, if basic services are only partially supplied "in the exercise of governmental authority" does such an arrangement expose them to liberalization under GATS? The WTO (1998b) notes that it would be:

> . . . unrealistic [. . .] to argue for continued application of Article I: 3 and/or maintain that no competitive relationship exists between the two groups of suppliers or services.

Further, the World Trade Organization (1998b) notes

> . . . this suggests that subsidies and any similar economic benefits conferred on one group would be subject to the national treatment obligation under Article XVII.

Thus, semipublic services would be subject to liberalization under GATS, with alarming material effects for poor communities, and the attainment of national and international equity, development, and human-rights goals more generally.

Conclusion

The new rules of the multilateral trading system reconceptualizes and recharts the relationships between international governance, the global economy, and national regulatory measures. In particular, the multilateral agreement regulating trade in services provides a framework for addressing a wide range of intersecting policy measures that affect market access for multinationals. This chapter argued that deployment of the General Agreement on Trade in Services heightens the ensuing tension between the rights of capital and state autonomy by prioritizing unrestricted market access of foreign-service providers.

This tension challenges the multilateral trading system and its members to secure any benefits of trade liberalization in services without infringing upon the authority of government to ensure access to basic services by women, men, and children living in poverty. In this regard, it is critical that WTO members engage in detailed and thoughtful analyses of the economic and social effects of liberalization in their services sector before making additional commitments to liberalize. Further, it is important that trade negotiators interpret new trade rules alongside equity and development goals.

Additionally, concrete steps must be taken in order for members to both maximize benefits of current liberalization and formulate future commitments that will prioritize the needs of all. This requires that national economic ministries substantively liase with social ministries in order to better ensure that economic and social needs are met. Unfortunately, GATS and TPRM put pressure on governments to adopt liberalization policies without this requirement. In this regard, the Trade Policy Review Mechanism can be used to better integrate economic and social issues into trade policy-making (Stichele, 1997), given its mandate to improve the quality of debate on issues of relevance to the multilateral trading system.

The implementation of GATS Articles I and XVII as written will erode the autonomy of member-states to address equity and development goals. Given that the GATS negotiations will continue, however, members have the opportunity to influence future negotiations to protect public services. This is particularly important for those countries that have adopted semi-private arrangements for the supply of basic services. For example, members can use the vagueness of the phrase in Article I, "[i]n fulfilling its obligations and commitments under the Agreement, each Member shall take such *reasonable measures as may be available to it* to ensure their observance," (GATT, 1994) to defend their public-services sector.

Therefore, dissolution of state authority in the public-services sector is a possibility, not an inevitability. However, if appropriate attention is not devoted to the conflicting priorities embedded in the new trade arrangements of the multilateral trading system, namely that of the rights of capital versus the regulatory rights of governments to address basic needs, GATS and the TPRM may serve to reinforce uneven development and increase inequality within and between member-states while at the same time formally integrating developing countries into the global economy.

References

Aharoni, Yair. 1997. "Changing Role of Government in Services," in Yair Aharoni, ed. *Changing Poles of State Intervention in Services in an Era of Open International Markets*. Albany: State University of New York Press.

Appadurai, Arjun. 1996. *Modernity at Large: Cultural Dimensions of Globalization*. Minneapolis: University of Minnesota Press.

Benería, Lourdes. 1999. "Global Markets, Gender and the Davos Man," in *Feminist Economics*, 5(3).

Bisnath, Savitri. 2002. "The WTO and the Liberalization of Trade in Services: Development, Equity and Governance." PhD dissertation, Cornell University.

Brookings-Wharton. 2000. "Papers on Financial Services: Comments and Discussion." Washington, D.C.: John Hopkins University Press.

Cuasch, J. Luis and Pablo Spiller. "Managing the Regulatory Process: Design, Concepts, Issues and the Latin America and Caribbean Story." Washington, D.C.: The World Bank.

Elson, Diane. 1998. "The Economic, the Political and the Domestic: Businesses, States and Households in the Organisation of Production," in *New Political Economy*, 3(2): 189–208.

Feketekuty, Geza. 2000. "Assessing and Improving the Architecture of GATS", in Pierre Sauve and Robert M. Stern, eds. *GATS 2000: New Directions in Services Trade Liberalisation*. Washington D.C.: Brookings Institute Press.

Feketekuty, Geza. 1998. "Trade in Services—Bringing Services into the Multilateral Trading System," in Jagdish Bhagwati and M. Hirsch eds. *The Uruguay Round and Beyond*. Michigan: Michigan University Press.

Ferber, Marianne and Julie Nelson eds. 1993. *Beyond Economic Man: Feminist Theory and Economics*. Chicago: The University of Chicago Press.

Fuchs, Gerhard and Andrew M. Koch. 1996. "The Globalisation of Telecommunications and the Issue of Regulatory Reform," in Eleonore Kofman and Gillian Youngs, eds. *Globalization: Theory and Practice*. London: Pinter.

GATT. 1994. *The Results of the Uruguay Round of Multilateral Trade Negotiations: The Legal Text*. Geneva: World Trade Organization.

Gill, Stephen. 2001. "Constitutionalising Inequality." Paper prepared for the conference on "Global Tensions." March 9–10, Cornell University, Ithaca, NY.

Global Water Partnership. 2002. "Dialogue on Effective Water Governance." Stockholm: Sweden.

Hirst, P. and G. Thompson. 1996. *Globalisation in Question: the International Economy and the Possibilities of Governance*. Cambridge: Polity Press.

Hoekman, Bernard. 1994. "Deregulation, Harmonization, and Liberalization: Implications for the International Marketing of Services", in Michel Kostecki, ed. *Marketing Strategies for Services: Globalisation, Client-Orientation, Deregulation*. Oxford: Pergamon Press.

Hoekman, Bernard. 1999. "Toward a more Balanced and Comprehensive Services Agreement." Washington, D.C.: The World Bank.

Hoekman, Bernard M. and Patrick A. Messerlin. 2000. "Liberalising Trade in Services: Reciprocal Negotiations and Regulatory Reform", in Pierre Sauve and Robert M. Stern eds. *GATS 2000: New Directions in Services Trade Liberalisation*. Washington, D.C.: Brookings Institute Press.

Kostecki, M.M. ed. 1994. *Marketing Strategies for Services: Globalisation, Client Orientation, Deregulation.* Oxford: Pergamon Press.

Low, Patrick and Aaditya Mattoo. 1998. "Reform in Basic Telecommunications and the WTO Negotiations: The Asian Experience." Staff Working Paper ERAD9801.WPF. Geneva: World Trade Organization.

Mattoo, Aaditya. 1999. "Developing Countries in the New Round of GATS Negotiations: from a Defensive to a Pro-active Role." Paper presented at the WTO/World Bank Conference on Developing Countries in a Millennium Round, Geneva 20–21 September.

Ostry, Sylvia. 1997. *The Post–Cold War Trading System: Who's on First.* Chicago: The University of Chicago Press.

Prakash, Aseem and Jeffery A. Hart. 1999. "Globalisation and Governance: an introduction", in Aseem Prakash and Jeffery A. Hart, eds. *Globalisation and Governance.* London: Routledge.

Qureshi, Asif H. 1996. *The World Trade Organization: Implementing International Trade Norms.* Manchester: Manchester University Press.

Rees, Judith. 1998. "Regulation and Private Participation in the Water and Sanitation Sector." TAC Background Paper no. 1. Stockholm: Global Water Partnership.

Ruggiero, Renato. 1998. "Toward GATS 2000—a European Strategy." Address given in Brussels to the Conference on Trade in Services, Organised by the European Commission. Geneva: World Trade Organization.

Sauve, Pierre and Robert M. Stern eds. 2000. *GATS 2000: New Directions in Services Trade Liberalisation.* Washington, D.C.: Brookings Institute Press.

Scholte, Jan Aart. 1999. "Globalisation: Prospects for a Paradigm Shift," in Martin Shaw, ed. *Politics and Globalisation: Knowledge, Ethics and Agency.* London: Routledge.

Schott, J. 1994. *The Uruguay Round: An Assessment.* Washington, D.C.: Institute for International Economics.

Shaw, Martin ed. 1999. *Politics and Globalisation: Knowledge, Ethics and Agency.* London: Routledge.

Stephenson, Sherry M. 1999. "Approaches to Liberalizing Services." Policy Research Working paper no. 2107. Washington D.C.: Organization of American States.

———. 2000. "Regional Agreements on Services in Multilateral Disciplines: Interpreting and Applying GATS Article V, in Sherry M. Stephenson, ed. *Services Trade in the Western Hemisphere: Liberalization, Integration and Reform.* Washington D.C.: Brookings Institute Press.

Stichele, Myriam Vander. 1997. "Globalisation, Marginalisation and the WTO." WTO Booklet Series, Vol. 2. Geneva: Transnational Institute.

UNCTAD. 1998. "Strengthening Capacities in Developing Countries to Development their Environmental Services Sector." Background note by the Secretariat. Geneva: UNCTAD.

World Trade Organization. 1998a. *Trading into the Future: Introduction to the WTO.* Geneva: World Trade Organization.

———. 1998b. "Health and Social Services." Background Note by the Secretariat S/C/W/50. Geneva: World Trade Organisation.

———. 1999. "Application of the Necessity Test: Issues for Consideration." Informal Noted by the Secretariat. Working Party on Domestic Regulation. Geneva: World Trade Organisation.

———. 2000. "A Review of Statistics on Trade Flows in Services." Note by the Secretariat, S/C/W/27/Add.1. Geneva: World Trade Organization.

Notes

1. The author wishes to thank David Alonzo-Maizlish, Esq. and Marzia Fontana for helpful comments on an earlier draft of this chapter.
2. The World Trade Organization, the International Monetary Fund, and the World Bank are the multilateral institutions that comprise the "multilateral trading system."
3. See "Economic, Social and Cultural Rights: Liberalization of Trade in Services and Human Rights," Report of the High Commissioner on Human Rights (2000), for a discussion of the links between trade liberalization and human rights.
4. The top 11 exporters of commercial services are: the United States of America, the United Kingdom, France, Germany, Japan, Italy, Spain, the Netherlands, Hong Kong, China, and Belgium-Luxembourg (World Trade Organization, 2000).

5. Freeman is a self-described "advocate of trade in services" in terms of "organizing private sectors around the world" (Brookings-Wharton, 2000).
6. Freeman notes that at that time the phrase "market access" had not been coined. He states that it is a phrase his coalition formulated.
7. The services sector is broken down into several subsectors: business; communication; construction and related engineering; distribution; educational; environmental; financial; health-related and social services; tourism and travel-related services; recreational, cultural and sporting; transport; and other services.
8. The multilateral trading system expects that the current round of negotiations will lead to significant commitments in the subsectors.
9. The "standstill" obligation "effectively prohibits the institution of new controls and binds significant levels of liberalization" in sectors that have no existing restrictions (Schott, 1994: 100).
10. The "built-in" agenda refers to "set timetables for future work" (World Trade Organization, 1998: 44).
11. Article XIX, Negotiation of Specific Commitments.
12. Article XX, Schedules of Specific Commitments.
13. Article II, Most-Favored-Nation Treatment.
14. Article XVI, Market Access and Article XVII, National Treatment.
15. The commitments of the member-states can be accessed at the World Trade Organization Web site (www.wto.org).
16. The distinction between National Treatment and Market Access is unclear given that some market access exceptions also violate national treatment. See Sauve and Stern (2000) and Mattoo (1999) for further discussion.
17. Article XXVIII, Definitions (b) defines "supply" to include the "production, distribution, marketing, sale and delivery of a service" (GATT, 1994).
18. The Annex to GATS notes that Mode 4 does not cover individuals in search of employment in another country, or citizenship and residence requirements (GATT, 1994).
19. Reviews are carried out every other year for the four largest trading areas (defined in terms of world market share, currently the European Union, the United States, Japan, and Canada), every 4 years for the next 16 largest trading nations, and every 6 years for other developing countries, with exceptions for the least developed countries (World Trade Organization, 1998).
20. Economic globalization is characterized by a deepening of markets across some borders, facilitated by a surge in technological innovations centered on information technology and decreases in communication costs. Globalization partially results in an increase in the scope of the market, the harmonization of legal and judicial norms and political and economic systems, as well as an intensification or deepening of the levels of interaction, interconnectedness, and interdependence, albeit uneven, between and within states. In addition, it is often invoked to define a set of processes, such as trade liberalization, that give it its spatial effects. See Prakash and Hart (1999), Scholte (1999), Shaw (1999), Appadurai (1996), and Hirst and Thompson (1996) for further discussion.
21. In their policymaking, trade economists and negotiators tend to compartmentalize "the economic" and "the social" despite the lack of ontological priority between the two. Most recently, feminist economists have been arguing against this artificial distinction (Beneria, 1999; Elson, 1998; and Ferber and Nelson, 1993).
22. The GATT regime did not enjoy this element, and it is arguable whether its lack of enforcement capability served to undermine its credibility, or alternatively will strengthen that of the WTO. As we have recently witnessed, the powerful trading nations continue to defy specific rulings of the Dispute Settlement panel, for example, the foreign sales corporation tax dispute between the European Union and the United States.
23. This often includes social regulation and standards. According to Cuasch and Spiller (1999: 22), "environmental and public health and safety regulations" are in this category.
24. For example, Corporate Europe Observatory and Transnational Institute jointly publish GATSwatch (http://www.gatswatch.org), a bulletin that provides a wealth of information on GATS-related news.
25. The extent to which public services will be affected will depend on the particular arrangements and commitments of each member, and the interpretation of the results of current and future negotiations.

26. Not all members have made specific commitments in these subsectors.
27. Water is a subsector of environmental services.
28. Health care is a subsector of health and social services.
29. The recent attempt by Bolivia to privatize its water sector in Cochbamba resulted in this problem. A subsidiary of a European service company purchased the rights to supply water to residents of Cochbamba. After the purchase the price of water increased by more than 35 percent, effectively making water inaccessible to the poor. The public held mass protests in response and the Government reversed its decision to liberalize in this subsector. The foreign company has sued the Bolivian Government and the case (Aguas del Tunari S.A. v Republic of Bolivia, Case ARB/02/3) is pending. www.pbs.org/frontlineworld/stories/bolivia/timeline.html. It is reasonable to assume that this case is a signal and example of what can happen under the GATS regime.
30. http://www.gwpforum.org/servlet/PSP

CHAPTER 10

Labor Standards, Women's Rights, Basic Needs

Challenges to Collective Action in a Globalizing World

NAILA KABEER

The Debate about Labor Standards

Globalization is a highly complex phenomenon encompassing the increasingly rapid flows of capital, goods, services, peoples, ideas, values, and images across national boundaries, and the greater integration of the global economy. This chapter focuses on two specific and interrelated aspects of this phenomenon—the ongoing globalization of production and the attempted globalization of labor standards—in order to explore a particular set of tensions that have been highlighted by them. These are the tensions among what appear to be a compatible set of social goals, which have been repeatedly endorsed at the international level: labor standards, women's rights, and poverty eradication. The existence of these tensions helps to explain why high levels of global collective action in support of labor standards coexist alongside relative inaction at the national level by those on whose behalf the demand for labor standards is being made.

The first section of this chapter documents recent changes in the international division of labor and their implications for North-South trade. These changes constitute the context in which demands for globally enforced labor standards have arisen. The next section uses the perspectives of women workers in Bangladesh's export-oriented garment industry as a point of entry "from below" into the international discourse on labor standards. It considers their needs and priorities and some of the factors that help to explain their low levels of collective action. The final section of this chapter argues that without some attention to the issue of basic needs, the campaign for global labor standards may end up eroding, rather than promoting, the rights of women workers in the poorer regions of the world's economy.

Changing Patterns of International Trade: The Reconstitution of Comparative Advantage

Textbook economics tells us that in a world of perfect competition, marginal returns to the various factors of production, including different kinds of labor, converge to equality. Market forces ration the use of scarce factors of production by raising their price while simultaneously encouraging the more intensive use of abundant factors by pricing them more cheaply. The logic of the market suggests that workers in areas of relative labor surplus can improve their wage rates by moving to areas of relative labor scarcity, either within national boundaries or across them.

In reality, of course, there are and always have been constraints on the movement of labor. The costs of such movements, formal controls, and informal restrictions are examples in point. Within countries, such constraints gave rise to segmented labor markets, reflecting and reproducing patterns of social inequalities along lines of class, gender, race, caste, and so on. Internationally, they led to the creation of high wage/low wage zones along lines that reflected inequalities in the international economic order. They also resulted in a pattern of international trade in which poorer countries specialized in the production of primary commodities using their abundant supplies of low-wage and unskilled labor, while higher-wage countries specialized in capital-intensive forms of production and the export of manufactured goods.

This pattern of trade began to change dramatically by the second half of the twentieth century, as the result of changes embodied in the processes of globalization. Two changes were particularly significant. The first being the changing technologies of transport and telecommunications, which served to compress time and space across the globe. The second was the dismantling of the regulatory frameworks that provided some degree of national stability in markets for labor and capital in the post-war decades. The result was a dramatic increase in the international mobility of capital. Capital flows in the industrial countries rose from around 5 percent of gross domestic product (GDP) in the early 1970s to around 10 percent in the early 1990s; the equivalent figures for transitional and developing countries were 7 percent and 9 percent (World Bank, 1995).

However, deregulation had less dramatic effects on the international mobility of labor, given that immigration controls remained largely intact. Migration per 1000 population declined from around 6.5 to 4.5 in the industrialized countries and remained static at around 1 elsewhere. Instead, the main effect of deregulation was the erosion of existing forms of social protection for labor within northern welfare states[1] and the "informalization" of labor markets as the concept of regular, full-time employment was replaced by more diverse patterns of work, including outsourcing, contract labor, casual, part-time, and home-based work.

As a result of these changes there has been a massive increase in world trade flows: trade now accounts for 45 percent of the world's GNP compared to 25 percent in 1970 (World Bank, 1995). A great deal of this increase is in manufacturing, which today accounts for 74 percent of world merchandise exports, compared to 59 percent in 1984 (World Trade Organization, 1995). In addition, labor-intensive stages of manufacturing industry have been relocated away from the "fortified enclaves" of formal, highly paid, and organized labor in the north to unprotected labor in their informal economies, and to the poorer, low-wage, labor-surplus economies of the south. The share of manufactures in developing country exports tripled between 1970 and 1990 from 20 percent to 60 percent (World Bank, 1995); 78 percent of exports from South and Southeast Asia now consists of manufactured goods. The decimation of older industries, such as textile and garments, in the OECD countries over the past few decades, and their reappearance in lower-income regions of the world, are particularly visible testimonies to this international reconstitution of comparative advantage.

Changing Discourses in International Trade: From Comparative Advantage to Unfair Advantage

The changing pattern of international trade has also altered the nature of trade relations between richer and poorer countries. In previous decades, trade across large distances was in dissimilar commodities and was consequently complementary in nature (Polanyi, 1957). In the current phase of globalization, however, labor-intensive manufactured goods are being traded by both rich and poor countries, bringing workers in geographically dispersed and economically differentiated locations into direct competition with each other. It is, therefore, not entirely coincidental that this phase has also seen the rise of a new discourse of "ethics" in international trade centered on working conditions in precisely those manufacturing industries in which poorer countries have gained a comparative advantage. A protectionist alliance of northern trade unionists, employers, and populist politicians deploy this new ethical discourse to mobilize public opinion against the indifference of some of the world's wealthiest multinationals to the conditions under which they employ some of the world's poorest workers.

These groups demand that certain minimum labor standards be observed by all multinationals, regardless of where they produce or buy their goods. Along with the core labor standards—freedom of association, the right to collective bargaining, and the banning of forced labor and discrimination—which have been widely endorsed at the international level as fundamental human rights and a shared vision of morality, they also make additional demands concerning hours of work, conditions at work, and "basic needs" standard for wages, rather than the legal minimum that prevails in most countries (Cavanagh, 1997; Bardhan, 2000).

Such standards would certainly improve the well-being of those workers for whom they apply, but they do not entail situations where workers are denied freedom of choice and have not received international endorsement. In addition, there have been demands by the northern labor movement that observation of labor standards be linked to international trade agreements in the form of a "social clause." This would enable the WTO, whose members hold the power to impose sanctions, to displace the ILO, which has traditionally exercised a supervisory function in this area, to take responsibility for the global harmonization of labor standards.

This new discourse of ethics in trade has succeeded in transforming what was once seen as the "comparative advantage" of poorer southern countries (cheap and abundant labor) into an "unfair advantage" (highly exploited labor). It has also been used to justify what (to use the concept formulated by Parkin [1979]) is essentially a form of double "social closure" at the international level: restrictions on the movement of labor out of low-wage economies combined with restrictions on the entry of goods produced by low-wage laborers into international trade.

Neoliberal economists generally oppose these demands. They see global free trade as a win-win solution that will maximize the gains from trade for both poor and rich countries, allowing each to concentrate on their comparative advantage. In addition, attempts to link trade and labor standards have been met with considerable hostility by southern governments who have seen too many examples of powerful countries imposing rules, defining them selectively, and then bending or breaking them when it suits their interests. Indeed, the history of the textile and garment industry is quintessentially a history of such behavior.

Britain was able to nurture its own textile and garment industry at the start of the industrial revolution through an elaborate system of restrictions and duties against textiles from its colonies, including what is now

Bangladesh. In time the U.S. put in place its own protectionist system to promote import substitution and developed an effective system of tariffs and embargoes over the nineteenth century (Ross, 1997). It subsequently joined up with the European producers, with whom it shared a gentleman's agreement to waive all import duties in order to ensure that the textile and apparel trade, the one area of manufacturing in which it was likely to face future competition from the poorer countries, was exempted from the key rules of GATT. This culminated in the Multi-Fiber Arrangement, which essentially controlled 70 percent of world trade in clothing and textiles on highly asymmetrical terms, placing strict limits on what poorer countries could export to the rich but no controls on what richer countries exported to each other.

However, disagreements over labor standards cannot simply be reduced to conflicts over protectionism versus free trade or between capital and labor. The United States government, for instance, is the world's most vigorous champion of free trade, taking sanctions against countries that operate trade barriers, and using its influence within the international financial institutions to press for the opening up of the world's economies to international capital. But it has simultaneously led attempts, supported by the American labor movement, to link trade to labor standards in order to protect American jobs from competition elsewhere.

Resistance to globally enforced labor standards has not only come from Southern governments and employers. Many Southern NGOs, even those working closely with organized labor groups to enhance rights of workers in their countries, have also been opposed to this proposal (Ghosh, 2000). The Third World Network (1996) has queried the impartiality of the WTO in enforcing labor standards in a world characterized by unequal trade relations, pointing out that:

> . . . whatever the theory, only the powerful can take retaliatory measures against the weaker partners and not vice versa [. . .] in the current power structure and relations in the world, all these instruments only work to the advantage of the powerful and the dominant, and make the world more oppressive.

Finally, development economists and research organizations, not known for their neoliberal sympathies, have also opposed attempts to link labor standards and trade agreements (South Centre, 1996; Basu, 1999; Bardhan, 2000; Ghosh, 2000). Singh and Zammit (2000:xv) argue that

> attempts to enforce labor standards through trade sanctions are likely to cause economic harm to most export developing countries, at least in the short to medium term, while doing little or nothing to improve their labor standards.

Indeed, under wholly plausible circumstances, this approach could be seriously counterproductive and reduce standards overall.

The Politics of (Mis)representation in International Trade

A detailed unpacking of the various strands of the arguments used to support or reject global labor standards by constituencies that are themselves internally diverse is beyond the scope of this chapter. Instead, this chapter confines itself to questioning the view that globally enforced labor standards is in the interests of all workers, particularly those who are unable to fight for such standards themselves. It argues that while such views may be genuinely held, they are based on an historical and uncontextualized understanding of what is at stake. An important factor influencing this understanding is the politics of representation that has been deployed in making the case for global labor standards by its supporters. They present their own version of win-win advocacy (Charnowitz, 1987; Cavanagh, 1997) maintaining that workers in the north would benefit from standards that increased the price of exports from late-industrializing countries and that reduced their attractiveness as low-cost production sites for northern investors. Workers in the south would benefit from higher wages and better working conditions, which would, in turn, lead to increases in aggregate demand and employment.

However, the success of such advocacy rests on the portrayal of working conditions in Third World export industries in such grim terms that anyone with a conscience is moved into supporting boycotts, trade sanctions, and other measures, all of which help to create a wider climate of acceptability for the idea of a social clause in trade agreements. The fact that many of the export industries in the south deal with consumer goods has worked to the advantage of this form of advocacy because consumers can be directly mobilized through their purchasing power. I have discussed elsewhere how easily this politics of representation around the rights of labor easily slips into a politics of misrepresentation (Kabeer, 2000).

The characterization of export-production in the Third World as dominated by sweatshops has paid considerable dividends, particularly in the universities of the U.S. where the antisweatshop campaign has been described as "the strongest surge of student activism since the anti-apartheid campaign of the 1980s" (Featherstone and Henwood, 2001). Although the United Students Against Sweatshops emphasizes that its goal is to improve workers' pay and working conditions in offshore factories rather than protect American jobs, there is a danger that a form of advocacy that relies on the terminology of sweatshops to tar all garment factories in poorer countries will lead in time to a more widespread version of the outcome recently reported in Occidental College. Here activists have pressed the college administrators to commission UNITE members in Pennsylvania to produce Occidental T-shirts on the grounds that the American union label provides the best available insurance that apparel is "sweat-free" (Featherstone and Henwood, 2001).

Such campaigns are, by their very nature, blunt instruments. Their success, as their supporters openly acknowledge, rests on their ability to portray Third World factories as "showcases of horrors for the labor abuses sanctioned by the global free trade economy, where child labor, wage slavery, and employer cruelty are legion" (Ross, 1997: 10). There is little mileage in presenting nuanced, balanced, and differentiated accounts of ground-level realities in low-income countries: distinguishing between situations where the problems are largely poverty and underdevelopment and those that entail the flagrant violation of basic human rights. Yet such a distinction is imperative if poor workers in the south are not to be penalized for their poverty or their country's position in the global economic order. The rest of this chapter tries to make such a distinction and asks how it can be used to reconcile the discourse of labor standards with advocacy for women's rights and the goal of global poverty eradication.

Problematizing Women's Work: The Bangladesh Garment Sector

The Rise of a Female Industrial Working Class in Bangladesh

The export-oriented manufacture of garments in Bangladesh began in the late 1970s and expanded rapidly. By the end of the 1990s its contribution to the country's export earnings had gone from around 1 percent in 1982 to approximately 70 percent. Even more remarkable, it created a first generation of female factory workers in a country where, by religion and culture, women had been secluded within the home and denied any form of economic opportunity in the public domain. Bangladesh is part of a region of the world that is characterized by extreme forms of patriarchy. Women are not merely denied access to mainstream economic opportunities, they are also deprived of access to education, health services, and even food, so much so that this region (unlike other parts of the developed and developing world) is characterized by excess levels of female mortality, lower female than male life expectancy and fewer women than men in the overall population. The adversity of its sex ratio makes it part of a region that accounts for what Amartya Sen calls the phenomenon of "the missing women."

There have been some important improvements in the country's situation over the past decade or so. It has moved from military rule to a fragile democracy. Poverty has also gone down, particularly in recent decades, and the country has moved to a position of food self-sufficiency. However, it remains one of the poorest countries in the world with around half of its population living below the poverty line. Even though processes of impoverishment and landlessness in previous decades have driven many women from poorer families to seek work, cultural restrictions on their mobility and the barriers they faced in the marketplace confined them to the most poorly paid and exploitative margins of the informal sector, where they worked as domestic servants, prostitutes, and casual wage laborers.

Given this history of invisibility in the public domain, the overnight emergence of young women onto the streets of the cities of Bangladesh with the advent of the export-oriented garment manufacturing defied all expectations. Current estimates suggest that the country employs around 1.8 million women and has additional direct and indirect employment of around 10 million. The women workers alone, it is estimated, support an additional 7 million people. This was not necessarily an intended effect, but the garment industry appears to have contributed far more to the reduction of poverty through the expansion of women's economic opportunities than the myriad of income-generating projects offered by government and nongovernment organizations (NGOs) to poor women in the past.

Conditions in Bangladesh's Garment Factories: The Perspectives of Women Workers

Studies carried out on the situation of women workers in Bangladesh's garment industry have made it clear that there are many aspects of factory work that women workers find problematic. Some of these represented violations of their rights as workers, others their rights as women, and still others their rights as human beings. However, many of these issues are not captured in the wider debates about labor standards. As Dannecker (2002:124) concluded on the basis of her research: "the complaints of the women focused on other issues than the ones discussed in the literature or mentioned by union or NGO representatives as the most significant problems."

For instance, wages cropped up frequently in women workers' accounts, but not necessarily in relation to the minimum wage for the sector. Indeed, it was the higher levels of wages prevailing in the garment sector, relative to most other jobs available to women, which explained their entry into the industry. The more frequent complaint related to irregularity of payments. Employers are not legally obliged to pay monthly wages on the same day each month, but there is a legal limit to delays in payment that many employers clearly violated. Wages were sometimes delayed by months (often because employers themselves faced delays in payments by buyers), and often cut if a worker arrived late to work.

Overtime was also a source of dissatisfaction, but not always for the same reasons. For married women it was its compulsory nature. Given a choice, many would have preferred to go home to attend to their children or to their domestic responsibilities. For unmarried women, on the other hand, working overtime was often welcomed as a means of supplementing their wages. Their dissatisfaction rose from the fact that overtime was seldom shown on their time cards, and hence there was a lack of clarity regarding the rate of remuneration.

In terms of health and safety, responses were largely about long-term effects of prolonged working hours in closed conditions on their health, rather than specific concerns. A great deal of attention has been given by outside observers to the issue of toilets, but for the women themselves, the number of toilets took second place to the fact that there were restrictions on their ability to use them. Many reported that their factories permitted workers only two toilet breaks a day; the key was kept with the supervisor to ensure enforcement. In some factories, women's access to drinking water was monitored to ensure they did not need to use the toilet too frequently. As Dannecker (2002:133) points out: "An increase in numbers of toilets per factory would not solve the problem described by the workers, since [. . .] the actual number is not the problem but the access."

Even though sexual harassment did occur in the factories, it was mentioned far more often in relation to the behavior on the streets than within the factory (Kabeer, 2000; Zohir and Paul-Majumder, 1996). Indeed, security on the streets appeared to be one of the most pressing problems women workers had to face. While Dannecker's study does note incidents of sexual harassment on the factory floor, she also cautions against the tendency in the literature to always perceive Bangladeshi women in a passive role with regard to sexuality. Some women engaged in romantic liaisons on the factory floor, others found husbands, and still others used their sexuality to promote their own interests within the workplace, forms of behavior that gave rise to a public perception of garment workers as "loose."

Child-care issues also emerged as a problem for women workers. Around half of the women in the garment industry were, or had been, married and between 40 and 50 percent had children. Some women left their children in their villages with their parents; others left them at home alone or in the care of older siblings or neighbors; still others brought them into the factories to work as "helpers" (Bissell and Sobhan, 1996). According to one survey, around 80 percent of children working in the factories were found to have relatives within the same factory (Paul-Majumder and Chowdhury, 1993). Employers claimed they only hired children at the insistence of their more skilled workers. One of the side effects of the sacking of children from garment factories, in the wake of threatened U.S. legislation against imports that used child labor, was that many women workers who had no alternative child support also lost their jobs.[2]

Other disadvantages highlighted by women workers were more cultur- ally specific in nature. They included anxieties about their reputation in the wider community; discomfort at having to work alongside men; the lack of provision of a place to pray; and so on. However, one factor that systematically emerges in research on working conditions is the disrespect meted out to women by their supervisors. As Dannecker (2002:135) notes, "all the interviewed women articulated their helplessness with regard to the way the supervisors addressed them, talked with them and treated them." Such disrespect has a gendered dimension; managers and supervi- sors are far more cautious toward male workers. For instance, Zohir and Paul-Majumder (1996) found that though 60 percent of male and female workers expressed satisfaction with their jobs, men were more likely to pri- oritize the level of wages as their reason for job satisfaction (perhaps be- cause many more of them were in the higher-skill categories), whereas women prioritized the behavior of management. Indeed, women were twice as likely as men to mention management behavior as their main rea- son for job satisfaction.

However, these problems notwithstanding, my own and other studies suggest that the majority of women workers rated their access to employ- ment in the garment factories in largely positive terms. They valued the satisfaction of a "proper" job and the opportunity to earn a living wage, compared to the casualized and poorly paid forms of employment that had previously been their only options. They also enjoyed the new social networks their employment made possible, the greater voice they enjoyed in household decision-making, the respect they received from other family members, including their husbands, an enhanced sense of self-worth and self-reliance as well as greater personal freedom and autonomy (Amin et al., 1997; Dannecker, 2002; Kabeer, 2000; Kibria, 1995 and 1998; Newby, 1998; Zohir and Paul-Chowdhury, 1996). Indeed, in a recent participatory consultation of the urban poor by the United Nations Development Pro- gramme, garment factories and NGOs were the only formal institutions that were reported to have a positive influence in the lives of the poor (Nabi et al., 1999).

Dannecker's (2002:255) conclusion on the basis of her investigation into women's perspectives on their working conditions was that

> . . . women workers do not romanticize their jobs, marriages, or other aspects of their lives. They are aware of the exploitation, that employment is poorly paid, that they are treated badly inside the factories and unfairly in many dif- ferent ways. Nevertheless, they are also certain that it has given them material and personal benefits, an aspect often neglected in the literature.

This paradox of broadly positive subjective evaluations of work in a con- text of negative objective conditions at work is not unique to Bangladesh.

It is to be found in other parts of the developing world. It is evident, for instance, in the conclusion arrived at by Wolf (1992: 256) on the basis of her detailed largely qualitative analysis of women workers in Java:

> the workers in my study are not likely to agree with previous researchers' judgments [. . .] that factory work is detrimental and alienating. [. . .] This, of course, does not mean that they are not aware of their exploitation. Javanese factory workers recognise that factory employment is poorly paid, unprotected, and unfair in those senses, yet they are also certain that it has brought them both material and personal benefits that few would give up.

It also characterized the experience of industrialization for women workers in the north. As Fraser (1997: 230) points out, feminists who equate the emergence of capitalist employment in Europe with "wage slavery" miss out on the contradictory and gender-specific implications of such employment in the lives of workers:

> To be sure, it was painfully experienced in just that way by some early-nineteenth century proletarianized (male) artisans and yeoman farmers who were losing not only tangible property in tools and in land but also prior control over their work. But their response was contextually specific and gendered. Consider, by way of contrast, the very different experience of young single women who left farms—with open-ended work hours, pervasive parental supervision, and little autonomous personal life—for mill towns, where intense supervision in the mill was combined with relative freedom from supervision outside it, as well the increased autonomy of personal life conferred by cash earnings. From their perspective, the employment contract was a liberation.

Fraser also makes the important point that then, as now, factory employment was just one sphere in the totality of women workers' lives. Other spheres included the consumer market to which their wages bought them entry, but also the domestic sphere, where they were expected to perform the unpaid work of social reproduction. In this arena particularly, itself permeated by power and inequality, women's wages functioned "as a resource and a leverage" (p. 230), helping them to transform the nature of the patriarchal contract at home. Research with women workers in the Bangladesh garment industry suggests that, in a different time and a different place, another group of newly proletarianized young women are attempting to undertake a similar transformation.

Therefore, the question that needs to be addressed is: What does the demand for global labor standards, as currently defined, offer young women who seek to escape the highly personalized tyranny of the patriarchal contract at home, to the somewhat more impersonal tyranny of the patriarchal contract in the workplace? From the perspective of those in the wealthier countries of the world, one rationale for the demand for global labor standards is to prevent what is widely referred to as "the race to the welfare bottom." But what is the rationale from the perspective of those who are already at the welfare bottom?

Labor Standards and Women's Rights: Global Discourses, Local Realities

One answer may be that such labor standards provide the end goal to which workers aspire. A second may be that it helps to overcome inequities in the labor market. As feminist economists have argued, the existence of a statutory minimum wage is particularly important for women who have less information about the market than men and are much more likely to underestimate their own worth (Elson, 1999). In addition, maternity benefits and child-care facilities help to offset preexisting distortions in market forces that do not factor in the cost of women's unpaid work in caring for their children and family. These are sound arguments, but they apply to all women workers, not just to those in the traded sectors, which is where global campaigns have focused their energies.

Moreover most countries, including Bangladesh, have various commitments to labor standards within their national legislation. The Industrial Relations Ordinance of 1969 provides legal protection for the right to form trade unions, and Bangladesh has ratified the core ILO Conventions 87 and 98, which give workers the basic rights of freedom of association and the right to organize and bargain collectively. The country also has legislation on minimum wage, child-care facilities, and other practices. Most of these are not observed in practice, but they are certainly far-reaching enough to constitute a starting point for workers' struggles to improve their conditions at work.

By contrast, labor standards that are imposed from outside, which take no account of what is feasible, possible, or desirable from the point of view of the workers they are meant to benefit, and that are enforced by the more powerful nations of the world, should not be confused with the promotion of workers rights. Rights entail self-determination; they express self-determination and contribute to its expression. This means that workers must be allowed to assess the trade-offs to different courses of action—on an *informed* basis—and make their decisions accordingly, since they are the ones who will have live with the consequences.

In his history of the English working class E. P. Thompson made the point that the working class did not simply "rise like the sun at an appointed time. It was present at its own making" (Thompson, 1963, cited in Singh and Zammit, 2000:37). It took workers in Britain and other industrialized countries several decades of struggle before they won the right to engage in collective action to improve their working conditions. If women workers in the poorer countries of the world are to engage in similar struggles to transform themselves from an isolated fraction of the labor force in their countries into an organized section of the labor movement, they too must be present "at their own making." However, these attempts will reflect their own priorities and constraints at a particular point of time: priorities determine the willingness to take action; constraints determine the form this action takes and what it is able to achieve.

Translating Standards into Rights: Voice and Organization

In the Bangladesh context, as far as priorities go, many aspects of their working conditions that violate women's sense of justice have been noted. Yet there has been no large-scale mobilization on women's part to translate this shared sense of injustice into rights at work. Hostility of employers to the trade unions is one obvious reason for this. However, employers' efforts to suppress union activity has been made far easier by the failure of the trade unions themselves to take women workers' concerns seriously. Trade unionism is over 100 years old in the region and most garment workers are aware of their existence. However, few are members. This is not a purely gender-specific phenomenon: less than 5 percent of male workers belong to trade unions. Rather, it reflects what trade unions represent in the context of South Asia generally.

Trade unions in the South Asian context have strong links with the major political parties.[3] They act as the industrial appendage of their political parties rather than as representatives of workers' interests. As far as women workers are concerned, not only are most male trade unionists largely indifferent to their needs and priorities as workers, they also tend to reproduce the norms and attitudes that maintain social, including gender, hierarchies in society and at work (Dannecker, 2002). It is not accidental that trade unions are a largely formal sector phenomenon in a region where the overwhelming majority of workers are in the informal sector. Breman (1996: 247) has described the attitudes of Indian trade unions toward such workers as one of "indifference, rising almost to enmity" underpinned by the "fear that pressure from below would lead to gradual erosion of the rights gained during a long struggle by the protected labor." Since the majority of women are in the informal sector, such exclusionary behavior has markedly gendered outcomes.

More responsive to the needs and rights of women workers are various nongovernmental organizations that have sought to provide secure, low-cost residential facilities for women workers (Nari Uddug Kendra), and community-based day-care centers for their children (Uthsao). In addition Phulki, a women's organization, has worked with employers to introduce child-care facilities in a number of factories, winning their support and contributions through a combination of moral arguments (employers' obligation), legal arguments (the existence of legislation that requires factories employing more than a certain number of women workers to provide child-care facilities) and, perhaps most effectively from the employers' point of view, through the "business case"—namely reduced absenteeism and higher productivity among mothers who would otherwise be concerned about their children.[4]

Further, although conventional trade unionism may have failed workers in general, and women workers in particular, new kinds of labor organizations based within the community and offering a wider range of support services, including legal literacy, are emerging. The Bangladesh Independent Garment Workers Union Federation, newly founded and funded by USAID, is the best resourced of these, but there are others, such as Kormojibi Nari, which is affiliated with left-wing parties that have come to realize the significance of gender in their work. As a result of these efforts, there are many more examples of collective action, including sporadic strikes, "downing of tools," and collective bargaining by women workers, than in the early years of the industry in Bangladesh. More recently, Nari Uddug Kendra has taken the initiative to bring together twenty-two organizations, including trade unions, research and nongovernmental organizations, and human rights activists, to help protect and promote the rights of women workers, and to ensure that their voices are heard in discussions about the industry's future. Nevertheless, it remains the case that mobilization by women workers remains sporadic, limited, and uneven.

Translating Needs into Rights: Voice and Exit

Although the failure of the trade union movement to represent the interests of women workers is one reason why women have failed to mobilize around labor standards, there are also other deeper constraints, rooted in the nature of underdevelopment in Bangladesh, and in the organization of gender relations. Like other low-income, labor-abundant economies, Bangladesh faces a stark trade-off between the quantity of employment it can generate for its population and the quality of this employment. Even though remittances from its workers abroad form an important source of foreign exchange, international migration is a limited option as long as immigration controls remain intact.

The trade-off is more differentiated at the level of individuals. Organized workers have been able to improve their standards at work *and* retain their jobs, by excluding less privileged workers. The fact that the minimum wage in some sectors in Bangladesh is more than double its per capita GNP, and several multiples of what prevails in the informal sector, is evidence of their success. However, those who have been excluded through various forms of discrimination and social closure, including those exercised by organized workers, face a harsh trade-off between the opportunity to work and improved conditions at work.

Women workers have therefore been slow to organize because of their fear of losing jobs in a society in which, as women, they have very few economic opportunities (Dannecker, 2002). Traditionally denied access to paid work in the public domain, it has been the garment industry that has provided them with their first entry into the formal labor market. In an era when the male breadwinner model is breaking down under the pressures of poverty, households are increasingly looking to women's economic contributions as an aspect of their livelihood strategies. Further, for women themselves, the options outside the garment industry are far more bleak. Despite their dissatisfaction with many aspects of their jobs, they would be reluctant to jeopardize the concrete gains they have made in the present for the uncertain gains of the future that the struggle for rights might bring. They know very well that for every woman who is prepared to fight for better conditions at work, there is another who is prepared to take her place on more acquiescent terms.

This reveals a major flaw in the way that labor standards are being posed in current debates. The focus is almost entirely on the traded sectors of southern countries, which are either conflated with the whole economy of the country or else treated in isolation from the rest of the economy. Comparisons are made between the wages that women earn in these industries and the prices their products sell for in richer countries, or else with the wages earned by workers in the equivalent sector in richer countries. Yet neither of these prices are the main influence on the labor market decisions of women workers in Bangladesh. It is the wages that prevail in the other jobs available to them, and the implications of not having a job that exercise the greatest influence. Consequently, it is conditions and options prevailing in the wider economy, rather than those in the garment sector, that will determine the extent of the risk that women are prepared to take.

Translating Standards into Rights: Toward Inclusive Citizenship

The successful implementation of global labor standards will most certainly lead to an upward harmonization of working conditions, but at a price. Many of Bangladesh's smaller factories would go out of business, thousands of jobs would be lost, and a large number of families would sink back into poverty. What would remain would be reduced industry, but one with globally acceptable labor standards. What would this imply for workers, including women workers, elsewhere in the economy? As Zadek (2000) has suggested, there are three alternative scenarios that might prevail: the "oasis" scenario (improvements of conditions for select groups of workers in specific consumer-sensitive industries); the "desert" scenario (pressure for labor codes does not lead to any significant improvements, but their implementation undermines government regulation); and the "mecca" scenario (consumer pressure and codes of conduct reinforce statutory regulation, leading to a sustained improvement in labor standards, nationally and internationally).

On the basis of the past history of the region, the oasis scenario seems the most plausible outcome. Indeed, it has existed for a number of years in the form of privileges and entitlements enjoyed by the organized sector, the product of collective action by largely male workers for a male-dominated formal sector. There is little evidence that these benefits spread to the rest of the economy. On the contrary, as noted earlier, the organized sector deliberately sought to exclude informal sector workers on grounds that they would bid down wages and erode their privileges.

The implications of the analysis here suggests the need to move away from the narrow preoccupation with labor standards in the traded sector—a very small percentage of the workforce in poorer countries—to labor conditions in the wider economy, which determine the willingness of workers, all workers, to stand up for their rights. If the struggle for better working conditions has become interdependent at the global level, it is certainly interdependent at the local. The struggle for labor standards needs to be broadened and made more inclusive through the institution of a universal "social floor" (Singh and Zammit, 2000) so that all workers, men as well as women, urban as well as rural, formal as well as informal, are able to organize around their rights without having to jeopardize their basic livelihoods.

A social floor in Bangladesh would, at a minimum, cover the basic needs of food and health. It could be operationalized by building on and improving existing social security measures, including employment guarantee schemes, food-for-work programs, public distribution systems, and low-cost basic health insurance. It could be partially financed by expanding the national tax to GDP ratio.[5] However, given the extremely low per capita incomes that prevail in the country, some degree of redistribution at the international level would be essential. A global social fund, administered through global contributions and taxes, appears to be an obvious solution to ensure equitable global social policy.

The institution of a universal "social floor" in Bangladesh—and other poor countries—would have a number of very clear benefits. From the national point of view, it would combine economic considerations (making the workforce more competitive internationally) with poverty concerns (meeting basic needs). From the employers' point of view, it would represent an investment in the productivity of their workforce, the costs of which they would share with the wider society. From the point of view of the poor, it would mean not having to sacrifice their dignity and self-respect in order to earn a living.

And finally, from the point of view of women, it would have implications for both their status and agency. It would acknowledge their status as citizens by making their claim to security independent of their relationships within the family (where they tend to be treated as dependants of men), and in the marketplace (where there was no recognition of their unpaid work in the home). Further, it would promote their agency as citizens by giving recognition to the fact that "voice" and "exit" are intrinsically related in the struggle for rights.

Entitlement to basic security would give women the leverage to renegotiate the patriarchal contract within the family, a leverage that they have otherwise had to acquire through participation in paid work in highly discriminatory labor markets. It would also strengthen their bargaining power vis-à-vis their employers, providing them with resources to fall back on, should their struggle for rights threaten to jeopardize their jobs. Without a credible exit option, women are far less likely to exercise "voice" in defense of their rights either at work or in the home.

From the perspective of multinational companies, wage-based comparative advantage might still lead them to invest in the poorer, labor-abundant companies of the world, but they would no longer face as compliant a labor force as they had in the past. We might even see an upward harmonization of wages and working conditions, but based on push factors from below rather than pull factors from above.

Conclusion: Social Policies for the Working Poor in Poor Countries

One of the major challenges posed by globalization is to find ways to support working men and women in their struggle for rights so that countries do not become locked in a race to the welfare bottom. This challenge is made more imperative by the prospect of intensified competition. However, the imposition of labor standards, which bear little relation to the conditions prevailing within a national economy, and hence to its capacity to finance such standards, is not a solution that is conducive to reducing poverty in poorer countries and meeting the basic needs of its workforce. Without some degree of redistribution from rich to poor, from capital to labor, particularly less privileged forms of labor, and from north to south, labor standards will merely generate unemployment in the poorer parts of the world.

The argument for a global "social floor," funded by global social funds, is the contemporary version of the argument that gave rise to national social policies in Europe in an earlier era of capitalism: As Esping-Andersen (1990) puts it,

> When workers are completely market-dependent, they are difficult to mobilise for solidaristic action. Since their resources mirror market inequalities, divisions emerge between the "ins" and the "outs," making labor-movement formation difficult. Decommodification strengthens the workers and weakens the absolute authority of the employer.

Decommodification, through the institution of collective social provision—the foundation of European welfare states—rescued workers from the status of commodities, reliant only on their ability to sell their labor to meet their basic needs.

These provisions are now under threat. As globalization erodes the capacity of the welfare states to maintain their own labor standards, they too face a version of the dilemma of "exploitation versus exclusion" outlined for Bangladesh. Van Parijs (1996) has pointed out that social policy in Europe had the dual objectives of bringing down unemployment, perceived as the major form of exclusion, and enforcing labor standards (minimum wages, etc.) in order to reduce exploitative conditions at work. Now, however, as European economies are subject to increasing international competition, they find that "the more [they] do to improve the material situation of the poorest among the workers, the scarcer the jobs become, and the more people there are who are deprived of the privilege of having one."

Apply this basic dilemma to poor, labor-abundant economies in which women have historically been denied access to employment, and locate these economies in the same globalizing world, and it becomes even sharper. If the principle of decommodification is to be defended today, if workers are to be treated as more than just commodities to be traded in the marketplace, social policies will clearly have to go global. But they will also have to be constructed "bottom-up." The institution of a "social floor," tailored to the conditions prevailing in different countries, and adjusted upward as these conditions improve, would help to protect workers from the worst insecurities of international market forces, without making unrealistic demands on poorer countries. In the North it may contribute to the willingness of workers to moderate protectionist demands to protect their jobs; in the South it would increase the reserve price of labor, and the ability to bargain for better standards at work. The core labor rights to voice, organization, and collective action—cornerstones of the right to self-determination—rest on workers' confidence that the exercise of these basic rights will not jeopardize their ability to meet their basic needs.

References
Amin, S., I. Diamond, R. T. Naved, and M. Newby. 1998. "Transition to Adulthood of Female Garment Factory Workers in Bangladesh." *Studies in Family Planning*, 29(22): 185–200.

Bardhan, P. 2000. "Social Justice in the Global Economy: Governance and Policy Issues." ILO Social Policy Lecture, September 1–6, University of the Western Cape, South Africa. http://www.ilo.org/public/english/bureau/inst/papers/sopolecs/bardhan/

Basu, K. 1999. "International Labor Standards and Child Labor." *Challenge*, 42(5): 80–93.

Bissell, S. and B. Sobhan. 1996. "Child Labour and Education Programming in the Garment Industry of Bangladesh: Experience and Issues." UNICEF: Dhaka.

Breman, J. 1996. *Footloose Labour. Working in India's Informal Economy.* Cambridge: Cambridge University Press.

Cavanagh, J. 1997. "The Global Resistance to Sweatshops," in A. Ross, ed. *No Sweat: Fashion, Free Trade and the Rights of Garment Workers.* London and New York: Verso.

Charnowitz, S. 1987. "The Influence of International Labour Standards on the World Trading Regime. A Historical Overview." *International Labor Review*, 126(5): 565–584.

Dannecker, P. 2002. *Between Conformity and Resistance: Women Garment Workers in Bangladesh.* University Press: Dhaka.

Elson, D. 1999. "Labor Markets as Gendered Institutions: Equality, Efficiency, and Empowerment Issues." in *World Development,* 27 (3): 611–627.

Esping-Andersen, G. 1990. *The Three Worlds of Welfare Capitalism.* Polity Press: Cambridge.

Featherstone, L. and D. Henwood. 2001. "Clothes Encounters. Activists and Economists Clash Over Sweatshops." *Lingua Franca,* March.

Fraser, N. 1997. *Justice Interruptus: Critical Reflections on the "Post-Socialist" Condition.* London and New York: Routledge.

Ghosh, J. 2000. "Rules of International Economic Integration and Human Rights." Background chapter for the Human Development Report, UNDP: New York.

Harriss-White, B. 2001. "Work and Social Policy with Special Reference to Indian Conditions." Paper presented at the UNRISD Workshop on Social Policy in a Development Context, Stockholm, September 23–24, 2000.

Kabeer, N. 2000. *The Power to Choose. Bangladeshi Women and Labour Market Decisions in London and Dhaka.* London and New York: Verso Press.

Kibria, N. 1995a. "Culture, Social Class and Income Control in the Lives of Women Garment Workers in Bangladesh." *Gender and Society* 9(3): 289–309.

———. 1995b. "Becoming a Garment Worker. The Mobilisation of Women into the Garments Factories of Bangladesh." UNRISD Occasional Chapter no. 9. UNRISD: Geneva.

Nabi, R., D. Datta, S. Chakrabarty, M. Begum and N. J. Chaudhury. 1999. "Consultation with the Poor. Participatory Poverty Assessment in Bangladesh." NGO Working Group on the World Bank. Dhaka: Bangladesh.

Newby, M .H. 1998. "Women in Bangladesh: A Study of the Effects of Garment Factory Work on Control over Income and Autonomy." Ph.D. dissertation, University of Southampton. Southampton.

Parkin, F. 1979. *Marxism and Class Theory: a Bourgeois Critique.* Oxford: Tavistock Publications.

Paul-Majumder, P. and J. H. Chowdhury. 1993. "Child Workers in the Garment Industry of Bangladesh." Associates for Community and Population Research: Dhaka. Mimeo.

Polanyi, K. 1957. *The Great Transformation. The Political and Economic Origins of Our Time.* Boston: Beacon Press.

Ross, A. 1997. "Introduction," in *No Sweat: Fashion, Free Trade and the Rights of Garment Workers.* A. Ross, ed. New York and London: Verso.

Singh, A. and A. Zammit. 2000. "The Global Labour Standards Controversy. Critical Issues for Developing Countries." Geneva: South Centre.

South Centre. 1996. "Liberalization and Globalization: Drawing Conclusions for Development." Geneva: South Centre.

Third World Network. 1996. "Barking up the Wrong Tree: Trade and Social Clause Links." http://www.twnside.org.sg/south/twn/title/tree-ch.htn

van Paijs, P. 1996. "Basic Income and the Two Dilemmas of the Welfare State." *Political Quarterly*, 61(1): 63–66.

Wolf, D. L. 1992. *Factory Daughters: Gender, Household Dynamics and Rural Industrialisation in Java.* Berkeley: University of California.

World Bank. 1995. *World Development Report: Workers in an Integrating World.* London and New York: Oxford University Press.

Zadek, S. 2000. *Ethical Trade Futures.* London: New Economics Foundation.

Zohir, S. C. and P. Paul-Majumder. 1996. "Garment Workers in Bangladesh: Economic, Social and Health Conditions." Research Monograph 18. Dhaka: Bangladesh Institute of Development Studies.

Notes

1. These changes are less significant in the poorer parts of the world where social protection measures only ever applied to a very small proportion of the labor force.
2. The issue of child-care support is discussed on p. 181.
3. See Harriss-White (2001) for description of situation in India.
4. Suraiya Haque, personal communication.
5. The GDP ratio is at present shockingly low at around 10 percent compared to 15–20 percent prevailing in the rest of the region.

CHAPTER 11

Contesting Global Trade Rules

*Social Movements and
the World Trade Organization*

MARC WILLIAMS

Introduction

The end of the Uruguay Round of multilateral trade negotiations ushered in the World Trade Organization (WTO) as the institutional nexus of the world trading system. From the outset, the increased scope of the WTO compared with its predecessor, the General Agreement on Tariffs and Trade (GATT), attracted sustained criticism from social-movement representatives. This continuing focus on the WTO, intense scrutiny of its activities, and a concerted effort to alter its agenda-setting and decision-making processes by social-movement activists have transformed the political context of global trade talks. The primary aim of this chapter is not to assess the impact of social-movement actors on the world trading system, but rather to explore one of the ways in which these actors affect the search for a regulatory framework for world trade.

The increasing politicization of world trade results from underlying tensions generated by the processes of globalization. As used here, globalization refers to a material and normative process. It is both a deepening of global economic integration, and a reconstruction of ideological frameworks of normalization and resistance. The political contest over the WTO thus arises in the context of an evolving global political economy, understood as a set of material and ideational practices.

Two tensions created by the shifting context of globalization provide parameters for the discussion that follows. One set of tensions arises from the impact of globalization on the nation-state. This is a contested issue with some analysts insisting that the state retains its significance with limited changes to autonomy and sovereignty whereas for others the state is in retreat and is being supplanted by forms of supranational governance. It is not necessary to subscribe to the "retreat of the state thesis" to note the transformation of sovereignty and state autonomy attendant on the processes of globalization. The effects of globalization are uneven, and states remain central. However, a focus exclusively, or even largely, on nation-states forecloses much of the relevance in contemporary international relations.

It is within this evolving framework that social movements have come to prominence in the practice of global politics. Within global political economy, globalization has generated conflicts among state and nonstate actors, and instigated a search for regulatory frameworks to lessen the impact of globalizing processes. The process of internationalizing national economies creates a search for new forms of transnational governance and regulation. Central to this process is the rise of social movements, linking civil society across national boundaries and thus actively shaping and reshaping international politics.

The expansion of the multilateral trading system creates another set of tensions. The extension of trade rules into new areas has reinvigorated the historical conflict between domestic interest groups supportive of trade liberalization and those groups intent on protecting national and sectional interests from further economic liberalization. Further, the strengthening of the international trade regime provides the political space in which social-movement activists have sought to challenge the liberal ideology of the hegemonic discourse on trade policy.

The World Trade Organization has emerged as one of the key structures of global governance in international political economy. As a successor to the GATT, the WTO widens and deepens global regulation of international trade and payments. It extends GATT disciplines into areas previously governed by protectionist devices in the post-war global trade regime (i.e., agriculture and textiles), and brings new issues such as intellectual property rights, services, and investment measures under regulatory control. The WTO's mandate brings it into conflict with a range of social-movement activists, representing consumer, development, labor, and environmental interests. The creation of the WTO, its mandate to further liberalize trade, and the apparent shift in regulatory authority from the national to international level, increases insecurities about the impact of globalization.

This chapter explores social-movement activism directed at the WTO. It charts the developments that have led social movements to contest world trade rules. The first section traces how the creation of the WTO as an institutional venue transformed the politics of the global regulation of trade, and as a consequence provides a site of contestation for competing groups and perspectives. The chapter next charts the criticisms made of the WTO by social-movement activists. This section focuses on the social-movement actors engaged in trying to influence the WTO through engagement strategies, rather than on those who adopt a rejectionist stance (Williams and Ford, 1999). This discussion focuses on demands for procedural reforms. The impact of social-movement activities on the WTO is examined in the following section. Consideration is given to the political significance of social-movement activities for the ability of the organization to perform its core functions.

The WTO and Global Governance

This section assesses the role played by the WTO in global governance through an analysis of the WTO as a regulatory instrument within the world trading system. To understand the importance of this institution in the international trade regime, it is necessary to examine two separate but related issues. The first concerns the organizational characteristics of the WTO that is, its key organizational features and the ways in which they enable or constrain its ability to influence member-states and outcomes in the world trading system. The second issue concerns the implicit and explicit normative framework inscribed in the WTO. International organizations embody and promote a specific set of values, and these value preferences constitute a key aspect of the political context within which global institutions operate.

The WTO: Scope and Domain

The WTO, like its predecessor the GATT, performs three key functions for the world trading system. First, it is the legal and institutional foundation of the world trading system. It is a legal agreement specifying the rights and obligations of its members. The agreements establishing the WTO, and subsequent decisions of the organization, form part of international economic law. Further, the WTO stands at the apex of the plethora of bilateral and multilateral trade agreements in the global economy. The legitimacy of other trade agreements depend on the extent to which they are compatible with the framework established by the WTO. Through its provision of rules, norms, and principles, the WTO is the main instrument designed by nation-states for the governance of the multilateral trading system.

Second, the WTO provides a forum for multilateral trade negotiations. The organization, itself the outcome of a round of multilateral trade

negotiations, presides over the process through which further trade liberalization is achieved. Negotiations under the auspices of the WTO specify
the principal contractual obligations determining trade negotiations and
trade legislation. Moreover, the Trade Policy Renewal Mechanism (TPRM)
facilitates the evolution of trade relations and policy through its surveillance of the policies of WTO member-states.

Third, the WTO performs the vital function of dispute resolution. The
Dispute Settlement Understanding (DSU) provides the machinery for set-
tling members' differences regarding rights and obligations. As a center for
the settlement of disputes, the WTO contributes to the stability and further evolution of the world trading system, since liberalization will not
take place in the absence of effective dispute settlement procedures. The
WTO also consists of a series of interlocking legal agreements, and (with
the exception of the Plurilateral Agreements) membership requires acceptance of these agreements as a single undertaking. Their breadth and
range, coupled with the requirement of a single undertaking, exemplify the
scope and complexity of the WTO. It is thus evident that the WTO impacts
on a wide range of policy sectors of considerable salience for national and
transnational actors.

In this context, the rules governing decision-making and the informal
practices that evolve in the Organization become issues of political significance. Although decision-making is by consensus, the dominant trading
nations wield the most influence in the WTO. The chief decision-making
body is the Ministerial Conference, comprising all 144 members of the Organization. The Ministerial Meetings often result in decisions on many issues covered by the WTO agreements. Since it meets every two years, it has
delegated its competence to the General Council which consists of all WTO
members, is the highest decision-making body in the interval between Ministerial Conferences. The General Council also acts as the dispute settlement
body and the trade-policies review body. The organizational structure of
the WTO is completed by three councils, each with a functional area of specialization, various committees, and a number of working groups and working
parties.

The WTO represents elements of continuity with the postwar trading
regime established by the GATT. Both organizations are based on the same
four key principles: nondiscrimination, reciprocity, transparency, and
multilateral cooperation. Nevertheless, the creation of the WTO transformed the management of world trade in three crucial respects. First, it
engineered a shift from trade liberalization based on tariff concessions
(shallow or negative integration) to discussions of domestic policies, institutional practices, and regulations (deep or positive integration). Second,
it constructed a new agenda that expanded the scope of trade liberalization

policy (through the inclusion of services, trade-related intellectual property rights, and domestic [nontrade] policies), and changed the character of negotiations from a focus on bargaining over products to negotiations over policies that shape the conditions of competition. Third, it initiated a movement toward policy harmonization, for example, in the areas of subsidies, trade-related investment measures, and services.

These changes essentially redefine the relationship between national authorities and the multilateral trading system, and heralds a shift from embedded liberalism to neoliberalism. This movement is not complete, and is by no means irreversible, but the transformation of the institutional basis of the world trading system, from the negative integration sanctioned under the GATT to the positive integration envisaged in the WTO, defines a movement in the form of liberalism underpinning global economic governance.

The WTO's Normative Framework

The WTO (and the GATT before it) is founded on liberal economic principles. The dominant position of liberal economic thought in academia and policy-making circles serves to normalize this orientation and renders this bias invisible. The contention herein is neither that liberal economics is a homogenous discipline nor that its analysis and prescriptions are incorrect. I am not concerned with the truth or falsity of liberal economic analysis, and space prohibits any discussion of different approaches to economic theory within the liberal economic perspective. The key point is to indicate the extent to which the values embedded within the WTO support certain discursive practices and marginalize particular values and orientations. In other words, I argue that the WTO represents a specific mobilization of bias in support of neoliberal economic policies.

The WTO is committed to the promotion of a liberal trading order. Its policies are predicated on an assumption that trade is better than no trade and that barriers to trade are harmful to national and international welfare. However, the WTO member-states do not always act in accordance with the prescriptions of trade theory, and this gives rise to a number of disputes. The WTO, like the GATT, remains an organization in pursuit of managed trade, rather than being a free trade institution. Many critics confuse its economic rationale with the policies it pursues. In the preceding section I argued that the WTO represents a specific mixture of national interests (protectionism) and international interests (free trade). This discussion on its normative framework necessarily concentrates on the underlying rationale for its policies, but rejects the assumption that the organization can be reduced to its ideology.

The theory of comparative advantage first enunciated by David Ricardo in the nineteenth century has proven to be one of the most durable theories in liberal economics. It has been challenged by empirical evidence and developments in economic structure and technology, but retains its position as the foundation for the theoretical understanding of international trade. The central contention of the theory is that specialization in the production of those goods in which one country enjoys a comparative advantage and their exchange for others, which would be produced in another country at relatively greater cost, will increase national and international welfare.

This theory, and its updated variant, which emphasizes factor endowments rather than comparative costs, provides the central set of assumptions for the analysis of trade policy. The restrictive assumptions on which the theory is based have at times been the subject of penetrating criticism by various liberal economists. The most recent assault on the liberal theory of trade came from the proponents of strategic trade theory (Krugman, 1986). But even the most strident advocate of strategic trade theory later concluded that liberal trade theory remained relevant, and free trade should provide the foundation for economic policy (Krugman, 1995: 21–32). From this perspective free trade is superior to no trade because the gains from trade outweigh the disadvantages. Further, a liberal trading regime is beneficial because it promotes increased consumption and opportunities to export surplus production.

This commitment to a vision of liberal trade privileges trade over nontrade issues, and economic issues over noneconomic ones. In its analysis of the gains from international specialization, the liberal theory does not inquire into the creation of comparative advantage, relegates distributional issues to secondary importance, and neglects the social consequences of trade. These are classified as domestic issues and therefore outside the focus on exchange. Alternatively, and although a standard social-movement critique of the WTO does not exist, a primary area of contestation arises from the tendency of consumer and human rights, and environmental, development, and labor activists to challenge the primacy of economics and demand attention to social issues.

Concern for these neglected aspects most animates social-movement critiques. For example, environmentalists are concerned with the ecological impact of trade; human-rights activists and trade unionists with the conditions of workers producing goods for export; consumer groups with health and safety issues; and development advocates with effects on development prospects and the possible suppression of indigenous production. Supporters of the traditional paradigm argue that it can address these concerns while critics insist that the liberal regime is based on an economistic approach to social issues in which the benefits of trade liberalization are given priority over noneconomic costs. Thus, differences concerning the relative importance of social and distributional issues remain between the contending approaches.

In the light of this examination, the WTO emerges as an intergovernmental organization embedded in a structure of evolving supranational governance. This dual character forms an important feature of the political contestation over it, with critics emphasizing its supranational aspects and defenders maintaining that it is merely the sum of its members. Both perspectives omit an important dimension of the complex characteristics of contemporary global governance. In many respects the WTO is not an independent entity separate from its member governments. It is a legal, contractual document assigning rights and obligations to its members, and a forum in which members can pursue their interests. Furthermore, the WTO is not a service organization, and compared with many international organizations, is staffed by a small secretariat. However, this portrait suggests that the WTO is solely system-dependent, and fails to capture the ways in which it transformed and continues to affect the trading regime.

The WTO is distinct from the GATT in terms of its permanence and rule-making authority. Not only has it expanded the number of policy sectors on which decisions are taken, the outcomes of its negotiating processes and dispute settlement procedures significantly influence the behavior of national and transnational actors. On some issues, the WTO has effected a shift in decision-making from the national to the global level. This movement is accompanied by the transformation in the compromise between nationalism and multilateralism. In pursuit of further trade liberalization, the WTO necessarily extends supranational surveillance and restricts national decision-making. Further, the WTO is a powerful instrument in the construction of global norms. Through its commitment to the free trade project, it reinforces trade liberalization and supports solutions that erode various forms of protection.

It is the supranational character of the WTO that has alarmed a number of social movement activists who fear that the organization and control of vital national decisions is being gradually and irretrievably displaced from national control to a supranational organization shrouded in secrecy. The engagement by social movements with the WTO arises in this context. This encounter is the subject of the next section, where the campaign by social-movement activists for expanded participation by civil society actors in the WTO will be examined.

Contra the WTO: The Social-Movement Critique

Social movements are not homogenous, but comprised of diverse organizations at local, national, and transnational levels. Nevertheless, despite the differences in size, resources, ideology, activities, and organizational forms, a certain commonality of values and commitment to a set of goals enable us to conceive of the existence of a social movement. The absence of homogeneity within social movements also indicates the lack of a single point of view that can be represented as expressing the perspective of a particular social movement. Thus, the arguments that follow do not presume rigid conformity in any specific social-movement approach to the WTO.

In what sense then, is it possible to talk about a social-movement perspective on the world trading system? The starting points are a recognition of both this diversity as well as the existence of social-movement activism directed at the WTO. Social-movement critique is evident in the various activities undertaken by social-movement actors. No singular social-movement critique of the WTO exists since there are a number of social-movements involved in trying to influence the organization. Representatives have developed and published critiques of the WTO, and are engaged in lobbying activities directed at national governments, regional organizations, as well as the WTO, in attempts to influence global and national regulation of trade.

We can distinguish between specific issue campaigns and a general democratic reform campaign. Issue campaigns are those in which a social movement focuses on specific linkage issues, such as the environment, labor issues, and human rights, and attempts to alter WTO policy in ways supportive to its objectives. Environmentalists campaign for, among other things, mainstreaming sustainable development throughout WTO policies, whereas human-rights activists and trade unionists seek the inclusion of core labor standards within the WTO rules. The democratic reform campaign is common to most social movement activists and will be the focus of the following subsection.

Transparency, Accountability, and Representation

Social-movement activists have initiated a debate on the democratic credentials of the WTO. These critics argue that the WTO lacks transparency and accountability, and is not sufficiently representative in so far as its operations are shrouded in secrecy, its decisions are removed from effective scrutiny by national legislatures, and it fails to provide participation for a wide range of stakeholders affected by its decisions (WWF, 1999a; Wallach, 1999; Stichele, 1998). Furthermore, they contend that the WTO plays an important role in legitimizing a specific protrade solution to the conflicts between trade and social issues.

Underpinning this critique is a rejection of the intergovernmental character of the WTO. This position rests on a perception that the supranational reach of the WTO effectively erodes sovereignty, and that the absence of civil society representation in its decision-making will serve to advance the interests of those groups, specifically transnational firms, who are most likely to profit from further liberalization and the absence of effective national control. Critics argue that the WTO should be accountable, not solely to its member-states, but also to communities around the world directly affected by trade liberalization.

They contend that representatives from civil-society organizations have a crucial role in making the world trading system more transparent (Bellman and Gerster, 1996; Enders, 1996; WWF, 1999a). This social-movement critique of the WTO consists of two interrelated parts. A negative critique focusing on the absence of transparency, accountability, and representation, supplemented by a positive set of arguments showing why greater transparency, accountability, and increased representation for civil-society groups will enhance democracy in the WTO, and lead to more effective decision-making.

The negative case links the democratic deficit with the policies pursued in the WTO. Critics allege that transparency is lacking in two respects: first, negotiations are conducted, dispute panels are convened, and decisions are taken solely in the presence of member-states. Thus, civil-society groups are effectively disbarred from providing a valuable watchdog function for the wider public. Second, although the WTO has moved toward the derestriction of most of its documents, and constructed a Web site that provides access to a wide range of its published output, critics contend that the provision to keep crucial documents restricted for six months after being issued, severely hampers the monitoring and advocacy functions of social-movement organizations.

An organization with a restricted membership and lacking in transparency, it is argued, cannot effectively be accountable to its constituents. Critics argue that the decision-making structure of the WTO privileges the interests of transnational corporations and enhances their power at the expense of local communities. If the WTO is accountable to any constituency it is to that of global capital (Stichele, 1998). Indeed, some allege that the WTO pursues a free-trade agenda responsible for environmental degradation, increases in global poverty, human-rights abuses, and erodes democratic scrutiny of trade policies (Wallach, 1999). In short, the WTO, as a pillar of global governance, is not subject to democratic accountability.

In addition, three broad claims have been made for the increased participation of civil-society groups in the WTO. The first is based on an assumption common to pluralist theories of democracy in which it is claimed that the more voices heard, the better the policy output. This claim has been made explicitly by Bullen and Van Dyke (1996), who contend that administrative structures that integrate public input will consistently produce better results than those where information input is restricted. Thus, opening WTO bodies to social-movement actors will provide decision-makers with more ideas and views, and improve the results of policy deliberations (Esty, 1997 and 1999). Further, proceedings that are not transparent, perpetuate a secretive image of the organization and diminishes public confidence and support for its work. Moreover, it leads to misunderstandings and suspicion of the deliberative processes of the multilateral trading system.

Second, social-movement representatives claim that they possess specialized knowledge and can constructively contribute to trade politics. In other words, increased participation of social-movement NGOs will ensure that a holistic range of potential consequences of trade liberalization are addressed, because they can provide information and technical expertise not necessarily available in intergovernmental deliberations (Esty, 1999).

The third claim concerns the necessity for broad public support for further trade liberalization. Both the trade community and its critics recognize the fragile nature of such support. Many social-movement representatives argue that their participation will increase public support for the organization since member-states rely on public support for the implementation of trade policies (Bullen and Van Dyke, 1996). Moreover, wider public participation counters the role of vested interests and therefore ensures that policies are taken in the public interest. Wary of the argument that commercial secrecy dictates the intergovernmental nature of trade negotiations, social-movement campaigners insist that increased participation need not jeopardize secrecy considerations.

In addition, social-movement representatives contend that greater and more substantive representation is also necessary at the domestic level. The WWF (1999b) calls on governments to be made more accountable to their populace. It argues that WTO policies should be scrutinized through extensive parliamentary procedures and consultations with stakeholders at the domestic level. The International Institute for Sustainable Development (1999) extends this critique arguing that it is "wrong to focus all attention at the WTO. Key problems rest at the national level [. . .] in the opaque processes that too often characterize trade policy development."

These claims have been disputed by supporters of the status quo who reject the assertions that WTO decision-making is secretive, lacks accountability, and fails to provide representation for citizens. Defenders of the current arrangements make three counterarguments. The first consists of a reassertion of the intergovernmental nature of the WTO. As an intergovernmental organization, the WTO depends for its continued functioning on the support of its state members. The growth in membership, from 76 at its inception to 144 (as of January 2002), demonstrates that potential members are not dissuaded from joining the organization because of concerns over its democratic credentials. Moreover, defenders argue, the high level of secrecy essential for trade negotiations can only be maintained if the state-centric nature of the organization remains in its current form. Multilateral trade negotiations require governments to forge compromises between various domestic interests, a strategy that would become increasingly complicated if nonstate actors are given a greater degree of representation within the formal organizational framework (Williams, 1999).

A second issue emphasized by supporters of the status quo concerns the conditions under which trade liberalization is furthered. They reject the contention that an increase in the number of groups represented will lead to improved decision-making. They argue that admission of nonstate actors into the negotiating process is likely to increase protectionist sentiments in the organization, since the new actors (social-movement NGOs and many firms) do not support the goal of trade liberalization. Any attempt to widen the membership will result in increased justification for protectionism.

Third, defenders of the current institutional structure query the representative nature of civil-society organizations. They claim that it will be difficult to devise a method of accrediting legitimate NGOs, and argue that many civil-society organizations do not represent a distinct community of interests. In addition, many governments from the developing world have expressed concern that any increase in the role given to NGOs will further strengthen Northern interests in the organization, since those NGOs possessing the expertise and financial resources to engage directly with the WTO are likely to be based in the North.

Responsiveness of the World Trading System

In what ways are social-movement criticisms of the WTO politically significant? In other words, to what extent have social movements affected the decision-making of key WTO members, and elicited a response from the organization? State interests and intersate conflicts were the primary reasons for the failure of the Seattle Ministerial Meeting in 1999, as well as the success of Doha in 2001, yet social-movement actors have impacted the functionings of the WTO.

The Doha Ministerial failed to ignite the trade liberalization agenda, and the WTO continues to face difficulties in furthering its mandate. It is widely acknowledged that one of the main reasons for its current malaise arises from continued questioning of its liberalization project, and scrutiny of its decision-making procedures. Social-movement actors have persistently challenged the liberalization project at the heart of the WTO, as well as its democratic credentials. They have pursued their critique through lobbying governments, the WTO, and the dissemination of information to journalists and the wider public.

These separate (and at times explicitly linked) campaigns have not on their own created the current malaise in the multilateral trading system. However, their efforts, especially their rejection of unfettered trade liberalization, and their promotion of a reform agenda centered on making the WTO more transparent and accountable, have contributed to the current situation. The political importance of social-movement protest is linked to the indispensable requirement of building public support for further trade liberalization. Although it is debatable whether contestation by social-movement activists over WTO policies have undermined the legitimacy of the organization, the evidence suggests that the debates just outlined have raised doubts concerning this legitimacy and that of the multilateral trading system. Social movements are significant in shaping the context within which the authority of the WTO is determined.

Moreover, it is apparent that WTO member-states have not dismissed these challenges. They have responded in ways that suggest concern for the organization's credibility. Governments have engaged with representatives of civil society, and improved access to the WTO, in attempts to widen the public base of support for increased liberalization. Although nonstate actors remain formally excluded from participating in WTO deliberations, the organization has revised its earlier policy of exclusion in response to critiques concerning its democratic credentials. The WTO has progressively expanded access for social-movement activists and corporate actors.

First, the secretariat is involved in initiating consultations and dialogues with civil-society organizations. This has resulted in direct contacts between the director-general and NGOs, as well as symposia for NGOs to discuss trade, development, and environmental issues. The facilities provided for NGOs at the Ministerial Meetings have also significantly improved over time. Second, the WTO initiated a process to make its documents more readily available to the public. Most WTO documents are circulated as unrestricted, some are derestricted automatically after a sixty-day period, others can be derestricted at the request of a member, but others, especially those pertaining to important current policy decisions, remain restricted.

In the aftermath of the Seattle Ministerial, Mike Moore, the former director-general, and the secretariat embarked on an offensive to demonstrate the virtues of trade liberalization for all sectors of the global economy. The debate on the WTO's openness and accountability has been active from its inception and remains an important one for supporters and opponents of the multilateral trading system. Powerful countries, especially the U.S., have shown awareness of the necessity for wide public support of further trade liberalization and the WTO. In the General Council, the U.S. has consistently supported increased access for NGOs and greater transparency. U.S. support was crucial in the decisions to derestrict documents, and expand dialogue between the secretariat and NGOs in 1996. At the May 1998 Ministerial, former president Clinton called for increased participation of civil-society groups in the WTO: He proposed that "the WTO for the first time, provide(s) a forum where business, labor, environmental, and consumer groups can speak out and help guide the further evolution of the WTO" (*Bridges Weekly Trade News Digest,* 1998). Additionally, in Seattle the U.S. position on labor and environmental issues owed much to the perceived necessity of support by these groups in domestic U.S. trade politics.

Conclusion

This chapter argued that the social-movement critique of the WTO is constructed at the intersection of two tensions created by the processes of globalization. The first concerns the increased political space for social-movement actors as the pace and scope of international economic liberalization and integration transform state sovereignty and autonomy. Transnational social movements have expanded their activities and increased in importance as a result of global economic liberalization and integration. A second tension arises from the expansion of the multilateral trading system through the incorporation of new issues, and the increase in regulatory control of the WTO.

Increased trade liberalization has brought into prominence the impact of trade on social issues and disadvantaged groups, and revitalized the conflict between protectionist forces and supporters of "free trade." The WTO as the institutional nexus of the multilateral trading system has attracted the attention of social movements. Social-movement organizations have targeted the policies and democratic credentials of the WTO. They contend that the WTO policies neglect and marginalize other values, such as protection of the environment and support for workers' rights. This is partially a product of the intergovernmental nature of the organization, and in part a result of its organizational ideology. Social-movement organizations are therefore campaigning for a democratization of the WTO, so that it can reflect interests beyond those narrowly conceived in the prevailing interstate, neoliberal paradigm.

Social-movement organizations, especially development and environmental groups, contend that activity at the national level fails to capture the complete nature of global governance and contemporary forms of regulation. Hence, there is a need to democratize international institutions so that they more completely reflect interests of stakeholders who are marginalized or excluded by traditional forms of international politics. However, the ability of social-movement activists to challenge the system of world trade rules remains constrained by the institutional context of the WTO and the discourse of free trade. The WTO is a relatively closed organization to participation by social-movement representatives. Its tradition of secrecy during negotiations, its intergovernmental nature, and its function as a negotiating forum mitigate against increased access for social-movement activists.

References

Bellman, C. and R. Gerster. 1996. "Accountability in the World Trade Organization." *Journal of World Trade Law*, l30(6): 31–74.

Bridges Weekly Trade News Digest. 1998. "Clinton Endorses Call for High-Level WTO Meeting on Trade-Environment and Calls for WTO Openness," 1.2(18).

Bullen, Sally and Brennan Van Dyke. 1996. "In Search of Sound Environment and Trade Policy: A Critique of Public Participation in the WTO." Geneva: Center for International Environmental Law.

Enders, Alice. 1996. "Openness and the WTO." IISD Working Paper.

Esty, Daniel C. 1997. "Why the World Trade Organization Needs Environmental NGOs." Geneva: International Center for Trade and Sustainable Development.

———. 1999. "Environmental Governance at the WTO: Outreach to Civil Society," in Gary P. Sampson and W. Bradnee Chambers, eds. *Trade, Environment and the Millennium*. Tokyo: United Nations Press.

International Institute for Sustainable Development. 1999. "Six Easy Pieces: Five Things the WTO Should Do—and One It Should Not." Winnipeg: IISD.

Krugman, Paul R. ed. 1986. *Strategic Trade Policy and the New International Economics.* Cambridge, MA: MIT Press.

———. 1995. "Is Free Trade Passé?" in P. King, ed. *International Economics and International Economic Policy.* New York: McGraw-Hill.

Stichele, Myriam Vander. 1998. "Towards a World Transnational Organisation?" WTO Booklet Series vol.3. Amsterdam: Transnational Institute.

Wallach, Lori. 1999. "Whose Trade Organization: Corporate Globalization and the Erosion of Democracy." Washington, D.C.: Public Citizen.

Williams, Marc. 1999. "The WTO and 'Democracy.'" in Annie Taylor and Caroline Thomas, eds. *Global Trade Issues.* London: Routledge.

Williams, Marc and Lucy Ford. 1999. "The WTO, the Environmental Social-Movement and Global Environmental Management," in *Environmental Politics*, 8(1): 268–289.

WWF. 1999a. "A Reform Agenda for the WTO Ministerial Conference." A Position Paper. Gland: WWF International.

———. 1999b. "Sustainable Trade for a Living Planet." Gland: WWF International.

PART 4

Gender, Globalization, and Development

CHAPTER 12

Utilizing Interdisciplinarity to Analyze Global Socio-Economic Change

A Tribute to Ester Boserup

IRENE TINKER

Ester Boserup was a truly original scholar who challenged many prevailing economic development theories and became the guru of the women and international development field. She was such a towering scholar, that her publications are more often quoted than read. Most people recall one or two ideas from her books and articles and overlook her many other insights. Boserup wove her examination of agriculture, technology, population, and women into a unified model that strengthened her analysis of the separate disciplines.

Not only does Boserup's model provide insight into current trends, her penetrating analyses have often anticipated contemporary debates. For example, her stance that food subsidies had a negative impact on agriculture has been a recurrent theme since she wrote about Denmark during World War II. Her observations that improvements in women's health and education were perhaps the best ways of achieving family planning were noted at the UN Population Conference in Bucharest in 1974, and anticipated resolutions made at the UN Population Conference in Cairo in 1994. Above all, Boserup demonstrated the interrelationship of technological changes on the farm, and in cities and factories with socially constructed roles for women, men, children, and the elderly.

The interrelated and interdisciplinary model that she propounded was particularly significant for feminist scholars concerned with the impact of economic development on women because it provided intellectual credibility to a new field. In the 1970s, policy studies about women were in their infancy and most women's studies on campuses were lodged in the humanities. For those of us trying to influence planning and programs of the major donors for development assistance, being able to set our arguments into the overarching Boserup model was of inestimable importance.

Equally important was the fact that this outstanding economist had insisted on considering noneconomic factors in the process of change, a view that challenged the narrow economic approach predominant at the time. Her research was thoroughly multidisciplinary, "viewing human societies as dynamic relationships between natural, economic, cultural, and political structures" (Boserup, 1999 and 1997). Boserup's skepticism of economic theories was grounded in the wrenching political changes on the European continent following World War I, as well as the intellectual ferment stirred by contending theories of socialism, communism, and democracy. Instead of relying on a single discipline or ideology, Boserup included strands of many perspectives in her model.

This approach is vividly portrayed on the cover of her intellectual autobiography, *My Professional Life and Publications 1929–1998* (1960), which shows a circle with topics around its edges all connected by arrows: culture, environment, technology, population, occupation, and family. In this volume, Boserup traces, in her typically concise form, the evolution of her thinking, illustrating her intellectual journey with references to her publications. Throughout her life she challenged conventional wisdom. Her earliest entries mention university honors papers in which she questioned some of the conclusions reached by both Marx and Keynes; perhaps because neither theory helped explain her childhood poverty caused by the double loss of her father and the family investments. The book's last paragraph reiterates her lifelong theme that rapid technological change radically influences cultural attitudes and behavior: "The importance of these problems for economic development is overlooked by economists, when they make the assumption that rational behavior is the rule whatever the circumstances."

The Boserup Model

Ester Boserup developed her model for economic development as a result of her work experiences trying to reconcile practical economics with theories she learned at the university. She worked for the Danish government from 1935 until 1947, an unsettled period that encompassed the depths of the depression, World War II, and the postwar recovery. As head of the planning office she was involved with trade policies and observed first-hand the effect of widespread government subsidies on Danish agriculture. In 1947 she moved to Geneva to work with the newly created UN Economic Commission of Europe (ECE), where her work again focused on trade, much of which, as in Denmark, was in agricultural products. In later years, she wrote extensively on the issues of food aid and their disastrous impact of agriculture in Africa. While working for the ECE, Boserup began to wonder whether the low rate of industrial growth in France might be related to its low population growth. Already the interrelationships between agriculture, population, trade, and industry were churning in her mind.

By 1957, after the Marshall Plan helped Europe to recover from the war, the international community began to focus on the newly independent countries. Boserup and her husband, Mogens, joined a project headed by Gunnar Myrdal, a colleague at ECE, to assess the future of India. Economic development assistance was at its zenith, Western models of development were in ascendancy, and India was the experiment. At the time, few people, Indian or Western, questioned the validity of the prevailing development theory, especially as it applied to agriculture; indeed, most of the economists in the Indian Planning Commission were Western-trained.

But Boserup held to her critical gaze. Traveling through the country she decided that what she had learned about agriculture in the West did not fit the Indian situation. She observed women working in the fields, noted the agricultural impact of various forms of tenure, and learned about the flexibility of agricultural labor. All this made her question many of the Western-based assumptions about agricultural production, particularly the theories relating to surplus labor, population density, and migration. Such observations provoked an increasing skepticism of the entire project, and the evaluations of the situation in India held by herself and her husband increasingly diverged from those held by Myrdal.[1] So after completing the chapters required by their contract, Boserup returned to Copenhagen to write.

Boserup's model for economic development is based both on practical experience in Europe and India, and extensive historical research. She argued that population densities compelled early societies to invent agricultural technologies in order to increase food production. New agricultural systems, in turn, required adaptations in the social structure, altering family work obligations and gender relationships. Changing agricultural methods also affected the environment. Increased food production, which resulted from improved technology, also fostered urbanization where social systems underwent even greater adjustment.

Agricultural Change

Ester Boserup first stated her development model in *Conditions of Agricultural Growth*, which appeared in 1965. Rejecting the idea of static primitive societies that modernized only with exogenous technology, she argued that such societies, under pressure from population growth, invent their own technologies to increase food production. More people means that existing land must be farmed more intensively than earlier systems, so long as fallow rotation is replaced with short fallow periods. These changes required more labor input into farming, though no one worked very hard. Gradually the forest became grasslands and required the application of nutrients and the turning of the soil. Long fallow systems demanded little weeding; men cleared the land and women grew the food. Women began to weed the fields as shorter fallow periods pertained. Increasing population density led to more intensive agricultural systems using animal draft power and plows, and the substitution of common land for private ownership. Under this farming system men had to spend more time growing food, although women continued to do much of the labor. These historic stages are familiar to readers of Boserup's books, as are the implications for social structure; but she warned that these changes are not predictive of the future without study of technologies still in the pipeline (Boserup, 1981).

Less familiar are her theories of urbanization. Food surpluses allowed the expansion of town centers. But these surpluses might be the result of many producers rather than new technology; hence towns could grow prior to technological innovation. However, for towns to grow, they needed adequate transport for trade (Boserup, 1990: 87). This gradualism, which Boserup documented in her research into ancient European and American growth patterns, became dislocated, she argued, with the abrupt introduction of modern technology into areas lacking requisite infrastructure or cultural receptivity. For these reasons, the introduction of modern farming techniques, such as the Green Revolution, has had very different impacts in Asia and Africa. With its limited infrastructure and sparse population, Africa benefited little from the new technologies in comparison to Asia, which had adequate transport, trained extension workers, and rural amenities. Continued low agricultural productivity in Africa led many governments to seek, and development agencies to provide, imported food for urban areas. These staples were sold at subsidized prices, thus further reducing incentives for food production: "The assumption of inelasticity of food production [. . .] made large-scale transfer of food from industrialized to developing countries look like a desirable solution to the agricultural problems of both the developing and developed countries" (Boserup,

1990: 281). Farmers leave the land and crowd into rapidly expanding urban agglomerations where misery reigns.

Population Increase

Boserup's theories about population growth also challenged contemporary wisdom. When she published *Population and Technological Change* in 1981 she reiterated the theory first presented in *Conditions of Agricultural Growth* (1965); with the new book, she sought to broaden and deepen it through discussions of the causes and effects of population increases. In the 1960s, the theories of Thomas Malthus dominated population policy: because people were increasing geometrically while food was increasing arithmetically, land for cultivation would soon be exhausted and starvation, wars, or pestilence would ensue.

However, Boserup argued that Malthus saw the world as static; she believed that population densities would result in new technologies that would increase food production on lands currently in production. Dense populations were also necessary if roads, schools, and health clinics were to be provided in remote rural areas. Population growth was therefore necessary for economic development. In the introduction to Boserup's collected essays, T. Paul Schultz (1990: 2) remarks that she, in effect, stood Malthus on his head:

> The historical record remains sufficiently varied and uncertain, so that neither the model of Malthus nor that of Boserup explains adequately all the evidence. But the last two decades have moved the mainstream interpretation of this process in the direction proposed by Boserup.

Boserup (1975:26) expounded the importance of population growth to economic development, but she also argued that women's ability to determine "when and how often to bear children" is a decisive element in women's efficient participation in the development process. To accomplish this, women needed access to education and health services. Active at the first UN World Population Conference in Bucharest in 1974, her views were incorporated in a consensus resolution declaring that an improvement in women's status and educational opportunities would promote women's health as well as a reduction of birth rates.

Such an approach was as important "regardless of whether the overall situation is one of strong pressure of population on resources or an insufficient population base for development" (Boserup, 1975:26) Further, she noted how traditional methods of spacing were often discarded during economic change leading to higher fertility per woman and often increased maternal and infant morbidity and mortality.[2] The importance of women's health and education to population programs was reiterated and expanded in 1994 at the Cairo UN Conference for Population and Development by a global coalition of women's organizations.

A Theoretical Base for Women in International Development

Ester Boserup's book on *Woman's Role in Economic Development* was first published in 1970, five years after *The Conditions of Agricultural Growth: The Economics of Agrarian Change under Population Pressure*. In this book Boserup explored linkages between industry and agriculture, and investigated the predominantly male migration to cities. Throughout, Boserup's interest in occupational distribution is obvious. Her first sentence states: "A main characteristic of economic development is the progress towards an increasingly intricate pattern of labor specialization" (Boserup, 1970: 15). She further emphasizes that the division of labor within the family is assigned by age and sex, and this distribution varies across regions and cultures. Criticizing generalizations made by Margaret Mead—that men are the providers of food while women prepare it—she distinguishes between male and female farming systems.

Women Farmers

Only the first third of her book is an examination of women's roles in these various farming systems, though this is the section most often quoted, as it makes women's subsistence and farmwork visible. Women's economic worth is related to their status: bride price is paid where women work in the fields; a dowry is offered to convince the groom to accept a nonworking wife. Where women farm and men can purchase their labor, and where land use rights can be expanded, polygamy continues. Cultural practices appear to trump religion in this regard for the countries with high levels of polygamous households are in West Africa.[3] In Muslim areas where dowry is the rule, the incidence of polygamy is largely confined to the wealthy. In these areas of male farming, upper caste/status women are in seclusion but women from the lower classes frequently work as casual laborers, an occupation that emphasizes the economic costs of female seclusion.

Boserup devotes an entire chapter to describing the loss of women's status under European colonialism. Two of her points stand out: first, the promotion of land ownership deprived women of land use rights in areas of Africa and South East Asia; second, the belief that men were superior farmers encouraged the introduction of technology and cash crops to men, especially in Africa, thus leaving women to continue using traditional low-yield methods for growing subsistence crops. Both actions continue to have current repercussions. Land rights and ownership have become highly contested, especially in Africa where the bride-price custom continues. In countries such as Rwanda or Uganda, where wars and/or HIV/AIDS have left grandmothers as the primary providers for their extended families, woman's right to control her own farmland is now being recognized.[4] On the second point, insufficient attention to subsistence food production in Africa is a primary cause for the decline in per capita food availability throughout the continent.

Women in Towns

Boserup differentiates between female and male towns in her discussions of farming systems. Female towns are centered on markets where women dominated trade. Male towns are of two types: they may have a surplus of men in the population or they may be towns where women are in seclusion and therefore unseen. A semimale town is one where women dominate the traditional markets while the modern sector is exclusively the domain of men. Further, most towns include migrants of ethnicities whose cultures diverge regarding women's occupations.

Market towns trade both agricultural and nonagricultural commodities. Because historically women produced many of the household products they needed, increased opportunities for trade encouraged specialization. Products may originate in rural areas but trading is done in towns. Women and men also offered their tailoring and food at markets. Boserup called this activity the "bazaar and service sector," which was a more focused concept than the more widely used residual category "informal sector." Her category is more accurate, for when the International Labor Organization (ILO) studies looked at the informal sector, they were searching for small enterprises that hired workers. This classification effectively screens out most women- or family-run microenterprises, such as street food vending home-based work, or urban agriculture.[5] Boserup notes that many women prefer such work to factory jobs because it more easily meshes with household responsibilities. This is also true of other economic activities that women can conduct from home.[6]

The impact of higher education on women's occupations reveals continued discrimination by sex. Boserup (1970:140) attributes the "polarization and hierarchization" of men and women's work roles to the maldistribution of technology between them. But she also notes how the age-sex-race-class hierarchies play out differently on different groups of women, and often reward some occupations while increasing discrimination against women in others.

Influencing the United Nations

After *Woman's Role* was published, the Danish government included Boserup in the Danish delegation to the UN. In 1972 she began an eight-year membership in the UN's Committee of Development Planning. This, in turn, led to her appointment as rapporteur to the first UN experts meeting that addressed the issue of women in international economic development. This meeting marked the first attempt by the Social Development Division of the UN's Economic and Social Affairs department to focus on the roles of women in development, or for the cosponsor, the UN Commission on the Status of Women (CSW), to address economic development issues as framed by the documents proclaiming the First Development Decade 1960–'70.[7] Ester Boserup's report of this meeting provided the UN with documentation that development was indeed a women's issue.

Also in 1972 and after many years of requests from the CSW, the general assembly finally passed a resolution declaring 1975 International Women's Year (IWY). During the debate, the themes of the year were articulated as equality, peace, and development: Equality for the West, peace for the East, and development for the global South. At first IWY was designated simply as a year, but the reinvigorated women's movements, especially in the United States, influenced their governments to support a World Conference for IWY, which subsequently took place in Mexico City in June 1975.[8]

Ester Boserup's Importance for Feminist Activists, Scholars, and Practitioners

Women globally were observing governmental policies that discriminated against women. Despite the fact that most newly independent countries gave women equal citizenship rights in their constitutions, prevailing customs allowed male dominance. In the U.S. the women's movement grew in strength and demanded equal wages, equal educational opportunities, particularly to professional schools, access to credit and mortgages, and so on. Women in newly independent countries wondered what happened to the nationalist rhetoric that promised equality for women and men. Deterioration rather than improvement of the status of women was observed in many countries as a result of development policies implemented in the 1960s and '70s. All of these trends were noted in Boserup's trenchant analysis of many studies by anthropologists and policy-makers that she utilized in her book to substantiate her conclusions.

During these tumultuous decades, women organized in many countries to change development programming and social policies of their governments. The evident scholarship of *Woman's Role* and the author's impressive credentials as a mainstream economist provided the burgeoning community of women in international development proponents with a convincingly academic reference. Once the awareness of Boserup's writings became widespread, her theories became the scholarly foundation of the women in international development field.[9]

As the second wave of the women's movement expanded around the world, the issue of women's roles in economic development programming gained momentum. Inga Thorsson had persuaded the Swedish Parliament to mandate government support for women in its foreign assistance programs as early as 1964. In the U.S. Congress, a group of feminists lobbied successfully for the inclusion of a paragraph in the U.S. Foreign Assistance Act of 1973 that directed administrators to integrate women into the new poverty-focused programs.[10] This paragraph was subsequently included in resolutions for many UN agencies as well as in the General Assembly, as these bodies began to anticipate the upcoming IWY. The activists and practitioners who promoted greater visibility for the issues of women and international development found in Ester Boserup's book the statistics and trends that gave credence to their demands for a policy shift.[11] The UNDP asked Boserup to summarize her major viewpoints in a short pamphlet for the IWY conference. "Integration of Women in Development: Why, When, How," written with assistance from Christina Liljencrantz, it was widely distributed and provided delegates with information to strengthen the conference document, the Plan of Action, regarding women and development.

A second activity that helped publicize both the topic and Boserup's major contributions was the Seminar on Women in Development held in Mexico City just prior to the IWY Conference. Sponsored by the American Association for the Advancement of Science (AAAS), and under my leadership, over 100 women[12] and men from around the world gathered to analyze development issues and propose recommendations to the UN.[13] These materials were also distributed at the governmental conference.

Ester Boserup's insights concerning population, agricultural changes, and women had immediate application during the 1976–1985 Decade for Women. During that period, planners perceived urban dwellers as less needy than rural people. As rapid migration produced squatter settlements filled with families struggling to provide a livelihood for their children, more attention was given to housing and available employment in the informal sector. As noted, the ILO studies focused on enterprises large enough to provide employment; for some time the microenterprises operated by a woman or her family were ignored or discounted. Today, Boserup's emphasis on the critical role that women's incomes, from the bazaar and service-sector play in urban survival, is broadly recognized. Home-based work in both rural and urban areas continue to provide millions of women with income; women at home are now being organized in both developed and developing countries for the purposes of more efficient enterprises, better wages, and health and retirement benefits.[14]

Critics of Boserup argue that her lack of feminist analysis weakens her model by omitting the heavy impact of male dominance. Both African and U.S. scholars have suggested that African women are not nearly as independent, either in farming or in fertility decisions, as Boserup portrays them.[15] Others see the economic system as the source of women's oppression while recognizing that gender inequalities intensify such women's subordinate position at all class levels.[16]

In reviewing such criticism, Jane Jaquette emphasizes that Boserup discounts male-female differences, an attitude widely held among educated women in the first half of the last century. Boserup had understood that education was her path out of poverty; universities in Europe were open to the talented as well as to the traditional elites. A good degree provided access to intellectual circles where women were more accepted as equals than they were among the middle and lower classes in what were still stratified societies. She excelled in her studies and considered herself equal with men. In addition, she seldom discussed how she balanced marriage and three children with her professional work. In fact, when her children were young she was able to work part-time even though no such provisions were generally available for this arrangement.[17]

Jaquette discusses the continuing debates among feminists between equality and difference, and between treating women as equals of men and recognizing the merit in demands for special provisions that recognize women's role in the family. "What is needed," Jaquette argues, "is a more complex theory of justice that will combine the best elements of equality and merit and make room for difference without forcing everyone to be alike."[18] Such issues were not of concern to Boserup, who simply accepted a dual role and surmounted any tension between family and work.

On the other hand, Boserup always recognized that economic changes have variable effects on the relative status of women and men. She analyzed this through age-sex-class-race hierarchies. She examined the conflicts among generations of women in her new introduction to the 1983 Spanish edition of *Woman's Role in Economic Development*. "Since the first edition of this book appeared in 1970," she notes such changes as greater "access to jobs in large-scale industries and modern-type services, the rapid spread of female education, and the access to health services and family planning" have altered their life experiences. Because young women benefit from such changes while their mothers do not, the status hierarchy between female family members has been upset. Indeed, some older women have supported patriarchal Islamic governments because they "have more to lose than to gain by improvements in the position of young women."[19]

Multidisciplinarity

Throughout her career Boserup "focused on the interplay of economic and noneconomic factors in the process of social change" (Boserup, 1999: 7), eschewing any attempt to confine her analyses to a few disciplines. This approach is even more critical today with the torrent of information available over the internet in every individual field. Yet despite her championing the use of scholarship from this multidisciplinary viewpoint, especially when trying to influence policy, she was wary of using monetary proxies for non-monetized transactions, a technique utilized by such publications as the *Human Development Report*, to convince policy-makers about the importance of social trends. Her concern was that such analyses might easily lead to false or simplified conclusions.

Often, she argues, government policy conflicts with economic change, and uses the examples of powerful agricultural lobbies that demand subsidies when "the government should promote structural reform" (Boserup, 1999: 29). Excess food production in high-income countries was exported to support subsidized food in urban areas in developing countries; though perceived as humanitarian, this policy overlooked the impact on food production and employment in rural areas. Subsequent reduction of world food surplus through policies that limited production further exacerbated the food situation around the world. Arguing for more attention to increased production in rural areas she writes that "[a]s long as economic infrastructure is more, it is not possible to modernize agriculture" (Boserup, 1990: 280).

Boserup criticizes formal economic models, widely used for development planning, as static. Analyses of land, labor, and capital may be sufficient for short-term plans, but

> long-term development analysis must take account of structural change, i.e., *change of the capacities themselves*, by land improvements or deterioration, population, natural or migratory changes, major changes in income distribution and political systems, etc. Moreover, long-term analysis must take into account the changes in those structures which economists usually leave to be studies by other scientific disciplines, for instance national cultures. [. . .] Rapid technological change created conflicts with national culture through its radical influence on the way of life: Cultural attitudes and behavior, which may have been rational before, are no more so [. . .] The importance of these problems for economic development is overlooked by

economists, when they make the assumption that rational behavior is the rule whatever the circumstances.

(Boserup, 1999: 58–9; 60)

Boserup tracked with interest the gains that women made. In 1996 she responded to my complaints about the backlash against the women's movement globally:

> I had never dreamt that there would be so (many) big changes in the position of both women and poor countries in my lifetime, and find it inevitable that such large changes will cause a lot of reaction and both short- and long-run counter movements. So don't become too gloomy a pessimist.[20]

However, in July 1999 she expressed growing concern about contemporary trends embedded in globalization:

> I think that today the greatest threat to women comes from the U.S. neoliberal campaign, which if it succeeds in privatizing schools, universities, child institutions, and culture will also "reprivatize women in their homes." I wonder how long the European governments can keep up their resistance against the American pressure.[21]

Conclusion

For many women active in influencing policy both inside and outside governments and international agencies, the existence of a scholarly base from which to argue cannot be overestimated. For example, Vina Mazumdar, who coordinated the 1979 India Commission on the Status of Women report, recalled learning of the Boserup book only after the report was in press. Reading that book made her feel more confident of the conclusions and recommendations found in the report. Muzumdar's discovery and identification that came from reading *Woman's Roles in Economic Development* is an experience similar to my own. Ester Boserup's book legitimized and documented many tentative ideas growing in the minds of many women as a result of their observations of changes affecting women in developing countries. Whatever their views of specific findings or analyses, the entire community of scholars, activists, and practitioners have benefited from the Boserup model.

References

Boserup, Ester. 1965. *Conditions of Agricultural Growth: The Economics of Agrarian Change Under Population Pressure,* London: George Allen and Unwin.

———. 1970. *Woman's Role in Economic Development.* London: George Allen and Unwin.

———. 1981. *Population and Technological Change: A Study of Long-term Trends.* Chicago: U. of Chicago Press.

———. 1990. *Economic and Demographic Relationships in Development: Essays selected and introduced by T. Paul Schultz,* Baltimore: Johns Hopkins Press.

———. 1999. *My Professional Life and Publications 1929–1998*. Copenhagen: Museum Tuscular-num Press.

Boserup, Ester and Christina Liljencrantz. 1975. *Integration of Women in Development: Why, When, How*. New York: UNDP.

Notes

1. Myrdal finally published his massive and influential *Asian Drama* in 1965.
2. "Population, the status of women and rural development," Boserup, 1990: 161–174.
3. About half of all married women live in polygamous marriages in Senegal, Togo, and Guinea, over 40 percent in Liberia, Nigeria, and Cameroon, and one-third in Ghana, Niger, and Uganda; Philippe Antoine and Jeanne Nanitelamio, "Can Polygyny Be Avoided?" in Kathleen Sheldon, ed., *Courtyards, Markets, and City Streets: Urban Women in Africa*. Boulder: Westview Press, 1996.
4. See my chapter in Irene Tinker and Gale Summerfield eds., *Women's Rights to House and Land: China, Laos, Vietnam*, Boulder, CO: Lynne Rienner, 1999.
5. See for example my *Street Foods: Urban Food and Employment in Developing Countries*, Oxford University Press, 1997; and Lisa Prugl and Irene Tinker's, "Microentrepreneurs and Homeworkers: Convergent Categories," *World Development*, 25(9): 1471–1482, 1997.
6. For a current reading of women's urban occupations see my "Feeding Megacities: a Worldwide Viewpoint," *The Urban Age*, World Bank, Winter 1998: 4–7; or "Beyond Economics: Sheltering the Whole Woman," in *Engendering Wealth and Well-Being*, Rae Blumberg, Cathy Rakowski, Irene Tinker, and Michael Monteon eds., Boulder, CO: Westview, 1995.
7. Issues related to women's rights to work and receive equal pay had been debated in the CSW as early as 1953. Reflecting the long-standing debate between labor women who promoted protective legislation for women, and the women's movement with its emphasis on equal rights, this dichotomy reappeared in the U.S. debate over the Equal Rights Amendment. See *Women in Washington: Advocates for Public Policy*, I. Tinker ed., Beverly Hills, CA: Sage Publications, 1983.
8. A useful history of the Commission on the Status of Women and the first three UN Conferences on women may be found in Anne Winslow ed., *Women, Politics, and the United Nations*, Westport CT: Greenwood, 1995. Also see Irene Tinker and Jane Jaquette's, "UN Decade for Women: Its Impact and Legacy", *World Development*, 15(3), 1987.
9. The book was published in limited numbers and was out of print for many years though its continuing demand has resulted in translations into Swedish (1971), Danish (1974), Italian (1982), German (1982), French (1983), Indonesian (1983), and Spanish (1993), the latter containing a new introduction by Boserup.
10. For the story of how this amendment was written and passed, and for an understanding of the euphoria of the U.S. women's movement in the 1970s, see my edited volume *Women in Washington: Advocates for Public Policy*, Beverly Hills, CA: Sage Publications, 1983.
11. See Irene Tinker's, "The Making of the Field: Advocates, Practitioners, and Scholars," in I. Tinker, ed., *Persistent Inequalities: Women and World Development*, New York: Oxford University Press, 1990.
12. Boserup participated in the symposium and it was the first time we met. Subsequently we represented our respective governments on the newly created Board of the UN International Instituted for the Research and Training for Women (INSTRAW) and met as several conferences and UN Experts Meetings.
13. Margaret Mead, then president of AAAS, gave generously of her support for my efforts as director of the office of international programs. Research papers and an annotated bibliography, prepared for the symposium, added to the growing studies in the field. Proceedings and papers were edited by I. Tinker and M. Bo Bramsen and published as *Women and World Development*, under the auspices of the AAAS by the Overseas Development Council: Washington, D.C., 1976. *Women and World Development: An Annotated Bibliography* is a companion volume, edited by Mayra Buvinic.
14. See in Prugl and Tinker, op. cit; my "Women and Power: The Symbiosis of In and Out," paper presented at a conference on Gender in International Relations at the University of Southern California, February 2–4, 2001.

15. For example, Simi Afonja's "Changing Patterns of Gender Stratification in West Africa," in Irene Tinker, ed., *Persistent Inequalities: Women and World Development,* Oxford U. Press, pp. 198–209, 1990; or Suellen Huntington's "Issues in Woman's Role in Economic Development," *Journal of Marriage and the Family,* 37(4): 1001–12, 1975.

16. See Lourdes Beneria and Gita Sen's, "Accumulation, Reproduction, and Women's Role in Economic Development: Boserup revisited," *Signs* 7(2): 279–98, 1981.

17. See my original paper for this conference, which includes details of Boserup's life gleaned from personal discussions and letters. For a copy, contact me at tinker@socrates.berkeley.edu

18. Jane Jaquette's "Gender and Justice in Economic Development," in Irene Tinker ed., *Persistent Inequalities: Women and World Development,* New York: Oxford University Press, 1990.

19. Original English text supplied to me by the author.

20. Letter from Ester Boserup to Irene Tinker, July 12, 1996.

21. Letter from Ester Boserup to Irene Tinker, July 11, 1999.

CHAPTER 13

Development and Productive Deprivation

Male Patriarchal Relations in Business Families and Their Implications for Women in South India[1]

BARBARA HARRISS-WHITE

Introduction

The late Ester Boserup started her germinal work *Woman's Role in Economic Development* with a depiction of development that is as relevant to the current era of globalization as it was in 1970:

> (e)conomic and social development unavoidably entails the disintegration of the division of labor among the two sexes traditionally established in the village. With modernisation of agriculture and with migration to the towns, a new sex pattern of productive work must emerge, for better or worse. The obvious danger is, however, that in the course of this transition women will be deprived of their productive functions, and the whole process of growth will thereby be retarded.
>
> (Boserup, 1989: 5)

Boserup's is an attempt to trace the distinctive regional patterns of this transition. My objective is to elaborate some consequences of this transition to productive deprivation, consequences that are not confined to growth. First, Boserup's account of the South Asian pattern is needed to situate my argument.

Boserup's narrative begins in the Indian village in which types of women are defined through their work. The highest status woman is veiled and nonworking; the second is confined to domestic work; the third is active on the farm and is an occasional wage worker; and the last and lowest in status is an independent wage worker. They are a "microcosm," reflecting, respectively, Middle Eastern, Latin American, Southeast Asian, and African female work patterns (Boserup, 1989:70). Boserup also divided the South Asian subcontinent into two regions: the North, redolent of the Middle Eastern and African work patterns, where female agricultural wage labor is supply-constrained; and the South, where, because of female farming and participation, work patterns are similar to Southeast Asia. However, when Boserup analyzes the progressive deprivation of productive work for women, neither the status categories nor the agrarian regions play much of a role.

The process of deprivation proceeds from the agriculturalization of the peasantry and the stripping of crafts from the work of agricultural households. Craft production becomes specialized, it increases in scale, production being organized either in households (and according to household division of tasks and authority) or through male wage labor. As the division of labor deepens and exchange becomes fundamental to social reproduction, tasks are progressively defined by categories of worker, in which skilled categories are dominated by men (Boserup, 1989: 69–76).

Boserup then shifts to towns. South Asian towns are male domains, either through selective male migration or because of the seclusion of women, or both. The prospects for women's work in towns is related to the rural gendered division of labor in the nonfarm economy so that while in North India "men even do the shopping" (Boserup, 1989:86), in the South, in what she defines as the "semimale town," retail trade may be in the hands of women. However, she notes that "to most Hindus the idea of female participation in trade is an abomination" (Boserup, 1989:87)[2] and "modern sector" bureaucracy, industry, and markets are dominated by men.

Even in South India, Boserup (1989: 98) recognizes a "deepening cultural resistance to women's participation in trade." Female work is then confined to unsecluded women from the lowest castes who provide artisanal, home-based, petty production, plus a variety of services. Boserup (1989:192) shows convincingly that women are progressively marginalized from wage work in factories and that female activity rates decline with development.[3] Both demand and supply factors play their role in this. Employment regulations for women increase their cost while the inflexibility of modern industrial discipline is incompatible with the rearing of children (Boserup, 1989: 110–17).[4]

She reaches a powerful conclusion: "If women are hired at all [. . .] it is usually for the unskilled, low-wage jobs, men holding skilled jobs. Thus the roles assigned to men and women even in the modern sector indicate a widening difference between the productivity and earnings of each" (Boserup, 1989: 139–40). She follows the implications of this conclusion for *growth* arguing in favor of women's education and predicting that educated women would work for wages. It follows, unconventionally, that increased urban, educated female employment would: reduce male migration, putting men to productive use in the rural economy; more conventionally it would reduce the per capita cost of provision of urban infrastructure and lower birth rates.

Boserup also explicitly recognizes that the structural transformations due to industrialization and urbanization would produce gendered *tensions* in "modern," urban households. Tension would result from burdens of urban women that were lighter than those of urban men (Boserup, 1989: 186). Her model of productive deprivation, in general, and the intimate domestic tension resulting from it, describes a *global* tension—but Boserup herself never pursued its implications.

Boserup's gendered economic history, geography, and sociology are both stylized and steeped in modernization theory. Migration, structural, and sectoral transformations, and the scaling-up of occupation and enterprise play central roles. In the process, the significance of the North-South Indian region for progressive productive deprivation of women disappears, the implications for class formation of the "microcosm" based upon work patterns are lost, and the progressive deprivation of the productive functions of women is sought in male control of the "modern sector" in its entirety.

Thirty years later, the productive deprivation of women remains a fundamental developmental *tension* in gendered relations of production and distribution. In this tribute to Ester Boserup's work, I will explore—in greater detail than that of her project—the consequences of the gender dynamics of the family business, not only for growth (as did Boserup) but also for well-being (which, apart from women's education she neglected). The family business is at the cutting edge of her argument, providing much of the kind of employment that marginalizes women in her account of the transition to modernity.

Women from business families are educated, sometimes to as high a level as their men. In family businesses and business families,[5] relations of control of men over men (neglected not only by Boserup but also by most theorists in feminist economics[6]) are of paramount importance. The family business is the concrete extension of the unit of reproduction into the market economy, as well as the unit of control over technology and money, a "combat unit designed for battle in the market" (White, 1993: 8). I will use Boserup's method of stylized descriptive modeling, but here it is developed at the microlevel.[7] Case material will be drawn from two sources: first, a field study of the reproduction of elite businesses in a South Indian town (where a random sample of businesses, stratified by ward, have been questioned every decade since 1973); and second, demographic and livelihood data from rural households in three of eleven randomly selected villages in the two surrounding districts whose development has also been followed since 1973.[8]

The Gendered Structure of a Family Business

Figure 13.1 shows the division of labor in a family business. The typical unorganized firm is regulated not by the state but by social custom and institutions. Its labor force is divided by extent and kind of security. Family labor will be described in the next section. Wage labor is divided between permanent and casual. Casual labor is divided by sex. Being a member of the permanent labor force is here a condition to be aspired to, in contrast to being permanent labor in agriculture, which is to be shunned.

Laborers are selected by origin (local), caste (usually not scheduled), and sex (male). Permanent work is not a matter of high skill and offers a diversity of livelihoods, ranging from the nightwatch to accountancy. All require the family labor force to trust the employee unsupervised. Contracts are individualized and verbal. They vary in their periods of payment and notice of dismissal; the first delayed (sometimes pay is yearly) and the other instant. Some permanent jobs can be part-time, some seasonal. Many bosses agree to time off for employees to work their own land or to do periodic trade, or they make working on the owner's land integral to the factory or workshop "contract."

A primitive form of occupational welfare is usually extended to this part of the labor force. Employers will give loans and "gifts" of petty cash for purposes such as medical expenditure, education, and marriages. Livelihoods are sometimes inherited. At one and the same time these acts parody state social protection, reveal how employers tie up labor they do not wish to lose, and transform employment contracts into relations of patronage and clientelage.

In stark contrast, the casual labor force is characterized by low and fluctuating pay, higher turnover, and insecurity. Although labor recruiters may be given annual bonuses and lent small sums of money, attempts are made to turn labor over so as to reduce its customary entitlement to annual gifts and avoid protective obligations. Male casual labor is occasionally unionized. Yet the multiplicity of unions invite the political mediation of disputes, which are rarely resolved in favor of labor. Labor laws tend to be enforced not by unions but by the state. The Factories Acts inspectors, with huge territories to cover and few resources with which to enforce the law, are more often than not found to be implicated with bosses in a nexus of corruption around the evasion of labor-protection laws and the erosion of labor rights.

Female casual labor is subjected to extremes of casualization, negligence, and harassment, as well as unsafe and unsanitary working conditions, their wages often reported by bosses as "pocket money." In firms, work has for decades been subcontracted, often exported to rural sites to avoid inspection and to profit from cheap or unwaged family labor, low

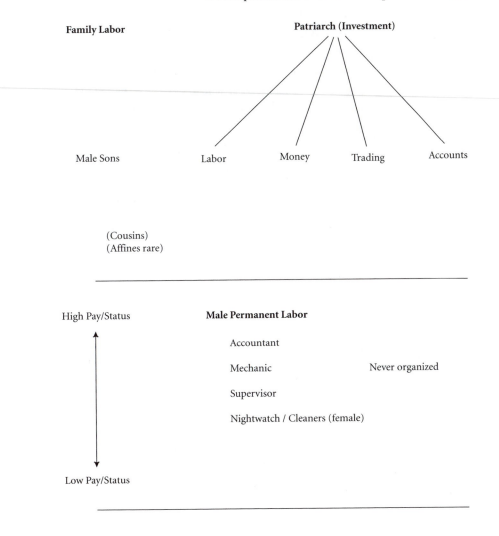

Figure 13.1: Division of Labor in a Family Business

Table 13.1: Caste and Gender in the Business Economy of a Town in South India, 1973–1993*
(% of total workforce)

1973 Caste	No. of firms sampled: 93				Workforce: 664	
	Family Labor		Permanent Wage		Casual Wage	
	Male	Female	Male	Female	Male	Female
Forward caste/other	9	0	4	0	0.7	0
Backward caste	6	0	15	5	0.1	0
Most backward caste	6	0	14	8	6	4
Scheduled castes	3	0	0.1	0	3	6
Muslims	3	0	2	0	2	0
	27	0	35.1	13	11.8	10

1983	No. of firms sampled: 126				Workforce: 1037	
FC	3	0	2	0	0	0
BC	12	0.3	17	3	3	2
MBC	4	0	17	3	5	3
SC	1	0	2	0	10	2
Muslims	3	0	3	0	2	0
	23	0.3	41	6	20	7

1993	No. of Firms Sampled: 253				Workforce: 1955	
FC	3	0.6	0.1	0		
BC	10	3	7	2		
MBC	5	2	4	0.5		
SC	2	0.4	0.6	0.1		
Muslims	1.5	0.2	0.7	0.1		
Caste + gender Unknown					57	
	21.5	6.2	12.4	2.7	57	

*Source: Basile and Harriss-White (2000)

rents, and the ease of evasion of any "welfare" obligations and taxes. Thus capital uses informal practices and the idiom of social protection highly selectively and deliberately so as to render the majority of the workforce insecure, and a minority less insecure.

Table 13.1 tracks changes over twenty years in a South Indian market town, which is also an administrative and service center (specializing in the wholesale trade of rice and groundnuts, sari weaving, and the crafting of gold ornaments, all of which are "clustered" inside the town). Though its census population is about 60,000, its real population is about 60 percent greater, with local villages resisting incorporation into the municipality for taxation reasons. The mass of businesses (85 percent) are small family firms. The average number of livelihoods (seven–eight per firm) has not changed much over the period 1973–'93. The proportion of small and *entirely* family-run businesses has risen from 28 to 35 percent over the period, whereas the proportion of family labor in the entire labor force has remained static at around a quarter. All the owners of capital are active workers, yet the composition of this work force has altered slightly, owing to the entry of a very small number of female family workers. They are hard to locate—working as washerwomen, tailors, jewel workers, sewers of leather goods in process-specialized flexible production, deep in the interiors of their homes. Casual labor, however, has increased from 23 percent of jobs to 57 percent between 1973 and 1993.

Forward caste control over business is stable in absolute terms and their apparent proportional decline masks the massive increase in the concentration of their capital. Backward castes have gained ground as owners, while most backward castes and scheduled castes comprise around 80 percent of the casual labor force. Ten to 15 percent of firms only employ their own caste as wage labor. So, counting firms without any wage labor, half the firms are still single-caste entities. In the other half, including larger businesses, workers form an emulsion of castes, though some employers still refuse to hire scheduled caste laborers (Basile and Harriss-White, 2000). Urban assets inequality has increased out of all proportion to that in villages. Whereas in 1973 the ratio of assets owned by the top 10 percent of businesses expressed as a multiple of those owned by the entire lowest 50 percent was 13:1, by 1983 it had widened to 66:1, and by 1994 to 117:1.

The Gendered Governance of the Family Firm

The family labor force is modeled in Figure 13.1 (see p. 227) and its relationships over the life cycle of a business family is summarized in Table 13.2. The family business is controlled through flexible, cross-generational configurations of agnates, which have a very strong collective identity. Irrespective of living arrangements, men negotiate authority based on the division of tasks and skill among them, while also deferring to authority based upon age. Tasks are divided between these men: accountancy, purchase, sales (and the negotiation and enforcement of contracts and credit relations), and the supervision of labor. Over thirty-five years ago it was "usual for a man to recruit his partners, managers and technical experts from among his close kindred," observed M. N. Srinivas (1966) of industrial entrepreneurs near Delhi, and this practice has changed but little, if at all.

These joint family firms *can* be explained in transactions costs terms: as lowering the costs of acquiring—and the risks of keeping—trade secrets,

Table 13.2: Gender Roles in Family Businesses

Males	Females
Firm	*Household*
Management and control by male family members	Strategic control by men
Permanent labor force (clientelized, males)	Tactical control and socialization by women
Casual labor force (sometimes unionized, males—largest single element of productive labor, deliberately casualized, female)	Female/child wage labor in domestic service
	Occasional male labor in domestic service
Life Cycle	
Youth	*Formation*
(Work) shop and home-based socialization into management of capital and labor	Home-based socialization into management of household (children, food, ceremony)
Apprenticeship	*Apprenticeship*
(Sometimes elided with schooling)	Educated for marriage alliance
Skills, contacts, networks, individual and collective elements of reputation (Higher education may be threatening)	
Entry into Business	*Marriage*
As member of family firm, with division of tasks based on male authority	Durables in dowry crucial to groom's status in family firm
As "independent" firm closely financed and controlled by male elders	Fungibles in dowry contribute to groom's starting capital
	Household reproductive labor
Death of Patriarch	Production of male labor crucial to: (*a*) power relations in division of property and (*b*) size of family firm
Splitting of family firm	
Vulnerability of property rights, finance, conflict over sites and rights	
Consolidation of Business	*Consolidation of Business*
Growth of firm	Social work
Formation of conglomerates with brothers and sons	Management of household
Complex overlapping forms of ownership	Reproductive work
Subcontracting, casualization of labor (esp. female labor)	
Amassing of dowries for daughters	
Investment in land	

information, accounts, and trustworthy relations. A few business heads can and do calculate both the transactions costs and the opportunity costs of their male-family-based forms of management and find them to be cheaper than market alternatives. At the same time, family firms are authoritarian units of capital and labor. They may also be social spaces where transactions costs logic does not apply.

Transaction costs cannot explain the equal and implicit returns to the different efforts of individual sons, especially when authority systems at work and home reinforce each other. At work the youngest son has lowest status, based on that of his job and irrespective of his productivity. At home he has least authority among men, based on his status in the household. His effort will not relate to his work status or domestic authority. Notional nominal rates of pay below those of the equivalent sector of the labor market and equal rights to family property also offer disincentives to effort. Nevertheless family labor tends to work hard. The gains from cooperation and compliance with authority prevail, or else jointly managed male firms would not be so commonplace. Factors such as a collective and individual interests in accumulation across generations, the security of employment, and noneconomic gains act as incentives, and the effect of patriarchal, social, and economic sanctions on alternative wage work act as deterrents. Together carrot and stick explain the supply of male family labor, its loyalty and cohesion (Harriss-White, 1996: 243–45).[9]

Accumulation is therefore the result of an intensely male, concentrated, and specialized set of relations of *cooperative control* for the production of the managerial labor, which also owns capital, sometimes in substantial conglomerates networked by kinship. Within these businesses, relations between men are carefully, almost "naturally," constructed so as to nurture cooperation and control—control over other men within and outside the household. It is by means of this control that control over capital is concentrated. Cooperation conceals control. *Conflict between men* is the most threatening aspect of the management of a family business. The partition of a family business is as vulnerable a moment in the development of a firm as is the initial start: not so much because of risks with labor relations or with contacts for commodity supplies, but because of unclear property rights and brotherly conflict over finance and market shares.

Rapid demographic change has intensified these relations of control. Increases in the age at marriage and the general halving of completed family size within a generation give rise to a *deficit of brothers/sons*.[10] The deficit of brothers can be shown to affect starting capital, firm size, and the ease of entry into trade or business of a young male adult. As a result, business coalitions between agnates and affines are having to become more common; in the local business elite we studied, sons-in-law or brothers-in-law had joined one-fifth of the family businesses in the latest generation.[11]

Relative age and marital status are important factors structuring male control over women. Marriages and alliances are carefully controlled to create and protect the resource flows crucial to capital accumulation. Laidlaw's description of Jain practice is worth quoting because it is widely relevant.

> A family's "credit" in business is its stock in the broadest sense, which includes social position, its reputation and the moral and religious as well as the business conduct of all its members. [. . .] When a family contracts a good marriage, its credit increases. [. . .] (T)he potential impacts on business confidence of particular potential alliances are explicit factors for consideration [. . .] because business practice depends [. . .] so much on trust, moral conduct and financial standing. [. . .] This means that a family's credit lies not only in the hands of the men who are actually engaged in business, but in that of its women too. When sons succeed automatically to their father's position in the family firm, the future of the business enterprise is, quite literally, in the women's hands.
>
> (Laidlaw, op. cit., 1995: 355–56)

The piety of their female family members then has implications for business.

The role played by gender in the accumulation of capital thus involves a hierarchy of power based upon the male control of both male labor and male and female sexuality and social behavior. In this arena of power, not only are women subordinated to men but young men are subordinated to older men. We find patriarchy in its original sense: the governance of male society by its elders. These male relations of patriarchy, relations among men in which gender identity is important, have consequences for development and well-being, which reinforce the productive deprivation of women in the class-controlling capital, and they do so by a variety of means.[12]

Paradoxes of Economic Development

Under these alignments of governance, gender relations are allocatively inefficient, and have complicated and contradictory consequences. Capital is controlled but less efficiently than it might be if women were able to work, as Boserup advocated, on terms commensurate not even with men but merely with their education. At best, some educated women work as teachers in private schools. For the most part they are also encouraged to be active in voluntary work in the Rotary and Lions' Clubs (as "Lionesses"). As a result of such inefficiency, the local economy is actually more labor-intensive than it otherwise might be.

The need to keep capital under tight patriarchal control discourages the business elite from sending sons (implicated in the ownership of firms by the time of their early adulthood) far away to higher education and out of direct male parental reach. Thus, they often lack the technical knowledge required to foster innovation. In consequence, technical changes in rice production, silk making, gold ornament manufacturing, and retailing, generally capital-biased and labor-displacing, are retarded.

The need to keep capital under tight patriarchal control also leads to unrisky diversifications, local in space and narrow in their commodity composition. This is one of several reasons for the intense commodity clustering apparent in the Indian economy (Cadene and Holmstrom, 1998; Schmitz and Nadvi, 1999). That strangers are generally still not welcome to cooperate follows from the structure of governance of family business. Last, the impacts of family firms governed in this way affect allocative efficiency. Competition between firms (superficially independent entities) networked by kinship is frequently suppressed. Collusive oligopolies can be created and enforced.

I do not wish to do more than speculate on how distinctively "Indian" these male patriarchal arrangements are. In his treatise on *Trust*, Fukuyama (1995) distinguishes France, Italy, Taiwan, and Hong Kong from the U.S., Germany, and Japan on the basis of general levels of trust. The first group, being societies with *low* levels of trust, have economies with a preponderance of relatively small-scale firms based on male family labor. Even in large corporations and public companies, the promoter family's shares constitute a large proportion, and professional managers are comparatively rare. The glass ceiling on accumulation constituted by family forms of accumulation is associated with decentralized and flexible, network-based forms of economic organization.

India is very conspicuous by its absence in *Trust*, but would belong to the low trust group. With respect to the Chinese commercial diaspora, Greenhalgh (1994), who examined family firms as part of her critique of the revisionist emphasis on (Confucianist) culture to explain East Asian capitalism, found, among other things, the same kind of structuring of male family labor—with male authority vested in seniority and women severely subordinated and exploited in the effort to keep production costs low. Women were confined to nonmanagerial and part-time work and excluded from inherited property relations. Therefore, in neither of these respects is India to be considered uniquely distinctive. India's distinction relates to demographic consequences.

Paradoxes of Human Development

There are three matters for male and female well-being and agency. First, the reinforcement of patriarchal relations in the class-controlling local *capital* has contradictory effects on the welfare of women. These have been theorized as positive for the female workforce or for upwardly mobile subaltern social classes but negative in the heart of the local business class itself. Second, the agent of what I have called female "gender-cleansing" (and what could also be called demographic structural adjustment) is itself female, for it is women who neglect or kill their daughters (Harris-White, 1999). Third, the increasingly male-biased and gendered accumulation of *capital* has an impact on well-being that is concealed by the analytical attention paid to *income*. Capital's gendered impact can be felt irrespective of the other ways in which the economy is structured—for example, through caste and religion (Basile and White, 2000).

Concerning the first paradox, survival chances are normally theorized in terms of returns to work (either by the flat binary category of economic participation, nonparticipation, proxies for "income," or gendered incomes). The orthodox hypothesis relates wealth to the withdrawal of women from economic participation in the interest of the status of the household. Seclusion is a public status attribute primarily reflecting upon men. It contrasts with the compulsions of wage labor among women of lower castes. Accumulation and seclusion have *also* been accompanied by the diffusion from North India of the dowry, not vested in the bride but taking the form of an unmediated transfer from bride givers to receivers. As the economic costs of women rise, their economic benefits fall, as do their relative status and survival chances. These propositions have received much attention in the literature on the economics of the household.[13]

Agnihotri (2000), exploring the hypothesis that there is a U-shaped curve in the relation of the antifemale sex ratio to increasing income and wealth, has discovered a few cases of kinks in the generally downward-sloping relationship (after which point the ratio of females to males recovers). But these inflexion points are at levels of income or wealth (land) that exclude all but the tiniest minority of the elite population and their "liberated" men and women (some of whom will be readers of this chapter).

In general, the sex ratio becomes ever more adverse to women as income or household wealth rises (Agnihotri, 2000). The slope is steeper in urban cases than in rural ones, and for children than adults. In other words, the association between development and disadvantage is worse where wealth is more concentrated and is anyway worsening over recent time. While the aggregate All-Indian sex ratio has recovered from 927 in 1991 to 933 in 2001, the juvenile (under 10) sex ratio has slipped nationwide from 945 to 917; and in states of the Northwest to *750* (Athreya, 2001).

Case-study research in rural and urban South India reveals complex economic logics at work among the *poor* (Nillesen, 1999). Complex logics specific to class and gendered wage work are likely to be required to explain survival differentials elsewhere.[14] As total income increases in *landless* households, so the survival differential *reduces*. But in rural *landed* households, increases in assets are associated with an increasing bias against girls in sex differentials in life chances. Prosperity reduces the survival chances of rural girls, not when it is in the form of income, but when it takes the form of landed property.

Contemporary historical research shows that this latter effect has appeared only recently and is intensifying as property ownership becomes more extensive and the possibility of inheritance diffuses (Harriss-White, 1999). Economic development and the amassing of inheritable property, even if on a small scale, act so as to disfavor women in certain class positions—in this instance, most intensely those women belonging to the numerically small class of the propertied elite.[15] My own work on the local rural landed elite of the dominant agrarian caste yielded an under-7 sex ratio in 1993–'94 of 645. That for the local agrocommercial elite gives an under-15 sex ratio in 1994 of 784. These are extremely low. It would seem that one in five girls there has been denied the freedom to live.[16]

Concerning the second paradox, we have to explain the act of maternal neglect of girls, and of women's hostility toward womanhood. Of this, Ashis Nandy (1990: 34) writes: "(m)an's cruelty toward man is exceeded only by man's cruelty toward woman. But even man's cruelty toward woman is no match for the cruelty of woman toward woman." He argues, however, that such behavior results not from low earnings, low self-valuation, or perceptions that weaken the female fallback position in intrahousehold bargaining, but rather from women turning against themselves and identifying with aggressive men. As well as being psychological victims of male aggression and male supremacist ideology, women are active agents in their self-repudiation.

Which brings me to the third and final problem. The use of continuous economic variables such as landholding, expenditure, or income to explain sex ratios does not illuminate the full range of patriarchal logics that may be brought to bear on women's life chances. First, consider dowries (regarded at least as a disabling economic shock to parents of daughters, at most a potentially mortal burden to daughters, and a massive threat to the latter's relative status). Among local elites, if income is derived only from a *salary*, the ratio of dowry to household assets is likely to be high and the conventional cost/benefit calculation may indeed account for sex discrimination.

By contrast, in the households of local elite business families, where income comes from *capital*, if total dowries ever disbursed for daughters are compared with net total assets for sons, the ratio will be much lower—my estimate of the dowry:assets for elite business families in 1994 was 1:12.[17] In these circumstances dowries are neither particularly burdensome, nor are they in any sense a premortem inheritance on a par with the prospects of sons. Here dowries enter the explanation at the level of *discourse*. If they have a real role as a disincentive for females, it is *ideological*. That culture and ideology may have powerful material consequences is not in dispute. Nor is the fact that women can be complicitous with an ideology that undermines them.

Now, consider the demand for male labor in the family firm in a context of rapid fertility decline. This provides a second material explanation for daughters not being valued by the local elite. In firms with deficits of family labor, the compensating introduction of male affines is not free because it carries the price of a dowry. Yet neither the gendered transfer of assets between generations nor the gendering of the division of managerial labor by themselves can explain such severe female disadvantages in life chances under conditions where total resources are relatively abundant. The cultural transfer to the South from the North of dowry, as an idiom of modernity (replacing bride price or small reciprocal transfers at marriage) battened onto customary norms barring women from managing family businesses, are first and foremost cultural constraints. They are lethal sets of ideas.

The relative deprivation from productive functioning and the exclusion of women from the ownership of capital are ironies of India's development, which would have vexed Ester Boserup. The creation of wealth means the expansion and diffusion of the male family business. Women are excluded from family business and the role they play in business families—though it is a significant social role—actively threatens their well-being. Their dowry is not theirs to control and it is a far smaller part of their natal family's capital than the portion accumulated for males. It is now not poverty, or Indian kinship practices, so much as the way local Indian capitalism is socially constructed and mediated by kinship practices and their own psychological complicity that poses the greatest relative danger to women.

What Is Being Done?

The 1961 Dowry Prohibition Act is not enforced. Dowries are ever more rarely vested in brides, local marriage patterns mix and match virilocality, village exogamy, and caste hypergamy in ways that increasingly isolate women,[18] women's rights to land and nonland property are widely disregarded, and sex identification and selective abortion centers are poorly regulated nation-wide. In Tamil Nadu, girl children may be abandoned at certain primary health centers for upbringing in orphanages, and reserved jobs in the state. The Scheme for the Protection of the Girl Child entitles poor couples with one or two daughters to benefits in education and employment, consequent to the mother's sterilization. These schemes treat symptoms rather than causes. The funding of both schemes reveal the state government's lack of serious intent.

To improve their relative status in the local business elite, women must work outside the home and the voluntary sector. Here the state is nothing but ambivalent. On the one hand female disadvantage is reproduced through disadvantageous access to state-administered health, education, food, and social security. The state is pro-male-biased in the way it goes about creating assets and registering collateral for credit. On the other hand, in the region I have addressed, educated women are employed disproportionately in the state than in the private sector. It is left to social and political activists and a small sensitized element in the media to counter the heavy weight of ideas by reason, shame, and ridicule through means such as theater, village debates, press reports, films, and counseling—and that not only of women but also increasingly of men.

References

Agnihotri, S. 2000. *Sex Ratio Patterns in the Indian Population.* New Delhi: Sage.

Athreya, V. 2001. "Census 2001: Some Progress, Some Concern," *Frontline,* April.

Basile, E. and B. Harriss-White. 2000. "Corporatist Capitalism: Civil Society and the Politics of Accumulation in Small Town India." QEH Working paper Series 38 (paper to the Gordon White Memorial Conference, IDS Sussex, 1999), www.qeh.ox.ac.uk

Boserup, E. 1989 (1970). *Women's Role in Economic Development.* London: Earthscan.

Cadene, P. and M. Homstrom, eds. 1998. *Decentralised Production in India: Industrial Districts, Flexible Specialisation and Employment.* New Delhi: Sage.

Dasgupta, M. 1987. "Selective Discrimination Against Female Children in Rural Punjab, India," *Population and Development Review,* 13(1): 77–100.

Dasgupta, M. and P.N. Bhat. 1995. "Intensified Gender Bias in India: A Consequence of Fertility Decline." Working paper no. 2, Center for Population and Development Studies, Harvard.

Fox, R. 1969. *From Zamindar to Ballot Box: Community Change in a North Indian Market Town.* Ithaca: Cornell University Press.

Fukuyama, F. 1995. *Trust: the Social Virtues and the Creation of Prosperity.* London: Penguin.

George S. ed. 1998. "Female Infanticide," Special Issue, *Search Bulletin,* XIII(3).

Greenhalgh, A. 1994. "De-orientalizing the Chinese Family Firm," *American Ethologist,* 21(4): 746–75.

Haddad, L., J. Hoddinott, and H. Alderman. 1997. *Intrahousehold Resource Allocation in Developing Countries: Models Methods and Policy.* Baltimore: Johns Hopkins.

Harriss-White, B. 1999. "Gender Cleansing: The Paradox of Development and Deteriorating Female Life Chances in Tamil Nadu," in R. Sunder Rajan, ed. *Signposts: Gender Issues in Post Independence India.* New Delhi: Kali for Women.

——— and S. Janakarajan. 1997. "From Green Revolution to Rural Industrial Revolution," *Economic and Political Weekly,* XXXII(25): 1469–77.

Hensman R. 1999. "How to Support the Rights of Women Workers in the Context of Trade Liberalization in India," in A. Hale ed., *Trade Myths and Gender Reality.* Uppsala: Global Publications Foundation.

Jackson, C. 1999. "Men's Work, Masculinities and the Gender Division of Labour," *Journal of Development Studies,* 36(1): 89–108.

Jackson, C. and R. Pearson eds. 1999. *Feminist Visions of Development.* London: Routledge.

Laidlaw, J. 1995. *Riches and Renunciation: Religion, Economy and Society among the Jains.* Clarendon: Oxford.

Nandy, A. 1990. "Woman Versus Womanliness in India: An Essay in Culture and Psychology," in A. Nandy ed., *At the Edge of Psychology: Essays in Politics and Culture.* New Delhi: Oxford University Press.

Nilleson, P. 1999. "The Survival of the Girl Child." M.Sc. Thesis in Economics for Development, Queen Elizabeth House, Oxford University.

Pearson, R. 1994. "Gender Relations, Capitalism and Third World Industrialisation," in L. Sklair ed. *Capitalism and Development.* London: Routledge.

Razavi, S. 1992. "Agrarian Change and Gender Power: A Comparative Study in Southeastern Iran." D. Phil. Thesis, Oxford University.

Schmitz, H. and K. Nadvi. 1999. "Clustering and Industrialisation: An Introduction," in H. Schmitz and K. Nadvi eds. *Industrial Clustering in Developing Countries*; also Special Issue, *World Development*, 27(9).

Sen, A. K. 1999. *Development as Freedom*. Oxford: Clarendon.

Srinivas, M. N. 1966. "A Sociological Study of Okhla Industrial Estate," in M. N. Srinivas ed. *Small Industries and Social Change*. New Delhi: UNESCO.

White, G. 1993. "Toward a Political Analysis of Markets," in *Bulletin*, Institute of Development Studies, 24(2): 4–12.

Notes

1. The empirical data is abridged from chapter five of my book *India Working* (forthcoming), Cambridge University Press, background papers for other chapters of which may be found on the Queen Elizabeth House Working Papers Web site: www.qeh.ox.ac.uk. I am very grateful for comments from participants at the Cornell Conference on Global Tensions and at seminars at the Dept. for International Development, London, Oberlin College, and Queen Elizabeth House.

2. By this Boserup must mean upper-caste Hindus.

3. This process of marginalization continues to this day (Hensman, 2000), despite the rise in female employment in S. Asian export-processing zones.

4. Demand disincentives include rules on maternity benefits, child care, and equal pay. Supply disincentives include fixed working hours and the location of sites. Pearson (1994: 339–58) comments critically that employment regulations do not act as disincentives where they have no reach in the vast informal sectors of developing economies. Nor are location and time constraints under flexible production.

5. The distinction was first made by Fox (1969: 143) and developed by Laidlaw (1995: 354–5).

6. Decades of research in feminist economics inspired by Boserup have shown how contradictory incentives inside households, differential returns on labor markets, and the gendering of marketing systems operate to subordinate women. See Haddad, Hoddinott, and Adler (1997) and Jackson and Pearson (1999) for the range of this field.

7. Boserup's models were regional and global in scope.

8. See, respectively, Basile and Harriss-White (2000) and Harriss-White and Janakarajan (1997).

9. Whether this elaborate set of authority relations is accurately captured as pure co-operation with its connotations of reasoned choice and voluntarism or as the valuable outcome of freedom to choose, or as the manifestation of the intrinsic and instrumental liberty of freedom to exchange and transact on markets, which Sen identifies in *Development and Freedom* as a goal of development (Sen, 1999: 4, 6, 18 and 27) is altogether another matter.

10. The reasons are complex and class-specific. They include the impact of education, fertility of poor, nutrition, poverty, ideas of modernity, the state social security system, which reduces the risks and costs of abandonment in old age, and experiments in incentive-based sterilization. That the wealthiest families have reduced their fertility as quickly as, or faster than, poor families is in all probability a testimony to the impact of education. However Monica Dasgupta's work (1987 and 1995) has long warned us against assuming that education is a factor encouraging equity in the right to life. Her most educated women were most likely to plan the gender composition as well as the size of their family. These will depend on sex sequences in birth orders. New technology allows sex selection to be done prenatally, while those excluded from access cull girls post-natally. Secular declines in the sex ratio at birth may also result from reduced fetal wastage, which is disproportionately male, this being the consequence of improvements in maternal health (D. Jayaraj and S. Subramanian, Pers. Comm., 2001).

11. One-fifth of the businesses of Arni's elite have drawn in affines. They are thought to occupy subordinate positions in such firms.

12. See Jackson (1999) for a general analysis of masculinity and work among laboring classes.

13. See Agnihotri (2000) chs. 1 and 2.

14. See Razavi (1992) for Iran.

15. The latter is a numerically smaller group than the class of landless agricultural laborers that it may suffer from lack of valuation as a development problem.
16. Unlike elsewhere in India, in this region of northern Tamil Nadu there is no evidence for sex selective feticide, and only patchy evidence of infanticide in more remote villages (George, 1998) though this practice is known to be spreading. The mechanism of death seems to be neglect.
17. Dowry norms for the merchant elite specify combinations of gold sovereigns and consumer durables (fridge, scooter, or moped, TV with home theater). A large local dowry in 1994 might have comprised Rs 2.6 lakhs in gold and Rs 1.03 lakhs in kind, Rs 3.6 lakhs in all (then over £7,000). The ratio was calculated by applying these dowries to all the daughters of present elite owners and dividing the net current assets (no doubt underestimated) between the total sons of the elite.
18. See Harriss-White (1999) for ethnographic material.

CHAPTER 14

Promoting Women's Capabilities

MARTHA NUSSBAUM[1]

It will be seen how in place of the wealth *and* poverty *of political economy come the* rich human being *and* rich human need. *The rich human being is [. . .] the human being* in *need of a totality of human life-activities.*
Marx, *Economic and Philosophical Manuscripts of 1844*

I found myself beautiful as a free human mind.
Mrinal, heroine of Rabindranath Tagore's "Letter from a Wife" (1914)

Development and Sex Equality

Women in much of the world lack support for fundamental functions of a human life. They are less well nourished and healthy than men and more vulnerable to physical violence and sexual abuse. They are much less likely than men to be literate, and still less likely to have preprofessional or technical education. Should they attempt to enter the workplace they face greater obstacles, including intimidation from family or spouse, sex discrimination in hiring, and sexual harassment in the workplace—all frequently without effective legal recourse. Similar obstacles often impede their effective participation in political life. In many nations women are not full equals under the law: they do not have the same property rights as men; the rights to make a contract; or the rights of association, mobility, and religious liberty.[2]

Burdened often with the "double day" of taxing employment and full responsibility for housework and child care, they lack opportunities for play and cultivation of their imaginative and cognitive faculties. All these factors take a toll on their emotional well-being. Women have fewer opportunities than men to live free from fear and enjoy rewarding types of love—especially when they are married without choice in childhood and have no recourse from a bad marriage. In all these ways, unequal social and political circumstances result in women's unequal human capabilities.[3]

Consider the examples of health and nutrition. There is pervasive evidence of discrimination against females in many nations of the developing world. Where equal nutrition and health care are present women live, on average, slightly longer than men: thus, we would expect a sex ratio of something like 102.2 women to 100 men (the actual sex ratio of Sub-Saharan Africa[4]). Many countries have a far lower sex ratio: India's, was 92.7 women to 100 men in the last census, the lowest sex ratio since the beginning of the census. The best estimate is that the current ratio is far lower, something like 85 to 100, on account of the availability of sex-selective abortion.

If we study such ratios and ask the question: "How many more women than are now present in Country C would be there if they had the same sex ratio as Sub-Saharan Africa?", We get a figure that economist Amartya Sen has graphically called the number of "missing women." There are many millions of missing women in the world today.[5] Using this rough index, the number of missing women in Southeast Asia is 2.4 million, Latin America 4.4, North Africa 2.4, Iran 1.4, China 44.0, Bangladesh 3.7, India 36.7, Pakistan 5.2, and West Asia 4.3.[6]

One area of life that greatly contributes to women's inequality is the area of care. Women are the world's primary, and usually only, caregivers for people in conditions of extreme dependency: young children; the elderly; and those whose physical or mental handicaps make them incapable of the relative (and often temporary) independence that characterizes so-called "normal" human lives. Women often perform this crucial work without pay and recognition that it is work. At the same time, the fact that they need to spend long hours caring for the physical needs of others makes it more difficult for them to do what they want to do in other areas of life, including employment, citizenship, play, and self-expression.[7]

The influential human-rights approach has a great deal to say about these inequalities, and the language of rights has proven enormously valuable for women, both in articulating their demands for justice and in linking those demands to the earlier demands of other subordinated groups. However, the rights framework is shaky in several respects. First, it is intellectually contested: There are many different conceptions of what rights are, and what it means to secure a right to someone. Are rights prepolitical, or artifacts of laws and institutions? Do they belong to individual persons only, or to groups as well? Are they always correlated with duties? And who has the duties correlated with human rights? What are human rights: to have freedom from state interference and a certain positive level of well-being and opportunity? To use the language of rights all by itself is not very helpful: it invites a host of further questions about what is being recommended.

Second, the language of rights has been historically associated with the idea of "negative liberty," or freedom from state intervention; many people use the language in this way today. Thus, it may prove a problematic conceptual framework within which to cast the idea of affirmative state duties to support human flourishing. Third, the human-rights approach has traditionally ignored urgent claims of women for protection from domestic violence and other abuses of their bodily integrity. Although this failure has to some extent been challenged (and corrected) by women who have insisted that "women's rights are human rights," there remains a reluctance to interfere in issues of distributive justice within the family.

This, I argue, is no accident since the human-rights paradigm is historically strongly connected with the traditional distinction between a public sphere regulated by law and a private sphere that the law should leave alone. This paradigm has not sufficiently challenged the traditional distribution of resources and opportunities among family members or insisted upon the recognition of women's work as work. Fourth and finally, the human-rights approach is often criticized for being Western and insensitive to non-Western traditions of thought. Even if one believes that these criticisms are in many ways mistaken (as I shall argue they are), one might still wish to search for a supplement to this contested language that would be free of this problem.

I shall argue that the supplement we need is the capabilities approach, an approach to issues of basic justice and the measurement of quality of life pioneered within economics by Amartya Sen, put into practice in the *Human Development Reports,* and developed by me in a slightly different way within feminist political theory.

The Need for Cross-Cultural Norms

Should we be looking for a set of cross-cultural norms where women's opportunities are concerned? In many areas women are already doing this. For example, women laboring in the informal sector are increasingly organizing on an international level to set goals and priorities.[8] Many other examples are provided by the international human-rights movement and international agreements such as CEDAW. But this process is both intellectually and politically controversial. Where do these normative categories come from? And how can they be justified as appropriate ones for cultures that have traditionally used different normative categories?

No critical social theory confines itself to the categories of each culture's daily life. If it did, it probably could not perform its special task as critical theory, which involves the systematization and critical scrutiny of intuitions that in daily life are often unexamined. Theory gives people a set of terms with which to criticize abuses that otherwise might lurk nameless in the background. Terms such as sexual harassment and hostile work environment are obvious examples of this point. But even if one defends theory as valuable for practice, it may still be problematic to use concepts that originate in one culture to describe and assess realities in another—and all the more problematic if the culture described has been colonized and oppressed by the describer's culture. Attempts by international feminists to use a universal language of justice, human rights, or human functioning to assess women's lives often encounter charges of Westernizing and colonizing—even when the universal categories are introduced by feminists who live and work within the nation in question. For it is said, such women are alienated from their culture and are faddishly aping a Western political agenda.[9]

I begin by asking whose interests are served by the implicit nostalgic image of a happy harmonious culture, and whose resistance and misery are being effaced? Nonetheless, when we advance a set of universal norms in connection with women's equality, we will also face three more respectable objections, which must be confronted. First, one hears what I call the *argument from culture*. Traditional cultures, the argument goes, contain their own norms of what women's lives should be: norms of female modesty, deference, obedience, and self-sacrifice. Feminists should not assume (without argument) that those are bad norms, incapable of constructing good and flourishing lives for women. By contrast, the norms proposed by feminists are seem as suspiciously Western because they involve emphasis on individuality, choice, and opportunity.

My answer to this argument does not preclude any woman's choice to lead a traditional life, so long as she does so with certain economic and political opportunities firmly in place. I should state at the outset that the opponent's notion of tradition is far too simple. Cultures are scenes of debate and contestation. They contain dominant voices, and the voices of women have not always been heard. It would be implausible to suggest that the many groups working to improve the employment conditions of women in the informal sector, are brainwashing women into striving for economic opportunities. Clearly they provide means to ends that women already want, and a context of female solidarity within which to pursue those ends. Cultures are also dynamic—struggle and change are deeply woven into them—thus the appeal to culture gives us questions rather than answers.

Now consider the argument that I call the *argument from the good of diversity*. This argument reminds us that our world is rich in part because we don't all agree on a single set of practices and norms. We think the world's different languages have worth and beauty, and that if any language should cease to exist, the expressive resources of human life is generally diminished. So too, cultural norms have their distinctive beauty; the world risks becoming impoverished as it becomes more homogeneous.

Here I distinguish two claims the objector might be making: first, that diversity is good as such; and second, there are problems with the values of economic efficiency and consumerism that are increasingly dominating our interlocking world. This second claim does not oppose cross-cultural norms; it just suggests that their content should be critical of some dominant economic norms. So the challenge to our enterprise lies in the first claim. To meet it we must ask: how similar are cultural and linguistic diversity?

The trouble with the analogy is that languages don't harm people, but cultural practices frequently do. We could think that threatened languages such as Cornish and Breton should be preserved, without thinking the same about domestic violence: it is not worth preserving simply because it is there and very old. In the end, the objection doesn't undermine the search for cross-cultural norms, it requires it. It invites us to ask: are the cultural values in question worth preserving? This entails a general cross-cultural framework of assessment that will tell us when we are better off letting a practice die.

Finally, we have the *argument from paternalism*. This argument says that when we use a set of cross-cultural norms as benchmarks for the world's varied societies, we show too little respect for people's freedom as agents and their role as democratic citizens. People are the best judges of what is good for them and if we say that their choices are not good for them, we treat them like children. This is an important point, and one that any viable cross-cultural proposal should bear in mind. However, it is not incompatible with the endorsement of cross-cultural norms. Indeed, it endorses some cross-cultural norms such as political liberties and other opportunities for choice. Paternalism gives us a strong reason to respect the variety of ways citizens choose to lead their lives in a pluralistic society, and seek a set of cross-cultural norms that protect freedom and choice. This means that we will value religious tolerance, associative freedom, and other liberties. These liberties are themselves cross-cultural norms and they are not compatible with views that many people and societies hold.

We can make a further claim: many existing value systems are themselves highly paternalistic, particularly toward women. They treat them as unequal under the law, as lacking full civil capacity, as having no associative liberties, or property, or employment rights of males. If we encounter such a system, it is in one sense paternalistic to say sorry, it is unacceptable under the universal norms of equality and liberty. In that way, any bill of rights is "paternalistic" vis à vis families, groups, practices, or pieces of legislation that treat people with insufficient or unequal respect. The Indian Constitution, for example, is in that sense paternalistic when it tells people that it is illegal to use caste or sex as grounds of discrimination. But that is hardly a good argument against fundamental constitutional rights or, more generally, opposing the attempts of some people to tyrannize others.

We dislike paternalism, insofar as we do, because there is something else that we like, namely liberty of choice in fundamental matters. It is fully consistent to reject some forms of paternalism while supporting those that underwrite these basic values.

The argument from paternalism indicates that we should prefer a cross-cultural normative account that focuses on empowerment and opportunity, leaving people plenty of space to determine their course in life once those opportunities are secured to them. It does not give us reason to reject the idea of cross-cultural norms. On the contrary, it provides strong reasons to seek such norms, including basic liberties and forms of economic empowerment that are crucial in making liberties available to everyone.

The argument also suggests that the account we search should seek empowerment and opportunity for each and every person, respecting each as an end, rather than simply as the agent or supporter of ends of others. Women are too often treated as members of an organic unit, such as the family or community is supposed to be, with their interests subordinated to the larger goals of that unit, which typically means those of male members.

Traditional Economic Approaches to Development: The Need for Human Norms

Another way of understanding why cross-cultural norms are needed in the international policy arena is to consider the current alternative. Prior to the shift in thinking that is associated with the work of Amartya Sen[10] and the *Human Development Reports* of the UNDP,[11] the most prevalent approach to measuring quality of life in a nation used to be to ask about gross national product (GNP) per capita. This approach tries to weasel out of making any cross-cultural claims about what has value—although it assumes the universal value of opulence. What it omits, however, is much more significant. We are not told about wealth and income distribution, or that countries with similar aggregate figures can exhibit great distributional variations. (South Africa always did very well among developing nations, despite its enormous inequalities and violations of basic justice.) Moreover, to see how people are really doing, we need to specify, beyond distributions of wealth and income, what parts of lives we ought to look at. Examples are life expectancy, infant mortality, educational and employment opportunities, health care, land rights, and political liberties. Identifying what is absent from GNP nudges us in the direction of mapping out these and other basic goods in a universal way, so that we can use a list of basic goods to compare quality of life across societies.

An additional problem with resource-based approaches, even those that are sensitive to distribution, is that individuals vary in their ability to convert resources into functionings. Some of these differences are straightforwardly physical: nutritional needs vary with age, occupation, and sex; a pregnant or lactating woman needs more nutrients than a nonpregnant woman; a child needs more protein than an adult. Some of the pertinent variations are social and connected with traditional hierarchies. If we wish to bring all citizens of a nation to the same level of educational attainment, we will need to devote more resources to those who encounter obstacles from traditional hierarchy or prejudice. Thus women's literacy will prove more expensive than men's literacy in many parts of the world. If we operate only with an index of resources we will frequently reinforce inequalities that are relevant to well-being.

If we turn from resource- to preference-based approaches, we encounter another set of difficulties.[12] Preferences are not exogenous, given independently of economic and social conditions. They are partially constructed by those conditions. Women often have no preference for economic independence before they learn about avenues through which women like them might pursue this goal. Nor do they think of themselves as citizens with rights that were being ignored, before they learn of their rights and are encouraged to believe in their equal worth. Men's preferences are also socially shaped and often misshaped. They frequently have a strong preference for their wives to do all the child care and housework—often in addition to working an eight-hour day. Such preferences are not fixed in the nature of things: They are constructed by social traditions of privilege and subordination. Thus a preference-based approach will reinforce inequalities, especially those inequalities that are entrenched enough to have crept into people's very desires. Looking at women's lives helps us see the inadequacy of traditional approaches. The urgency of women's problems gives us a very strong motivation to prefer a nontraditional approach.

Human Dignity and Human Capabilities

I now argue that a reasonable answer to all these concerns—capable of giving good guidance to governments establishing basic constitutional principles and to international agencies assessing the quality of life—is given by a version of the capabilities approach. The central question asked by the capabilities approach is not: "How satisfied is this woman?" or even "How much in the way of resources is she able to command?" It is: "What is she actually able to do and to be?" Taking a political stand on a working list of functions that would appear to be of central importance in human life, users of this approach ask: "Is the person capable of this, or not?" They ask not only about the person's satisfaction with what she does, but about what she does, and what she is in a position to do (what her opportunities and liberties are). They ask not just about the resources that are present, but about how those do or do not enable the woman to function.

To introduce the intuitive idea behind the approach, it is useful to start from this passage of Marx's 1844 *Economic and Philosophical Manuscripts*, written at a time when he was reading Aristotle and was profoundly influenced by Aristotelian ideas of human capability and functioning:

> It is obvious that the *human* eye gratifies itself in a way different from the crude, nonhuman eye; the human *ear* different from the crude ear, etc [. . .] The *sense* caught up in crude practical need has only a *restricted* sense. For the starving man, it is not the human form of food that exists, but only its abstract being as food; it could just as well be there in its crudest form, and it would be impossible to say wherein this feeding activity differs from that of *animals*.

Marx here singles out certain human functions—eating and the uses of the senses—that seem to have a particular centrality in any life one might live. He then claims that it is significant to be able to perform these activities in a fully human way, by which he means a way infused with reasoning and sociability. But human beings don't automatically have the opportunity to perform their human functions in a fully human way. Some conditions in which people live, conditions of starvation or educational deprivation, result in humans having to live in a subhuman way. Of course what Marx is saying is that these conditions are unacceptable, and should be changed.

Similarly, the intuitive idea behind my version of the capabilities approach is twofold. First, there are certain functions that are particularly central in human life such that their presence or absence is understood to be a mark of the presence or absence of human life. Second, and this is what Marx found in Aristotle, it is significant to be in a position to do these functions in a truly human way. The core idea is that of the human being as a dignified free being who shapes his or her own life, rather than being passively shaped or pushed around in the manner of a flock or herd animal. This approach makes each person a bearer and an end of value. Marx, like his bourgeois forebears, holds that it is profoundly wrong to subordinate the ends of some individuals to those of others. That is at the core of what exploitation is: To treat a person as a mere object for the use of others. What this approach promotes is a society in which individuals are treated as worthy of regard and in which each has been put in a position to live humanly.

I submit that we can produce an account of necessary elements of human functioning that commands a broad cross-cultural consensus, a list that can be endorsed for political purposes by people who have different views of what is a good life for a human being. The list provides a focus for quality of life assessment and political planning, and aims to select capabilities that are of central importance, whatever else the person pursues. The list in its current form represents the result of years of cross-cultural discussion,[13] and comparisons between earlier and later versions will show that the input of other voices has shaped its content in many ways. It remains open-ended and humble. It does not deny that the items listed are to some extent differently constructed by different societies. Indeed, part of the idea of the list is that its members can be more concretely specified in accordance with local beliefs and circumstances. Here is the current version:

Central Human Functional Capabilities

1. **Life.** Being able to live to the end of a human life of normal length; not dying prematurely or before one's life is so reduced as to be not worth living.
2. **Bodily Health.** Being able to have good health, including reproductive health;[14] be adequately nourished; and have adequate shelter.
3. **Bodily Integrity.** Being able to move freely from place to place; to be secure against violent assault, including sexual assault and domestic violence; having opportunities for sexual satisfaction and choice in matters of reproduction.
4. **Senses, Imagination, and Thought.** Being able to use the senses to imagine, think, and reason; and to do these things in a "truly human" way—a way informed and cultivated by an adequate education, including literacy and basic mathematical and scientific training. Being able to use imagination and thought in connection with experiencing and producing works and events of one's own choice: religious, literary, musical, and so forth. Being able to use one's mind in ways protected by guarantees of freedom of expression with respect to both political and artistic speech, and freedom of religious exercise. Being able to have pleasurable experiences and to avoid non-necessary pain.
5. **Emotions.** Being able to have attachments to things and people outside ourselves; to love those who love and care for us, to grieve at their absence. In general to love, grieve, experience longing, gratitude, and justified anger. Not having one's emotional development blighted by fear and anxiety. Supporting this capability means supporting forms of human association that can be shown to be crucial in their development.
6. **Practical Reason.** Being able to form a conception of the good and engage in critical reflection about the planning of one's life. (This entails protection for the liberty of conscience.)
7. **Affiliation.**

    A. Being able to live with and toward others, to recognize and show concern for other human beings, to engage in various forms of social interaction; to be able to imagine the situation of another and to have compassion for that situation; to have the capability for both justice and friendship. Protecting this capability means protecting institutions that constitute and nourish such forms of affiliation, and protecting freedom of assembly and political speech.

   B. Having the social bases of self-respect and nonhumiliation; being able to be treated as a dignified being whose worth is equal to that of others. This entails protections against discrimination on the basis of race, sex, sexual orientation, religion, caste, ethnicity, or national origin.
8. **Other Species.** Being able to live with concern for and in relation to animals, plants, and the world of nature.
9. **Play.** Being able to laugh, play, and enjoy recreational activities.
10. **Control Over One's Environment.**

   A. Political. Being able to effectively participate in political choices that govern one's life; having protections of free speech and association.

   B. Material. Being able to hold property (both land and movable goods); having the right to seek employment on an equal basis with others; having the freedom from unwarranted search and seizure. In work, being able to work as a human being, exercising practical reason, and entering into meaningful relationships of mutual recognition with other workers.

The list is, emphatically, a list of separate components. We cannot satisfy the need for one of them by giving people a larger amount of another one. All are of central importance and all are distinct in quality. The irreducible plurality of the list limits the trade-offs that it will be reasonable to make, and thus limits the applicability of quantitative cost-benefit analysis.[15] At the same time, the items on the list are related to one another in many complex ways. One of the most effective ways of promoting women's control over their environment and their right of political participation is to promote women's literacy. Women who can seek employment outside the home have more resources in protecting their bodily integrity from assaults within it. Such facts give us reason to *not* promote one capability at the expense of others.

Two capabilities, practical reason and affiliation, are especially important since they both organize and suffuse all the others. To use one's senses in a way not infused by the characteristically human use of thought and planning is to use them in an incomplete human manner. At the same time, to reason for oneself without considering the circumstances and needs of others is to behave in an incomplete human way.

The basic intuition from which the capability approach begins in the political arena is that human abilities exert a moral claim that they should be developed. Human beings are creatures such that provided with the right educational and material support they can become fully capable of human functions. That is, they are creatures with certain lower-level capabilities (which I call basic capabilities) to perform the functions in question. When these capabilities are deprived of the nourishment that would transform them into the high-level capabilities that figure on my list, they are fruitless, cut off, in some way but a shadow of themselves. If a turtle is given a life that afforded it an animal level of functioning we would have no indignation, no sense of waste and tragedy. When a human being is given a life that blights powers of human action and expression, we experience a sense of waste and tragedy.

The capabilities are sought for *each and every person* not, in the first instance, for groups, families, states, or corporate bodies. Such institutions may be important in promoting human capabilities and, as such, they may deservedly gain our support. However, it is because of what they do for people that they are worthy, and the ultimate political goal is always the promotion of the capabilities of every one.[16]

We begin with a sense for the worth and dignity of basic human powers, thinking of them as claims to a chance for functioning, claims that give rise to correlated social and political duties. Three types of capabilities are important in the analysis. First, *basic capabilities*: the innate equipment of individuals that is the necessary basis for developing the more advanced capability, and a ground of moral concern. Second, *internal capabilities*: states of the person herself that are personally sufficient for the exercise of the requisite functions. Most adult humans have the internal capability for religious freedom and the freedom of speech. Finally, there are *combined capabilities*: defined as internal capabilities combined with suitable external conditions for the exercise of the function. Citizens of repressive nondemocratic regimes have the internal, but not the combined capability to exercise thought and speech in accordance with their conscience. The list is thus one of *combined capabilities*. To realize one of the items on the list entails not only promoting appropriate development of people's internal powers, but also preparing the environment so that it is favorable for the exercise of practical reason and the other major functions.

Capability, not functioning, is the political goal. Although the state ought to make opportunities available, in a material not merely formal way, it is inappropriate to dragoon people into functioning in accordance with these capabilities. For many reasons—religious, familial, or personal—citizens may not prefer to exercise a given capability. This conception leaves that choice to them.

Capabilities and Care

All human beings begin their lives as helpless children and if they live long enough they are likely to end their lives in helplessness, whether physical or mental. During the prime of life most humans encounter periods of extreme dependency while some remain dependent on the daily bodily care of others throughout their lives. This articulation suggests that "normal" human beings do not depend on others for bodily care and survival. However, political thought should recognize that some phases of life, and some lives, generate more profound dependency than others.

The capabilities approach sees human beings from the first as animal beings whose lives are characterized by profound neediness as well as dignity. It addresses the issue of care in many ways: under "life" it is stressed that people should be enabled to complete a normal human life span. Under "health" and "bodily integrity," the needs of different phases of life are implicitly recognized. Under "sense," "emotions," and "affiliation," needs that vary with life's stage are targeted. "Affiliation" is of particular importance since it mentions the need for compassion, self-respect, and nondiscrimination. Thus, care must be provided in such a way that the capability for self-respect of the receiver is not injured, and that the caregiver is not exploited and discriminated against on account of performing that role. In other words, a good society must arrange to provide care for those in a condition of extreme dependency, without exploiting women (the primary caregivers) and depriving them of other capabilities.[17]

In this area the capabilities approach has an advantage over traditional liberal approaches that use the idea of a social contract. Such approaches typically generate basic political principles from a hypothetical contract situation in which all participants are independent adults. John Rawls, for example, uses the phrase "fully cooperating members of society over a complete life."[18] But, of course, no human being is that. And this fiction distorts the choice of principles in a central way, effacing the issue of extreme dependency and care from the agenda of the contracting parties when they choose the principles that shape society's basic structure. This fundamental issue profoundly shapes the way social institutions will be designed.[19] The capabilities approach, using a concept of the human being that builds in need and dependency into the first phases of political thinking, is better suited to deliberation on this urgent set of issues.

Capabilities as Goals for Women's Development

I have argued that legitimate concerns for diversity, pluralism, and personal freedom are not incompatible with the recognition of cross-cultural norms, and that cross-cultural norms are required if we are to protect diversity, pluralism, and freedom—treating each human being as an agent and an end. The best way to hold these concerns together is to formulate norms as a set of capabilities for full human functioning, emphasizing the fact that capabilities protect, and do not foreclose, spheres of human freedom.

Used to evaluate the lives of women who are struggling for equality in many developing and developed countries, the capabilities framework is not an alien importation. It is consistent with demands women are making in many global and national political contexts. It might therefore seem superfluous to put these items on a list: Why not just let women decide what they will demand in each case? To answer this question I should point out that the international development debate is already using normative language. Where the capabilities approach has not caught on—as it has in the human development reports—a less-adequate theoretical language still prevails—whether it is the language of preference-satisfaction or economic growth. We need the capabilities approach as a humanly rich alternative to these inadequate theories of human development.

The capabilities approach supplies norms for human development in general, not just for women's development. However, women's issues are not only worthy of focus because of their remarkable urgency, they also help us identify more clearly the inadequacy of various other approaches to development, and the reasons for preferring the capabilities approach. *Preference-based approaches* do not enable us to criticize preferences that have been shaped by a legacy of injustice and hierarchy. The capabilities approach, by contrast, looks at what women are actually able to do and be, undeterred by the fact that oppressed and uneducated women may say, or think, that some of these capabilities are not for them.

Similarly, *resource-based approaches* have a bias in the direction of protecting the status quo. In other words they do not take account of the special needs for aid that some groups may have on account of their subordinate status. The capabilities approach sees this fact clearly.[20] *Human-rights approaches* are close allies of the capabilities approach because they take a stand on certain fundamental entitlements of citizens, and hold that such entitlements may be demanded as a matter of basic justice. However, in comparison, the capabilities approach is both more definite, specifying what it means to secure a right to someone, and more comprehensive, spelling out those rights that are of particular importance to women.

The capabilities approach seem to have one disadvantage: It is difficult to measure human capabilities. We know that anything worth measuring in terms of quality of life is difficult to measure. Resource-based approaches simply substitute what is easy to measure for what really ought to be measured. The capabilities measures developed in the human development reports are admittedly not perfect: years of schooling are an imperfect proxy for education. We may expect that other proxies will be imperfect. On the other hand, we are working in the right place and on the right thing. Over time, as data-gathering responds to our concerns, we expect increasingly adequate data and better methods of aggregation. As has already happened with human-rights approaches, we need to rely on the ingenuity of those who suffer from deprivation; they will help us find ways to describe and quantify their realities.

Women all over the world have lacked support for central human functions, and that lack of support is to some extent caused by their gender. But women, given sufficient nutrition, education, and other support, like men—and unlike rocks, trees, and even horses and dogs—have the potential to become capable of these human functions. This is why their unequal failure in capability is a problem of justice. It is up to all human beings to solve this problem. I claim that the capabilities approach, and a list of the central capabilities, give us good guidance as we pursue this difficult task.

Notes

1. Ernst Freund Distinguished Service Professor of Law and Ethics, Department of Philosophy, Law School, and Divinity School, the University of Chicago. The present chapter is closely related to the arguments of my book *Women and Human Development: The Capabilities Approach* (Cambridge and New York: Cambridge University Press, 2000).
2. For examples see *Women and Human Development*, and my "Religion and Women's Human Rights," in Paul Weithman ed., *Religion and Contemporary Liberalism* (Notre Dame: University of Notre Dame Press, 1997), and in Nussbaum, *Sex and Social Justice* (New York: Oxford University Press, 1999).
3. For recent overall data see *Human Development Report 2001*, United Nations Development Programme (Oxford and New York: Oxford University Press, 2001).
4. Sub-Saharan Africa was chosen as the "baseline" because it might be thought inappropriate to compare developed with developing countries. Europe and North America have an even higher ratio of women to men: about 105:100. Sub-Saharan Africa's relatively high female/male ratio, compared to other parts of the developing world, is very likely explained by the central role women play in productive economic activity, which gives women a claim to food in time of scarcity. For a classic study of this issue, see Ester Boserup, *Women's Role in Economic Development* (New York: St. Martin's Press, 1970; second edition Aldershot: Gower Publishing, 1986). For a set of valuable responses to Boserup's work see *Persistent Inequalities*, Irene Tinker ed., (New York: Oxford University Press, 1990).
5. The statistics in this paragraph are taken from Jean Drèze and Amartya Sen's, *Hunger and Public Action* (Oxford: Clarendon Press, 1989) and Drèze and Sen's, *India: Economic Development and Social Opportunity* (Delhi: Oxford University Press, 1995). Sen's estimated total number of missing women is 100 million; the India chapter discusses alternative estimates.
6. See Drèze and Sen, *Hunger*, p. 52.
7. See Eva Kittay, *Love's Labor: Essays on Women, Equality, and Dependency* (New York: Routledge, 1999); Nancy Folbre, *The Invisible Heart: Economics and Family Values* (New York: The New Press, 2001); Mona Harrington, *Care and Equality: Inventing a New Family Politics* (New York: Knopf, 1999); Joan Williams, *Unbending Gender: Why Family and Work Conflict and What to Do About It* (New York: Oxford University Press, 1999).
8. See *Women in Informal Employment: Globalizing and Organizing*, publication of a public seminar, April 1999, Ottowa, Canada; the steering committee of WIEGO includes Ela Bhatt of SEWA and Martha Chen, who has been a leading participant in discussions of the "capabilities approach": see her "A Matter of Survival: Women's Right to Work in India and Bangladesh," in WCD, and *A Quiet Revolution: Women in Transition in Rural Bangladesh* (Cambridge, MA: Schenkman, 1983).

9. See the excellent discussion of these attacks in the essay "Contesting Cultures" in Uma Narayan, *Dislocating Cultures: Identities, Traditions, and Third World Feminism* (New York: Routledge, 1997).

10. The initial statement is in Sen, "Equality of What?" in S. McMurrin ed., *Tanner Lectures on Human Values 1* (Cambridge: Cambridge University Press, 1980), reprinted in Sen's, *Choice, Welfare, and Measurement* (Oxford and Cambridge, MA: Basil Blackwell and MIT Press, 1982), hereafter CWM; see also various essays in *Resources, Values, and Development* (Oxford and Cambridge, MA: Basil Blackwell and MIT Press, 1984), hereafter RVD; *Commodities and Capabilities* (Amsterdam: North-Holland, 1985); "Well-Being, Agency, and Freedom: The Dewey Lectures 1984," *The Journal of Philosophy* 82 (1985); "Capability and Well-Being," in QL, 30–53; "Gender Inequality and Theories of Justice," in J. Glover and M. Nussbaum eds., *Women, Culture, and Development* (Oxford: Clarendon Press, 1995) hereafter WCD; *Inequality Reexamined* (Oxford and Cambridge, MA: Clarendon Press and Harvard University Press, 1992). See J. Drèze and A. Sen's, *Hunger and Public Action* (Oxford: Clarendon Press, 1989), and *India: Economic Development and Social Opportunity* (Delhi: Oxford University Press, 1995).

11. *Human Development Reports: 1993, 1994, 1995, 1996* (New York: United Nations Development Program). For related approaches in economics see Partha Dasgupta, *An Inquiry into Well-Being and Destitution* (Oxford: Clarendon Press, 1993); Bina Agarwal's, *A Field of One's Own: Gender and Land Rights in South Asia* (Cambridge: Cambridge University Press, 1994); Sabina Alkire's "Operationalizing Amartya Sen's Capability Approach to Human Development: A Framework for Identifying Valuable Capabilities," D. Phil. Dissertation, Oxford University, 1999; S. Anand and C. Harris, "Choosing a Welfare Indicator," *American Economic Association Papers and Proceedings* 84 (199), 226–49; Frances Stewart, "Basic Needs, Capabilities, and Human Development," in *In Pursuit of the Quality of Life*, Avner Offer ed. (Oxford: Oxford University Press, 1996); Prasanta Pattanaik, "Cultural Indicators of Well-Being: Some Conceptual Issues," in UNESCO, *World Culture Report: Culture, Creativity, and Markets* (Paris, UNESCO Publishing, 1998); Meghnad Desai, "Poverty and Capability: Towards an Empirically Implementable Measure," Suntory-Toyota International Centre Discussion Paper no. 27, London School of Economics Development Economics Research Program, 1990; Achin Chakraborty, "The Concept and Measurement of the Standard of Living," Ph.D. Thesis, University of California at Riverside, 1996. For discussion of the approach see K. Aman ed. *Ethical Principles for Development: Needs, Capabilities or Rights* (Montclair, N.J.: Montclair State University Press, 1991); *Choice, Welfare, and Development: A Festschrift in Honour of Amartya K. Sen*, K. Basu, P. Pattanaik, and K. Suzumura eds. (Oxford: Clarendon Press, 1995).

12. Chapter 2 of *Women and Human Development* gives an extensive critique of economic preference-based approaches. Sen has repeatedly stressed this theme.

13. For some examples of the academic part of these discussions see the papers by Roop Rekha Verma, Martha A. Chen, Nkiru Nzegwu, Margarita Valdes, and Xiaorong Li in *Women, Culture and Development*.

14. The 1994 International Conference on Population and Development (ICPD) adopted a definition of reproductive health that fits well with the intuitive idea of human functioning that guides this list: "Reproductive health is a state of complete physical, mental and social well-being and not merely the absence of disease or infirmity, in all matters relating to the reproductive system and its processes. Reproductive health therefore implies that people are able to have a satisfying and safe sex life and that they have the capability to reproduce and the freedom to decide if, when, and how often to do so." The definition goes on say that it also implies information and access to family planning methods of their choice. A brief summary of the ICPD's recommendations, adopted by the Panel on Reproductive Health of the Committee on Population established by the National Research Council, specifies three requirements of reproductive health: "1. Every sex act should be free of coercion and infection. 2. Every pregnancy should be intended. 3. Every birth should be healthy." See Amy O. Tsui, Judith N. Wasserheit, and John G. Haaga eds. *Reproductive Health in Developing Countries* (Washington: National Academy Press, 1997).

15. See Nussbaum, "The Costs of Tragedy: Some Moral Limits of Cost-Benefit Analysis," in *Cost-Benefit Analysis: Legal, Economic, and Philosophical Perspectives*, M. A. Adler and E. Posner eds. (Chicago: University of Chicago Press, 2001).

16. Chapters 3 and 4 of *Women and Human Development* confront the difficult issues raised by religion and the family for this approach.

17. This problem will shape the way states think about all other capabilities. See the varied proposals in the works cited in note 12, and also my "The Future of Feminist Liberalism," a Presidential Address to the Central Division of the American Philosophical Association, *Proceedings and Addresses of the American Philosophical Association* 74 (2000), 47–79.

18. Rawls, *Political Liberalism* (above), a frequent phrase. For detailed discussion of this question see my "Rawls and Feminism," forthcoming in *The Cambridge Companion to Rawls*, Samuel Freeman ed.; and "The Future of Feminist Liberalism."

19. See the excellent argument in Kittay.

20. That is my account of the political goal: one might of course retain the capabilities approach while defining the goal differently—in terms, e.g., of complete capability equality. I recommend the threshold only as a *partial theory of justice*, not a complete theory. If all citizens are over the threshold, my account does not yet take a stand on what distributive principle should govern.

PART 5

Urban and Global Linkages

CHAPTER 15

The Global City

Strategic Site/New Frontier[1]

SASKIA SASSEN

Introduction

Globalization and digitization are resulting in an incipient unbundling of the exclusive authority over territory and people that we have long associated with the nation-state. The most strategic instantiation of this unbundling is probably the global city, which has emerged as a partly denationalized platform for global capital and a diverse mix of people from all over the world. This process brings with it operational and conceptual openings for the participation of nonstate actors in transboundary domains once exclusive to the national state; among such actors are nongovernmental organizations (NGOs), first-nation peoples, and antiglobalization activists. They also include immigrants and refugees who are subjects of adjudication in human-rights decisions and as such, are a type of international legal persona. Further, they include multinational corporations and global markets that can engage in direct transactions with each other, bypassing many of the strictures of the interstate system that until recently were the necessary frameworks for cross-border activities. These diverse nonstate actors can gain international visibility as individuals and organizations, and thereby overcome the type of invisibility entailed by aggregate membership in a nation-state. The nation-state was, until recently, the exclusive representative in the international domain; now individuals and groups can have direct representation in international fora.

The large city of today emerges as a strategic site for these new types of practices. It is one nexus where the formation of new claims materializes and assumes concrete forms (Isin, 2000; Magnusson, 1994; Hagedorn 2003). The loss of power at the national level produces the possibility for new forms of power and politics at the subnational level (Sum, 1999; Brenner, 1998) and at the supernational level (e.g., Ferguson and Jones, 2002). The national, as container of social process and power, is cracked (Taylor, 2000 Abu-Lughod, 2000); it was never as unitary a category as its representations suggested. However, today the unbundling goes further than it did in earlier phases. This cracked casing opens up possibilities for a geography of politics that links a variety of subnational spaces. One question this engenders is how and whether we are seeing the formation of new types of transnational politics enacted by the variety of nonstate actors concentrated in cities (Hamilton and Chinchilla, 2000; Guarnizo, 1994; Cordero-Guzman et al., 2001), and often enabled by network technologies, particularly public-access Internet (Mele, 1999). Beyond being a strategic site, the city also emerges as a post-modern frontier zone where a variety of often nonformal political subjects engage in types of politics for which the rules of engagement have not quite been shaped or fully formalized (Sassen, 2002a).

Recovering Place

Including cities in the analysis of economic globalization is not without its analytic consequences. Economic globalization has mostly been conceptualized in terms of the national-global duality, where the latter gains at the expense of the former. Further, it is largely theorized in terms of the internationalization of capital, and then only the upper circuits of capital. Introducing cities in traditional analysis of globalization allows us to reconceptualize processes of economic globalization as concrete economic complexes partly situated in specific places (Orum and Chen, 2002; Abu-Lughod, 1999; Knox and Taylor, 1995). This contrasts with the mainstream account of globalization where place is seen as neutralized by the capacity for global communications and control. A focus on cities decomposes the nation-state into a variety of subnational components, some profoundly articulated with the global economy and others not (Parnreiter, 2002; Yeung, 2000; Harris and Fabricius, 1996).

Why does it matter to recover place in analyses of the global economy, particularly place as constituted in major cities? It allows us to see the multiplicity of economies and work cultures in which the global information economy is embedded (Marcuse and Van Kempen, 2000; Low, 1999; Eade, 1996; Hagedorn, 2003). It also allows us to recover the concrete, localized processes through which much of globalization exists, and to argue that much of the multiculturalism in large cities is as constitutive of globalization as is international finance—though in ways that sharply differ from the latter (Cordero-Guzman, Grossfogel, and Smith, 2001; Sassen, 1998; King, 1996; Tardanico and Lungo, 1995). Finally, focusing on cities allows us to specify a geography of strategic places bound to each other, largely by the dynamics of economic globalization and cross-border migrations. I refer to this as a new geography of centrality, at the heart of which is the new worldwide grid of global cities. This is a geography that cuts across national borders and the old North-South divide. However, it does so along bounded channels: It is a set of specific and partial, rather than all-encompassing dynamics.

The centrality of place in the context of global processes makes possible a transnational economic and political opening for the formation of new claims and the constitution of entitlements—notably rights to place. At the limit this could be an opening for new forms of "citizenship." The city has emerged as a site for new claims: by global capital that uses the city as an "organizational commodity," but also by disadvantaged sectors of the urban population, frequently as internationalized a presence in large cities as capital. The denationalizing of urban space, and the formation of new claims by diverse transnational actors, raises the question: Whose city is it?

This type of political opening contains unifying capacities across national boundaries and sharpening conflicts within such boundaries. Global capital and the new immigrant workforce are transnationalized actors that have unifying properties internally, and find themselves in contestation with each other in global cities. Global cities are sites for the overvalorization of corporate capital and the devalorization of disadvantaged workers. But they are also sites for new types of politics that allow the latter to emerge as political subjects.

A New Geography of Centrality and Marginality

The new economic geography of centrality partly reproduces existing inequalities but is also the outcome of a dynamic specific to the current forms of economic growth. It assumes many forms and operates in many terrains: from the distribution of telecommunications facilities to the structure of the economy and employment. Global cities are sites for immense concentrations of economic power and command centers in a global economy whereas cities that were once major manufacturing centers have suffered inordinate declines.

The most powerful of these new geographies of centrality at the interurban level binds the major international financial and business centers: New

York, London, Tokyo, Paris, Frankfurt, Zurich, Amsterdam, Los Angeles, Sydney, Hong Kong, among others. But this geography now also includes cities such as São Paulo, Shanghai, Bombay, Bangkok, Taipei, and Mexico City. The intensity of transactions among them—particularly through the financial markets and transactions in services and investments—has sharply increased, as have the orders of magnitude involved. At the same time, there is a sharpening inequality in the concentrations of strategic resources and activities between these cities and others in the same country.

The growth of global markets for finance and specialized services, the need for transnational servicing networks due to sharp increases in international investment, the reduced role of the government in the regulation of international economic activities, and the corresponding ascendance of other institutional arenas (notably global markets and corporate headquarters) all point to the existence of transnational economic processes with multiple locations in more than one country. Although this may always have been part of the world economy in its many phases, today it has spread to far more sites and sectors. We can now see the formation, at least incipient, of a transnational urban system. These cities are not simply in a relation of competition to each other, they are part of emergent global divisions of labor (Sassen, 2001).

Global cities are centers for the *servicing* and *financing* of international trade, investment, and headquarter operations. That is to say, the multiplicity of specialized activities present in global cities are crucial in the valorization, indeed overvalorization of leading sectors of capital today. In this sense they are also strategic production sites for today's leading economic sectors. This function is reflected in the ascendance of these activities in their economies.[2] Whether at the global or regional level, urban centers—central and edge cities—are adequate and often the best production sites for such specialized services. When it comes to the production of services for the leading globalized sectors, the advantages of location in cities are particularly strong. The rapid growth and disproportionate concentration of such services in cities signals that the latter have reemerged as significant "production" sites, after losing this role in the period when mass manufacturing was the dominant sector of the economy.[3]

The growing digitization of economic activities has not eliminated the need for major international business and financial centers and the material resources they concentrate, from state-of-the-art telematics infrastructure to brain talent (Graham, 2002; Castells, 1996).[4] The reshaping ranges from the spatial virtualization of a growing number of economic activities to the reconfiguration of the geography of the built environment for economic activity. Whether in electronic space or in the geography of the built environment, the reshaping involves organizational and structural changes. The vast new economic topography that is being implemented through electronic space is one moment, one fragment, of an even vaster economic chain that is in good part embedded in nonelectronic spaces.

There is no fully dematerialized firm or industry. Even the most advanced information industries, such as finance, are only partly installed in electronic space—as are industries that produce digital products, such as software design. One of the organizing hypotheses in the global city model is that precisely because of the territorial dispersal facilitated by telecommunication advances, we see a sharpening in the agglomeration of centralizing activities. This is not a mere continuation of old patterns of agglomeration but a new logic for agglomeration. Many of the leading sectors in the economy operate globally, in uncertain markets, under conditions of rapid changes in other countries (e.g., deregulation and privatization), and are subject to enormous speculative pressures. Global cities function as nested communities with multiple networks and often tacit systems of trust that allow firms and markets to cope with the new conditions of uncertainty and risk. What glues these conditions together into a new logic for spatial agglomeration is the added pressure of speed.

A focus on the *work* behind command functions, on the actual *production process* in the finance and services complex and on global market *places,* has the effect of incorporating the material facilities underlying globalization and the infrastructure of jobs typically not marked as belonging to the corporate sector of the economy. An economic configuration very different from that suggested by the concept information economy emerges. We recover the material conditions, production sites, and place-boundedness that are also part of globalization and the information economy. Alongside these new global and regional hierarchies of cities is a vast territory part of which is increasingly peripheral and excluded from the major processes that fuel economic growth in the global economy. Many important manufacturing centers and port cities have lost functions and are in decline, not only in the less-developed countries but also in the most advanced economies. The formation of these new geographies of marginality is yet another feature of economic globalization.

Further, in global cities we see both new geographies of centrality and marginality (Buechler 2002; Sassen 2001: *Journal of Urban Technology,* 1995; Hagedorn 2003). The downtowns of cities and key nodes in metropolitan areas receive massive investments in real estate and telecommunications whereas low-income city areas and many older suburbs are starved for resources. Highly educated workers see their incomes rise to unusually high levels whereas low- or medium-skilled workers see theirs sink. Financial services produce superprofits whereas industrial services barely survive. These trends are evident, with different levels of intensity, in a growing number of cities in the developed world and increasingly in those developing countries that are integrated into global markets (Ciccolella and Mignaqui, 2002; Schiffer, 2002; Cohen, 1996).

The new urban economy is highly problematic; this is particularly evident in global cities and their regional counterparts. It sets in motion a series of new dynamics of inequality. The new growth sectors—specialized services and finance—contain capabilities for profit making vastly superior to those of more traditional economic sectors. However, many of the latter remain essential to the operation of the urban economy and the daily needs of residents, but their survival is threatened in a situation where finance and specialized services can earn superprofits and bid-up prices.[5]

Polarization in the profit-making capabilities of different sectors of the economy has always existed. However, what we see today takes place on another order of magnitude and is engendering massive distortions in the operations of various markets, from real estate to labor (Fainstein, 2001; Peraldi and Perrin, 1996; Hitz et al., 1995; Munger, 2002). This has sharply increased the distance between the valorized, indeed overvalorized, sectors of the economy and devalorized sectors, even when the latter are part of leading global industries (Ehrenreich and Hochschild, 2003; Parrenas, 2001; Chang and Abramovitz, 2000). This devalorization of growing sectors of the urban economy is embedded in a massive demographic transition toward a growing presence of women, African-Americans, and global south immigrants in the urban workforce (Sassen, 2001: chs. 8 and 9; Valle and Torres, 2000; Kempen and Ozuekren, 1998).

We see here an interesting correspondence between great concentrations of corporate power and large concentrations of "others." Large cities in the highly developed world are the terrain where a multiplicity of globalization processes assume concrete, localized forms. A focus on cities allows us to further capture not only the upper but also the lower circuits of globalization.

The Less-Visible Localizations of the Global

Cities make legible multiple localizations of a variety of globalization processes that are typically not coded as such in mainstream accounts. The global city is a strategic site for these instantiations of globalization in a double sense. First, these cities make some of these dynamics more legible than other types of spaces, such as suburbs and rural areas. Second, urban space enables the formation of many of these dynamics and in this regard is productive space (Lefebvre 1996).

Many of these less-legible localizations of globalization are embedded in the demographic transition evident in cities, where a majority of resident workers are today immigrants and women, often women of color. For instance, Ehrenreich and Hochschild (2003) examine the formation of a global supply of maids and nannies in response to the new expanded demand for such workers by the new high-income professional households in global cities (Sassen 2001; Parrenas, 2001; Chang and Abramovitz, 2000). These cities are seeing an expansion of low-wage jobs that do not fit the master images about globalization, and yet are part of it. Their embeddedness in the demographic transition is evident in all cities. The fact that the low-wage jobs are filled by women who are also immigrants render them invisible and contribute to the legitimization of their devalorization and that of their work cultures. This can be read as a rupture of the traditional dynamic whereby membership in leading economic sectors contributes conditions toward the formation of a labor aristocracy—a process long evident in Western industrialized economies. "Women and immigrants" come to replace the Fordist/family wage category of "women and children" (Sassen, 1998).[6]

The above can be seen as one of the localizations of the dynamics of globalization resulting from the process of economic restructuring in global cities. The associated socioeconomic polarization has generated a large growth in the demand for low-wage workers and jobs that offer few advancement possibilities. This, amidst an explosion in the wealth and power concentrated in cities—that is in conditions where there is also a visible expansion in high-income jobs and high-priced urban space. "Women and immigrants" emerge as the labor supply that facilitates the imposition of low-wages and powerlessness under conditions of high demand for those workers and the location of those jobs in high-growth sectors. It breaks the historic nexus that would have led to empowering such workers and legitimates this break culturally.

Another localization that is rarely associated with globalization—informalization—reintroduces the community and the household as an important economic space in global cities. I see informalization in this setting as the low-cost (and often feminized) equivalent of deregulation at the top of the system (Sassen, 1998). As with deregulation (e.g., financial deregulation), informalization introduces flexibility, reduces the "burdens" of regulation, and lowers costs, in this case especially the costs of labor.[7] Informalization in major cities of highly developed countries—whether New York, London, Paris, or Berlin—can be seen as a downgrading of a variety of activities for which there is an effective demand, and as a devaluing of these activities, given low-entry costs, intense competition and few alternative forms of employment. Going informal is one way of producing and distributing goods and services at a lower cost and with greater flexibility thereby further devaluing these types of activities. Immigrants and women are important actors in the new informal economies of cities. They absorb the costs of informalizing these activities: they are willing to work overtime and for low wages because they pool household resources, which allows them to survive in expensive cities. If they are entrepreneurs, they often engage in self-exploitation (Sassen, 1998; Benería and Roldán [1987] for the case in LDCs).

The reconfiguration of economic spaces associated with globalization in major cities has had differential impacts on women and men, on male-typed and female-typed work cultures, and on male- and female-centered forms of power and empowerment. The restructuring of the labor-market brings with it a shift of labor market functions to the household and community. Women and households emerge as sites in the larger economy in ways that had been superceded by standardized mass-manufacturing and large white-collar firms. These informal locations should be part of the theorization of the particular forms that these elements in labor-market dynamics assume today in advanced urban economies—not only in the global South, as is typically assumed.

These transformations contain possibilities, even if limited, for women's autonomy and empowerment. For instance, we might ask whether the growth of informalization in advanced urban economies reconfigures some types of economic relations between men and women. This condition has its own dynamic possibilities for women. Economic downgrading through informalization creates "opportunities" for low-income women entrepreneurs and workers, and therewith reconfigures some work and household hierarchies in which women find themselves. This becomes particularly clear in the case of immigrant women from countries with traditional male-centered cultures.

There is a large literature showing that immigrant women's regular wage work and improved access to other public realms have an impact on gender relations (Hamilton and Chinchilla, 2000; Hondagneu-Sotelo, 1994; Pessar, 1995; Salzinger, 1995). Women gain greater personal autonomy and independence while men lose ground. Women gain more control over budgeting and other domestic decisions and greater leverage in requesting help from men in domestic chores. Also, their access to public services and other public resources gives them a chance to become incorporated in the mainstream society. They are often the ones in the household who mediate this process. It is likely that some women benefit more than others from these circumstances; we need more research to establish the impact of class, education, and income on these gendered outcomes.

Besides the relatively greater empowerment of women in the household associated with waged employment, there is a second important outcome: their greater participation in the public sphere and their possible emergence as public actors. There are two arenas where immigrant women are active: institutions for public and private assistance, and the immigrant/ethnic community. The incorporation of women in the migration process strengthens the settlement likelihood and contributes to greater immigrant participation in their communities and with the state. For instance, Hondagneu-Sotelo (1994) found immigrant women come to assume more active public and social roles that further reinforces their status in the household and the settlement process. Women are more active in community building and community activism, and they are positioned differently from men regarding the broader economy and the state. They are the ones who are likely to handle the legal vulnerability of their families in the process of seeking public and social services. This greater participation by women suggests the possibility that they may emerge as more forceful and visible actors, and make their role in the labor market more visible as well.

There is, to some extent, a joining of two dynamics in the condition of women in global cities described in the foregoing. On the one hand, they are constituted as an invisible and disempowered class of workers in the service of the strategic sectors constituting the global economy. This invisibility keeps them from emerging as whatever would be the contemporary equivalent of the "labor aristocracy" of earlier forms of economic organization, when a low-wage worker's position in leading sectors had the effect of empowering that worker, as in the possibility of unionizing. On the other hand, the access to (albeit low) wages and salaries, and the growing feminization of the job supply and business opportunities brought about with informalization, do alter the gender hierarchies in which they find themselves.[8]

A Space of Power and of Empowerment

What makes the localization of the preceding processes strategic and potentially constitutive of a new kind of transnational politics (even though they involve powerless and often invisible workers), is that these same cities are also the strategic sites for the valorization of the new forms of global corporate capital. The partial loss of power at the national level produces the possibility for new forms of power and politics at the subnational level, especially in global cities. Global corporate capital emerges as one of the actors that can engage in cross-border politics, partly bypassing the domain of the interstate system.

However, the global city is also becoming a space of empowerment for the disadvantaged. Generally, the space of the city is a far more concrete space for politics than that of the nation (Isin, 2000; Fincher and Jacobs,

1998; Dunn, 1994; Magnusson, 1994). It is a space where nonformal political actors are part of the political scene in a way that is much more difficult at the national level. National politics needs to run through existing formal systems—whether the electoral political system or the judiciary (taking state agencies to court). Nonformal political actors are rendered invisible in national politics. The space of the city accommodates a broad range of political activities, for example, squatting; demonstrations against police brutality; fighting for the rights of immigrants and the homeless; the politics of culture and identity; gay and lesbian and queer politics. Much of this becomes visible on the street because much of urban politics is concrete, enacted by people rather than dependent on mass-media technologies. Street-level politics make possible the formation of new types of political subjects that often do not go through the formal political system.

There is something to be captured here—a distinction between powerlessness and a condition of being an actor even though lacking formal power. I use the term "presence" to name this condition. In the context of a strategic space, such as the global city, the types of disadvantaged people described here are not simply marginal; they acquire presence in a broader political process that escapes the boundaries of the formal polity.[9] This presence signals the possibility of a politics. What this politics will be depends on the specific projects and practices of various communities. Insofar as the sense of membership of these communities is not subsumed under the national, it may well signal the possibility of a transnational politics centered in concrete localities (Hamilton and Chinchilla, 2001; Levitt, 2001; Guarnizo, 1994; Schuster and Solomos, 2002). The Internet has enabled a new type of cross-border politics that can bypass interstate politics (Mele, 1999; Cleaver, 1998), even though such political activities can also thrive without this particular type of connectivity as Keck and Sikkink (1998) have shown us.

That even small, resource-poor organizations and individuals can become participants in global networks signals the possibility of a sharp growth in cross-border politics by actors other than states. The particular feature that interests me here is that through the Internet, *localized* initiatives can become part of cross-border networks. This produces a specific kind of activism, one centered in multiple localities, yet intensely connected digitally. Activists can develop networks for circulating not only information (about environmental, housing, political issues, etc.) but also political work and strategies. There are many examples of such types of cross-border political work. For instance SPARC, started by and centered on women, began as an effort to organize slum dwellers in Bombay to get housing (for a description, see Glasius et al., 2002: p. 219, p. 225). Now there is a network of such groups throughout Asia as well as some cities in Latin America and Africa. This is one of the key forms of critical politics that the Internet can make possible: A politics of the local with a big differ-ence—these are localities that are connected with each other across a re-gion, a country, or the world. Because the network is global it does not mean that it all has to happen at the global level. These forms of activism contribute in multiple microlevel ways to an incipient unbundling of the exclusive authority over territory and people we have long associated with the nation-state (Hamel et al., 2000; Schuster and Solomos, 2002; Muet-zelfeld and Smith, 2002; Brysk, 2002).

We can think of this mix of conditions and resources as facilitating a place-specific politics with global span. It is a type of political work deeply embedded in peoples' actions and activities but made possible partly by the existence of global digital linkages, particularly low-cost Internet con-nectivity. Further, it is a form of political and institution-building work centered in cities, networks of cities, and on nonformal political actors. We see here the potential transformation of a range of "local" conditions or in-stitutional domains (such as the household, the community, the neighbor-hood, the local school, and health-care entities) where individuals "confined" to domestic or local roles remain the key actors (e.g., Bastani, 2000). From being lived or experienced as nonpolitical, or domestic, these places are tranformed into "microenvironments with global span" (Sassen, 2002b).

What I mean by this construct is that technical connectivity will create a variety of links with other similar local entities in other neighborhoods in the same city, and in neighborhoods in other cities and in other countries. A partly deterritorialized ideational space or even community of practice can emerge that creates multiple lateral, horizontal communications, col-laborations, solidarities, and supports arising out of their specific localized struggles or concerns. People can experience themselves as part of global nonstate networks in their daily localized political work. They enact some features of "global civil society" in the microspaces of daily life rather than on some putative global stage (Sassen, 2002a).

One of the most radical forms assumed today by the transformations in the linkages that connect people to territory is the loosening of identities from what have been traditional sources of identity, such as the nation or the village. This unmooring in the process of identity formation is, at this time, a condition probably affecting only a minority of people, including the types of groups that concern me here. For these groups it has the capa-bility of engendering new notions of community of membership and enti-tlement. The mix of focused activism and local/global networks creates conditions for the emergence of partial transnational identities.[10] From the perspective of my concerns in this chapter, we might think of the en-ablement of transnational identities as a condition that can facilitate cross-border relations that at least partly bypass the world of interstate relations.

Conclusion

Economic globalization and the new network technologies have contributed to produce a spatiality for the urban that pivots on deterritorialized cross-border networks and territorial locations with massive concentrations of resources. This is not a completely new feature. Over the centuries, cities have been at the intersection of processes with supra-urban and even intercontinental scalings. What is different today is the intensity, complexity, and global span of these networks, and the extent to which significant portions of economies are now dematerialized and digitized and hence can travel at great speeds through these networks. Also new is the growing use of digital networks by a broad range of often resource-poor organizations to pursue a variety of cross-border initiatives. This has increased the number of cities that are part of cross-border networks operating at often vast geographic scales. Under these conditions, much of what we experience and represent as the local turns out to be a microenvironment with global span.

This new geography of centrality constituted by the worldwide grid of global cities and marked by sharp imbrications of digital and nondigital conditions, is one of the most strategic spaces for the formation of new types of political actors and politics. Global cities concentrate key sectors of global corporate capital and a vast mix of often disadvantaged people and organizations from around the world. This is a cross-border geography characterized by increasing density and diversity of transactions and actors. It is a space with new economic and political potentialities that is both place-centered (because it is embedded in particular and strategic cities) and transterritorial (because it connects sites that are not geographically proximate yet are intensely connected to each other).

It is not only the transmigration of capital that takes place in this cross-border geography but also that of people—both rich (the new transnational professional workforce) and poor (most migrant workers). It is also a space for the transmigration of cultural forms, for the reterritorialization of "local" subcultures. Although these types of developments do not necessarily neutralize attachments to a country or national cause, they do shift this attachment to include translocal communities of practice and/or membership, whether they are the new transnational professionals of global finance or activist organizations.

Globalization is a contradictory process; it is characterized by contestation, internal differentiation, and continuous border crossings. The global city is emblematic of this condition. Global cities concentrate a disproportionate share of global corporate power and are a key site for its overvalorization. They also concentrate a disproportionate share of the disadvantaged and are an important site for both their devalorization and their politicization. This joint presence happens in a context where the globalization of the economy has grown sharply; cities have become increasingly strategic for global capital; and marginalized people have found their voice and are making claims on the city. This joint presence is further brought into focus by the sharpening of the distance between the two. The center now concentrates immense power, a power that rests on the capability for global control and the ability to produce superprofits. But marginality, notwithstanding little economic and political power, has become an increasingly strong presence through a proliferation of new types of politics and an emergent transnational politics embedded in the new geography of economic globalization. Both actors, increasingly transnational and in contestation, find in the global city the strategic terrain for their operations.[11]

References

Abu-Lughod, Janet L. 1999. *New York, Los Angeles, Chicago: America's Global Cities.* Minnesota: University of Minnesota Press.

———. ed. 2000. *Sociology for the 21st Century.* Chicago: University of Chicago Press.

Appadurai, Arjun. 1996. *Modernity at Large.* Minneapolis: University of Minnesota Press.

Bastani, S. 2000. "Muslim Women On-Line," *Arab World Geographer* 3(1): 40–59.

Benería, Lourdes and Marta Roldán. 1987. *The Crossroads of Class and Gender.* Chicago: University of Chicago Press.

Body-Gendrot, Sophie. 1999. *Controlling Cities.* Oxford: Blackwell.

Brenner, Neil. 1998. "Global Cities, Global States: Global City Formation and State Territorial Restructuring in Contemporary Europe," *Review of International Political Economy.* 5, nr.2: 1–37.

Brysk, Alison (ed) 2002. *Globalization and Human Rights.* Berkeley, CA: University of California Press.

Buechler, Simone. 2002. "Women in the Informal Economy of São Paulo." Paper prepared for the National Academy of Sciences, forthcoming in *Background Papers. Panel on Cities.* Washington, D.C.: National Academy of Sciences.

Castells, M. 1996. *The Networked Society.* Oxford: Blackwell.

Chang, Grace and Mimi Abramovitz. 2000. *Disposable Domestics: Immigrant Women Workers in the Global Economy.* Boston: South End Press.

Cicollela, Pablo and Iliana Mignaqui. 2002. "The Spatial Reorganization of Buenos Aires," in Saskia Sassen ed., *Global Networks/Linked Cities.* New York and London: Routledge.

Cleaver, Harry. 1998. "The Zapatista Effect: The Internet and the Rise of an Alternative Political Fabric," *Journal of International Affairs* 51(2): 621–640.

Cohen, Robin. 1996. "Diasporas and the Nation-State: From Victims to Challenges," *International Affairs*, 72.

Cordero-Guzman, Hector R., Robert C. Smith, and Ramon Grosfoguel eds. 2001. *Migration, Transnationalization, and Race in a Changing New York.* Philadelphia: Temple University Press.

Dunn, Seamus ed. 1994. *Managing Divided Cities.* Staffs, UK: Keele University Press.

Eade, John ed. 1996. *Living the Global City: Globalization as a Local Process.* London: Routledge.

Ehrenreich, Barbara, and Arlie Hochschild (eds). 2003. *Global Woman.* New York: Metropolitan Books.

Fainstein, S. 2001. *The City Builders* (2nd Ed.). Lawrence, KS: Kansas University Press.

Ferguson, Yale. H. and R. J. Barry Jones (eds). 2002. *Political Space: Frontiers of Change and Governance in a Globalizing World.* Albany, NY: SUNY Press.

Fincher, Ruth and Jane M. Jacobs eds. 1998. *Cities of Difference.* New York: Guilford Press.

Futur Anterieur. 1995. Special issue: *La Ville-Monde Aujourd'hui: Entre Virtualite et Ancrage.* Thierry Pillon and Anne Querrien eds. Vols. 30–32. Paris: L'Harmattan.

Glasius, Marlies, Mary Kaldor, and Helmut Anheier (eds). 2002. *Global Civil Society Yearbook 2002.* London: Oxford University Press.

Guarnizo, Luis E. 1994. "Los Dominicanyorks: The Making of a Binational Society," *Annals, AAPSS,* 533: 70–86. May.

Hagedorn, John (ed) 2003. *Gangs in the Global City.* Chicago: University of Illinois Press.

Hamel, P., Henri Lustiger-Thaler, and Margit Mayer (eds). 2000. *Urban Movements in a Globalizing World.* London: Routledge.

Hamilton, Nora and Norma Stoltz Chinchilla. 2001. *Seeking Community in a Global City: Guatemalans and Salvadorans in Los Angeles.* Philadelphia: Temple University Press.

Harris, Nigel and I. Fabricius eds. 1996. *Cities and Structural Adjustment.* London: University College London.

Hitz, Keil, Ronneberger, Lehrer, Wolff, Schmid eds. 1995. *Capitales Fatales.* Zurich: Rotpunkt Verlag.

Hondagneu-Sotelo, Pierrette. 1994. *Gendered Transitions.* Berkeley: University of California Press.

Isin, Engin F. ed. 2000. *Democracy, Citizenship and the Global City.* London and New York: Routledge.

Journal of Urban Technology. 1995. Special Issue: *Information Technologies and Inner-City Communities.* 3, nr. 1 9. Fall.

Keck, Margaret E. and Kathryn Sikkink. 1998. *Activists Beyond Borders: Advocacy Networks in International Politics.* Ithaca, NY: Cornell University Press.

Kempen, Ronald van and Sule A.Ozuekren. 1998. "Ethnic Segregation in Cities: New Forms and Explanations in a Dynamic World," *Urban Studies,* 35(10): 1631–1657.

King, A.D. ed. 1996. *Representing the City: Ethnicity, Capital, and Culture in the 21st Century.* New York: New York University Press.

Knox, Paul L. and Peter J. Taylor eds. 1995. *World Cities in a World-System.* Cambridge: Cambridge University Press.

Lefebvre, Henri. 1996. *Writings in Cities.* (Transl. Eleonore Kofman and Elizabeth Levas). Oxford: Blackwell.

Levitt, Peggy. 2001. *The Transnational Villagers.* Berkeley: University of California Press.

Low, Setha M. 1999. "Theorizing the City," in Low ed., *Theorizing the City.* New Brunswick, NJ: Rutgers University Press.

Magnusson, Warren. 1994. *The Search for Political Space.* Toronto: University of Toronto Press.

Marcuse, Peter and Ronald van Kempen. 2000. *Globalizing Cities. A New Spatial Order.* Oxford: Blackwell.

Mele, C. 1999. "Cyberspace and Disadvantaged Communities: The Internet as a Tool for Collective Action," in M. A. Smith and P. Kollock eds., *Communities in Cyberspace.* London: Routledge.

Merrifield, Andy and Erik Swyngedouw eds. 1997. *The Urbanization of Injustice.* New York: New York University Press.

Muetzelfeld, Michael and Gary Smith. 2002. "Civil Society and Global Governance: The Possibilities for Global Citizenship." *Citizenship Studies* 6, 1:55–75.

Munger, Frank (ed). 2002. *Laboring Under the Line.* New York: Russell Sage Foundation.

Ong, Aihwa. 1996. "Globalization and Women's Rights: The Asian Debate on Citizenship and Communitarianism," in *Indiana Journal of Global Legal Studies.* Special Symposium on *Feminism and Globalization: The Impact of The Global Economy on Women and Feminist Theory.* 4(1). Fall.

———. 1999. *Flexible Citizenship: The Cultural Logics of Transnationality.* Durham, NC: Duke University Press.

Orum, Anthony and Xianming Chen. 2002. *Urban Places.* Malden, MA: Blackwell.

Parnreiter, Christoff. 2002. "The Making of a Global City: Mexico City," in Saskia Sassen ed., *Global Networks/Linked Cities.* New York and London: Routledge.

Parrenas, Rhacel Salazar ed. 2001. *Servants of Globalization: Women, Migration and Domestic Workers.* Stanford: Stanford University Press.

Peraldi, Michel and Evelyne Perrin eds. 1996. *Reseaux Productifs et Territoires Urbains.* Toulouse: Presses Universitaires du Mirail.

Pessar, Patricia. 1995. "On the Homefront and in the Workplace: Integrating Immigrant Women into Feminist Discourse." *Anthropological Quarterly* 68, nr. 1, pp. 37–47.

Salzinger, Leslie. 1995. "A Maid by Any Other Name: The Transformation of 'Dirty Work' by Central American Immigrants," in Burawoy, M. et al. *Ethnography Unbound: Power and Resistance in the Modern Metropolis.* Berkeley: University of California Press.

Sassen, Saskia. 1998. *Globalization and Its Discontents.* New York: New Press.
———. 2001. *The Global City.* (2nd Edition). Princeton: Princeton University Press.
———. 2002a. "The Repositioning of Citizenship: Emergent Subjects and Spaces for Politics." *Berkeley Journal of Sociology: A Critical Review* vol. 46: 4–26.
———. 2002b. "Toward a Sociology of Information Technology," in *Current Sociology. Special Issue: Sociology and Technology.* Summer.
Schiffer Ramos, Sueli. 2002. "Sao Paulo: Articulating a Cross-Border Regional Economy," in Saskia Sassen ed. *Global Networks/Linked Cities.* New York and London: Routledge.
Schuster, Liza and John Solomos. 2002. "Rights and Wrongs across European Borders: Migrants, Minorities and Citizenship." *Citizenship Studies* 6, 1: 37–54.
Soysal, Yasemin Nohuglu. 1994. *Limits of Citizenship: Migrants and Postnational Membership in Europe.* Chicago: University of Chicago Press.
Staeheli, Lynn A. 1999. "Globalization and the Scales of Citizenship," in *Geography Research Forum,* 19: 60–77. Special Issue *On Geography and the Nation-State,* Dennis Pringle and Oren Yiftachel eds.
Sum, Ngai-Ling. 1999. "Rethinking Globalisation: Re-articulating the Spatial Scale and Temporal Horizons of Trans-border Spaces," in Kris Olds, Peter Dicken, Philip F. Kelly, Lilly Kong, and Henry Wai-Chung Yeung eds. *Globalization and the Asian Pacific: Contested Territories.* London: Routledge.
Tabak, Faruk and Michaeline A. Chrichlow eds. 2000. *Informalization: Process and structure.* Baltimore: The Johns Hopkins Press.
Tardanico, Richard and Mario Lungo. 1995. "Local Dimensions of Global Restructuring in Urban Costa Rica," in *International Journal of Urban and Regional Research* 19(2): 223–249.
Taylor, Peter J. 2000. "World Cities and Territorial States Under Conditions of Contemporary Globalization," in *Political Geography* 19(5): 5–32.
Torres, Maria de los Angeles. 1998. "Transnational Political and Cultural Identities: Crossing Theoretical Borders," in Frank Bonilla, Edwin Melendez, Rebecca Morales, and Maria de los Angeles Torres eds. *Borderless Borders.* Philadelphia: Temple University Press.
Valle, Victor M. and Rodolfo D. Torres. 2000. *Latino Metropolis.* Minneapolis: University of Minnesota Press.
Yeung, Yue-man. 2000. *Globalization and Networked Societies.* Hawaii: University of Hawaii Press.

Notes

1. The first half of this chapter is a revised version of an article originally published in the *Journal of American Studies.* Sassen, S. 2000. "The Global City: Strategic Site/New Frontier." *Journal of American Studies.* (Special issue edited by David Katzman and Norman Yetman). Vol. 41: 79–95.

2. In my analysis what is specific about the shift to services is not merely the growth in service jobs but, most important, the growing service intensity in the organization of advanced economies: firms in all industries, from mining to wholesale, buy more accounting, legal, advertising, financial, economic forecasting services today than they did twenty years ago (Sassen, 2001: chapter 5).

3. Under mass manufacturing and fordism the strategic spaces of the economy were the large-scale integrated factory and the government through its fordist/keynesian functions.

4. Telematics and globalization have emerged as two shaping dynamics in the actual organization of work, but also in discourse formation presenting capital as hypermobile and footloose. (For a critical examination of these representations, see Sassen, 2001: chapter 2; 2002b).

5. Elsewhere I have tried to show how these new inequalities in profit-making capacities of economic sectors, earnings capacities of households, and prices in upscale and downscale markets have contributed to the formation of informal economies in cities of highly developed countries (Sassen, 1998: chaper 8). These informal economies negotiate between new economic trends and regulatory frameworks that were engendered in response to older economic conditions.

6. This newer case brings out more brutally than did the Fordist contract the economic significance of these types of actors, a significance veiled or softened in the case of the Fordist contract through the provision of the family wage.

7. For a broader treatment of the informal economy, including a focus on its re-emergence with the end of the so-called Pax Americana see Tabak and Chrichlow (2000). For an in-depth examination of how globalization has reorganized the informal economy in the global south see Benería and Roldán (1987) and Buechler (2002).

8. Another important localization of the dynamics of globalization is that of the new professional women stratum. Elsewhere I have examined the impact of the growth of top-level professional women in high-income gentrification in global cities—both residential and commercial—as well as in the re-urbanization of middle-class family life (Sassen, 2001: chapter 9).

9. This can take multiple forms, including the definition of certain types of activities and in-dividuals as criminal (Body-Gendrot, 1999) and the accumulation in cities of occasions for unjust treatment and definitions (Merrifield and Swyngedouw, 1997).

10. A growing number of scholars concerned with identity and solidarity posit the rise of transnational identities (Torres, 1998), translocal loyalties (Appadurai, 1996: 165), and transnational citizenship (Staeheli, 1999; Ong, 1996, 1999; and Soysal, 1994). This litera-ture provides us with a broader conceptual landscape within which we can place the more specific types of organizations and practices that concern me here.

11. See Soja's chapter (16) in this book for further discussion on this point.

CHAPTER **16**

Urban Tensions

*Globalization, Economic Restructuring, and the
Postmetropolitan Transition*

EDWARD W. SOJA

Soon after the 1992 Los Angeles riots that followed the Rodney King ver-
dict, the *Los Angeles Times* published an article by Robin Wright entitled
"Riots Called Symptom of Worldwide Urban Trend." The article focused
on a recently issued United Nations report on world urbanization trends
and argued that what happened in 1992 was the outgrowth of "an urban
revolution taking place on all six inhabited continents, brought about by
conditions very similar to those in Los Angeles: crime; racial and ethnic
tensions; economic woes; vast disparities of wealth; shortages of social services; and deteriorating infrastructure." Expanding on the UN report, it
was bluntly stated that the U.S. had the largest gap between wealth and
poverty in the developed world, that this gap was widest in New York and
Los Angeles, and that the urban polarity characterizing the country's two
largest cities is now comparable to that found in Karachi, Bombay, and
Mexico City. Pointedly, the report went on to predict that "urban poverty
will become the most significant and politically explosive problem of the
next century."[1]

What I propose to do here is elaborate on a number of key themes
opened up in these attempts to explore the global implications of a specifically urban event, what today is described by many as the Justice Riots that
took place in Los Angeles in late April and early May of 1992. These themes

275

include the worldwide urban transformations that have been occurring over the past thirty years; the degree to which these transformations are integrally associated with increasing social and spatial inequalities and polarization; how these changes work to exacerbate specifically urban tensions; and how what happened in Los Angeles in 1992 was representative of these urbanization trends.[2]

Defining Specifically Urban Tensions

In any assessment of the major "global tensions" affecting life in the twenty-first century, a strong argument can be made—and will be made here—that *specifically urban tensions* must be ranked among the most socially explosive, culturally complex, and politically challenging. By describing the tensions associated with increasing poverty and social polarization as "specifically urban," I mean not only that they happen to occur in cities rather than in rural or nonurbanized areas, although this statistical difference is in itself important to recognize.[3] That they are specifically urban also implies that they arise from, and to a significant extent are caused by, contemporary urban conditions and the social and spatial processes producing these conditions. This is not an innocent distinction, for it defines two very different approaches to urban theory and analysis: one that views the city as just a neutral backdrop to essentially social processes and relations; the other sees urbanism itself, its social and spatial specificities or attributes, as a significant part of the explanation of the phenomena being studied. The latter will be the approach taken here.[4]

Two additional assumptions guide the present analysis. The first recognizes the globality of contemporary urban tensions and the conditions that give rise to them. In other words, these specifically urban conditions and tensions are not confined exclusively to cities or to what is often narrowly defined as the urban or local scale. Today, perhaps more than ever before, urban tensions reverberate on regional, national, and global scales. In this sense, urban tensions *are* global tensions and need to be interpreted as such. This leads directly to the second assumption, that urban tensions and their immediate causes are today significantly different from what they were thirty years ago. This means that they must be addressed in ways that recognize the distinctive properties of the contemporary urban condition and the imprint of the new and different urbanization processes that have been reshaping cities and urban life over the past three decades. This has been a period in which cities have changed more dramatically than in almost any other equivalent period in the past 200 years. If the many problems associated with these changes are going to be effectively understood and addressed, long-established approaches to studying cities and developing ameliorative urban policies will have to be critically re-evaluated and revised.

To make this claim is not to ignore the past. That urban poverty is a significant and politically explosive problem is certainly not a new idea. For many parts of the world this statement could have been made at almost any time in the past two centuries. What is new and different from the past, however, is that it is now of sufficient magnitude to demand primary attention and particularities must not be swept aside as mere minor variations on long-established trends and historical continuities. Appreciating how and why the current causes and expressions of urban poverty are no longer what they were three decades ago begins with a recognition of the emphatically shared globality of contemporary urbanism, as well as a foregrounding of the particular changes that have been taking place in cities since the worldwide urban crises of the 1960s.

As noted earlier, something akin to an urban revolution has been happening to cities everywhere in the inhabited world, so that today an increasing number of the world's major cities are experiencing similarly volatile conditions of urban poverty and sociospatial polarization. Looked at in a slightly different way, what this suggests is that never before has the general urban condition been so similar among the major metropolitan areas of what we have traditionally called the First, Second, and Third Worlds. All processes of change are geographically unevenly developed and significant differences remain across cultures and continents, but the distinctive qualities of urbanism as a way of life are shared worldwide to a degree never before achieved, at least since the origins of the industrial capitalist city.

The Urban Impact of Globalization and Economic Restructuring

This increasingly shared urbanity is largely the product of two major forces that have been dramatically reshaping nearly every aspect of contemporary life over the past three decades. The most widely studied of these forces of change, and probably also the most often overemphasized, is globalization, or more specifically the *globalization of capital, labor, and culture*. The geographically uneven impacts of globalization have not been confined to what is called world or global cities, but has been affecting to varying degrees virtually every place on earth. Indeed, it can be argued that an integral but relatively understudied constituent of these globalization processes has been the worldwide diffusion of urban industrial capitalism itself. Stated differently, more so than ever before, every part of the world is to some degree feeling the impact of a particular form of advanced urban-based industrialization that had hitherto been almost entirely confined to First World countries and cities.

There is no doubt, however, that the effects of globalization are intensely concentrated and most visible in the world's major urban agglomerations. This concentration of globalizing capital, labor, and cultural diversity has been associated with a dramatic change in the size of cities, some of which now surpass 25 million in population—a size considered almost inconceivable thirty years ago. It has also led to the formation of new networks and hierarchies of *global city-regions*, which increasingly tend to interact transnationally—that is—they interact economically among themselves as much as or more than with other cities within their respective nation-states. Reflecting this new wave of urbanization and the massive transnational migration flows associated with it is the startling realization that within the next decade the majority of the world's population, for the first time in history, will be living in metropolitan regions of more than a million inhabitants. This helps to explain why poverty is becoming more urban-centered and consequently less rural than it used to be, and adds to sustain the notion that urban tensions are now also global tensions.

Closely intertwined with globalization and similarly stimulated by the revolution in information and communications technology (ICT) has been a pronounced and more endogenously generated urban and regional *economic restructuring.* The past thirty years has seen a dramatic transformation of the economic base of First World cities. This transformation has come to be described as a shift from Fordist and Keynesian systems of mass production and consumption concentrated in large urban-industrial regions such as the Ruhr, Northeast England, and the American Manufacturing Belt, to post-Fordist systems of flexible and information-intensive industrialization, associated with the vertical disintegration of the production process and the spatial re-agglomeration of firms in new clusters or districts, many of which had never been industrialized before. In the advanced industrial countries this still evolving "New Economy" is the product of combined processes of *deindustrialization*, primarily affecting the older Fordist urban and regional economies and *reindustrialization*, mainly in new post-Fordist industrial city-regions.[5]

Significantly, advanced forms of the New Economy have been selectively globalizing, spilling over into areas that never before experienced advanced urban industrialism. The most prominent of these "new industrial spaces" are the NICs, the growing number of Newly Industrialized Countries that have been significantly blurring the once very clear boundary between First and Third Worlds. At a different scale are such recently industrialized suburban or "greenfield" sites as Silicon Valley in California and many of the "technopoles" of Europe and Japan. Contributing still further to this growing urban-industrial convergence, the New Economy has been extending its effects into the urban fabrics of the former Second World in ways we are only beginning to comprehend. There can be no doubt that the international division of labor that for so long sustained the familiar partitioning into First, Second, and Third Worlds has not disappeared, but it is also clear that what were once fairly stable boundaries have become increasingly blurred and redefined by the combined effects of globalization and economic restructuring.

Urban Tensions and the Postmetropolitan Transition

Consider the internal urban changes generated by globalization and economic restructuring, and examine how they contribute to the growing urban tensions associated with deepening poverty and inequality. As many have noted, cities and urbanism have been changing at an extraordinarily rapid pace, instigating what some contend is the most striking transformation in the industrial capitalist city since its origin more than 200 years ago. I summarily describe this major reconfiguration of the modern metropolis, what the UN called an "urban revolution," as the *postmetropolitan transition*, and will try to explain why and how intensifying urban tensions and a politically volatile expansion of urban poverty and polarization have seemingly been built into this still ongoing social and spatial restructuring. To illustrate this analysis I mainly draw on the particular ways the postmetropolitan transition has been played out in the urbanized region of Los Angeles, keeping in mind what happened in the "violent spring" of 1992.

A key factor associated with growing urban tensions in nearly all the world's major city-regions has been the *increasing cultural heterogeneity* of urban populations, arising primarily from extraordinary increases in transnational migrations, or what some have called the globalization of labor. These combined forces have created what are surely the most culturally and ethnically heterogeneous cities the world has ever known. To give an extreme example, the adjacent small cities of Carson and Gardena in Los Angeles County have achieved and maintained over the past thirty years the unprecedented distinction of having a population that is almost perfectly quartered across the four major ethnoracial groupings: Anglo (non-Hispanic white); Latino; African-American; and Asian-Pacific Islander, each of which is itself a category of great diversity. Within the population labeled Asian-Pacific Islander, for example, there are significant numbers of Japanese, Chinese, Koreans, Vietnamese, Thais, Hawaiians, and Samoans. Many dozens of different languages are spoken in the schools, on the playgrounds, and sports fields, as well as at the nearby California State University at Dominguez Hills, recently ranked as the second most ethnically diverse campus in the U.S. Even though the boundedness and distinctive cultures of these ethnic groupings have certainly not disappeared, there has been a measurable increase in what might be called intercultural contacts and hybridities, as well as a growing consciousness of diversity itself. Illustrative of this contextual consciousness, the first explicitly named Museum of Diversity was recently opened in Carson.

At the other extreme from this concentrated diversity is the multiplication of ethnic enclaves, where a single ethnicity dominates. In a swathe of cities in southwest Los Angeles County, resident populations have changed from nearly 80 percent Anglo at the time of the Watts Riots in 1965 to over 90 percent Latino today. Nearby, once predominantly African-American communities such as Watts and much of the rest of South-Central Los Angeles now have majority Latino populations. Both the concentration and the spread of different ethnic and national groups have made Greater Los Angeles the location of the largest Mexican, Salvadoran, Guatemalan, Korean, Vietnamese, Thai, Samoan, Armenian, and Iranian populations outside their home countries. It should be noted, however, that this increasing cultural heterogeneity has not only been confined to North American cities. Many European cities are also experiencing similar increases, with one of the most stunning recent examples being Amsterdam. Here it was recently projected that with current trends continuing, the population will be predominantly Muslim within the next twenty years.

For many, such cultural heterogeneity is a source of survival as well as creativity and social mobility, but it also has the effect of multiplying the possibilities for intercultural conflicts and violence. As immigrant populations, preponderantly from poor countries, become an increasing part of urban life and livelihoods, there is too often triggered a resurgence of antagonism from "domestic" residents defending their economic and political turfs in the city. This has generated new rounds of racism and anti-immigrant xenophobia in many city-regions, often in association with nativistic movements aimed at expelling the immigrant newcomers. As the urban landscape becomes increasingly filled with a dense multiplicity of cultural and economic cleavages, it becomes the arena not just for struggles over local resources but also for many of the conflicts and confrontations that arise in the global geopolitical economy. Many regional wars around the world are today also fought on the streets of Los Angeles, New York, London, and Paris. The older dualisms of class and race remain, but are now overlain and cross-cut with a much more complex and variegated set of polarizations, producing an urban landscape that is no longer describable as a simple mosaic but rather as a constantly shifting fractal geography.[6]

Increasing cultural heterogeneity and its popular expression in the term multiculturalism are generating a new form of urban politics that revolves around complex questions of cultural difference, representation, and identity. This new "cultural politics" encompasses both resurgent and assertive traditionalism, aimed at preserving older cultural values and practices, as well as creative new forms of cultural hybridity and transnational identity formation. Such now widely accepted terms as Latino and Asian-Pacific Islander are themselves the product of a cultural politics aimed at achieving greater representation and more powerful collective identity. The more progressive offshoots of this politics of difference are also contributing to the recent resurgence of interest in rethinking the concept of citizenship and redefining notions of local democracy.[7] It is too early to say much more about this cultural politics, but even while its progressive possibilities are recognized, it is also clear that its development has already come into conflict with older and more-established structures of power and authority in the global city-region, multiplying still further the sources of urban tension both between and within different urban cultures.

Post-Fordist industrial restructuring has also had major effects on the urban landscape, increasing its potential for generating conflict and confrontation. It has led, for example, to radical changes in the structure, composition, and spatial organization of *urban labor markets*, contributing to further fragmentation, inequality, competition, and polarization. Once describable as a pyramid with a bulging middle, the distributional pattern of incomes and occupations in most First World city-regions has been developing a new shape, with a small bulge at the top, reflecting the increasing number of high-income jobs in the New Economy and an enormous bloating at the bottom, filled with a largely immigrant population composed mainly of the working poor. Far from unemployed, the working poor reside in multijob households that cannot accumulate enough income to rise significantly above the poverty line. They also tensely overlap with the welfare-dependent often homeless population that survives outside the formal labor market, varyingly described as the "truly disadvantaged" or the "permanent urban underclass," to use the terms associated with the work of William Julius Wilson.[8]

The once-bulging middle of the labor-market pyramid has been concurrently squeezed in two directions as growing numbers of formerly middle-class workers filter down toward the poverty line while, in much smaller numbers, others move up into the high-end category defined most popularly by the term yuppies, or young urban professionals. In Los Angeles, New York, Miami, and many other large global city-regions in North America, the majority of the urban population now consists of a conspicuously contrasting population of the working poor (estimated by some to be as much as 40 percent of the population of Los Angeles County) and what some call the professional-managerial-executive class. Although reminiscent of the simpler urban duality of bourgeoisie and proletariat, this class split is much more complex, blurrier in its boundaries, more overlapping in its constituents, and less predictable in its politics.

This double squeeze on the middle class, a dramatic reversal of postwar economic trends in most advanced industrial countries, is the source of enormous pressures on the majority of the urban population to maintain long-standing lifestyles and household incomes. The markedly polarizing middle of the urban labor market is now also being filled with specialized ethnic niches, adding to patterns of fragmentation and polarization, as some groups are given an additional boost in social mobility through such ethnic specialization while others are left with little more than dead-end jobs. This pattern is most pronounced in the U.S., where the welfare state has been much weaker than in Europe, and has been further weakened in recent years. Nevertheless, some degree of middle-class contraction and the emergence of a distinctive ethnic division of labor are experienced in most major urban areas in advanced industrial countries. Elsewhere, in those cities without a significant middle-class bulge in their labor markets, pre-existing polarities between the rich and the poor have often become exacerbated.

Rising immigrant populations, along with other causes of labor-market polarization, have triggered a major increase not just in multijob households but also in part-time or contingent workers. In the U.S., in particular, this is accompanied by an extraordinary expansion in the number of women with children entering the labor market, and a concurrent reduction of so-called traditional nuclear family households with one breadwinner. This has added many new terms and phrases to our urban vocabulary, among them DINKs (double-income, no kids households), the new orphans (teenagers and the elderly abandoned by their families), and the feminization of poverty. It has also led in some rapidly growing cities to a revival of slavery or at least domestic servitude, as immigrants are smuggled into the city, with their passports held by their "owners," to work for bare sustenance in sweatshops or as servants in wealthy households. The formation of the New Economy of flexible capitalism has become associated with increasing psychological stress and family tensions at every income level, as households struggle to avoid the persistent pressures of downward mobility.

At the top of the restratified income ladder something else has been happening to contribute to a worsening of urban problems, especially in the U.S. Today, the richest 10 percent of the population controls proportionately more wealth than it has at any other time since the Great Depression. This startling concentration of wealth and power, fostered by federal policies and corporate greed, constitutes a problem in itself. When the changing lifestyles of the elite are examined more closely, however, the problem becomes even more insidious in its effects on the political and economic lives of cities. Larger numbers of the rich are abandoning their civic responsibilities to dwell in secluded and vigorously protected privatized communities, what Evan Mackenzie calls private residential governments or *privatopias*.[9] Seeking and having the means to escape from real and/or imagined urban tensions, the insulated wealthy contribute less and less of their wealth to the resolution of urban problems.

The "secession of the rich" and the multiplication of armed guarded and gated communities are only a small part of a much larger process affecting the geographical form of the contemporary metropolis. Stated most simply, the postmetropolis has become increasingly characterized as well as most directly defined by what can be described as the *urbanization of suburbia* as new cities mushroom outside established urban cores, in large part based on the formation of new industrial and commercial employment agglomerations such as Silicon Valley, Orange County, and other high-technology complexes around Boston, London, Paris, Tokyo, and São Paulo. Now known familiarly as Edge Cities or Outer Cities or even Postsuburbia, this more regionally defined urbanization process has blurred many of the conventional boundaries of the metropolis, especially that between the urban and the suburban. Further, it has generated other effects both inside and outside the more successful examples of Outer City development.

Most of the attention given to the problems arising from this restructuring of urban form has centered on poor populations, mainly minorities and immigrants, who are concentrated in inner-city neighborhoods increasingly distanced from better paying jobs now clustered primarily in Outer Cities. This condition of highly concentrated urban poverty has created what scholars call a *spatial mismatch*: a damaging distortion in the distribution of jobs, housing, and public transit that is reinforced by similar skills and education mismatches as well as a more recently recognized "digital divide" having to do with access to the resources of cyberspace. Herein is another indication of how the new urbanization processes work to magnify social and economic inequalities and intensify urban tensions.

Less well studied are other problem areas arising from the restructuring of urban form, and what can be called the geographically uneven urbanization of suburbia. To take an extreme case, several outer cities surrounding Los Angeles have rapidly grown as a result of huge concentrations of relatively cheap housing. Although increased local employment opportunities were promised by the developers, inspired by successful nearby Outer Cities, the jobs did not materialize, forcing many workers to travel up to two and a half hours each way to their old job sites. These off-the-edge cities, as I call them, despite their bright (post)suburban appearances, have become among the most psychologically and socially stressful places in the postmetropolis, with exceedingly high rates of suicide, spouse and child abuse, divorce, delinquency, and other signs of family and community dysfunction.

The cumulative effect of these multiple sources of urban tension has been the creation and dissemination of what Mike Davis calls *security-obsessed urbanism*, borne of and bred through the spatial specificities of what he also describes as an *ecology of fear*.[10] This anxiety-ridden obsession with security is intensified by the increasing visibility of the poor, the newcomer, the stranger, the "other," as traditional patterns of urban segregation and containment no longer work as effectively as they once did. In the increasingly volatile and fractal urban landscape, fear is in the air. It not only thickens urban tensions everywhere in the city, but it also leads to major changes in the built environment, from the detailed patterning of streets and buildings to the larger reconfigurations of urban form. Housing developments as well as shopping malls are increasingly designed as fortresses, and are visually and aurally policed as such, with cameras and loudspeakers positioned in strategic places. In nearly every city the extent of truly public space is shrinking as waves of deregulated privatization drench the public sphere with intensified efforts at social control. The latter is symbolized most invasively by the surveillance camera, now as much a part of the everyday streetscape as the traffic light or the parking meter.

Although Los Angeles may epitomize the "Carceral City" with its security-obsessed urbanism, similar developments are occurring in most of the world's major urban regions. In *Splintering Urbanism*, Graham and Marvin survey the "exploding peripheries" of such global megacities as Jakarta, Istanbul, Manila, and Johannesburg, where prepackaged New Town complexes are proliferating to insulate the rich.[11] Building on the work of Teresa Caldeira, they also look at another representative postmetropolis, São Paulo, with its "fortified enclaves" located with similar insularity in its now multiple city centers.[12] As with so much of the postmetropolitan transition, this fortressing of the urban landscape can be traced back to the forces of globalization and economic restructuring, and seen as a contributing factor to the growing tensions arising from the new urban order.

A New Period of Urban Crises?

As noted, the package of problems associated with deepening poverty and the prolific urban tensions they generate are not in themselves entirely new, however they are different enough in qualitative and quantitative terms to demand new ways of understanding, analysis, and public response. I am not suggesting that long-established approaches to these problems and attempts to resolve them should be discarded, but rather that they must be restructured in ways that are more attuned to the new urban contexts that have taken shape over the past thirty years.

Simply put, urban poverty (and practically everything else associated with it) is no longer exactly what it used to be, and this difference matters. Making theoretical and practical sense of the rising urban tensions of the twenty-first century requires an effective understanding of the new urbanization processes generated by complex forces associated with globalization and economic restructuring. This understanding becomes even more urgent today as there are signs that, after thirty years of crisis-generated restructuring affecting every scale of our lives from the local to the global, we may have entered a *new period of crisis formation* generated by restructuring processes, globalization, the formation of the New Economy, and the changes associated with the postmetropolitan transition.

In many ways the violent uprising that took place in Los Angeles in 1992 was a vivid harbinger of this new kind of urban crisis. That this event took place in the global city-region of Los Angeles is not surprising since it is in this urban space that the postmetropolitan transition has reached one of its most advanced and fulsome forms. Although immediately rooted in continuing problems of racism and police violence, the "Justice Riots" of 1992 also contained within them a mass protest against the localized effects of globalization and economic restructuring—that is, against the growing disparities of wealth, deteriorating housing and public services, increasing inter-ethnic tensions, unresponsive local government, spatial mismatches, the rise of privatopias at the expense of public space, and other tensions and injustices inherent to the new rather than the old urban order.

In other words, whereas the Watts uprising in 1965 and the worldwide urban unrest of the 1960s were outgrowths of problems specific to the modern metropolis and the national capitalisms in which they were embedded, the Justice Riots of Los Angeles and many other politically explosive urban events since the fall of the Berlin Wall in 1989 are more appropriately interpreted as crises of the postmetropolis (or postmodern urbanism), and the reconfigured global and flexible capitalism that has been primarily responsible for the urban transformations of the past thirty years.

In the eleven years since 1992, simpler and more directly focused protests against globalization and its negative impacts on the physical environment and global poverty have multiplied in cities such as Seattle, Genoa, and Prague. However, these protests are almost entirely disconnected from the specifically urban conditions in which they take place, at least in comparison to what happened in Los Angeles. This leads me to suggest, in conclusion, that the growing movements against the negative effects of globalization and the specifically neoliberal model of the New Economy can be strengthened and extended by becoming more consciously and specifically urban. By this I mean more aware of the problems of poverty and injustice arising from the postmetropolitan transition, and more comprehensively spatial in terms of goals and strategies. This change in the scope of how globalization and economic restructuring are conceptualized helps to avoid the simplistic dichotomization of the global and the local, with globalization seen as the exclusive and all-inclusive enemy and the local romanticized into an equally exclusive-inclusive site of resistance. Cities and regions need to be understood as the places where the global and the local come together in distinctive ways, where global and local struggles converge in a distinctive political arena of its own. The primary objective here is not simply to prohibit globalization and flexible capitalism, but to find ways to make their continuing social and spatial impacts more democratic and just. To indicate the progressive potential of such urban and regional strategies I look again to Los Angeles.

In recent years Los Angeles has become a major center of innovation in the national labor movement, especially with regard to the formation of new alliances aimed at achieving greater social and spatial justice for the largely immigrant working poor. Led for the most part by innovative Latinas, organizations such as the Service Employees International Union (SEIU) and Hotel Employees and Restaurant Employees (HERE) have become the focal points of pan-ethnic labor and community coalitions such as the Los Angeles Alliance for a New Economy (LAANE). These coalitions cross traditional class and racial lines and contingently combine groups that in the past would rarely work together. Further, they use their knowledge of the restructured and globalized geography and economy of Los Angeles to develop new spatially conscious strategies to struggle for the rights of immigrants, the working poor, and other populations suffering in various ways within the new urban order. These strategies played a key role in making the regional living-wage movement and related campaigns for "development with justice" among the strongest and most successful in the country.

Increasingly, these new coalitions view their rights as residential or locational to both the city and the resources of the urban region. These rights include: the right to live in areas not threatened by nearby hazardous waste concentrations and other environmental dangers; the right to a living wage and appropriate health benefits; the rights as local taxpayers to full access to basic public services such as hospitals, schools, and suitable public transport; and the rights to participate and vote in local elections that directly affect living conditions and family well-being, even when not U.S. citizens. In a recent court case brought by a new organization called the

Bus Riders Union (BRU), the struggles for spatial justice and what might be called regional democracy succeeded in redirecting the investment plans and priorities of the Metropolitan Transit Authority from a costly fixed rail-transportation system that would primarily benefit white and relatively wealthy suburban residents and do little to resolve the spatial mismatch problem in the inner city, to a multibillion-dollar program to improve bus services, reduce journeys to work, and improve access to basic public services for the working poor.[13]

One of the many achievements of the BRU was to attach to the legal notion of civil rights an explicitly urban and spatial concept of justice, wherein the geography of the urban region (in this case the geography of a mass transit plan) becomes recognized as, in itself, a source that creates and maintains injustice and discrimination. There are continuing problems in implementing this court agreement, but the building of the metrorail system has stopped and huge amounts of public funds have begun to shift to policies that benefit the poor more than the wealthy. Indicative of the optimism this victory induced, one of the leaders of the Bus Riders Union is writing a book with the tentative title *Driving the Bus of History: The LA Bus Riders Union Models a New Theory of Urban Insurgency in the Age of Transnational Capitalism.* This chapter began with claims that the urban uprising of 1992 in Los Angeles was indicative of worldwide urban trends. It ends with the hope that some of the more recent developments taking place in the aftermath of 1992 will similarly have a global reach.

Postscript

As this chapter was written before the events of September 11, 2001, I have not commented directly on how these events relate to the broader discussion of urban tensions and their links to globalization, economic restructuring, and the postmetropolitan transition. Although some of the connections are fairly obvious, there are others that I would like to comment upon briefly in this necessary postscript.

Like the events in Los Angeles in 1992, what happened in New York and at the Pentagon can be seen as still another outcome of the worldwide problems and tensions associated with the negative effects of globalization and the uneven development of the New Economy, especially in its neoliberal form. However, except for the obvious symbolism of the sites selected for attack and the transformation of the city of New York (and its mayor) into icons of national patriotism, there has been relatively little attention given in the aftermath of the events to the specifically urban conditions that may have contributed to what occurred; in particular the growing tensions associated with increasing poverty and polarization in New York

City, Washington D.C., and the country as a whole. Further, what has happened since September 11 has worked against nearly all forms of progressive protest against the sources of these urban problems and tensions. Instead of an emerging spatial awareness of the uneven effects of globalization and an intensified search for greater spatial justice and regional democracy, there appears to be an extension of the security-obsessed urbanism and a fearful fortress mentality to the national scale, with New York City serving as the urban symbol for a reactionary patriotism seemingly bent on making the whole country a giant version of an armed-guarded gated community.

Behind these hardening shields there is emerging a concerted attack on the most successful achievements of earlier struggles, especially with regard to civil rights and civil liberties, to use two concepts that are intrinsically rooted in cities and urbanism. More than ever before there is a need to restore this specifically urban understanding of democracy, freedom, and justice, especially as we move deeper into a period of restructuring-generated urban crises. In this sense, the events of September 11 can be seen in retrospect as the most recent and most brutal manifestation of what was predicted in the UN report on the meaning of the Los Angeles riots in 1992, that "urban poverty will become the most significant and politically explosive problem of the next century."

Notes

1. Robin Wright. 1992. "Riots Called Symptoms of Worldwide Urban Trend," in *Los Angeles Times*, May 25.
2. Much of what follows is drawn from *Postmetropolis* where many of the same themes are addressed in greater detail. See Edward W. Soja. 2000. *Postmetropolis: Critical Studies of Cities and Regions*. Oxford and Malden, MA: Blackwell Publishers.
3. For example, a report issued by the Milton S. Eisenhower Foundation in 1998 noted that in the previous three decades (1968–98) the proportion of the U.S. poor living in metropolitan areas increased by 50 percent, from nearly half to 77 percent of the total. For further discussion of this report see Alissa J. Rubin. 1998. "Racial Divide Widens, Study Says," in *Los Angeles Times*, March 1.
4. For more on this distinction see Soja's, *Postmetropolis*, op.cit, pp. 3–18.
5. For an overview of the literature dealing with this industrial restructuring process see Chapter 6, "The Postfordist Industrial Metropolis: Restructuring the Geopolitical Economy of Urbanism," in Soja, *Postmetropolis*, op.cit., pp. 156–188.
6. One example of the new kind of polarization in this fractal urban landscape is that between Filipino and Cambodian immigrants in Los Angeles. Coming from two countries that face each other across the South China Sea, Cambodians have the lowest average family income among all major immigrant groups in Los Angeles, whereas immigrants from the Philippines have very close to the highest. For more discussion of the fractal city, see *Postmetropolis*, pp. 264–97.
7. See for example, Engin F. Isin ed. 2000. *Democracy, Citizenship, and the Global City*. Routledge: London and New York.
8. William Julius Wilson. 1996. *When Work Disappears: The World of the New Urban Poor*. New York: Vintage; and *The Truly Disadvantage: The Inner City, the Underclass, and Public Policy*. Chicago: University of Chicago Press, 1987.

9. Evan Mackenzie. 1994. *Privatopia: Homeowner Associations and the Rise of Residential Private Government.* New Haven and London: Yale University Press.
10. Mike Davis. 1990. *City of Quartz: Excavating the Future in Los Angeles.* London: Verso.
11. Stephen Graham and Simon Marvin. 2001. *Splintering Urbanism: Networked Infrastructures, Technological Mobilities, and the Urban Condition.* London and New York: Routledge.
12. Teresa Caldeira. 1996. "Fortified Enclaves: The New Urban Segregation," in *Public Culture* 8: 303–328; and *City of Walls: Crime, Segregation, and Citizenship in Sao Paulo.* Berkeley and Los Angeles: University of California Press, 1999.
13. For further discussion of these recent developments in Los Angeles see *Postmetropolis*, pp. 407–415.

CHAPTER 17

Urban Transport and Tensions in Developing Countries[1]

EDUARDO ALCÂNTARA DE VASCONCELLOS

Scope and Objectives

Major cities in developing countries have been experiencing profound physical, social, and economic transformations brought about by the globalization of the economy and related processes. Changes in economic investments, income distribution, the labor market and labor relations, and access to land and urban services have been at the center of such processes. Increasing unemployment and underemployment; persistent (and sometimes aggravated) poverty; occupation of peripheral areas lacking basic services; poor public-transport supply; and increasing congestion, pollution, and accidents—mainly related to the increasing and irresponsible use of automobiles—are common consequences in most large cities.

A social analysis of urban transport must evolve around actual mobility and accessibility conditions, their distribution among social groups and classes, how road space is used, and what sorts of externalities are generated and experienced. On general grounds, mobility and accessibility are constrained by disposable income, gender, age, individual level of education and employment conditions, household division of tasks, and the location of working sites and urban services. Mobility and accessibility are also affected by the supply of sidewalks, roads, and transport means, especially with respect to the share of public and private ones.

This chapter first summarizes the main structural factors and tensions that are currently challenging large urban areas in developing countries. Second, it analyzes how such factors and tensions are related to actual urban transport conditions, emphasizing mobility, accessibility, social, and equity issues. Five types of tensions are scrutinized: structural tensions (poverty); political tensions (institutional and class conflicts); transport-supply tensions (financing and regulation); economic tensions (expenses); and equity tensions (externalities). Third, this chapter analyzes the tendencies related to current tensions and the patterns of supply in urban transport and its use. Finally, it discusses the obstacles to be faced and the actions that may be adopted to minimize or overcome current transport-related tensions and problems.

Current Tensions

Current urban transport conditions in developing countries reveal a wide variety of different situations. They may be related to five types of tensions: structural, political, supply, economic, and equity. These are explored in the following.

Structural Tensions

Structural tensions relate to characteristics of social and economic development that affect society as a whole, with corresponding impacts on mobility. The first one is the long-lasting urbanization process, which, between 1950 and 1990, increased the urban population share in all countries in Asia, Latin America, and Africa. The second is persistent unemployment and subemployment in unstable informal activities. Intense urban growth leads to the severe problems of housing shortages, environmental degradation, and infrastructural deficiencies (Halfani, 1996).

Two particular features of this process are related to urban transport: sociospatial segregation, and different distribution of public services. In the case of the former, the wealthy, the middle classes, and the poor occupy different areas in urban spaces, with special regard to the occupation of peripheral areas by increasing numbers of poor migrants. In the latter case, public investments, driven by the uneven distribution of political power, generate sharp differences in the availability of and accessibility to public goods such as schools, hospitals, roads, and public transport, resulting in direct impacts on mobility and travel patterns.

Such physical transformations have definite impacts on transport demand. Pre-automotive cities allowed for space consumption by every person. However, modern, large cities made it more difficult to rely on nonmotorized means of transport once distances could not be walked or even cycled. The dependence on motorized transport, and public transport in particular, has become inevitable to most people. Further, as the physical and economic access to transport are biased toward those with higher incomes, deep accessibility inequities are generated.

Political Tensions

The political system is failing to ensure democratic representation of the conflicting interests. States are highly centralized and where formal democracies exist, they are fragile. The decision-making processes favors the elite and middle classes who have direct and indirect means of influencing policy outcomes, especially through the technocracy and bureaucracy that are closely related to middle-class interests. Other important agents also interfere, such as the highway and automotive industry lobbies and foreign-related interests, forming alliances that drive policy outcomes.

Social movements to support nonmotorized and public-transport means are weakened by fragile democratization environments, poorly developed citizenship, and political repression. They are also affected by public transport being one among several deprivations experienced by poor people. At the ideological side, demand for automobiles is artificially transformed into something "naturally humane" and the planners' role is seen as that of providing for such "desire." Consequently, contemporary space has been shaped in ways that reinforce and induce the need for the car—serving middle class's needs—while making nonmotorized and alternate public-transport means impractical.

The attempts to coordinate policy efforts face many obstacles: few cities have agencies in charge of such duties; technical resources are rare and badly trained; human resources working in the field oppose human and technical sciences knowledge traditions; technical requirements and time spans for implementing actions for each area often conflict; and agencies overlap in their jurisdictions and conflicts around common issues are frequent. The problem is very serious in large metropolitan areas such as Mexico City, Bangkok, and São Paulo, where coordinated efforts are essential to ensure the implementation of large-scale transport systems.

Transport Supply Tensions

The provision of transport infrastructure (roads) and means (vehicles) are essential to accessibility. The first tension is that in many cases there is no support for walking as a form of travel. Sidewalks, when they exist, are inadequate and badly maintained, with pedestrians having either to use narrow, dangerous areas, or share space with all sorts of vehicles. Crossings are either nonexistent or installed in ways that disregard pedestrian needs.

Pedestrians are treated as second-class citizens and the result is imprinted on space.

Support for nonmotorized vehicles (NMV) such as the bicycle is also deficient, with few cities having adequate road treatment for them. This problem becomes critical where motorized transport is being increasingly supported. Conditions to use NMV are also affected by unfavorable regulation such as taxes, import duties, and financing that have been used in many places to restrain or ban NMV. Lack of integration facilities to public transport also deeply affects the convenience of using bicycles.

The support to use buses, by far the most important public-transport mode in developing countries, is also deficient. Most peripheral areas do not have adequate roads for regular buses to use, making it necessary to use small trucks or jeeps. Vehicle technology is appallingly poor, as most vehicles are old private cars, adapted trucks with benches, or low-quality microbuses. Bus terminals are often physical points in space where vehicles and passengers try to find each other. Users have no information on services other than that provided by other users or by small, handmade plates hanging on the windshield of trucks and microbuses that are supposed to provide public transport. Bus operation is often marked by the instability of supply and unstable traffic conditions. Priority treatment on roads is rare and limited to few bus corridors implemented in some large cities. Public agencies in charge of transport have no monitoring systems, and information on public-transport performance is seen as a luxury. Conversely, efficient traffic management and monitoring techniques are developed to support automobile traffic.

The decisions about where and how to build infrastructure are based on traditional techniques that are inherently conservative, as they are directed to propose solutions to accommodate present tendencies in the future, without questioning the factors that shape transport demand. The investment in road expansion is both supported by forecasting techniques that reproduce current conditions as "natural," and justified by making economic appraisals based on the large wage-rate differential between car and public-transport users. Public investments in roads are then voiced as "corresponding to the public interest," whereas investments on public transport are often left to the market. Also, transport planning has been based on peak-hour-demand, particularly harming women's travel that is often related to more diversified, out-of-peak travel needs.

The way road infrastructure is distributed is also a source of tension. Traffic management is highly influenced by the myth of neutrality: using technical tools that avoid social and political considerations and pursuing the distribution of the circulation space supposedly to the benefit of "everybody." It ends up providing circulation space where the needs of the

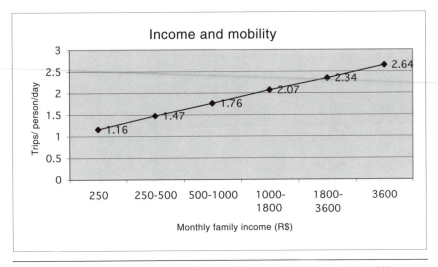

Income and mobility

Figure 17.1 Mobility and income, São Paulo metropolitan area, 1997. Source: CMSP, 1998.

weakest—pedestrians, cyclists, and bus passengers—are severely harmed, to enable efficient conditions for enacting dominant roles attached to private transport, especially that of the automobile driver.

Economic Tensions

Economic tensions are related to conditions to purchase and use private modes, such as the bicycle, and to pay public-transport fares. The continued poverty of most of the population, which lowers general mobility, prevents access to convenient public transport, and limits access to space and social services. In developing countries most people make about 1–1.5 trips per day, as compared to 3 trips for people in high-income societies. Female mobility is always lower than male's, reflecting the family division of tasks (Figures 17.1 and 17.2).

Trip purposes vary according to social, cultural, and economic factors. Work and school seem to be the universal single-most important purposes, regardless of geography and wealth, corresponding to about 70 percent of all trips. Modal split present large variations and three main groups may be devised: cities with predominantly nonmotorized trips (e.g., Beijing, Hanoi, and La Habana); cities where public transport responds for the majority of trips (e.g., Buenos Aires, Lagos, and Pretoria); and cities where motorized private modes play an important role (e.g., Caracas, Ouagadougou, and São Paulo). The use of a mode is highly constrained by income and gender: motorized means are used more extensively by higher-income strata and by men irrespective of income. When motorized trips

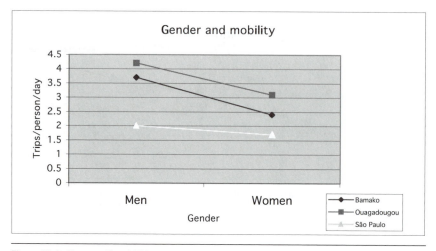

Figure 17.2 Vasconcellos, 2001.

are analyzed, most cities have more than 50 percent of trips made by public transport. Few have trains and metros and the bus is the main mode.

To fulfill their daily needs people have to use private-transport means or pay public means. Costs to own and use a nonmotorized vehicle are usually low whereas motorcycles and cars are much more expensive. Absolute transport expenses increases with income, as higher-income families are more mobile and use faster or more expensive modes. However, the participation of these expenses in total family income decreases with increasing wealth (Figure 17.3).

Equity Tensions

Equity tensions are related to the different conditions faced by people while using roads and the differential distribution of negative impacts of transport. Energy and equity are strongly related (Illich, 1974), and the increase in energy provided by motorized transport has a profound negative impact on equity. Mechanized transport allows for increased speed and hence in the number of destinations that can be reached. It also dramatically increases the consumption of space and the facilities demanded. Considering the unequal distribution of transport means, the ability to consume space is highly biased toward those with access to energy, and especially that from private transport. Accessibility is a scarce good, demanding the purchase of "transport kilometers" (Illich, 1974: 45).

The differential time needed to access public-transport means, as opposed to private motorized transport, is also important. Walking and waiting times for buses can be higher than 30 minutes, especially in peripheral

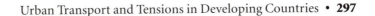

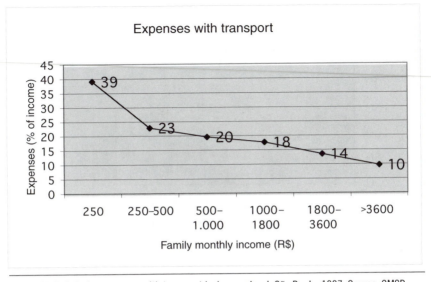

Figure 17.3 Relative expenses with transport by income level, São Paulo, 1997. Source: CMSP, 1998.

areas, and transfer times between two buses may increase discomfort and cost: up to 25 percent of users do not find services directly linking origin and destination. Trips by private modes always take much less time than that of public modes, and nonmotorized trips correspond to the lowest travel times (in face of people's physical limitations). Bus speeds usually fall in the 10–20 km/h range, due to the stop-run operation, poor traffic operational conditions, and congestion. Average door-to-door travel time may be 50 percent higher than that of the car. In noncongested cities the difference in speed between cars and buses can go up to 200 percent, with buses traveling at 20 km/h and cars at 60 km/h. In more congested cities, the mean speed of cars can still be double or triple that of buses.

The comfort of using roads is also highly differential and mainly relates to the conditions of sidewalks and the differential passenger density inside buses or automobiles (and the possibility of traveling seated). The low quality or lack of sidewalks severely harm most people, especially women and children, who enact the role of pedestrians more frequently. Overcrowded vehicles are a daily reality, and in several cities buses carry up to 2,000 passengers a day, implying high internal load and discomfort. Conventional maximum allowable densities (5 to 6 passengers per m^2) are frequently surpassed.

Space appropriation also reveals clear inequities related to different modes having highly distinct spatial consumption rates. On the one hand,

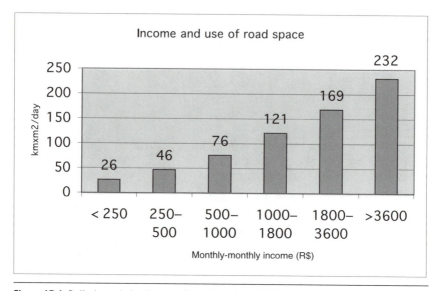

Figure 17.4 Daily dynamic family space budgets and income, São Paulo, 1997. Source: CMSP, 1998.

most people use roads in the role of pedestrians or cyclists and consume low quantities of space. Conversely, few use roads in the role of auto drivers and consume several times more space per person than those using standard buses or bicycles. That is, the consumption of road space is highly variable according to income and social status, and the assumption of streets as means of collective consumption that should be paid by everybody turns out to be a myth. When the space needed for parking and circulating is compared for four modes—train, bus, car, and bike—it is revealed that the most expensive or most energy-consuming is the automobile, using thirty times more area than a bus and about five times that of a two-wheeler (Vivier, 1999).

In Brazil, comprehensive, city-wide surveys show that people using automobiles (the minority) take approximately 70 to 80 percent of the road space (IPEA/ANTP, 1998). When the daily space consumption of families (space budget) is computed for several income levels and transport modes, the ratio between the lowest and highest income levels is almost 1:4 in the case of São Paulo (CMSP, 1998). When linear distances are multiplied by the specific personal-space correspondent to each motorized mode, the ratio between the lowest and highest income levels increases to 1:9 (Figure 17.4).

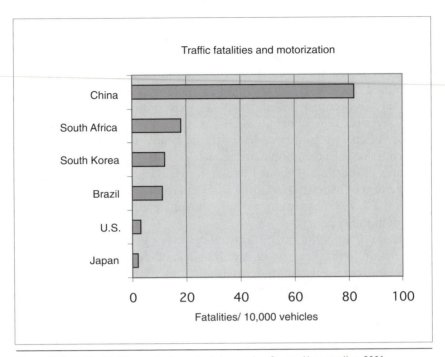

Figure 17.5 Traffic fatalities and rates, selected countries. Source: Vasconcellos, 2001.

The continued degradation of the quality of life in urban areas, represented by high traffic-accident rates, increasing pollution, and the disruption of urban space, is also a source of many tensions and inequities. In the context of safety, hundreds of thousands of people die every year and a much greater number get injured, a large part of them permanently disabled, as a consequence of the "death account" attached to irresponsible motorization. The importance of the problem places traffic accidents as the worse environmentally related transport problem in developing countries. When overall accident rates are analyzed, developed countries present rates of around 3 to 6 fatalities per 10,000 vehicles whereas developing ones may go as high as 82 (Figure 17.5). Several large cities present extremely high annual fatality figures: São Paulo (1500), and Bogotá, New Delhi, and Bangkok (about 1000 each). Recent trends are of great concern, especially in countries where motorized transport is rapidly growing.

Between 1968 and 1985 while road-accident fatalities decreased by around 20 percent in developed countries, they increased by 300 percent in Africa, and by almost 200 percent in Asia (TRRL, 1991) Studies show that pedestrians, cyclists, and motorcyclists (the most vulnerable) are the most harmed, accounting in most cases for about 50 percent of fatalities, as compared to 20–30 percent in developed countries (Guitink and Flora, 1995). Traffic accidents also cause several physical damages to those who survive. In São Paulo, for every person killed in 1997, there were twenty-two injured. For every pedestrian killed there were ten injured, and for every vehicle occupant killed, thirty-six were injured. There are about 14,000 seriously injured people every year (CET, 1997). Using gender as a category of analysis in the Americas, traffic-fatality rates adjusted for age and gender reveal a common pattern: male rates are always higher than female, in a proportion of about 1 to 3 or 4. In São Paulo, males correspond to 76 percent of pedestrian fatalities and 86 percent of vehicle-occupant fatalities (CET, 1997), revealing a disproportionate exposure to danger because of mobility patterns.

In terms of air pollution, inequity relates to few people producing most of the pollution that impacts all. Automobiles and motorcycles are responsible for most of the transport-related emissions. Air pollution has reached extremely high levels in several large cities, often exceeding the recommended limits of the World Health Organization (WHO). Cities differ both in the nature of their air-pollution problems and in the excess pollution produced. However, in most cases, transport is the main source of pollution. Most pollutants are related to serious respiratory diseases and several forms of cancer. Available data on one of the most harmful pollutants at the local level, Suspended Particulate Matter (SPM), show that it is much more highly concentrated in the large cities of the developing world as compared to those in developed countries (Figure 17.6).

Finally, social relations can be severely affected by traffic, once people are forced to reorganize their traveling behavior to adapt to new conditions. Increases in the number and speed of vehicles force people to reorganize their traveling behavior to protect themselves, resulting in reductions in both social interaction and the use of public spaces (Appleyard, 1981). Such effect is labeled the barrier effect (traffic severance). There is also a need to define strategies for reducing the risk of accidents (Hillman, 1988), especially among children, teenagers, and the elderly.

Trucks and buses, for their dimensions and engine power, often cause nuisances and building vibrations. However, the most pervasive negative influences are caused by automobiles, in the face of their numbers and need to negotiate space to survive. The disruption of the urban tissue occurs by destroying historical and architectural heritage for extensive road and transport infrastructure construction. This barrier effect represents a pervasive, although disguised impact, that affects residential and living spaces.

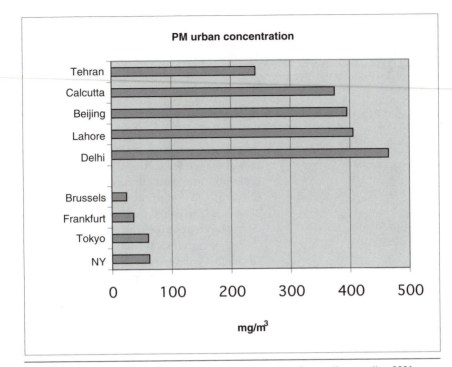

Figure 17.6 Concentration of particulate matter in urban areas. Source: Vasconcellos, 2001.

Future Trends and Possibilities

Changes fueled by globalization tend to affect urban-transport conditions, especially the reorganization of production processes, the expansion of the informal sector, increases in the female workforce, and state deregulation of markets (Castells, 1999). Most relevant for us are changes in the labor market, income levels, and distribution. These changes have important implications for shifts in both time use and the household division of tasks, which directly impact on travel demand. In addition, motorization is expected to increase throughout the developing world. Such changes reveal that urban transport problems in the developing world may significantly worsen in the coming years.

Long-term solutions to current urban transport problems in developing countries rely on complex structural changes, and depend on factors beyond the direct influence of urban and transport polices, such as enhanced democracy and citizenship, extensive access to education and health care, increased wealth for the poor, and better income distribution.

Table 17.1 Transport-related Tensions in Developing Countries

Dimension	Tension
Structural	Chaotic urbanization and lack of infrastructure
	Poverty and deprivation
	Unemployment and subemployment
Political	Fragile political systems
	Biased decision-making processes
	Poor institutional arrangements and coordination
Transport supply	Lack of support for walking and cycling
	Poor public-transport infrastructure and services
	Children's and women's needs not attended
	Biased road division toward automobile users
Economic	Cost of owning and using bicycles
	Cost of public transport fares
Equity	Discomfort while using public transport
	Low speed of public transport vehicles
	Uneven distribution of externalities:
	Traffic accidents
	Congestion
	Air pollution
	Urban and social disruption

Of course this does not preclude the articulation of specific policies and actions. The differences among, and particularities of, developing countries will naturally lead to different choices regarding specific solutions.

Structural Conditions

Economic transformations will have profound impacts on demographic and social conditions: a large number of cities will be unable to accommodate growth and will face severe infrastructural and environmental problems. Urban physical changes will have definite impacts on transport demand: increasing the amount of trips and further overcrowding public-transport vehicles. The dependence on motorized transport will increase and accessibility inequities will worsen.

There is not much to do to countervail such tendencies and impacts once political systems are biased. States are weakly organized and resources are scarce. The more promising action is the attempt to coordinate urban and transport policies, by ensuring that new urban growth occurs in a way that minimizes environmental impacts and social exclusion. This is the case of providing new housing areas for the poor with minimum social infrastructure, sidewalks, roads, schools, and medical services, and convenient public transport.

Poverty and unemployment may increase and the fiscal crisis of the state may worsen in several countries, as recently happened with Mexico, Thailand, and Argentina. Consequently, pressures both for and against public investments will increase and reactions against all sorts of subsidies will be enhanced, further restraining the implementation of equitable urban transport policies. Adequate transport planning and provision may minimize or eliminate some of the crucial barriers faced by the poor or deprived. Whereas poverty may be seen more in quantitative terms, relating to lack of material resources (including money), deprivation is more qualitative and relates to lack of access to economic opportunities, social services, and interaction. It is possible to associate mobility impairment with poverty and accessibility impairment with deprivation.

Therefore the agenda has to properly address the treatment of both conditions, contrasting needs related to strict physical reproduction of people and needs related to ensuring social and economic relations (Diaz Olvera et al., 1997). Transport investments may affect both, however in different ways: although subsidies to bus fares may improve mobility, it will be useless if there are no schools or jobs available or services that are open at convenient periods for those willing to use them.

Political Conditions

Formal democracies that are replacing authoritarian regimes do not seem to be more representative, and many developing countries will continue to face disruptions in their political systems. Therefore, true democratic representation of conflicting interests may not materialize, and the restricted educational system will continue to select those who will have access to relevant positions in the state and private sectors, thereby influencing policy outcomes. Social movements tend to be fragmented, local, and ephemeral—related mainly to cultural, ethnic, or religious identities (Castells, 1999). Although the importance of fragmented powers must not be ignored (Soja, 1997), I believe the dynamics of social change in developing countries will be primarily shaped by the creation of middle-class sectors, and their corresponding conflicts with the majority of the poor. However, the strengthening of citizenship brought about by such conflicts may countervail the inequities to some extent.

The main actions are to open public agencies to community participation and public accountability, and submit transport and traffic programs to social controls. This may be pursued through specific, day-to-day interactions of planners and community representatives, as well as through comprehensive public hearings on yearly transport plans, such as those adopted in Porto Alegre and other Brazilian cities under the Workers' Party administration.

Technocrats and expertise are trapped in the "world" of biased planning and modeling techniques, whose use is strengthened in the face of closed decision-making processes. However, the strong attachment to current practices may be eroded by increasing environmental and social concerns, including gender issues, that have been forging alternative approaches and introducing additional variables in the planning exercise. In pursuing new planning techniques, equity should be given priority attention, provided that a socially accorded efficiency level is attained. All projects, especially road building, should be submitted to "equity auditing" and made to answer the question: efficiency and sustainability for whom? Further, modeling techniques should be adapted to developing countries' conditions and limited to short- and medium-term forecasting exercises.

The planning process will have to develop new ways of promoting and controlling urban growth, in order to both address nonmotorized and public transport as priority means and define restraints to undesirable uses of private transport. The needs of women, the elderly, and children have to be an essential part of the planning exercise. For these changes to be accomplished, it is vital that the internal and external alliances that maintain and reproduce inequities are opposed.

Efforts to organize technical agencies or coordinate policies will be affected by the pressures to dismantle existent public agencies and lessen public-planning capabilities. This tendency may be opposed in large cities—where chaotic urban transport conditions hamper economic development—by gathering support from dominant groups to improve such conditions. The attachments of the bureaucracy and technocracy to elite and middle-class interests may be countervailed by pressures from organized groups, and the inherent conflicts and tensions that emerge from the increasing desires for equity and quality of life. The feasibility of new solutions may also benefit from the emergence of the environmental movement and its impact on the way urban transport is seen, as well as from the urban transport crisis itself. These emerging developments may help support alternative policies that were never adopted before or are facing opposition.

Transport Supply

The ideological prejudice against all nonmotorized means resists change and may be strengthened as motorization pressures increases. The main action in this case is to propel the political discussion on who has the right to use public roads, and reorganize the traveling environment to recapture public space for the priority use of the majority of those walking, cycling, or using public transport. A key related action is to submit such reorganization to a new computation procedure that divides space according to the number of people, as opposed to vehicles, as has been the usual practice of traditional automobile-supporting traffic engineering.

The supply of public transport may be subject to continuing instability in the face of deregulation and lack of investment. In addition, deregulation will confine bus technology to low-quality vehicles, which is compatible to a market-oriented approach within economically deprived environments. The aforementioned difficulty in organizing public agencies will negatively affect the organization of priority treatment for public transport and the control of quality of service, which will be affected by the chaotic supply emerging from a deregulated system.

Of special concern is the debate over the public or private supply of public transport. Negative consequences of public operation have been extensively portrayed in the literature. Mismanagement leads to inefficiency, with service unreliability, crowded vehicles, passenger discomfort, and underused equipment. Political interests and undue union pressures frequently lead to overstaffing, placing further pressures on costs. Disregard for market opportunities prevents the creation of new services. Inappropriate subsidization channels resources to those who are less in need or to support corporate interests. The need to define fares and control private operators, opens space for collusion. In addition, corruption may cause severe financial and credibility problems, often taking companies to bankruptcy.

Informal, deregulated transport supply has also been subjected to intense criticism. Most of the time the entrepreneurship of informal transit providers in developing countries is praised by foreign expertise. Reality, however, shows that the fast increase in informal transport leads, in the first moment, to typical consequences such as savage competition, degenerating work conditions, and poor vehicle maintenance and, in a second step, to attempts of self-regulation that evolve into private monopolies. Operators understand that they have a private business and any public interference is seen as an intrusion in the business freedom. Any tool is used to protect their personal interests, be it illegal or violent.

The immediate consequence is that those who are able to pay are served whereas those who cannot pay are not served. Further, and contrary to some expectations, deregulated markets often have a negative impact on fares, once organized operators—after expelling new competitors—use their monopolistic power to increase revenues. Service integration can seldom be achieved, both for the nature of political conflicts and the quantity of private operators that have to negotiate policy decisions. Difficulties in cooperation extend to difficulties in promoting technological changes and/or enforcing compliance to legally defined limits, for example, when individual operators refuse changes or external controls.

Therefore, the relationship between the state and the private sector in supplying public transport has to be carefully analyzed. The role of the public sector in regulating and enforcing public-transport operations has to be preserved and used, primarily to ensure that the transport needs of the majority are fulfilled, that public transport works in support of urban social and economic life, and in accordance to equity and efficiency objectives. The main proposal is that of seeing public transport as an essential public service, subject to societal and public controls, which implies the progressive replacement of informal/illegal supply by a regulated one. The regulatory environment should be flexible in order to provide services better suited to the market, and should be tailored to stimulate mode diversity and physical and operational integration to attract automobile users.

Economic Conditions

The use of bicycles may be supported by building appropriate infrastructure, ensuring safe traveling environments, and providing financial and taxation support for their purchase and use. As a general principle, daily operation of public transport should be financially self-sustaining through fares. Most bus systems in developing countries survive on their own, although based on poor, low-quality services constricted by an economically deprived environment. Thus, when self-sustainability is not possible and services are considered essential, external resources have to be used, especially in the form of subsidies.

Subsidization is justified as a way to provide minimum services to those most in need, who otherwise could not afford to pay for them in market-oriented transport operations. This includes the poor in general, women in particular situations, the elderly, students, handicapped persons, and geographically isolated people. Care must be taken to exert social control over subsidies, to avoid inefficiency, private accumulation, or appropriation by higher income levels. Subsidies have to be considered as *investments*, a means to ensure that people are integrated in economic and social life. This proposal is aligned with the view that public transport is a public issue that affects important social and economic dimensions in every society.

Equity Conditions

Increased motorization is expected to lead to worsening safety and environmental problems. In the last twenty-five years, fatalities have increased 106 percent in Brazil, 364 percent in India, and 665 percent in China (Vasconcellos, 2001). Congestion is increasing at a fast pace, with severe impacts on bus performance. Increased motorization will also lead to increased pollution: the World Bank estimates that carbon monoxide (CO) emissions may be multiplied by five until 2010 as compared to 1986 levels, with the main increases located in the former Soviet Union, China, and centrally planned Asia (World Bank, 1996).

The key actions here are: first, treat traffic safety as the main environmental challenge; second, improve bus-traveling conditions through priority treatment; and third, organize motorized transport supply and use in order to minimize air pollution. All actions are in line with the reorganization of the use of roads toward the most numerable users—pedestrians, cyclists, and bus users. This may include the control and charging of externalities caused by private transport. All measures may face strong opposition. However, increased traffic accidents and severance may fuel open social movements to protect quality of life, especially in residential areas violated by undue traffic.

Conclusions

Urban transport conditions in developing countries remain highly inadequate and inequitable for most of the population. Traditional procedures, along with political and technical alliances, have been generating transport systems that propagate an unfair distribution of accessibility and reproduce inequities. Private transport is often privileged and nonmotorized whereas local public transport means have been neglected. These problems have been aggravated since the 1980s, in face of economic restructuring and fiscal crises of states.

Problems and inequities concerning transport and traffic conditions in developing countries can be attributed first to structural factors, such as intense and uncontrolled urbanization, persistent poverty, fragile democracies, closed decision-making processes, poor citizenship conscience, inequitable economic development, and the denial of education for most. They are also related to urban and transport policies, specifically two historical processes: the dominance of private transport and the submission of public transport to the market approach. The dominance of private transport lies behind safety, environmental, and space inequities. The market approach to public transport precludes a social approach and translates into deficient accessibility and quality: to deny access to space is a means of maintaining the historical exclusion of most.

The major challenge to change current conditions is to modify roadway building and use by reassessing them according to social and equity concerns, to ensure that the most numerous and vulnerable roles are granted priority. The planning process will have to: develop new approaches to drive and control urban growth; address nonmotorized and public transport as priority means; and define restraints to undesirable use of private transport. The role of the public sector in regulating and enforcing public-transport operations has to be preserved and used primarily to ensure that public transport works in support of the urban social and economic life, and in accordance to equity and efficiency objectives. The urban transport crisis, coupled with increasing equity concerns, may promote alternative policies that were never adopted before or that have been facing opposition.

References

Appleyard, D. 1981. *Liveable Streets*. Berkeley: University of California Press.

Castells, M. 1999. *A sociedade em rede*, Volume 1. São Paulo: Paz e Terra.

Cia de Engenharia de Tráfego. 1997. *Corredores de Ônibus, Volumes e Velocidades Médias 1995* (internal report). São Paulo.

Cia do Metropolitano de São Paulo. 1998. *Pesquisa Origem—Destino 1987*. São Paulo.

Diaz Olvera, L., D. Plat, and P. Pochet. 1997. "Les Mobilités Quotidiennes Deux Pauvres à Bamako et Ouagadougou," in *Mobilité et Politiques de: Transport das les Villes en Dévelopement*. IN-RETS, Paris.

Guitink, P. and J. Flora. 1995. "Nonmotorized Transportation in Transportation Systems: Back to the Future?" Paper presented at the Transportation Research Board 74th Conference, Washington, D.C, January.

Halfani, M. 1996. "Marginality and Dynamism: Prospects for the Sub-Saharan African City," in *Preparing for the Urban Future—Global Pressures and Local Changes*. Michael Cohen, et al. eds. Washington, D.C.: Woodrow Wilson Center.

Hillman, M. 1988. "Foul Play for Children: A Price of Mobility," in *Town and Country Planning*, October, pp. 331–332.

Illich, Ivan. 1974. *Energy and Equity*. New York: Harper and Row.

IPEA/ANTP. 1998. *Redução das Deseconomias Urbanas com a Melhoria do Transporte Público*, Brasília.

Soja, Edward. 1997. Margin/Alia: "Social Justice and the New Cultural Politics," in A. Merrifield and E. Swyngedounw. *The Urbanization of Injustice*. New York: New York University Press.

TRRL—Transport and Road Research Laboratory. 1991. *Towards Safety Roads in Developing Countries*. UK.

Vasconcellos, Eduardo A. 2001. *Urban Transport, Environment and Equity—the Case for Developing Countries*. London: Earthscan.

Vivier, J. 1999. "Comparaison des Coûts Externes du Transport Public et l'Automobile en Milieu Urbain," *Transport Public International*, 48(5): 36—39.

World Bank. 1996. *Sustainable Transport—Priorities for Policy Action*. Washington, D.C.: World Bank.

Note

1. Part of the content of this chapter is based on specific parts of the author's book. See Vasconcellos (2001).

About the Authors

Lourdes Benería
Cornell University
Lourdes Benería is professor of city and regional planning and women's studies and director of the Gender and Global Change Program at Cornell University. She has written numerous books and articles on issues related to women's paid and unpaid work, gender and development, globalization, and structural adjustment. Benería is currently the president of IAFFE (International Association for Feminist Economics) and a member of the International Advisory Committee for the ILO's Program on Socio-Economic Security. Her book *Gender, Development, and Globalization: Economics as If All People Mattered* (2003) has also been published by Routledge. She has served as adviser and has worked with different international organizations, NGOs, and governmental bodies, including the ILO, UNDP, UNIFEM, UNRISD, and others.

Savitri Bisnath
Oak Philanthropy
Bisnath's research focuses on the multilateral trading system and the General Agreement on Trade in Services. She is co-editor, with Lourdes Benería, of the *Gender and Development Reader* Vols. I & II (Edward Elgar, 2001), and co-author of *Women's Empowerment Revisited* with Diane Elson (UNIFEM, 1999). Her article, "Poverty and Gender: An Analysis for Action," written with Lourdes Benería, appears in *The Globalization Reader*

(F. J. Lechner and J. Boli editors, Blackwell, 1999). Dr. Bisnath has worked with several United Nations agencies as well as philanthropic and non-governmental organizations. She holds a doctoral degree from Cornell University and a B.A. in economics from the University of California, Los Angeles. She was born and raised in Trinidad and Tobago, and currently resides in Switzerland, where she works for an international philanthropic organization.

Iwan J. Azis
Cornell University
Iwan J. Azis is a professor at Cornell University, where he is teaches at the Johnson Graduate School of Management. He also holds a professorship in the department of economics, University of Indonesia. Dr. Azis has addressed topics such as financial economics, macro-micro linkages, and macroeconomic forecasting. From 1984 to 1993, he served as director of the World Bank–funded Inter-University Center. He is an economic forecaster in the LINK World Econometric Group and in the Pacific Economic Outlook (under PECC) group. In early 1998, along with the deputy prime ministers of Thailand and Korea, he was invited to speak before the Joint Economic Committee (JEC) of the U.S. Congress on the Asian Crisis in relation to the U.S. contributions to the IMF. One of his works on impact analysis was adopted by the UN General Assembly (the 53rd session) on the "Implementation of Provisions of the Charter Related to Assistance to Third States Affected by the Application of Sanctions," (UN report A/53/312, August, 1998). He serves as a council member in the East Asian Economic Association (EAEA), and is a research fellow at the Rural Development Research Consortium (RDRC), University of California, Berkeley. Azis is an editor of *Review of Urban and Regional Development Studies*, Tokyo, and international editor of *Bulletin of Indonesian Economic Studies*, Australian National University. He is currently completing a book on Asian Development Paradigm.

Diane Elson
University of Essex
Diane Elson is a professor in the department of sociology at the University of Essex, UK. She has written numerous books and articles on gender, globalization, and development. Dr. Elson's most recent publications are a report for the United Nations Development Fund for Women, *Progress of the World's Women* (2000), and co-edited a special issue of the journal, *World Development*, on growth, trade, finance, and gender inequality (July 2000). She has served as adviser to numerous governmental and intergovernmental bodies, including the governments of the Netherlands, Sweden, and the UK, as well as UNIFEM, UNDP, the ILO, and FAO. She is currently

advising UNIFEM and the Commonwealth Secretariat on a program of support to Gender Budget Initiatives in Africa, Asia, and Latin America. She also works with NGOs, and is a member of the UK Women's Budget Group and the international network Women in Informal Employment Globalizing and Organizing (WIEGO).

Stephen Gill
York University
Stephen Gill is professor of political science at York University, Canada, specializing in international political economy and international relations. He is also a senior associate member of St. Anthony's College, Oxford University, UK. Dr. Gill's published work includes over sixty articles and chapters in edited collections as well as the following books: *The Global Political Economy* (with David Law, Johns Hopkins University Press, 1988); *Atlantic Relations: Beyond the Reagan Era* (Harvester-Wheatsheaf, 1989); *American Hegemony and the Trilateral Commission* (Cambridge University Press, 1991); *Gramsci, Historical Materialism and International Relations* (Cambridge University Press, 1993); *Restructuring Global Politics* (Asahi Shimbun Sha, 1996, in Japanese, translated by Seiji Endo); *Globalization, Democratization, and Multilateralism* (United Nations University Press & Macmillan, 1997); *Innovation and Transformation in International Studies*, (co-editor with James Mittelman, Cambridge University Press, 1997). His latest work is *Power and Resistance in the New World Order* (Palgrave Macmillan, 2003), and he has a book in press with Isabella Bakker: *Power, Production, and Social Reproduction* (Palgrave Macmillan, 2003). He is currently completing a new book: *The Constitution of Global Capitalism.*

Stephany Griffith-Jones
University of Sussex
Dr. Griffith-Jones is a professorial fellow at the Institute of Development Studies, University of Sussex. Her research focuses on global capital flows, with special reference to emerging markets, and the macroeconomic management of capital flows in Latin America, Eastern Europe, and sub-Saharan Africa. Professor Griffith-Jones is the author of numerous publications, including *Short-Term Capital Flows and Economic Crises*, with Manuel F. Montes and Anwar Nasution (Oxford University Press, 2001). She has also consulted with several multilateral organizations. Griffith-Jones holds a Ph.D. from Cambridge University.

Barbara Harriss-White
Oxford University
Barbara Harriss-White is professor of development studies at Oxford University, UK, and was the founder and director of Oxford's M.Phil. in devel-

opment studies. She is also a fellow of Wolfson College, Oxford. Trained in agricultural science and development economics, Dr. Harriss-White is committed to the interdisciplinary study of development and has spent a total of six out of the last thirty years carrying out firsthand fieldwork involving the business histories of over 2,000 traders, moneylenders, and (agro) industrialists, as well as hundreds of interviews with local policymakers and implementers in India, Sri Lanka, and Bangladesh. She has also worked more briefly in Francophone West Africa. Her interests are in the transformation of the economy (especially the informal economy and the food economy); markets and their political and social regulation; and social welfare (especially gender issues, nutrition, social security, and disability). Dr. Harriss-White sits on the editorial boards of *Journal of Development Studies*, *Oxford Development Studies*, the *Journal of Agrarian Change*, and other academic journals. She is a trustee of ActionAid, and the author, co-author, and/or editor of twenty-five books and monographs. Dr. Harriss-White has published 145 academic papers/chapters.

Naila Kabeer
University of Sussex
Naila Kabeer is a professorial fellow at the Institute of Development Studies, University of Sussex, UK. She has worked extensively on issues related to gender, poverty, household economics, and population. She is the author of *Reversed Realities: Gender Hierarchies in Development Thought* (Verso, 1994). Her recent book, *The Power to Choose: Bangladeshi Women and Labour Market Decisions in London and Dhaka*, also published by Verso, explores ways in which the voices of women workers in different contexts might influence thinking on global labor standards.

Ravi Kanbur
Cornell University
Ravi Kanbur is T. H. Lee Professor of World Affairs and professor of economics at Cornell University. He holds a joint appointment between the department of agricultural, resource, and managerial economics in the College of Agriculture and Life Sciences, and the department of economics in the College of Arts and Sciences. Dr. Kanbur holds a bachelor's degree in economics from the University of Cambridge and a doctorate in economics from the University of Oxford. From 1989 to 1997, Professor Kanbur was on the staff of the World Bank, serving successively as economic adviser, senior economic adviser, resident representative in Ghana, chief economist of the African Region, and principal adviser to the chief economist. Prior to joining the Bank, he was professor of economics and director of the Development Economics Research Center at the University of Warwick, UK, hav-

ing previously taught at the Universities of Oxford, Cambridge, Essex, and Princeton. Professor Kanbur's main areas of interest are public, development, and agricultural economics. His work spans conceptual, empirical, and policy analyses. He is particularly interested in bridging the worlds of rigorous analysis and practical policy-making. Dr. Kanbur's vita lists over seventy-five publications, covering topics such as risk-taking, inequality, poverty, structural adjustment, debt, agriculture, and political economy. The honors he has received include the Quality of Research Discovery Award of the American Agricultural Economics Association.

Philip McMichael
Cornell University
Philip McMichael is professor and chair of development sociology at Cornell University. His books include *Development and Social Change: A Global Perspective* and *The Global Restructuring of Agro-Food Systems*. Dr. McMichael is former president of the Research Committee on Agriculture and Food of the International Sociological Association.

Martha Nussbaum
University of Chicago
Martha Nussbaum is the Ernst Freund Professor of Law and Ethics at the University of Chicago, with appointments in the philosophy department, the law school, and divinity school. She is an associate of the classics and political science departments, a member of the Board of the Human Rights Program, an affiliate of the Committee on Southern Asian Studies, and the founder and coordinator of the new Center for Comparative Constitutionalism. She has an M.A. and Ph.D. from Harvard University. Dr. Nussbaum is a philosopher whose work has focused on ancient Greek philosophy, contemporary moral and political philosophy, and the connections between philosophy and literature. Her books are *Aristotle's "De Motu Animalium"; The Fragility of Goodness; Love's Knowledge; The Therapy of Desire; Poetic Justice: The Literary Imagination and Public Life; Cultivating Humanity: A Classical Defense of Reform in Liberal Education; Sex and Social Justice; Women and Human Development: The Capabilities Approach*, and *Upheavals of Thought: The Intelligence of Emotions*. Among her edited volumes are *Quality of Life* (with Amartya Sen) and *Women, Culture and Development* (with Jonathan Glover).

Saskia Sassen
University of Chicago
Saskia Sassen is the Ralph Lewis Professor of Sociology at the University of Chicago, and Centennial Visiting Professor at the London School of

Economics. She is currently completing her forthcoming book, *Denationalization: Territory, Authority, and Rights in a Global Digital Age* (Princeton University Press, 2003), based on her five-year project on governance and accountability in a global economy. She has recently completed, for UNESCO, a five-year project on sustainable human settlement for which she set up a network of researchers and activists in over fifty countries. Her most recent books are *Guests and Aliens* (New Press, 1999) and *Global Networks, Linked Cities* (Routledge, 2002), which she edited. *The Global City* is available in a new updated edition (2001). Her books are translated into fourteen languages. Dr. Sassen is a member of the U.S. National Academy of Sciences Panel on Cities, and chair of the Information Technology, International Cooperation and Global Security Committee of the Social Science Research Council (USA).

Edward W. Soja
University of California, Los Angeles
Edward W. Soja is a professor in the regional and international development (RID) area of urban planning. His courses address issues of urban political economy, regional planning, and planning theory. After starting his academic career as a specialist on Africa, Dr. Soja has focused his research and writing—over the past twenty years—on urban restructuring in Los Angeles, and more broadly on the critical study of cities and regions. His wide-ranging studies of Los Angeles bring together traditional political economy approaches and recent trends in critical cultural studies. Of particular interest to him are the ways issues of class, race, gender, and sexuality intersect with what he calls the spatiality of social life, and with the new cultural politics of difference and identity that this generates. In addition to his work on urban restructuring, Dr. Soja continues to write on how social scientists and philosophers think about space and geography, especially in relation to how they think about time and history. His latest book brings these various research strands together in a comprehensive look at the geohistory of cities, from their earliest origins to the more recent development of what he calls the "postmetropolis." His policy interests are primarily involved with questions of regional development, planning, and governance, and with the local effects of ethnic and cultural diversity in Los Angeles. His publications include: *Postmetropolis: Critical Studies of Cities and Regions* (Blackwell, 2000); *Thirdspace: Journeys to Los Angeles and Other Real-and-Imagined Places* (Blackwell, 1996); *The City: Los Angeles and Urban Theory at the End of the Twentieth Century* (University of California Press, 1996) with A. J. Scott; and *Postmodern Geographies: The Reassertion of Space in Critical Social Theory* (Verso, 1989).

Guy Standing
International Labor Organization
Guy Standing is director of the Socio-Economic Security Program of the International Labor Organization (ILO). In 1998–99 he was in the "transition team" assisting the ILO's new director general in preparing the restructuring of the ILO. Dr. Standing was previously director of the ILO's Labor Market Policies Branch, and director of the ILO's Central and Eastern European team, based in Budapest. He is chairman of the Basic Income European Network (BIEN). Standing has a doctorate in economics from the University of Cambridge and a master's degree in industrial relations. He has written and/or edited several books on labor economics, labor market policy, unemployment, labor market flexibility, and structural adjustment and social protection policies. Recent books include: *Restructuring the Labour Market: The South African Challenge* (with J. Sender and J. Weeks) and *Russian Unemployment and Enterprise Restructuring: Reviving Dead Souls* (1996). Recent articles include "The Folly of Social Safety Nets" (*Social Research*, 1998); "Global Feminization through Flexible Labor: A Theme Revisited" (*World Development*, 1999), and "Brave New Worlds?: A Critique of a World Bank Rethink" (*Development and Change*, September 2000). Dr. Standing is on the editorial boards of several academic journals. He was a member of Bruno Kreisky's Commission on European Employment and has worked with many governments and international bodies, including UNDP, the World Bank, ICFTU, the European Commission, and the UN Commission on Human Rights. Standing was economic adviser in the prime minister's department in Malaysia in the 1980s, and has worked with various other governments around the world. Dr. Standing's latest book is *Beyond the New Paternalism: Basic Security as Equality* (Verso, 2002).

Irene Tinker
Dr. Irene Tinker has focused much of her career on the differential impact of development on women and men. An activist as well as a scholar, she has lobbied for policy change and encouraged collaborative research with scholars worldwide. Such an approach is examined in *Street Foods: Urban Food and Employment in Developing Countries* (Oxford, 1997). The outcome of the original studies was to recommend ways to improve the income of vendors and/or the safety of the food they sold. Tinker later returned to the countries to evaluate the long-term impact of recommended interventions. The studies, her analysis, and selected street-food recipes are included in her book, *Women's Rights to House and Land: China, Laos, Vietnam* (Lynne Rienner, 1999), edited with Gale Summerfield, which is a result of collaboration with women in those countries.

Eduardo Alcântara de Vasconcellos

Dr. Eduardo Alcântara de Vasconcellos is a civil engineer (1974) and a sociologist (1983). He obtained his master's and doctoral degrees in political science (Public Policy in Transport) at the University of São Paulo, Brazil (1988 and 1993), and conducted his postdoctoral research at Cornell University, in the department of city and regional planning, from 1993 to 1995. He has been working since 1975 as a transport planner for several public and private transportation organizations in Brazil. Vasconcellos is currently associate director of ANTP, the Brazilian National Public Transportation Association, and consultant for the São Paulo Subway Company on studies covering mobility and accessibility in the metropolitan area. He has published several papers on urban transport in Brazilian and international journals. Dr. Vasconcellos has also written four books on the issue.

Howard M. Wachtel
American University

Professor of economics at American University, Howard M. Wachtel writes about globalization in the world economy, international money, labor, the American economy, and economic transformation in the planned economies of East-Central Europe, the former Soviet Union, and the Third World. In 1999–2000, he was a distinguished visiting scholar at the American Academy in Berlin and academic visitor at the Truman Institute of Hebrew University. He is the author of four books: *Street of Dreams—Boulevard of Broken Hearts: Wall Street's First Century* (Pluto Press, 2003); *The Money Mandarins: The Making of a New Supranational Economic Order* (Pantheon, 1986); *Labor and the Economy* (Harcourt Brace Jovanovich, third edition, 1992); and *Workers' Management and Workers' Wages in Yugoslavia* (Cornell University Press, 1973). He has published two monographs as a fellow of the Transnational Institute in Amsterdam: *The New Gnomes: Multinational Banks in the Third World* (1977) and *The Politics of International Money* (1987). Dr. Wachtel has published more than sixty articles for such leading academic journals as the *American Economic Review, Review of International Political Economy, Journal of Political Economy, Review of Economics and Statistics,* and *Theory and Society.* He has written for *The Nation,* the *New York Times,* the *International Herald Tribune, Le Monde Diplomatique, The Guardian* (London), and *Der Tagesspiegel* (Berlin). He has testified on economic concentration before the Senate Committee on the Judiciary, and written a report on inflation and unemployment for the Joint Economic Committee of Congress. Professor Wachtel has lectured widely in the United States and abroad, including Harvard University, Cornell University, University of California at

Berkeley and Riverside, Smith College, Central European University (Budapest), the Institute for Social Studies (the Hague), Copenhagen Business School, and Free University (Berlin). He was also an academic visitor at the London School of Economics and Cambridge University, and the Gould Visiting Scholar at the American University of Paris. He received a Ph.D. from the University of Michigan.

Marc Williams
University of New South Wales
Marc Williams is head of the School of Politics and International Relations and professor of international relations, University of New South Wales, Sydney, Australia. Dr. Williams has written extensively on international political economy, international organizations, and global environmental politics. His most recent book (co-authored) is *Contesting Global Governance: Multilateral Economic Institutions and Global Social Movements* (2000).

Index